EDWIN DICKINSON

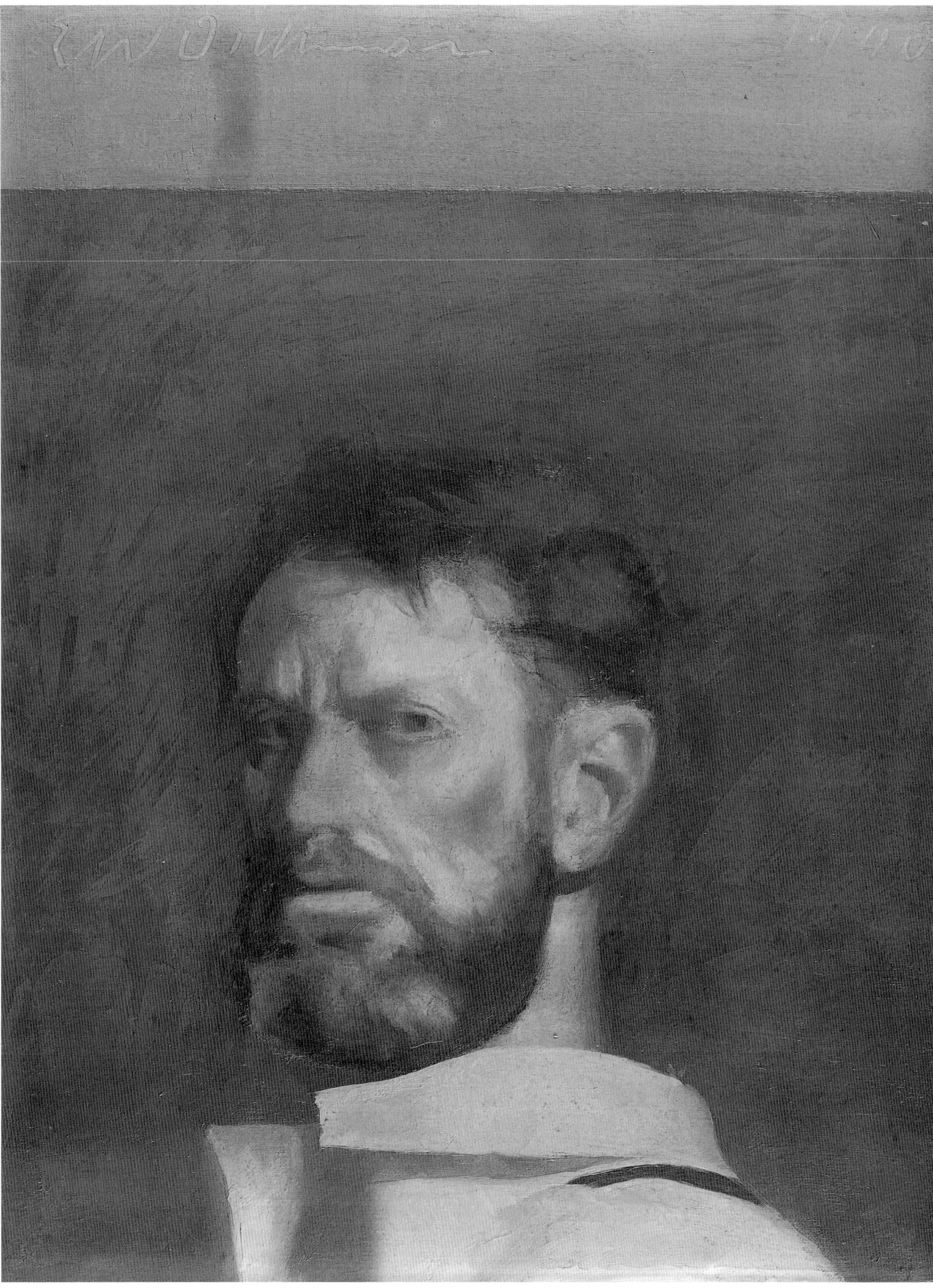

EDWIN DICKINSON Dreams and Realities

An exhibition organized by
DOUGLAS DREISHPOON

With essays by
Douglas Dreishpoon
Francis V. O'Connor
Mary Ellen Abell

Recollections and appreciations by
Elaine de Kooning
John Ashbery
Norman A. Geske
Michael Mazur

Chronology by
Helen Dickinson Baldwin

HUDSON HILLS PRESS, NEW YORK
IN ASSOCIATION WITH THE Albright-Knox Art Gallery | Buffalo, New York

This exhibition and its publication were supported by a major grant from The Henry Luce Foundation, with additional support from The Judith Rothschild Foundation.

In Buffalo, this exhibition is made possible through the generous support of Ferguson Electric Construction Co., Inc., JP Morgan Chase, and Walsh Duffield & M Insurance, Inc.

The Albright-Knox Art Gallery is supported, in part, by public funds from the New York State Council on the Arts, and by grants-in-aid from the County of Erie and the City of Buffalo.

Albright-Knox Art Gallery
Buffalo, New York
April 27–July 14, 2002

The Pennsylvania Academy of the Fine Arts
Philadelphia, Pennsylvania
September 14–December 1, 2002

National Academy of Design
New York, New York
January 31–April 13, 2003

Arkansas Arts Center
Little Rock, Arkansas
May 9–July 20, 2003

Sheldon Memorial Art Gallery and Sculpture Garden, University of Nebraska–Lincoln
Lincoln, Nebraska
August 29–November 9, 2003

First Edition

Published in the United States by Hudson Hills Press, Inc., 1133 Broadway, Suite 1301, New York, New York 10010-8001.

Distributed in the United States, its territories and possessions,
Canada, Mexico, and Central and South America by National Book Network.

Distributed in the United Kingdom and Eire by Windsor Books International.

Editor and Publisher: Paul Anbinder
Editor, Albright-Knox Art Gallery: Karen Lee Spaulding
Copy Editor: Nancy Preu
Proofreader: Lydia Edwards
Indexer: Karla J. Knight
Designer: Christopher Kuntze
Composition: Angela Taormina
Manufactured in Japan by Toppan Printing Company.

LIBRARY OF CONGRESS CATALOGUING-IN-PUBLICATION DATA

Dreishpoon, Douglas.
Edwin Dickinson : dreams and realities / essays by Douglas Dreishpoon, Mary Ellen Abell, Francis V. O'Connor ; with recollections and appreciations by Elaine de Kooning . . . [et al.].— 1st ed.
p. cm.
Published in connection with an exhibition at the Albright-Knox Art Gallery.
Includes bibliographical references and index.
ISBN 1-887457-00-3 (pbk. : alk. paper)
1. Dickinson, Edwin Walter, 1891—Exhibitions. 2. Dickinson, Edwin Walter, 1891—Criticism and interpretation. I. Dickinson, Edwin Walter, 1891– II. Abell, Mary Ellen, 1949– III. O'Connor, Francis V. IV. Albright-Knox Art Gallery. V. Title.
N6537.D44694 A4 2002
759.13—dc21 2001024654

Cover illustrations: Front—*Woodland Scene* (detail), 1929–35, Collection Herbert F. Johnson Museum of Art, Cornell University, Ithaca, N.Y. Back—*Staircase, The Manse of Ulysses,* 1928, Collection Robert C. Graham, Jr.

Frontispiece: *Self-Portrait,* 1940

CONTENTS

LENDERS TO THE EXHIBITION

AXA Financial, Inc., through its subsidiary
The Equitable Life Assurance Society of the United States

Peter A. Baldwin

Robert A. Baldwin

Harvey and Deborah Breverman

Dr. and Mrs. Philip L. Brewer

Estate of Janice Brustlein

Mr. and Mrs. Daniel W. Dietrich II

Esther Ewing

Mr. and Mrs. W. Thomas Gossett

Robert C. Graham, Jr.

Dr. and Mrs. Arthur E. Kahn, New York

Maurice and Margery Katz

Morris Collection

John O'Connor

Scharf Family Collection

Gilbert and Ruth Scharf

Shein Collection

Theodore and Eleanor Waddell

Merrill Wagner and Robert Ryman

Addison Gallery of American Art, Phillips Academy, Andover, Massachusetts

Albright-Knox Art Gallery, Buffalo, New York

The Arkansas Arts Center, Little Rock

The Art Students League of New York

Brooklyn Museum of Art, New York

Burchfield-Penney Art Center, Buffalo, New York

Clark Atlanta University Art Galleries, Georgia

Emerson Gallery, Hamilton College, Clinton, New York

Fine Arts Museums of San Francisco

Herbert F. Johnson Museum of Art, Cornell University, Ithaca, New York

Hirshhorn Museum and Sculpture Garden, Smithsonian Institution, Washington, D.C.

The Metropolitan Museum of Art, New York

Middlebury College Museum of Art, Vermont

Museum of Fine Arts, Springfield, Massachusetts

The Museum of Modern Art, New York

National Academy of Design, New York

The Nelson-Atkins Museum of Art, Kansas City, Missouri

The Pennsylvania Academy of the Fine Arts, Philadelphia

Philadelphia Museum of Art

Sheldon Memorial Art Gallery and Sculpture Garden,
University of Nebraska–Lincoln

The David and Alfred Smart Museum of Art, The University of Chicago

Smithsonian American Art Museum, Washington, D.C.

Sweet Briar College Collection, Virginia

Whitney Museum of American Art, New York

Babcock Galleries, New York

Curtis Galleries, Minneapolis, Minnesota

James Graham & Sons, New York

Julie Heller Gallery, Provincetown, Massachusetts

Michael Rosenfeld Gallery, New York

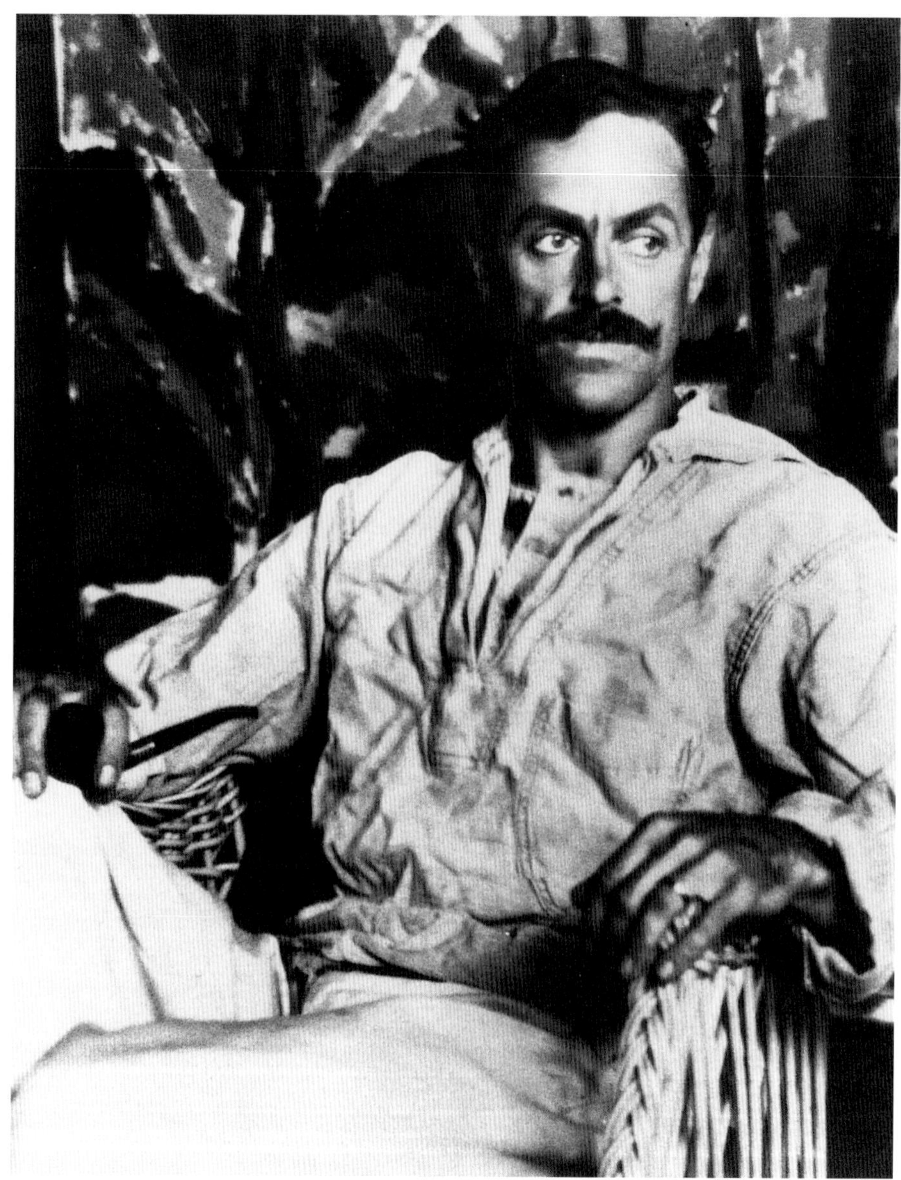

Edwin Dickinson, 1929. Courtesy Dickinson Family Archive

FOREWORD

Among contemporary American artists few of our younger men are more gifted, and their ability less appreciated, than is Edwin Dickinson. An excellent draftsman, he could easily have steered his course as to have become not only a popular, but a successful portrait painter. Nature, however, does not seem to have destined this artist for a popular career.

So wrote my esteemed predecessor William M. Hekking, director of the then Albright Art Gallery, in the catalogue introduction that accompanied a one-artist exhibition of Dickinson's work here in 1927. Today, three-quarters of a century later, these words still ring true, for Edwin Dickinson continues to be a singular artist, one of exceptional integrity, and one who was held in the highest regard by his fellow artists—indeed, by all—who were privileged to know him.

Edwin Dickinson had a deep affection and abiding affinity for Buffalo, a place where "he first started to draw, first studied painting and where he first taught painting," wrote his wife Frances Dickinson in 1977. In fact, it was in Buffalo in 1927 that *An Anniversary,* 1920–21, became the first of his paintings to enter a museum collection. It is, therefore, with the greatest pleasure that the Albright-Knox Art Gallery, in the first part of this new century, has organized this major exhibition of Dickinson's paintings and drawings. A gifted scholar of twentieth-century American art, Gallery Curator Douglas Dreishpoon proposed this exhibition in 1998 and has worked with unwavering conviction to bring it to fruition. His work was made not only possible but also infinitely richer through the essential collaboration of the artist's daughter, Helen Dickinson Baldwin. Her participation in this endeavor has been gratifying to all of those involved in the project, and we extend to Helen our immeasurable appreciation for her time, her interest and enthusiasm, and her critical support of all of our efforts.

My colleagues at the institutions that will host this exhibition after its opening in Buffalo have been most enthusiastic, and we are grateful for their collegiality and endorsement: Derek Gillman, Director, and Sylvia Yount, Chief Curator, The Pennsylvania Academy of the Fine Arts, Philadelphia; Annette Blaugrund, Director, and David Dearinger, Chief Curator, National Academy of Design, New York; Townsend Wolfe, Director, and Brian Young, Curator, Arkansas Arts Center, Little Rock; and Janice Driesbach, Director, Sheldon Memorial Art Gallery and Sculpture Garden, University of Nebraska–Lincoln. To the many lenders—private collectors, public institutions, and galleries—who are parting with their important works for such an extended period of time, we offer our sincerest thanks.

To say that foundation support for this exhibition has been outstanding is an understatement. The Henry Luce Foundation and the Judith Rothschild Foundation, through their superb generosity, have affirmed our belief that it was the right time to review Dickinson's work. In Buffalo, the sponsorships of Ferguson Electric Construction Co., Inc., JP Morgan Chase, and Walsh Duffield & M Insurance, Inc., once again underscore the importance of corporate partnerships. And, as always, support of public funds from the New York State Council on the Arts makes projects such as this an ongoing reality.

In the introductory text that Frances Dickinson wrote in Buffalo's Burchfield Center catalogue in 1977, she said: Buffalo and Sheldrake have been central to the life and work of Edwin Dickinson. . . . It was Buffalo friends who were his first and most important patrons and the geography of the area left a lasting impression on his work. . . . Recalling those years and our winters and many visits in Buffalo has given me pleasure, the deep pleasure of remembering warm friendships. Writing about those times is my tribute to the city, the region and above all to our friends."

It is the privilege of the Albright-Knox Art Gallery to return the tribute and pay honor to Edwin Dickinson in Buffalo, his early home.

Douglas G. Schultz
Director
Albright-Knox Art Gallery

PREFACE

Edwin Dickinson embodied an unlikely combination of artistic personalities. Described in his obituary as "an important representational American artist highly regarded by painters and critics as a 'master of painting in the Romantic tradition,' but one whose work stirred an equally deep interest among those drawn to the Abstract and Modernist schools,"[1] he came to represent different things to different people. Born in 1891, he came of age in the twenties and as a young painter susceptible to mysterious muses, was immediately classified by critics as a Romantic. Romantic he was, but his romanticism issued from such a deeply personal source, was at times so subjective, that viewers were often baffled by what they saw. Undaunted by a bewildered public, he persisted in his own universe. In doing so, he entered a distinguished pantheon of eccentric dreamers whose nocturnal visions threw shadows across what might otherwise be considered the more conventional history of American art.

Most people are drawn to light. Light dispels shadows, disperses superstitions, inspires optimism. If light signifies acute visibility, all that is knowable, darkness has the opposite connotation; its terrain is unknown, obscure, disorienting. Darkness implies another world, of dream and association, of death even, a realm without rational constraints. Dickinson gravitated to darkness the way others are drawn to light. It spoke to him in personal terms and became a ubiquitous chord in his pictorial repertoire. Darkness signified the substrata of his mind, and its appearance in compositions, symbolical paintings, and the *premier coups* through microtones of gray and black was a natural extension of his poetic sensibility. At times he was able to keep darkness at bay, especially painting outdoors when the landscape was bathed in color and light. But even in the best of circumstances, darkness seeped into his canvases like an insidious condition.

Dickinson's exploration of his darker side, a melancholy persona with many faces, is what made his work so compelling when it was first exhibited and what continues to make it so relevant today. His willingness to mine this aspect of his subconscious is what differentiates him from his neighbor in Truro, Edward Hopper, whose own melancholic tendencies were tempered by brilliant Cape light, and what aligns him with older visionary painters—Washington Allston and Albert Pinkham Ryder—as well as with younger abstract painters—Clyfford Still and Mark Rothko—who recognized black as a color of profound import. The blacks in a composition like *Andrée's Balloon*, 1929–30 (cat. no. 15), or a *premier coup* like *Surf, Point Lookout*, 1953 (cat. no. 62), or even those in a late self-portrait from 1954 (cat. no. 65), whether laid on densely with a palette knife or brushed on thinly, have the same ominous overtones, the same poetic inflections as the expansive blacks in a monumental abstraction by Still (fig. 1). Dickinson's romanticism is synonymous with the somber registers of his palette.

The painter's romantic tendencies, however, were balanced by a rigorous preoccupation with analytical tools in the form of perspectival studies. Perspective—the matrix through which many images, paintings as well as drawings, were conceived—stabilized an otherwise mercurial vision. Even as a young adult, he marveled at perspective's potential (fig. 2), and as time went on, it became a kind of mental game, an ongoing

Fig. 1
Clyfford Still
American, 1904–1980
1954, 1954
oil on canvas, 113½ × 156 (288.3 × 396.2)
Collection Albright-Knox Art Gallery, Buffalo, New York
Gift of Seymour H. Knox, 1957

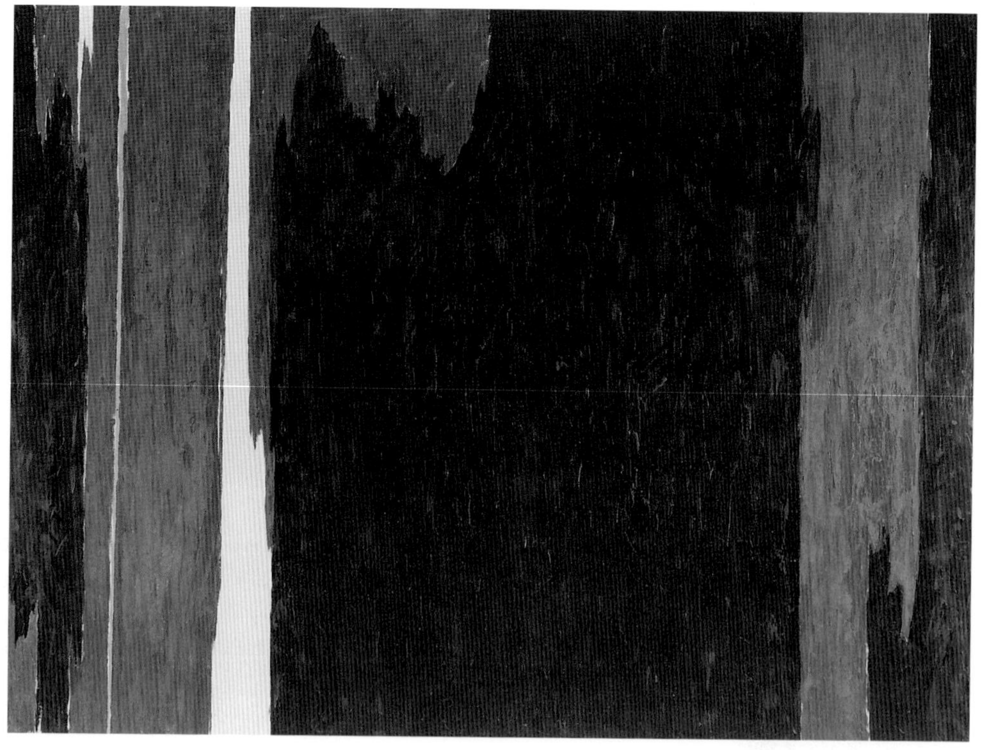

minated in *Ruin at Daphne*, 1943–53 (cat. no. 50), a picture based on one of the most complex perspectival schemes imaginable. Although never resolved to his satisfaction, the painting assumed an almost mythic status during his lifetime. Begun in Wellfleet in 1943, and brought with him to New York a year later when the family moved there, its ongoing progress was tracked by none other than Elaine de Kooning, who had it photographed in various stages by Rudolph Burckhardt for her 1949 article in *Art News*.[2] What distinguished this picture, besides its fantastic content, perpetual state of becoming, and empirical execution, was its elaborate perspectival machinations—the implications of an idiosyncratic world where intuition and science commingled. Dickinson's complex mental geography—part-representation, part-abstraction—shares a kinship with such later developments as Willem de Kooning's gestural abstraction, Robert Smithson's and Sol LeWitt's entropic and systemic landscapes, and even his close friend Jack Tworkov's late geometry-based painting. Having arrived at the right place at the right time later in his life, Dickinson's unbridled subjectivity did not go unnoticed by a younger generation of New York painters, especially de Kooning and Tworkov, who recognized and lauded its prescient nature.

* * *

Dickinson's unique sensibility captivated me in the early eighties when I first encountered his work at Hirschl & Adler Modern in New York. My curiosity was piqued, and from then on I sought out examples wherever they could be found. It was an auspicious confluence, corresponding with my arrival at the Albright-Knox Art Gallery in 1998, that I discovered an important early symbolical painting, *An Anniversary*, 1920–21, in the Gallery's permanent collection and realized that the artist, born in Seneca Falls only a few hours from Buffalo, had spent his formative years in Western and Central New York.

Sheldrake, on the west side of Cayuga Lake, and Buffalo were central to the artist's life and work. In Buffalo, where his family moved when he was six years old, he learned to draw, and the environs of both locations had a sustained impact on everything he

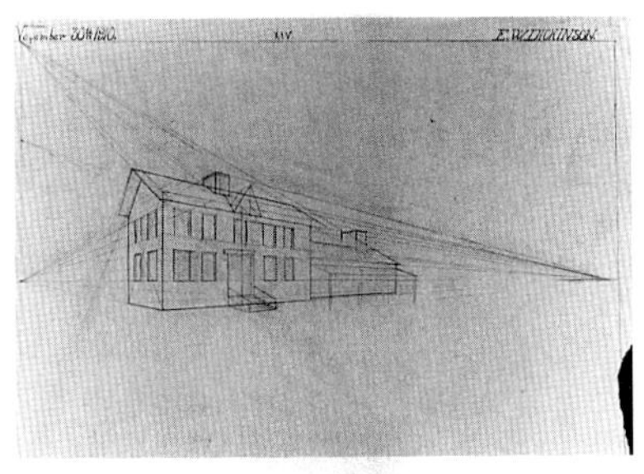

Fig. 2
Edwin Dickinson
Perspective drawing, 1910
graphite on paper, 11 × 15 (28 × 38.1)
Courtesy Dickinson Family Archive

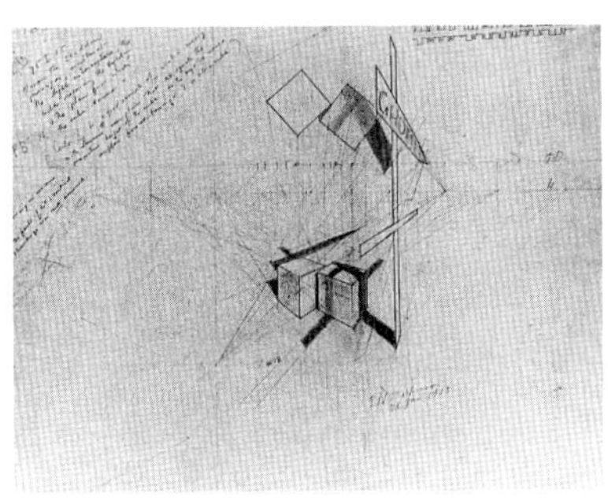

Fig. 3
Edwin Dickinson
Perspective drawing, 1950s
graphite on paper, 8 × 10 (20.3 × 25.4)
Courtesy Dickinson Family Archive

did. All his life, his spiritual homes were the end of Cape Cod, from Wellfleet to Provincetown, and the Finger Lakes of his birth, especially Sheldrake, where he spent boyhood summers at his father's cottage on Cayuga Lake. Year after year he returned to Sheldrake and Buffalo—where he did his first teaching in the summer of 1916 at the Buffalo Fine Arts Academy and had his first one-artist exhibition at the Albright Art Gallery in 1927. That same year, the Sawyer family donated *An Anniversary* to the Gallery, making it the first public collection to own a major work by him.

Dickinson's close association with the Albright Art Gallery and the city of Buffalo is the catalyst for the present retrospective, which defers respectfully to the major retrospective organized by Lloyd Goodrich and the artist in 1965 at the Whitney Museum of American Art. Composed of 104 paintings, 2 early watercolors, and 37 drawings, spanning the years 1915 to 1962, that show, Dickinson's swan song, was a fitting tribute to a stellar career. After his death in 1978, two important exhibitions were held: a selection of landscapes organized by Joe Shannon at the Hirshhorn Museum and Sculpture Garden in Washington, D.C., in 1980, and two years later, a smaller retrospective organized by John Dobkin for the National Academy of Design in New York. The artist described himself as a "general painter in oil," which was meant to explain his persistent interest in large-scale, multifigured compositions, landscapes, nudes, still lifes, portraits, and self-portraits. For this occasion, I set out to present the full spectrum of Dickinson's production from a fresh perspective, trying whenever possible to include less familiar examples, and focusing on the symbolical paintings as the main thread.

During his lifetime, the artist refused to have his paintings reproduced in anything other than black and white, fearing that poor color would only mislead the viewer. This was, and still is, a reasonable concern, and we have made every effort in this publication to get the color right. It is my hope that the exhibition and its catalogue will once again spotlight an artist whose work deserves communion with compassionate eyes.

Douglas Dreishpoon
Curator
Albright-Knox Art Gallery

NOTES

1. George Goodman, Jr., "Edwin W. Dickinson Dies at 87; Noted Representational Artist," *New York Times*, Dec. 3, 1978, p. 44.

2. Elaine de Kooning, "Edwin Dickinson Paints a Picture," *Art News* (New York), Sept. 1949, pp. 26–28, 50–51.

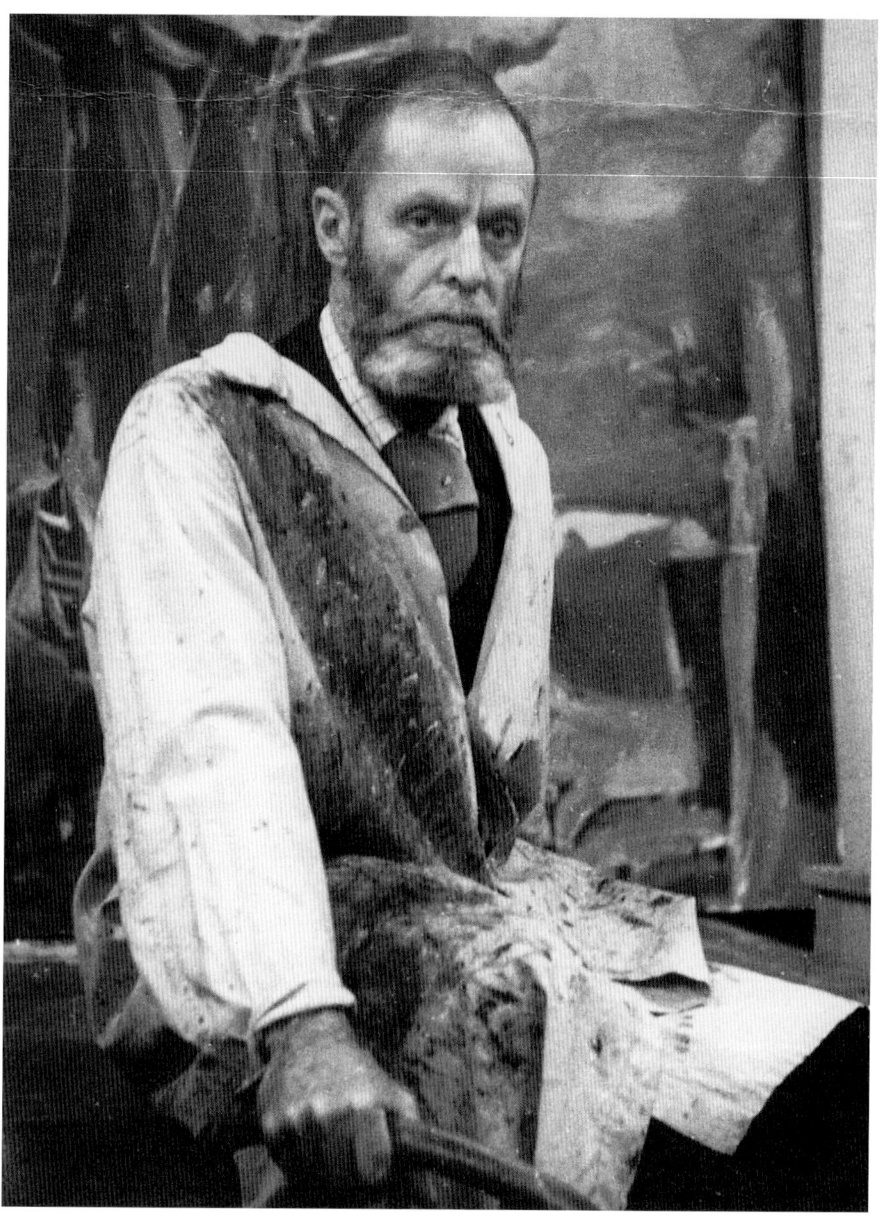

The artist and teacher posing for a class at the Brooklyn Museum, December 1956.
Courtesy Dickinson Family Archive

ACKNOWLEDGMENTS

Douglas Schultz was the first person to hear my Edwin Dickinson pitch during an impromptu conversation outside the Gallery in the waning light of a November day in 1998. I had recently arrived at the Albright-Knox Art Gallery and was elated by the artist's representation in the permanent collection and his connection to Buffalo and Central New York, and very much aware that nothing substantive had been done on his work in the last twenty-five years. Although I had not even contacted the artist's family, I proposed a major retrospective that would travel. All I knew then was that something had to be done, and we should be the ones to do it. Doug sensed my enthusiasm, saw my point, and encouraged me to proceed. As the project gained momentum, so did his support.

On the heels of our discussion, I contacted the artist's daughter, Helen Dickinson Baldwin, in Nashville, Tennessee, and made arrangements to meet with her, her late brother Constant Dickinson, and John Driscoll, at Babcock Galleries in New York. That was in December 1998. By April 1999 I was in Nashville, discussing ideas for the show and developing a preliminary checklist. Helen is committed to her father's career and reputation. Ten years ago she initiated a catalogue raisonné and since then has singlehandedly tackled this immense undertaking. Without her extensive archives, inherited from her mother Pat, comprehensive photographic files and data sheets, and her own exhaustive research, this project would have been unthinkable. Helen was an essential collaborator, contributing the chronology and extensive research for both the selected exhibition histories and the bibliography printed here. She also fact-checked all essays and appreciations, provided research material, addresses, and telephone numbers for lenders, located photographic prints and transparencies (archival and contemporary), and in every conceivable way facilitated the exhibition and its catalogue. It was not an easy journey at times, but she rose to the challenge, a stalwart and gracious spirit, and the enterprise bears her indelible stamp.

A trip to Provincetown and Wellfleet in August 2000 set the project on its final course. During a whirlwind three days, I met with Mary Ellen Abell, one of the essayists for the catalogue, who was then finishing her doctoral dissertation on Dickinson, and with her help scheduled interviews with Ruth Hatch, Gilly Hatch Gretton and Thomas Gretton, Caro Hawthorne, Jack Hall, and the late Martha Malicoat Dunigan, whose recollections greatly enhanced my understanding of Edwin Dickinson and his love for the Cape. At this time I also met with Helen in Wellfleet, confirmed the Gallery's commitment to the project, and began a series of interviews that we continued in Nashville and Buffalo.

Colleagues at various institutions, generous with their time, assisted in numerous ways. Sylvia Yount, former Chief Curator at the Pennsylvania Academy of the Fine Arts, expressed an early interest in taking the show, even before proposals had been sent out. She not only committed her institution's resources but intervened on my behalf to ensure the loan of several major works. Pari Stave, Vice President and Director of AXA Gallery, guided Francis O'Connor and me to Dickinson works in Equitable Life Assurance Company's collection and fielded subsequent queries, as did Pam Koob,

Metropolitan Museum of Art. Richard A. Born, Senior Curator at the David and Alfred Smart Museum of Art, The University of Chicago, accommodated my request to see their Dickinsons during a trip to Chicago in November 2000. Likewise, Sarah Powers, Curatorial Assistant at the Philadelphia Museum of Art, kindly provided access to their three Dickinsons. And the cooperation of Anne-Louise Marquis, Research Associate at the Hirshhorn Museum and Sculpture Garden, Jim Concha and James Sousa, Collection Managers at the Smithsonian American Art Museum, Stefanii Ruta Atkins, in the Office of the Registrar at the Museum of Modern Art, Barbie Spieler and Larry Giacoletti, Registrar and Assistant Registrar, and Alan Myers, Manager of Off-site Collection Storage at the Whitney Museum of American Art, facilitated my viewing of works in their collections and helped to fulfill our loan requests.

Several New York art dealers generously assisted. John Driscoll, Director and owner of Babcock Galleries, and a longtime advocate for Dickinson's work, in 1985 completed his doctoral dissertation on Dickinson, which remains one of the most cogent and sensitive texts on the artist. John's early endorsement of the project, coupled with his willingness to contact lenders and secure color transparencies and photographs for the catalogue, made a difference. Elizabeth Moore, former Associate Director at ACA Galleries, came on board as well with encouraging advice and in the final stretch negotiated critical loans. She also lent color transparencies for the catalogue. Andrew Arnot at Tibor de Nagy offered his support and pertinent information. Leigh Morse and Eric T. Larsen at Salander-O'Reilly Galleries procured permission to reprint Elaine de Kooning's essay, and Adrian Turner at Mitchell-Innes & Nash complied with my request for color transparencies of Jack Tworkov and his work and, in cooperation with the Janice Biala Tworkov estate, provided color transparencies of Dickinson's *Cap Fréhel, La Fauconnière, C. du N.* and *Portrait of Janice Tworkov.*

Each of the writers for the catalogue deserves special thanks: Francis O'Connor for his psychodynamic interpretation of the major symbolical paintings and self-portraits; Mary Ellen Abell for her informed discussion of Dickinson's teaching career and pedagogical methods; Norman A. Geske for his heartfelt recollection; Michael Mazur for his insightful appreciation; John Ashbery and the estate of Elaine de Kooning for allowing us to reprint their appreciations of Dickinson for this publication.

Others contributed in equally significant ways. John O'Connor not only lent important works to the show, but it was his propitious call in 1998 that propelled me to undertake the project. Peter J. Crego, minister of the First Presbyterian Church in Seneca Falls, was kind enough to meet with my wife and me on a Saturday afternoon in the fall of 2000 and give us a tour through the church where Dickinson's father served from 1889 to 1897. Hermine Tworkov Ford spoke with me about her father and granted permission to reproduce an early example of his work as well as a family photo. Mrs. William B. H. Sawyer graciously opened her Buffalo home to me so that I could view Dickinson works in the family's collection. Caroline Davis, Librarian at the Syracuse University Library, Department of Special Collections, made Dickinson's journals available during a three-day research stint. David Tatham, Professor of Art History at Syracuse University, welcomed me in his home during this visit. The painter Lennart Anderson kindly shared his recollections about Dickinson. Jenny Sponberg at the Curtis Galleries promptly processed loan requests and forwarded essential color transparencies, as did Anita Duquette of the Whitney Museum of American Art. Joseph Ketner, Director of the Rose Art Museum at Brandeis University, with the help of Registrar Stephanie LaMore, accommodated my eleventh-hour request to photograph two Dickinson works from a private collection in nearby Needham.

To the library staff, the technology and image resources, publications, and accounting departments, and to the registrars at the Albright-Knox I offer my heartfelt appreciation. Editor for Special Projects Karen Lee Spaulding once again defied all odds and obstacles in bringing the publication to completion. Her superlative skills, above and beyond those of an editor, not only ensured the project's timely resolution, but also assured everyone's sanity in the process. Head Librarian Janice Lurie marshaled the forces of her able staff—Amy Hezel, Eric Gangloff, and Conan Cerretani—who responded cheerfully to my ongoing requests for research materials while conducting painstaking authority- and fact-checking for the bibliography and exhibition histories. In the technology and image resources department, Richard Cherry, Bryan Gawronski, Yvonne Widenor, Kelly Frank, and Tom Loonan processed all digitized files for picture research, converted document files, duplicated slides for promotion and black-and-white prints for reproduction, and in general kept glitches in the image flow and electronic world under control. Registrars Laura Fleischmann and Daisy Stroud processed and consolidated all loans for the exhibition and its tour, which they helped to coordinate. In the accounting department, Susan Griffin magically produced checks for all of our urgent requests. In the final stages of manuscript preparation, Editor of Publications Sarah Hezel contributed her considerable skills to a careful review of all documentation and became an invaluable member of the Dickinson team.

Curatorial Assistant Holly Hughes leapt into the trenches early on, tackling all phases of the project's development from start to finish. She prepared loan forms, wrote query letters, contacted lenders and photographers, gathered photographs and color transparencies, and helped to proof galleys and layouts. In other words, she did it all. Hers was a formidable contribution.

To each of the lenders, I extend sincere thanks. Without their cooperation and trust, there would be no Dickinson retrospective.

To Paul Anbinder, President of Hudson Hills Press, we offer our appreciation for his abiding interest in all projects at the Gallery and for watching over this endeavor with such care.

My good friend Christopher Teasdale kindly read a preliminary draft of my essay and offered many constructive suggestions.

On the home front, my wife, Lisa Rafalson, deserves more than thanks for keeping me in the fold for the past eight months. In the midst of the madness, her optimism and encouragement were comforting.

D. D.

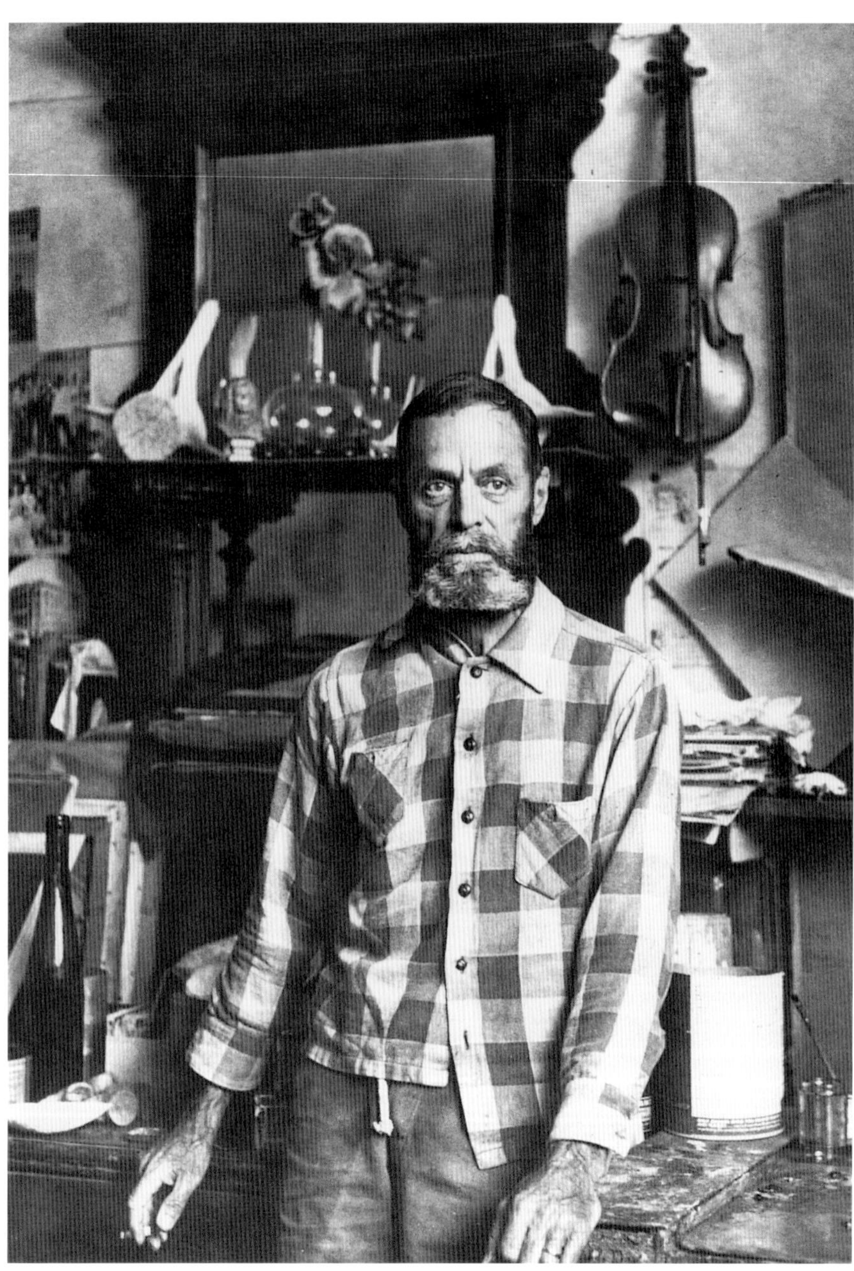

The artist in his studio at Wellfleet, ca. 1941.
Photograph by George Yater. Courtesy Dickinson Family Archive

STRIKING MEMORY

Douglas Dreishpoon

Edwin Dickinson's inclusion at the age of sixty-one in Dorothy Miller's *15 Americans* exhibition at the Museum of Modern Art in 1952 probably seemed to some like a curious coup. By this time his exhibition track record, extending back to 1914, was extensive. He had already devoted more than forty years to making art. Born in the nineteenth century to come of age in the twentieth, he straddled two worlds. Most of his creative life had been spent on the periphery of the art establishment, in the relative quiet of his own universe. Although known in New York art circles through a series of earlier exhibitions at the Georgette Passedoit Gallery between 1936 and 1942, his inclusion in *15 Americans* was something altogether different. It came late in his already distinguished career and signaled an auspicious turn of events.

This was not the first time Dickinson had been featured at the Museum of Modern Art with Miller's curatorial blessing. Nine years earlier, in 1943, she had selected two works—a self-portrait (cat. no. 40) and a symbolic allegory titled *Composition with Still Life* (cat. no. 20)—for *Romantic Painting in America*, an exhibition she coorganized with James Thrall Soby. A sprawling enterprise that set out to embrace every conceivable tenet of Romanticism, *Romantic Painting* was not without its curatorial shortcomings. It did, however, provide the first sympathetic context for Dickinson's poetic sensibility.[1] Within this visual smorgasbord, he found his designated place among the "International Tradition," along with such historical and contemporary figures as Washington Allston, A. B. Davies, Marsden Hartley, William Morris Hunt, John La Farge, John Marin, William Page, Benjamin West, and James Abbott McNeill Whistler. The only individual missing from this stellar constellation was Albert Pinkham Ryder, who was assigned another category, the "High Romantic," along with Albert Blakelock and the now-obscure Robert Newmann.

An artist like Dickinson stands out as an anomaly within the conventional history of American art. Like his predecessors Allston, Page, and Ryder, he seemed to walk on different air, to live by his own conventions. Like these kindred spirits, he courted subjectivity, imagination with no constraints. He observed life through a unique lens. Even the most mundane phenomenon, he might have said, when captured from the right angle under the right circumstances, could yield something marvelous. He never questioned this way of seeing, just as he never considered himself anything other than a "general painter in oil." He seemed to take what he did for granted, as though it were a natural extension of his being. Still the work perplexed. When some viewers, confronted by the baffling content of his symbolical paintings, requested explanations, he demurred, letting the works speak for themselves. When others saw abstraction in the *premier coups* ("first strikes," or canvases painted on the spot), he pointed out their origins in specific sites. Some pictures, it seemed, at least in his own mind, could be easily explained. Others, however, remained impenetrable.

Dorothy Miller became an avid supporter of Dickinson's work, and her curatorial endorsement in the forties was a boon to his career. By the time of *15 Americans*, she had already initiated a series of landmark shows that focused on contemporary American artists.[2] As with her other productions, *15 Americans* traversed a wide spec-

and calligraphic canvases by Jackson Pollock and Bradley Walker Tomlin, with sculptural counterparts by Herbert Ferber; biomorphic fantasy worlds by William Baziotes; Frederick Kiesler's primordial *Galaxy*; and Richard Lippold's delicate sculptural models, constructivist marriages of science and poetry through time and space. The representational and figurative canvases of Joseph Glasco, Herbert Katzman, Irving Kriesberg, and Herman Rose combined elements of Expressionism, Primitivism, Fauvism, and American scene painting. And Thomas Wilfred's light experiments with the Clavilux, called Lumia Compositions, projected light on ground glass, adding yet another, ephemeral dimension to the mix.

Dickinson was represented by five symbolical paintings (cat. nos. 16, 20, 21, 34, 50), three *premier coups* (*Château at Ollioules, Villa le Printemps,* and *Villa la Mouette*), the latter while he lived in France in 1938, and one self-portrait from 1941 (cat. no. 40)—the same self-portrait, it turns out, featured nine years earlier in *Romantic Painting in America*. It probably seemed like an odd assortment of pictures, but then, Dickinson's approach to art had a bipolar inflection. In Miller's "Americans" series, it was standard procedure for artists to contribute a personal statement about their work. Most participants did so themselves or, as in the case of Pollock and Tomlin in *15 Americans*, had someone else write on their behalf. Apart from an abbreviated biographical sketch, Dickinson's entry is without any statement whatsoever. Instead, he chose to include a frontal self-portrait from 1941, the only artist to do so. Reproduced in the catalogue, this image of him mediated between his labor-intensive, multifigured symbolical paintings and his more spontaneous *premier coups.*

Most *premier coups* originated in the landscape and took anywhere from two to four hours to complete. Compared with his symbolical paintings, they were a quick fix that either survived or did not. Those that made it were inscribed along one side (with the blunt end of a brush) with his signature, the date of completion and, in some instances, location. Those deemed unsuccessful were scraped out, painted over, or destroyed. Their rapid execution offered a reprieve from the laborious work of a symbolical painting—described by the artist in a letter to a close friend as a "big one."[3]

The symbolical paintings were an entirely different entity. The result of many sittings (a designation roughly equivalent to the time required to paint one *premier coup*), they often took years to complete and in most cases were never considered finished. This was certainly the case with *Ruin at Daphne* (cat. no. 50), one of the most talked-about pictures in *15 Americans*. It was begun in the small Cape Cod village of Wellfleet on January 1, 1943, and by 1952 had already undergone multiple revisions. Described in the catalogue checklist as "Unfinished composition. Begun 1943—still in progress," it might have remained in progress had it not been sold to the Metropolitan Museum of Art two years later in 1954. Like most of Dickinson's symbolical paintings, the work was a complex amalgam of perceptions and associations. Compared with preceding ones, it was of modest size. This fact had not stopped Elaine de Kooning from describing the picture as a "heroic canvas" three years earlier, in 1949, for a feature article in *Art News*.[4]

AN ARTIST AMONG NARROW STREETS

Years before the Great War, before the onslaught of tourism, and even before eager students came in the thirties to sit at the feet of Hans Hofmann, Provincetown was a sleepy and picturesque town perched at the terminal hook of Cape Cod. With its narrow streets shaded by majestic elms, poplars, and willows, its endless beaches, and, just outside town, its hand-tended vegetable gardens, small fields, pasture lands with dairy cattle, rushy ponds, and ramshackle icehouses, Provincetown had the aura of a magical place. Some of its earliest settlers, even before the Pilgrims set up temporary residence there in 1620, were Portuguese fishermen, whose rugged lifestyle and exotic customs gave the village a distinct ambience. When Dickinson arrived there in the summer of 1912 to study with Charles Hawthorne, who had opened his own school in 1899, artists were still a curiosity, an alien though not unappreciated addition to the local population.[5]

Many artists have been drawn to Provincetown for its indescribable light. "People tend to forget," Robert Motherwell wrote in 1978, "that Provincetown is (roughly) on the forty-two degree meridian [*sic*], as is Barcelona and Oporto and Cannes and Rome (almost exactly) and Macedonia and Istanbul and Peking (more or less), a distinctly warm southern light compared to Northern Europe, a light as seductive to painters in the modernist tradition as geometry was to the ancient Greek philosophers and musicians, not to mention Mohammedan designers."[6] Motherwell began summering at Provincetown in 1953, and his nostalgic perception of the place and its light was that of a warm-weather, seasonal resident. Roughing it out year-round was another proposition entirely. Winters could be formidable, and when Dickinson made his home there, they were a force to be reckoned with.

"Living on Cape Cod as much as I have has been beneficial," Dickinson remarked to Katharine Kuh later in his life. "I can think of many places that would not have done as well for me. I lived there a long time; I went there because I thought I would like it and I did. One of the reasons: there weren't many towns with so very many artists' studios in them, all of which were not good, of course."[7] It is true that Provincetown, even in the early days, offered abundant studio space to fledgling artists. In Dickinson's case, however, there were other, equally compelling reasons why he chose to make Provincetown his home for more than twenty-four years, from 1913 to 1937, before relocating to nearby Wellfleet in 1939. To review the circumstances that led to his arrival in 1912 and his decision the following summer to live there year-round is to realize that Provincetown was more than just a convenient place to launch a career; it was a haven for a life at loose ends.

At the age of nineteen, Dickinson had only recently committed himself to art. After two failed attempts, in 1909 and 1910, at entering the United States Naval Academy at Annapolis, he paid a visit to his father, a Presbyterian minister, who was then summering in Asheville, North Carolina. That a man of Dickinson's innate intelligence was unable to pass an entrance exam in mathematics on two consecutive occasions seems hard to believe. Helen Dickinson Baldwin, the artist's daughter, suggested that her father might have failed both exams because he just did not prepare enough. As a revealing aside, she also mentioned: "My father grew up under the assumption that he would become a minister like his father, because that was the way it usually went in families; one son was supposed to follow in the father's footsteps. His two brothers [Howard and Burgess] had not and it was assumed he would."[8] Apparently, it was

ond attempt to get into Annapolis, and with little else to do, he joined his father in the North Carolina mountains.

While in Asheville, he met an artist willing to instruct him in commercial art. It must have been an experience of epiphanic proportions for he not only committed his future to the fine art of painting but that fall, with purposeful ambition, made a beeline to New York, where he lived with his brothers and enrolled at Pratt Institute in Brooklyn. The following year, in 1911, after completing preliminary drawing classes at Pratt, he transferred to the Art Students League. Once there, he had his choice of teachers and elected to study with William Merritt Chase and Frank V. DuMond. He could have studied with Robert Henri, who had recently arrived at the League with a stellar reputation after having run his own school since 1909. "I chose Chase," Dickinson later told Dorothy Seckler, "without knowing what was, perhaps, the greater suitability for me in studying with Henri. I didn't know. And I've never thought that I chose wrong. Either one would have done well. I wanted to go to the League."[9] Life might have taken a different course had Dickinson selected Henri. Outwardly, Chase and Henri were as different as night and day: Chase was a dandy, urbane and cosmopolitan; the unpretentious Henri affected a plebeian, rough-around-the-edges persona. When it came to pedagogical points of view, they had more in common. Both encouraged students to trust their intuition, to tackle subjects outside the academic canon, and to paint spontaneously—lessons Dickinson would take to heart. In the twilight of his career, Chase by 1912 had passed the pedagogical torch to his most gifted student, Charles Hawthorne. Dickinson must have sensed the transition. Rather than follow Chase to his renowned summer school at Shinnecock, Long Island, or settle into one of the other already established artist colonies in Cos Cob or Lyme, Connecticut, or even Gloucester, Massachusetts, he cast his lot with the younger Hawthorne and set out for Provincetown.

His arrival there as a full-time student was far from carefree. "I started studying with Charles W. Hawthorne in the summer of 1912," he told Carol Gruber in 1957. "My brother, Burgess, with whom I was intimate, died tragically, so I wanted to leave New York, which I was able to do."[10] The summer of 1912 was Dickinson's initiation to Provincetown. In the wake of his brother's tragic suicide on January 28, 1913, he fled New York and spent the next five months in Buffalo with his family. Summer found him again in Provincetown, and by the fall, he had decided to remain on the Cape year-round. Burgess's suicide had a profound effect on Dickinson's entire life and artistic career. So did the earlier death of his mother, whom he had lovingly accompanied from sanatorium to sanatorium, from Saranac Lake, New York, to Pinehurst, North Carolina, until she finally succumbed to what was thought to be "tuberculosis of the bone" in 1903, when he was only eleven. The psychic fallout from his mother's and Burgess's deaths stayed with Dickinson on the Cape, and he recalled the anniversaries of his losses each year in a journal that he began in 1915, as a New Year's resolution to friends, and continued religiously until 1971, when advanced stages of Alzheimer's made coherent writing impossible.[11]

To open any one of the journals is to enter a mysterious and idiosyncratic world in which divergent realms coexist: the temporal and the timeless, the phenomenological world outside the studio and the subjective universe within his mind. The notations tell us a great deal about the man—his daily thoughts and his rituals— but for all they reveal, much is left unsaid. The first entry begins January 27, 1916, in volume two. (Apparently, volume one, covering the period from January 27, 1915, to January 26, 1916, was lost before Dickinson went off to war.) As with most entries, this one is brief, only a few lines on a ruled page: "Still feeling ill—up late painted myself AM. PM painted eve home." Days are divided by A.M. and P.M., and in many entries, along with painting and social activities, the weather is noted: [February 15, 1916] "AM painted—PM painted. eve saw Manon [a friend]. Rec'd valentine scarf from Tibi [his sister Antoinette]. Bright moonlight on snow. Cold." There might have been an evening dance at the Masonic Hall or dinner at a friend's house; he might have gone to church in the morning, after cleaning the studio; in the afternoon he might have skated or walked along the beach; Saturday evenings he was off to the Beachcombers' Club to hear music, have supper, or play chess. A good day, it seems, began and ended with painting, quality time spent in the studio, usually alone. Days are differentiated, or not, by weather conditions—rain, wind, snow, gray, squall, sun, thunderstorm; for Dickinson, who painted only by daylight, weather conditions mattered a great deal. Entries are factual, personal to a point, but in no way confessional, except on rare occasions—for instance, on May 25, 1916, when he wrote: "AM in & out—walk on dunes. Wretched day. PM worked at office. eve at Tibi's." As to why the day was "wretched," we remain in the dark.

In spite of their emphasis on quotidian matters, the journals are shadowed by the past, with former events—deaths, birthdays, anniversaries—perennially recorded. On May 17, 1945, Dickinson wrote "my journal has value for me." Indeed, his journals were an extension of his very being—a compendium of observations, facts, recollections, projections, simple and complex notations, calculations, chores accomplished or pending, a year's summary, including the total number of sittings for one of the symbolical paintings, income earned, debts still owed or paid. One can easily envision the journal for any given year somewhere in the artist's home, an essential part of his creative milieu, always accessible.

Fig. 1
Saturday morning criticism in Charles W. Hawthorne's class, Provincetown, Massachusetts, 1912 or 1913
Courtesy Dickinson Family Archive

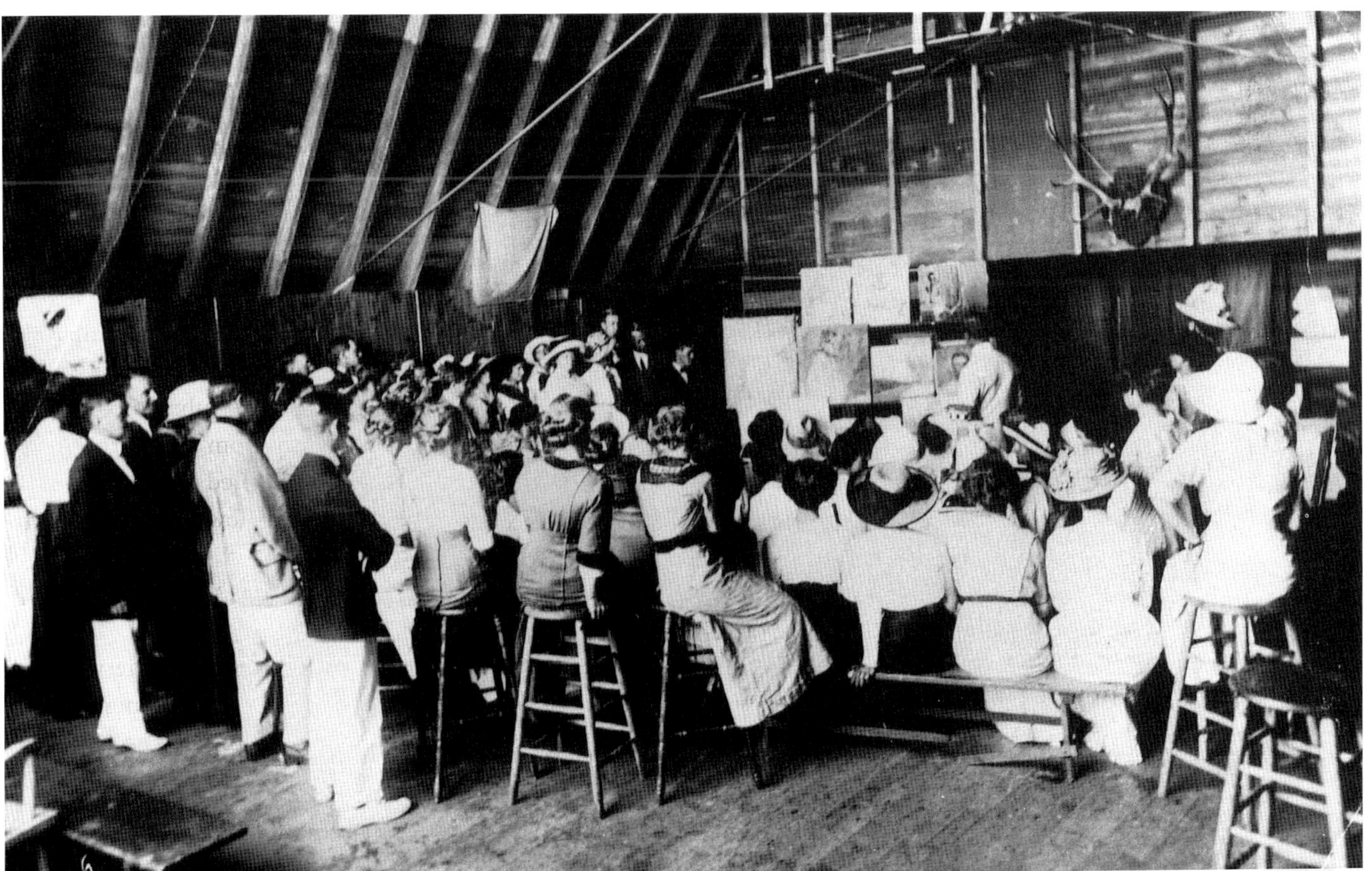

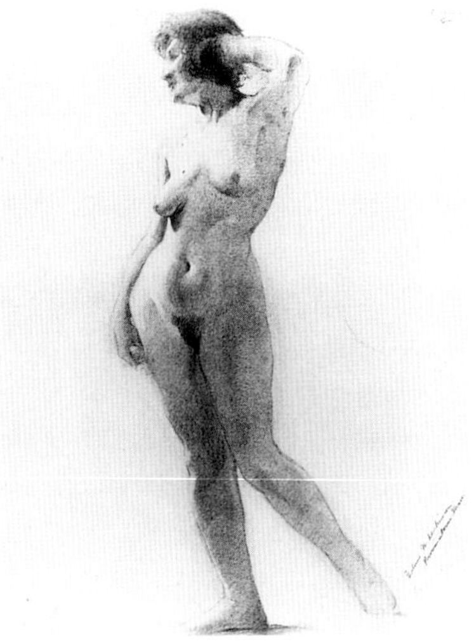

Fig. 2
Edwin Dickinson
Life Study, Female Nude with Upright Arm, 1913
charcoal on paper, 18¾ × 12½ (47.6 × 31.8)
Collection Edward Giobbi
Courtesy Dickinson Family Archive

Dickinson emerges from the journals as a disciplined and hardworking artist. During the first three summers, Saturday mornings were spent in the company of Hawthorne, who gathered a large group of students under the timbered roof of a spacious barn (fig. 1) or on the beach, where he critiqued the work of about six of them each week. What might have been an intimidating experience given the large crowd was in actuality a constructive exercise. Summers, when it was possible to work outdoors, were one thing. Winters were another, and the recollections of those brave enough to persevere ring like rites of initiation. "I studied three summers with Hawthorne," Dickinson recalled, "working winters by myself, in a studio, in which I lived alone, or sometimes with another painter or two. It was heated by a coal stove, no running water, and not insulated. We lined it with building paper. And it was cold. Of course, there was nothing to it because we were young and our circulation was way up, bang, good, you know. We liked it, and we did it voluntarily, by choice, and lucky to be able to. . . . The young fellows weren't married, most of them. We did lots of work. I painted a good many still lifes; I painted the local people. Lots of time was given to painting not from nature but from compositional invention in such ways as I could—gropingly."[12]

It must have been an exhilarating time as he drew from live models (fig. 2), and painted *premier coups* outdoors and compositions from his imagination indoors. During 1916 he also took up printmaking, creating etchings and monotypes. Though he did not sustain this interest, he did produce some notable things (figs. 3 and 4) over the course of about a year, working closely with his friend and studio mate, Ross Moffett.[13]

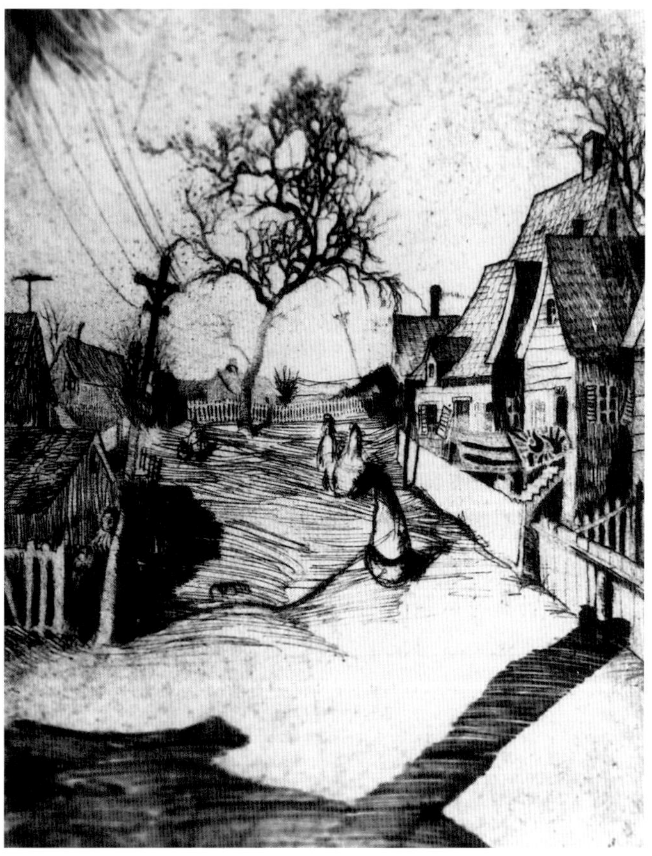

Fig. 3
Edwin Dickinson
Montello Street, 1916
drypoint on paper, 8¹⁵⁄16 × 6⅞ (22.7 × 17.5)
Collection The Metropolitan Museum of Art, New York
John B. Turner Fund, 1967

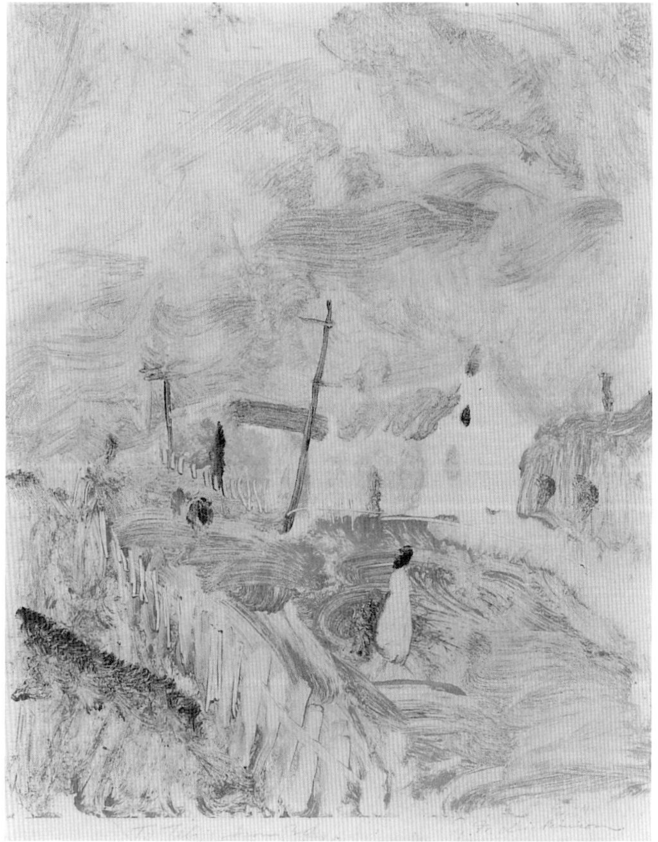

Fig. 4
Edwin Dickinson
Standish Street, 1916
monotype on paper, 14 15/16 × 12 (37.9 × 30.5)
Collection The Metropolitan Museum of Art, New York
John B. Turner Fund, 1967

STRIKING INTO AMERICA

Through his association with Hawthorne, Dickinson entered the world of art at an auspicious time. During the teens and twenties, with artists questioning the essential character of American art, a debate ensued around what constituted viable subject matter and technique. Geographical locale also entered the fray. The country and the city were at odds, it seemed. For some, the city had become the epicenter, a melting pot for everything —highbrow and lowbrow—that configured the American way of life. For others, the metropolis was a festering world of decadence and degradation—congested, unstable, polluted. Money and materialism had warped and distorted basic humanitarian values. The ideological discourse between urban centers and rural lands was waged by visual artists, poets, and writers. In magazines such as the *Seven Arts*, the *Dial*, and the *New Republic*, the terminology signified an anti-urban, anti-technological stance. Other magazines, such as *Broom*, *Secession*, and the *Little Review*, were more receptive to and positive about machines, technology, and the urban milieu.[14]

Writers and cultural critics such as Van Wyck Brooks, Waldo Frank, Lewis Mumford, and Paul Rosenfeld played an instrumental role in articulating an agrarian cultural nationalism. Words and phrases like *roots*, *native soil*, and *the American earth* rallied artists in search of a usable past. Rural outposts became places of refuge, a salvation from the metropolis, and offered a cornucopia of motifs appropriate for indigenous American art. Proposed as a grass-roots ideology by Mumford, regionalism emerged in the late twenties as a cultural battle cry, a critical response to the modernity of the age.[15]

As the urban-rural debate gained momentum after World War I, a central axis revolved around the photographer-philosopher-dealer Alfred Stieglitz and his coterie of artists and writers—Frank and Rosenfeld, along with Arthur Dove, Marsden Hartley, John Marin, and Georgia O'Keeffe. Stieglitz aggressively endorsed an art of painting and photography that issued from American soil, even though his notion of the "soil" was biased toward abstraction in its expression through equivalence, metaphor, and obscure symbolism. Stieglitz's vision for American art, articulated through the writings of Frank and Rosenfeld, was exclusive, the rarefied domain of insiders and intellectuals.[16]

Others were more inclusive when it came to codifying something as inchoate as American art at the threshold of a new century. Like Stieglitz, Henri proselytized for an art "with deep roots" grounded in "the soil of the nation" and responsive to a culture in flux. He, too, was ready to jettison European conventions for homegrown expressions but unwilling to limit how this might be accomplished. In Henri's worldview, the art spirit signified personal expression but was egalitarian at its core. He recognized early that America was rapidly becoming a nation of wildly diverse ethnicities and habits. This was true democracy, and he urged his students to embrace its every incarnation, urban and rural, to seize what they saw in paint, even at the expense of technical mistakes or failures.[17]

Although far removed from the polemical arena of New York City, Provincetown harbored individuals who espoused radical ideas.[18] Hawthorne shared Henri's yen for subject matter that exposed the hypocrisy of middle-class decorum, the equivalent of pictorial slumming, and he passed this interest on to Dickinson, who began to incorporate Portuguese West End residents into his compositions. Socioeconomic overtones permeate *The Rival Beauties* (cat. no. 2), *Interior* (cat. no. 4), *Imaginary Azores Scene,*

with autobiographical innuendo. That Dickinson gravitated to local subjects because they were accessible to him is not surprising. That these became the basis for more personal narratives is of greater significance—and the basis for Francis V. O'Connor's text in this book.

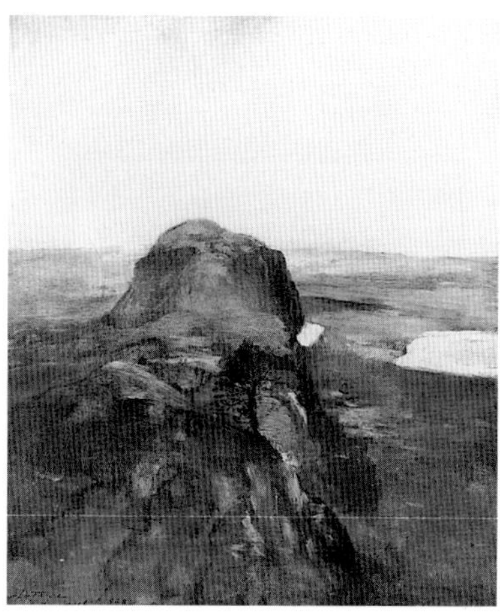

Fig. 5
John La Farge
American, 1835–1910
Autumn Study, View over Hanging Rock, Newport, R.I. (Bishop Berkeley's Rock), 1868
oil on canvas, 30¼ × 25¼ (76.8 × 64.1)
Collection The Metropolitan Museum of Art, New York
Gift of Dr. Frank Jewett Mather, Jr., 1949. (49.76)

Hawthorne and Henri had something else in common: they shared an approach to painting that relied heavily on intuition and spontaneity. We tend to think that the marriage of improvisation and the visual arts occurred after World War II, with the advent of Abstract Expressionism.[19] However, the impulse to improvise, to strike an image into existence spontaneously, on the spot, had begun nearly a century before. Intimations of this sensibility appear in Henri Bergson's notion of élan vital (life force) and Benedetto Croce's belief in the supremacy of intuition over scientific rationalism.[20] And some of the earliest expressions, analogs to this way of thinking, came from visual artists.

In Europe, the art of spontaneous painting became known as *premier coup*. Militaristic in tone, *premier coup* signified an all-out attack on nature—one that required complete immersion in the elements.[21] Perhaps it was inevitable that painters would bolt from the controlled environs of the atelier to test their skills *en plein air.* A by-product of traditional pedagogy, and to some extent a reaction to the escalating influence of photography, the *premier coup* issued out of staid academies in Munich, Paris, and London, where it was embraced by maverick teachers such as Wilhelm Leibl and Charles Emile Auguste Carolus-Duran, who realized that for painting to survive, for it to overcome the inherent stasis of academic precepts, it had to reconnect with nature, indeed with life, head-on.[22]

The impulse to paint *premier coup* migrated to the United States as early as the mid-1860s, via Barbizon, with William Morris Hunt and John La Farge (fig. 5), whose remarkable views of the Newport coast were never exhibited publicly because they were considered too unfinished. The criterion of finish was a monumental stumbling block to the acceptance of this kind of painting. It took decades, critical endorsement, and new eyes before the virtues of the *premier coup* were finally accepted by a recalcitrant public. In the end, their reluctance did not matter; by 1900 the incorporation of the approach into the curriculum of an institution like the Art Students League assured its propagation.

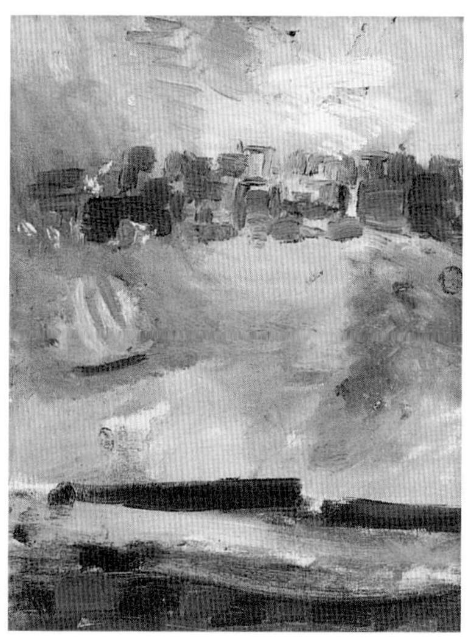

Fig. 6
John Marin
American, 1870–1953
Weehawken Sequence No. 80, ca. 1916
oil on canvas board, 12¼ × 9½ (31.1 × 24.1)
Collection The University of Maine at Machias
© 2001 Estate of John Marin/Artists Rights Society (ARS), New York

Once transplanted to Yankee soil, the *premier coup* assumed another meaning. For someone like Henri, it became a trope for individuality and democracy, a way to bypass moribund traditions. It aspired to speed, like the burgeoning machine age, but was ruled by intuition. Signaling a culture in transition, the *premier coup* could be seen as one of many survival tactics for life in the new century. It required thinking on one's feet, negotiating ever-changing circumstances on all fronts, and most importantly, and especially where art was concerned, creating in the process.[23] The origin of gestural abstraction began with painting *premier coups*. In the hands of someone like John Marin, who early on sensed its potential, it opened the perceptual doors to more subjective projections (fig. 6).

The technique appealed to Dickinson when he encountered it in Chase's painting class at the League. "All students worked in oil," he told Seckler. "And almost all of them premier coup. We did, in other words, five or six a week, many of which we painted out, some of which we might work on a second time."[24] His enthusiasm for this approach was reinforced by Hawthorne, who had students traipse all over Provincetown with their equipment in search of an appropriate motif. These student exercises—the front facade and screen door of a simple Cape Cod house or a model posed at the beach (figs. 7 and 8)—over time developed into highly abstract impressions of nature. Dickinson painted hundreds of canvases in this way. Seen together, they constitute a visual diary of places lived and visited: Provincetown, Wellfleet, Sheldrake, Buffalo, and various locations in France. Varying in size from ten by eleven to thirty by thirty-six inches, these works were an essential part of Dickinson's creative cycle and were included in many one-artist and group exhibitions from the twenties on.

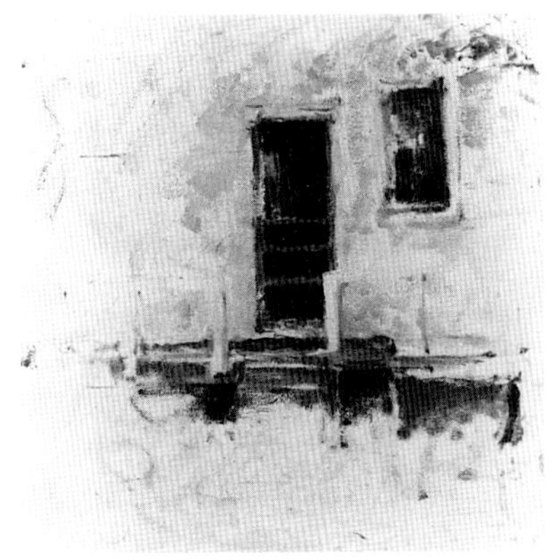

Fig. 7
Edwin Dickinson
Screen Door, Provincetown, 1912
oil on canvas, 24 × 23¼ (61 × 59)
Private Collection, New York
Courtesy Dickinson Family Archive

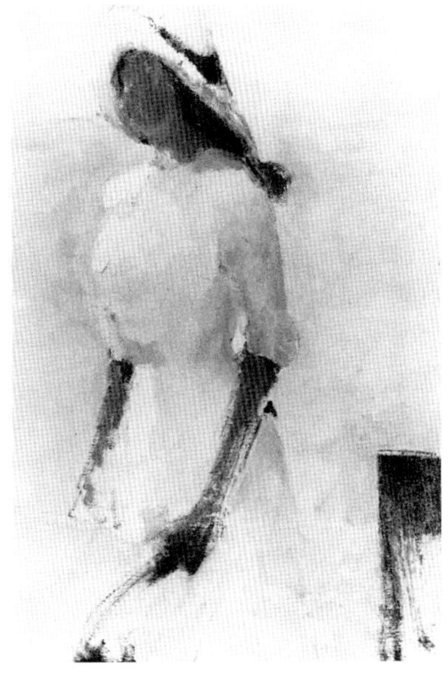

Fig. 8
Edwin Dickinson
Model on Beach, 1912
oil on canvas, 24 × 17 (61 × 43.2)
Collection Mr. and Mrs. Roderick Cushman
Courtesy Dickinson Family Archive

Painting spontaneously forced Dickinson outside of himself, freed him from his past, from the demons of death, from the salonlike machines that occupied so much of his studio time and seemed to weigh so heavily on him. His forays into the countryside required a different orientation. He walked for miles to secure the optimal site, and walking was cathartic; he did it religiously regardless of season. He was peripatetic by nature, a trait inherited, no doubt, from his father. He was always, it seemed, on the move, with or without his family. Travel refreshed him, presented him with new subjects, and kept him creatively in flux. The *premier coup*, in its rapid-fire execution, its all-or-nothing-at-all mandate, suited him perfectly. It was, however, only one dimension of a far more complex production.

DISTILLING MEMORY

Dickinson's symbolical paintings were another proposition altogether, and they challenged him in myriad ways. With them, he left the specificity of site, the immediacy of the first strike, and the particularity of circumstance for another kind of world, where memories and environments conflate, objects take on metaphorical meaning, natural light fades, and shadows descend. Many required multiple sittings and remained on the easel for years. Once released from the studio, they often circulated until purchased, submitted to juried international exhibitions at the Carnegie Institute, as well as to other annual and biennial venues at the Pennsylvania Academy of the Fine Arts, the Art Institute of Chicago, the Corcoran Gallery of Art, and the National Academy of Design. The symbolical paintings were the bedrock of Dickinson's career, though in other ways, they were the bane of his existence.

Most began without preliminary fanfare. "No preliminary drawings were made for these compositions," Dickinson noted in one of his few published statements, "nor were objects to be represented planned before starting. It was always intended, however, that human models, as well as other things, were to be painted. Plans that preceded even the stretching of the canvas included predetermination of the keys, the stretch of values, the color-schemes, the number and grouping of the spots, their sizes and their shapes and their variety."[25] Once begun, a symbolical painting acquired a life of its own as it underwent multiple transformations and revisions. Particularly with those from the twenties and thirties, the notion of completion is elusive. "None of the large paintings is really finished," he confessed to Kuh. "There comes a time when I stop because to go on would mean reorganizing the canvas from the bottom up. I can't throw away the investment of so many years—nine years in the case of *Ruin at Daphne*. So I make the best of a bad job by finishing them as well as I can. In other words, they all topple over when they're about three-fifths done."[26]

Dickinson seemed to accept the work's unresolved nature, just as he seemed to court

self changed, his interest in the painting might lessen. Again to Kuh: "If a painting takes many years, one hasn't stood still from the beginning to the end. As time goes by, one starts to disapprove of the earlier work. But even so, I prefer doing long ones to short ones."[27] Time became a relative construct with the symbolical paintings, as he layered and distilled, scraped out when necessary, and built up again. Such compositions functioned as vehicles for association, arenas for ideas assimilated through time.

The earliest surviving works—*The Rival Beauties, Interior, Inland Lake, Imaginary Azores Scene, An Anniversary*, and *The Cello Player*—already signal Dickinson's unorthodox methodology, his preoccupation with ambitious designs, multifigured arrangements, fantastic perspectives, and sundry still-life objects. One senses strange worlds in the making, but for all their idiosyncrasies, they hold together pictorially. Even *The Cello Player* (cat. no. 8), developed around one of the most complex perspectival schemes imaginable, is resolved in every detail.

With *The Fossil Hunters, Woodland Scene*, and *Composition with Still Life* (cat. nos. 12, 16, and 20), other forces enter to create perplexing worlds. Recognizable cues exist—wooded glades, shale cliffs, turbulent seas—but the context appears helter-skelter. Figures are cropped and obscured in bizarre ways, rendered in contorted positions that defy gravity. Some seem to float, as though suspended in water. Nocturnal light has replaced natural light. Grays dominate the palette. Dickinson, like Francisco Goya before and Mark Rothko after him, deployed the darker registers of his palette micro-tones of gray and black—to produce unsettling worlds of haunting intensity. Fragmentation and dislocation create baffling tensions. Nothing seems familiar. Who are these people? Why are they here? How do they relate to their environment? How does one explain such improbable juxtapositions?

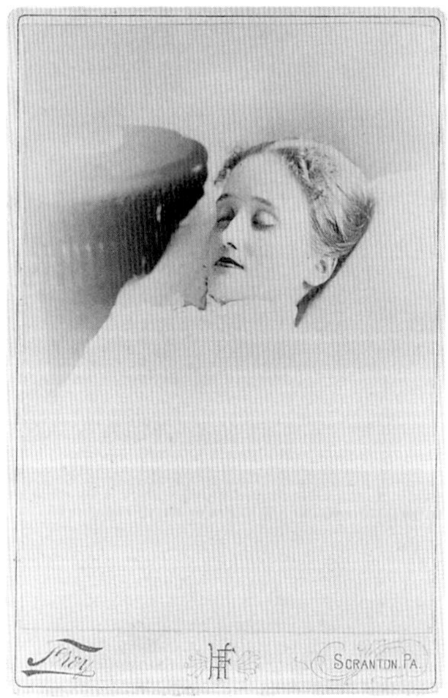

Fig. 9
Henry Frey
Portrait of deceased young adult female,
late 19th century
albumen cabinet card
Courtesy George Eastman House, Rochester, New York

Any attempt to decipher these paintings (by far the most peculiar of the symbolical paintings and a triad unto themselves) must take into account their exceedingly long gestation and polysemous character. One could say that in these monumental canvases, Dickinson meditated on life and death and that death hovers around these images in a spectral cloud. Out of the fertile imagination of a minister's son came haunting memento mori that recall the death portraits produced en masse by the Victorians to honor and memorialize the dead (fig. 9). Still, such an ethos does not account for the disorienting internal structure of these composite images.

In the solitude of his Provincetown studio, Dickinson free-associated his own dream worlds well before Parisian Surrealism migrated to the United States. Another influence, however, lay closer to home, and it is mentioned in the journals as early as 1917. Dickinson loved movies. They figured large in his social life, and he saw them whenever and wherever he could—in New York, Buffalo, Provincetown, even Paris. At times he frequented the cinema twice in a day, sometimes accompanied by his sister Tibi, brother Howard, his father, or a girlfriend, depending on the occasion and circumstances. It is hard to say what pictures he might have seen; most journal entries refer to "movie" without any mention of specific titles.[28] In less than twenty years, between 1912 and 1929, silent films had an enormous cultural impact in the United States.[29] In Dickinson they found an avid fan. He was drawn to their silent dimension, the monochromatic austerity of their black-and-white prints, and, most importantly, their unique structural logic. Movies projected another world—linear narrative through montage—and their magic was not lost on Dickinson, who eventually concocted an analog uniquely his own.

LAUNCHING A CAREER

With the exception of *Ruin at Daphne* and *South Wellfleet Inn* (cat. nos. 50 and 67), all of Dickinson's major symbolical paintings were completed on the Cape, his base of operations until the family's departure for New York in 1944. After his discharge from the navy in July 1919, and a seven-month sojourn in France, Dickinson returned to Provincetown and settled into a productive routine. He took a studio at Days lumberyard, for which he paid fifty dollars a year, a sizable amount for a struggling artist. When it came to finances, however, the graces of fate smiled on him. Family money, in the form of an inheritance from his maternal grandfather, had sponsored his early enrollment at the League and relocation to Provincetown to study with Hawthorne. His trip to Europe after the war had been funded, in part, by the army life insurance given to him by the parents and widow of Herbert Groesbeck.[30] And in 1924, his Buffalo friends and patrons, the Sawyers, initiated a monthly stipend of fifty dollars, which they continued through 1944 in exchange for art work.

Yet, even with this help from family and friends, eking out an existence in Provincetown during the twenties and thirties was a challenge. Dickinson realized early that teaching could provide him with a livelihood and took whatever jobs came up. He taught an evening life class at the Art Students League in New York in 1922–23. A founding member of the Provincetown Art Association, he was able to teach classes there during the summer and winter months starting in 1929. And in 1935, he signed on for an evening painting class, as well as a life drawing class, in Buffalo. What began as a pragmatic necessity developed into a lifelong passion. Teaching fulfilled him; it provided him with a forum for presenting his ideas and an opportunity to guide students. His own role models, Chase, DuMond, and Hawthorne, had given the profession an elevated status. His commitment to it over the course of fifty years, as Mary Ellen Abell makes clear in her text in this volume, was equally impressive.

Dickinson came of age in Provincetown emotionally and artistically. Many of the people he encountered became lasting friends. One member of his intimate group, Frances [Pat] Foley (fig. 10), whom he met in 1926, became his wife and the mother of his two children, Helen and Constant. When he was not teaching or socializing, he was painting and drawing. Between 1915 and 1916, the Provincetown Art Association exhibited some of his first professional works. And in Buffalo, in 1924, his work was featured in a two-artist show at the Garret Club, followed, in 1927, by his first museum show, at the Albright Art Gallery. At least four paintings were exhibited on this occasion, among them *Inland Lake, An Anniversary*, and *The Cello Player*. Dickinson's expectations were high for the paintings, which he circulated to various exhibitions around the country during the teens and twenties. For the young, aspiring artist, juried shows could launch a career. In theory, the best works received prizes, honorable mentions, and with a little luck, some favorable press. Dickinson entered this arena with precocious results. *Old Ben and Mrs. Marks,* 1916 (cat. no. 3), first exhibited at the Society of Independent Artists in 1917, was subsequently selected in 1919 to represent the school of new American art at the Musée National du Luxembourg in Paris. And *The Fossil Hunters* (cat. no. 12), first shown in 1928 at the Carnegie International Exhibition, was awarded the Second Altman Prize for Landscape a year later by the National Academy of Design.[31] Recognition through juried shows did not necessarily translate to dollars, however, and the same was true for gallery representation if one were lucky enough to secure it. For the first twenty-one years of his career, Dickinson remained commercially unaffiliated. That situation changed in 1936 when Georgette Passedoit offered

Fig. 10
Edwin Dickinson
Frances Foley, 1927
oil on canvas, 50 × 40 (127 × 101.6)
Collection Mr. and Mrs. N. J. Nicholas, Jr., New York
Courtesy Dickinson Family Archive

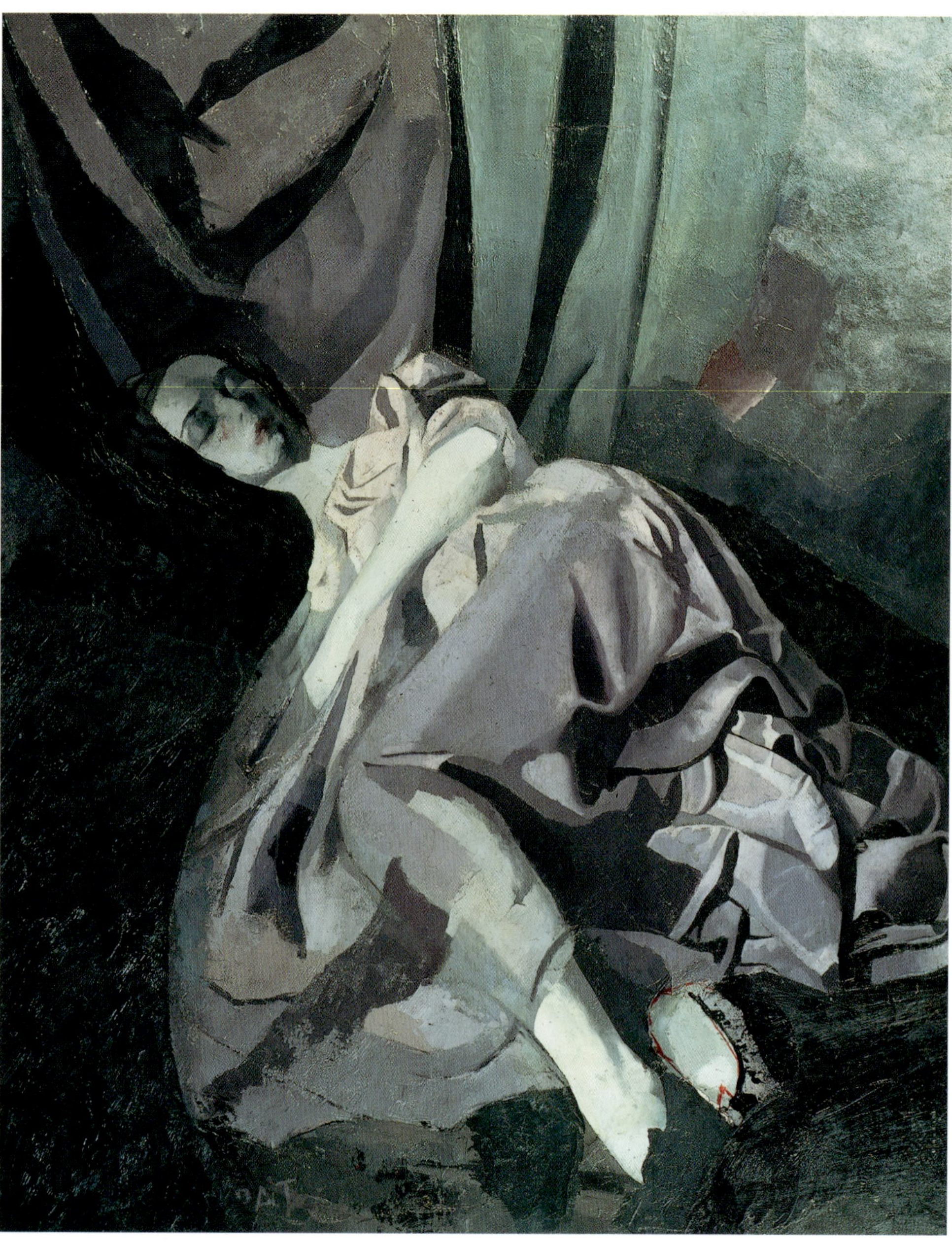

For the first of seven shows at Passedoit, Dickinson elected to exhibit drawings of various sites in Provincetown and Sheldrake. Even if Passedoit had requested only drawings, in retrospect, it seems like an odd choice. Why would an artist, for his inaugural show at a prestigious New York gallery, present only drawings? The reason may be quite simple. It was the thirties, after all, and with the Depression still in force, art was considered a luxury in most people's minds. So perhaps they elected to exhibit works on paper at a price people might be able to afford? Although the show received positive reviews, apparently, close to nothing sold.[33]

Dickinson took drawing seriously and did it conscientiously, and he would continue to include drawings in subsequent exhibitions at Passedoit and elsewhere. According to Helen Dickinson Baldwin, he never traveled anywhere without his drawing kit. Drawing brought out another side of his creativity by mediating between labor-intensive compositions and impulsive *premier coups*, between dream and reality. Anyone who has spent time with Dickinson's drawings knows their allure. They display impeccable control. They can be architectonic and linear, diaphanous and ethereal. Using only graphite and charcoal, and when necessary smudging the medium with his little finger, he achieved palpable textures and a broad tonal range. The world as represented in a Dickinson drawing is deceptive, reflecting the "weirdness" that John Ashbery describes in his poignant piece on the artist reprinted herein. Reflections deflect expectations. Strange twists of vision produce subtle distortions. Unexplainable things happen in the drawings that do not occur in other works.

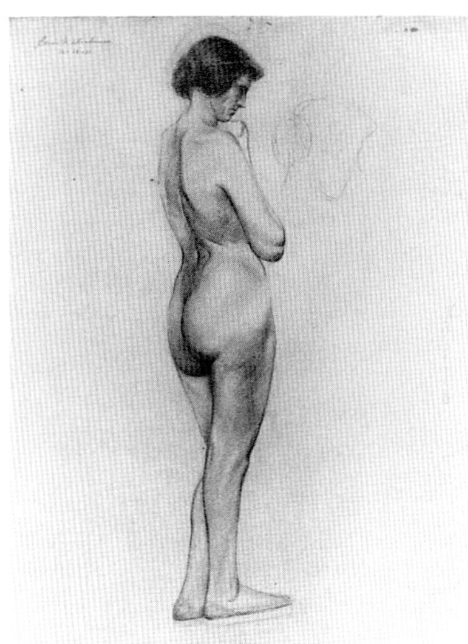

Fig. 11
Edwin Dickinson
Standing Female, Rear View, 1911
graphite and charcoal on paper, 24 × 18 (61 × 45.7)
Scharf Family Collection
Courtesy Dickinson Family Archive

"I was just an average boy," he reminisced to Gruber. "Mostly I was interested in football, and social life, and all those things—I'm glad I was. But I had always drawn more than other boys and was considered good at it. Any boys who also drew, we would draw together. Not art drawing, but soldiers and regiments—little figures in ink. Sometimes I would copy something. I ran across some pen and ink drawings of England, done in 1907, which are the earliest things I have."[34] What started as a childhood hobby developed into a serious course of study. In Frank DuMond's class at the League, in 1911, he drew from live models (fig. 11), a practice he continued in Provincetown. After arriving in Paris, December 29, 1919, he could be found drawing at the Académie de la Grande Chaumière (cat. no. 69). In these Parisian works he began to crop and simplify, to emphasize negative and positive space, and to use the figure as a vehicle for more abstract configurations. During his European travels, he also experimented with watercolor, producing notable works in St. Tropez (cat. no. 70). As he made his way through southern France and Spain, he filled his notebook with sketches. It was an intense period of drawing, the fruits of which remained for the most part obscure until James Graham & Sons exhibited a selection of these in 1968.

By the mid-twenties, Dickinson's unique draughtsmanship distinguished his works on paper. Like the symbolical paintings, some drawings evolved over multiple sittings. However, unlike the paintings, most were completed in fewer than six. Their affinity to his compositions resides in their composite constitution, layered with innuendo. This is certainly true of *Staircase, The Manse at Ulysses* (cat. no. 74), a drawing begun in Trumansburg, New York, January 2, 1928, two months after his marriage to Frances Foley, who was known as Pat.

Dickinson's father was then pastor of the First Presbyterian Church of Ulysses in Trumansburg. After their marriage on October 31, Edwin and his bride took the midnight train to Sheldrake, where they spent the winter in the family cottage. From Sheldrake they made numerous trips to Trumansburg. *Staircase* was drawn during one of these visits, from January 2 to 6. Natural light wafts through windows. Multiple reflections imply multiple levels of being. Certain areas (balustrade, stairs, windowsills and panes, moldings, and other architectural elements) are carefully delineated in perspective. Others (reflections off windows, mirrors and walls, drapes over windows) remain more suggestive. Dickinson's line displays quirky aspects, especially when it strays from definition and meanders over the paper's surface. Implications are made, only to be relinquished. Questions arise. What, for instance, is the rectangular form in the lower right? A mirror? A doorway? A picture frame without its image? Does the shading around it have any significance? And what is the faceless bust doing on the stairwell that spirals heavenward to a skylight where the artist's signature appears?

A drawing like *Staircase*, akin to *The Fossil Hunters*, in which the initials *B.D.* [Burgess Dickinson] appear under Beethoven's death mask, as well as perennial entries in the journals, was Dickinson's way of evoking the memory of loved ones deceased. In his mind, life and death were inextricably bound, like two sides of the same coin. Even in his most joyous moments, married only two months and still on his honey-

teen years earlier on January 28, 1913, assumed renewed meaning in January 1928. Though seemingly ordered by laws of perspective, *Staircase* is inhabited by mysterious and poignant muses. Such muses, inseparable from Dickinson's creative cycles, may explain on some level his continual wanderlust and why, given the opportunity to explore less familiar terrain, he did.

FREE TO PAINT UP A STORM

One opportunity to explore came in 1937, shortly after *Composition with Still Life* was finished. Using the money advanced to him by Esther and Ansley Sawyer, the entire family departed for Europe, intending to stay for two to three years. Landing in Rotterdam on December 2, they were in Paris by the next day and remained there for about two weeks before heading south to Arles in time for Christmas. From the moment they arrived in Paris, Dickinson felt relaxed and invigorated. It was his first time back since the war and now, with the Louvre entirely accessible, as it had not been in 1920, he was awestruck. "We spent more time at the Louvre than anywhere else," he wrote from Arles to his friends Esther and Ansley. "Much stimulated and informed; humility emphasized."[35] Copious letters to the Sawyers during this period confirm a close relationship that had begun twenty-five years earlier when Edwin and Esther met as students in Chase's class. With Esther's marriage to Ansley, a prominent Buffalo lawyer, in 1915, the friendship expanded. As an engagement present, Esther had given her husband-to-be a Dickinson painting. In time, the Sawyers not only provided Dickinson with a monthly stipend for twenty years and bought his drawings as gifts for others but also donated major paintings to museums, beginning with *An Anniversary* to the Albright Art Gallery in 1927, *Composition with Still Life* to the Museum of Modern Art in 1952, and finally *Woodland Scene* to Cornell in 1954.

Dickinson arrived in Arles with an ample supply of linen canvas and stretchers that had been purchased in Paris. It took a little while, however, before he finally got down to work. It was no easy task to find suitable living quarters for the family, and one of the children had contracted a cold in Arles that escalated into bronchitis. They would have stayed in Arles, but inclement weather and forty-mile-an-hour winds made painting outdoors impossible. So they proceeded south to Sanary-sur-Mer, where they rented a villa called Sinaia. Before the end of 1937, Dickinson was painting up a storm. "Sanary is a perfect place for a landscape painter, which is what Dick now is," Frances wrote to the Sawyers. "Rocks—sea—olive trees—grape vine stumps and many many villas. Everyday is warm enough for painting and we ride with the sea."[36] Frances took a photograph at this time of her bearded husband in beret and their two young children posed on the red granite cliffs of Port Issol (fig. 12). They had surely discovered a painter's paradise.

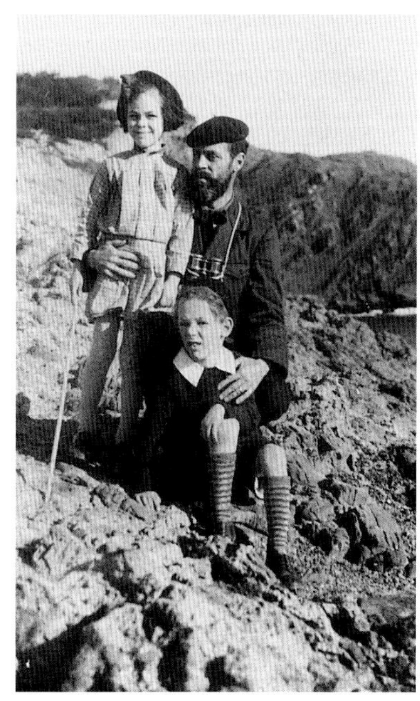

Fig. 12
Helen, Constant, and Edwin on cliffs at Port Issol, France, February 1938
Photograph by Frances Dickinson
Courtesy Dickinson Family Archive

Dickinson had been painting the landscape *premier coup* since 1912, but in France he had a breakthrough. Actually, the breakthrough had begun the summer before, after finishing *Composition with Still Life* and returning once again to the landscape and more spontaneous painting. The results, however, were not entirely gratifying. "The last summer's landscapes," he wrote to the Sawyers, "weren't very good, but they turned me over and began the steady practice. I had not had this before, because of the big one always on my back.... What used to fill my mind doing landscapes was to a larger extent the exercise of experience applied to the new fresh experience that I wanted to get something from. There is no doing without that exercise, but I was wild to have it go along without taking up most of the room.... I got to work as soon as I could following our arrival in Europe. We have no friends [here], the days revolve around painting. The experiments I produced myself when the big one was done, I have had, am having & shall for some time. I am painting very much better."[37]

Dickinson arrived in Sanary unfettered and with a definite purpose in the form of another one-artist show at Passedoit scheduled for early April. His expectations for a second show were far greater; he envisioned a mini-retrospective—earlier compositions combined with the landscapes he was painting at a steady pace. By February 20, he had completed twenty-three canvases, some in three or four sittings but most *premier coup*. Sometimes walking for miles with all his gear, he gravitated to several motifs: villas painted on clear, bright days, and coastal and interior scenes. Compared with earlier *premier coups*, the canvases painted in France are distinguished by a lighter touch, thinner paint application, and greater experimentation through the manipulation of paint with brush and fingers. Incorporating a broad range of perspectives and terrains, from the windy cliffs of Port Issol and sun-drenched villas to the intimate clearing of a wooded glade, these works display clear vision and dead-on concentration. By March 10, in less than two months and with only one month until the show opened, he had finished thirty works, sixteen of which were boxed for shipment to the States via Marseilles. In his mind's eye, he knew what the show should be and said so to Esther Sawyer: "The total for the exhibit is 35 oils, 22 of which are for sale and 13 loaned. . . . I am intent that Passedoit makes no changes, and that she crowd matters so that they may all be shown. . . . It is my first showing of the kind in New York; the new work will be better understood for better or worse when shown with the previous."[38]

On April 7, with selected canvases en route to New York, the family visited Italy for one week. By the end of the month, they were back in Sanary, where they remained for more than a month before moving to Paris for three weeks. With spring in full swing, they left for the Côtes du Nord and rented a stone farmhouse in Brittany, near Lancieux. Meanwhile, good news arrived from New York; the Metropolitan Museum of Art had purchased *Villa la Mouette,* 1938.[39] As it turned out, not every work shipped from France made it onto the walls at Passedoit, but this did not lessen the show's coverage in the major newspapers and art magazines. Some writers noticed the difference in personality between the symbolical paintings and the *premier coups*. One critic went so far as to say, that the landscapes "might have been painted by another hand."[40] Another anonymous writer described Dickinson as a visionary painter and went on to make some very astute observations: "Dickinson contrasts blurred landscapes of southern France with symbolic pictures of intermingled images. Centralizing on a distinguishable theme, the painter builds a composition of unusual patterns in an orchestration of funerary grays. Always there is a feeling of sinking into space, into an unreal world—a world inhabited by images of lean-faced men and white-breasted women. Occasionally gusts of smoke, fog or fire may be perceived in Dickinson's abysmal regions. . . . The art of this painter with its subdued color and indistinct forms seems to have been dreamed and developed from behind lowered curtains, in the coolness of a darkened parlor filled with familiar family objects."[41] Reviews such as these put Dickinson on the map, making his subsequent shows anticipated events.

The rest of the summer was spent in Lancieux, with the children enjoying the farm and Dickinson painting in nearby orchards sheltered from disruptive winds. In August he returned from a trip to Paris with unsettling news about the Czechoslovakian crisis. Using the radio in their farmhouse, he was able to monitor Morse code messages.

they soon realized they must depart. Securing visas proved impossible; with hordes of people already fleeing from French ports, the bureaucratic process took weeks. So they departed for England without visas, leaving from Dieppe on September 24. Landing at Newhaven later that morning, they were ushered into a cavernous customs room, where they waited and waited. It was a trying experience, remembers Helen Baldwin: "Father thought we had a better chance to clear customs without visas if there weren't people clamoring behind us, so we waited most of the night until we were the only ones left. He had a letter from the secretary of state, Cordell Hull, urging all possible courtesies for us. When it came our turn, all the customs officials gathered around and after much discussion finally let us through. In London, we stood for days in steamship lines until October 1, when we finally secured passage on the TSS *Transylvania* from Glasgow to Boston."[42] Safely back in the States, with very little money and nowhere to go, they hired a taxi to take them to Provincetown to stay with Pat's mother, who lived on Cook Street. She paid the hundred-dollar fare. Home they were, but far from settled.

PAINTING TO SURVIVE

After a short time in Provincetown, they decided to move to Buffalo. The Sawyers provided lodging and a studio for them there, but it was a grueling winter, with terrible weather and much sickness. When spring finally arrived, they were on the move again, this time in search of a permanent home. Together with his father, Dickinson scouted the northeast, looking as far south as Baltimore, Maryland. In the end, drawn back to the Cape, they found and bought a modest old house off Cove Road in Wellfleet. Dickinson had always wanted a house by the water and kept this one until 1980. Wellfleet may have been a painter's paradise, but with a wife and two young children, its rustic environs proved a formidable challenge. The first year was spent on improvement. Pat's mother provided the money for a kitchen, bathroom, and running water. The next fall, in 1940, and with a loan from their old friend Richard Parmenter, they were able to purchase additional land and build a painting studio that was finished later that year. Though settled for the most part, they were still struggling.

Wellfleet was not far from Provincetown, yet at times it felt like the other side of the moon, especially when the last rays of summer faded to winter. Summer was a glorious time, with rambunctious beach picnics that often peaked well into the night. Winter had a beauty all its own, but for some, the prospect of damp cold weather and shorter days was intimidating. For the Dickinson family, winter meant lean times, even with the Sawyers' monthly stipend and an annual, though variable, check from Pat's family, who owned a hotel in Winter Park, Florida. "We were as poor as church mice," Helen Baldwin recalled. "Those five years were difficult for all of us but especially my mother, who out of necessity raised chickens and shucked scallops."[43] At one point, when the situation became dire, the children were told that their family dog, Whistle, would have to go because they could no longer afford to feed her. Devastated, they pleaded, even offering to forgo their allowance. In the end, Whistle was allowed to stay.

Confronted with such conditions, Dickinson once again resorted to teaching. Twice a week he drove to Boston, to the Stuart School. He substituted for Arnold Geissbuhler's classes at Wellesley College; met with students at the Association for Music and Art on the Cape, in Centerville, and at the Art Center in Dennis; and voluntarily conducted a telegraphy class for Wellfleeters as part of the war effort. His affiliation with Passedoit probably seemed a godsend during these difficult years, even though annual shows meant additional pressure to produce. "That time [1939–1942]," he told Gruber, "was the beginning of having one [show] a year, for two or three years, and it was very taxing on me. The reason for doing it was to assist economically, living very limitedly with small children. We had no running water in the house, and we used kerosene and a coal stove, and it was cold. It was no hardship for me, but it was certainly not easy for the others. The exhibitions, one a year, were for the purpose of making money, at which I succeeded slightly."[44]

Even if these exhibitions did not put money in the bank, they brought recognition and mostly favorable reviews. The first show, shortly after their return from Europe, took place in April 1939, while the family lived in Buffalo. For this occasion, about sixteen paintings were exhibited, mostly *premier coup* landscapes from his prolific stint in France. One writer responded to the work's evocative quality. "A series of vapory oils in dusky greens, greys, and browns, with forms barely emerging from the mistiness of the landscape scenes," he wrote, "makes an unusually poetic show."[45] Another praised Dickinson's supple technique but questioned his success rate: ". . . in doing these quick and sometimes amazingly suggestive impressions of fleeting mood and light of the out-of-doors," he wrote, "he is not always completely successful. . . . He is at work in a borderland of flux and fluidity in an experimental world where the statements of his sensitive brush will be watched with much interest."[46] The *premier coups* were a hit-or-miss proposition. That was their challenge and, when everything came together, their brilliance. Critics responded accordingly.

In December, *New York Times* critic Howard Devree lauded a second installation of about seventeen drawings, describing the show as one "for connoisseurs, students, and all enthusiasts of the black-and-white medium."[47] Some stunning works were produced for this occasion, four of which—*View from a Wellfleet Window, Cottage Window, South Wellfleet Inn*, and *Roses*, all from 1939 (cat. nos. 81, 82, 83, and 84)—epitomize Dickinson's distinctive touch and imagination. The following two shows, mounted a year apart in April 1940 and 1941, were devoted exclusively to paintings. In both of these, Dickinson's tendency to abstract the landscape had become more pronounced. "Always heading in that direction," the critic for the *Times* wrote, "the artist has at length entered upon an abstract phase that is virtually uncompromising."[48] Another kind of landscape, begun in situ and transformed through successive sittings, also emerged as a new direction at this time. *The Finger Lakes*, 1940 (cat. no. 34), is an example of this composite entity. In this work, additional sittings introduced a more complex iconography in the form of a rose at the bottom of the image and a hot-air balloon at the top.[49] Several frontal self-portraits found their way into the 1941 show, as well. One of these, reproduced in the *Art Digest*, was described as "a detached study of a man who has looked long and searchingly at himself. With its deathly blacks and chalk white face, it is like looking down into a coffin."[50] The same self-portrait would represent the artist two years later in Dorothy Miller's *Romantic Painting in America*.

Most critics recognized the bipolar character of Dickinson's symbolical paintings and *premier coups*. Some saw, with the *premier coups*, a tendency toward distillation and abstraction. Edward Alden Jewell said as much in 1941, when he wrote, "Mr. Dickinson does not define, he does not incorporate detail; instead his art is entirely, or very largely, a distillation—a matter of essences." A year later, in another review, he added that the work "reveals no change, but fortifies the mood of clairvoyant sensitiveness established years ago. These are for the most part true 'essence' abstractions."[51] By the early forties, Dickinson's distinct vision was registering sympathetically not only with critics but with curators and, especially, a younger generation of painters.

A PAINTER RETURNS TO NEW YORK

Seven one-artist shows at Passedoit had been Dickinson's introduction to a New York audience. However, by the end of 1942, his relationship with the gallery was tenuous. Around that time, Georgette Passedoit had taken on a new partner, John Blair, and apparently the relationship between him and Dickinson was strained. Dickinson continued to keep work at the gallery on consignment until 1949, but he stopped exhibiting there after 1942. For nineteen years, until his retrospective at James Graham & Sons in 1961, he remained by choice unaffiliated.

By the end of World War II, New York had begun a dramatic cultural transformation. The art world was changing and so was the role of the commercial art gallery and its influence on an artist's career. What had been customary for an aspiring artist during Dickinson's youth—the juried exhibition—was becoming a thing of the past. In a letter to Esther Sawyer posted from Wellfleet on February 23, 1943, he bemoaned the fact that museums in New York had abandoned jury-selected exhibitions. "They [the museums] appoint a jury, however, which visits the dealers and invites from among painters who have dealers the making of the exhibition. This does away with anything new, better from younger men, and is, I surely hope, a practice that will soon overthrow itself. It is the product, Esther, of the type of museum director who is now the most accepted type in the highest places."[52] The waning relationship with Passedoit only exacerbated this exclusionary perception.

In a postscript to the same letter, Dickinson mentioned a woman well connected in the art world and a memorable studio visit he recently made: "Last fall [1942] in New York, a woman very much in the smart, international modern art whirl said she knew someone who knew me—it was [Jackson] Pollock, a zany fellow by whom I saw a canvas at the time I was assembling the exhibition for our association (the Bairds bought it I think—cotton pickers subject).[53] I take it that Pollock has pushed himself along but being in New York so little I have never seen anything by him. At that time (last fall) I went to the studio of a young Dutchman (35) who is quite unknown, but not among one division of painters. A remarkable fellow—de Kooning."[54] The woman may have been Elaine Fried (soon to be Elaine de Kooning), and with their introduction began a cordial friendship.

In June 1943, Dickinson wrote to Ansley and Esther, again from Wellfleet: "The Museum of Modern Art in New York is to have an exhibition of 'American Romantic Painters' this fall, and has asked me to send them eight paintings 'to see'—entirely, of course, at their own expense. The large 'Figures & Still Life' is in their hands now."[55] *Figures & Still Life* (later retitled *Composition with Still Life*) had been at the Paul Rosenberg Gallery for consideration since February and from there was delivered directly to the Museum of Modern Art. By September, Dorothy Miller had made her selection. "The Museum of Modern Art," he wrote to Esther, "is going to show the *Figures & Still Life* & a self portrait. They wrote me that they are showing but two because of the size of the large one. . . . They seem interested in the large one and have asked questions about it."[56]

Romantic Painting in America premiered in November. Having missed the opening, Dickinson did not get to New York to see the show until February 1, five days before it closed. On February 2 he wrote in his journal: "To MoMA to see show—Breakfast at the Park Lane—walked, lunched with Sid, Mary, Thorn; to symphony—Cooper Union and ASL—Picked up two photos of Pompeii."[57] It was a whirlwind visit, one of many over the next six months. The family had decided to leave Wellfleet for a larger city. Better schools were sought for the children, and Dickinson realized that his livelihood would benefit from more opportunities. New York should have been their logical destination, given Dickinson's familiarity with it and its already positive influence on his career, but they were also considering Boston, where he and Geissbuhler were hoping to open their own art school. By 1944, signs seemed to point toward Boston, where Pat had already landed a job.

Dickinson had been traveling back and forth to New York since March, looking for a place to live and, more importantly, some kind of employment. "I have been to NY twice in the last 10 days," he wrote to Ansley from Wellfleet, "looking for a teaching position. These trips were short ones & the 2nd one not planned."[58] Both, it turned out, were fruitless, and he did not return to New York until late June, when he settled in for a month. "As is imaginable," he wrote to Esther and Ansley from his temporary lodgings at 350 East Thirty-third Street, "there are reasons why it would be better for each one of us four to be in a large city now, and this late spring, we decided that I should spend the summer in New York in an effort to secure an amount per month in addition to what we have, which would enable us to be here."[59] Apart from a portrait commission (done from a photograph) and another commission (later canceled) from a French magazine, *Tricolor*, to produce a suite of drawings of New York subjects (cat. nos. 87–89),[60] he found little work and no teaching. He did, however, locate an apartment just before he left for Wellfleet on August 15 and took it on the spot. He wrote to Ansley the day after he returned to Wellfleet: "We think it expedient that we leave Wellfleet. I went to New York at the end of June to look for a teaching position and ascertain whether or not we could venture going there, if, a teaching position failing, I could get other work in my field to do. I want a teaching position, but I did not get one. I now feel sure that the yearly trip to New York for this purpose is fruitless—one must be there in order to get one, and I expect to have one for the winter following this one." He then added: "Apartments in New York are exceedingly difficult to find. I found one, suitable for us, at $55 a month, and it was necessary that I decide to take, or not to take and at once I took it."[61]

So, on September 2, the entire family moved into a small apartment at 420 West 119th Street. Pat was the first to find work and by October 2 was teaching at the Hewitt School. It took a little while longer for Dickinson, who meanwhile settled for commissions. "Since coming to NY," he wrote to Esther later that month, "I have done only work that I had received orders to do. I am painting in our apartment and brought no work from Wellfleet as I shall not have a studio for a little time yet." Toward the end of the letter, he returned to what was becoming a pet peeve: the dearth of juried shows and the all-too-powerful influence of dealers and galleries in determining who got shown. "There is now," he declared, "hardly such a thing as an 'open' show to which a young or unknown man can send in the hope of attracting some attention or gaining prestige through participation."[62]

In spite of the art world's seemingly capricious dynamics, Dickinson had every reason to be optimistic. His visibility through annual exhibitions may have been on hold but not his reputation. Living in New York required a stable livelihood, however, and before too long he had returned to teaching. The first offer to come through in March was from the Cooper Union, and by the fall of 1945 he was teaching classes there on Tuesdays and Fridays, and at his alma mater, the Art Students League, on Mondays and Thursdays. A year later, the Midtown School offered him two classes on Wednesdays and Fridays and before the decade ended, he was also employed at the Art School of

because of his tendency to relinquish these during the summer when the family returned to Wellfleet) and resumed work on *Ruin at Daphne*.

Work was balanced by an active social life. Dickinson never had a problem keeping himself busy, morning, noon, or night. Even his earliest years in Provincetown, as recorded in the journals, read like an impressive social calendar. Once in New York and settled into a consistent teaching schedule, he and Pat began to explore the town. They went to art openings. Movies were a once-a-week pastime, with or without the children. Relishing animated company and good conversation, they developed a close circle of friends who came from many walks of life.

One of their closest friends, Janice Tworkov, had been a student of Dickinson's in Provincetown during the twenties.[63] Her professional name was *Biala*, after the small town of her birth in eastern Poland, from where she and her brother, Jack Tworkov, had emigrated to the United States, with their mother, in 1913. By the mid-twenties, both were committed to art and had found their way to Provincetown, where they continued their studies during the summers. Biala had heard about Dickinson and came to Provincetown to study with him. A portrait he made of her in 1924 documents their early association (fig. 13), and he would paint her again on the beach at Wellfleet in the summer of 1940 (cat. no. 37). After a brief stint with Charles Hawthorne at the

Fig. 13
Edwin Dickinson
Portrait of Janice Tworkov, 1924
oil on canvas, 30 × 25 (76.2 × 63.5)
Courtesy Mitchell-Innes & Nash, New York

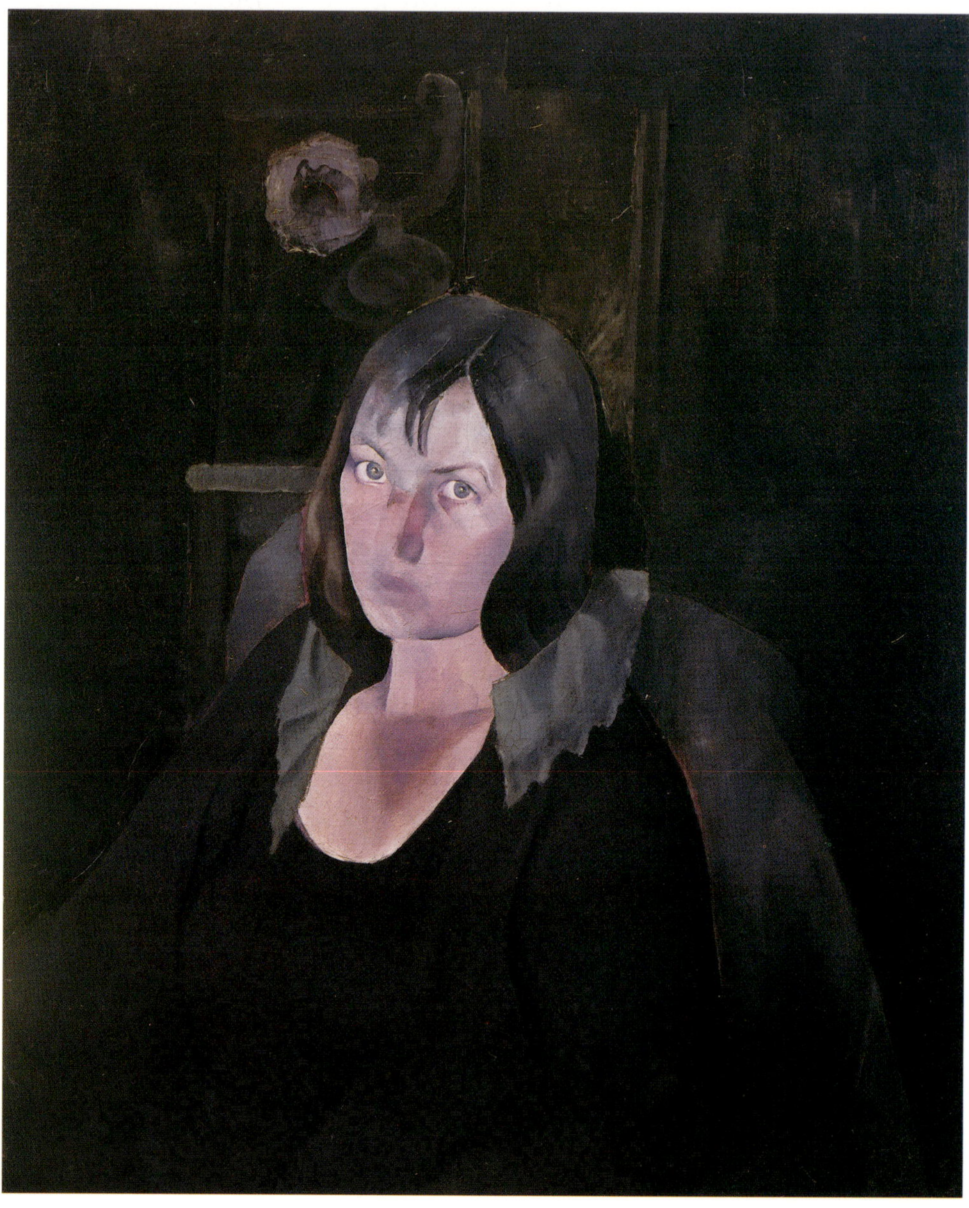

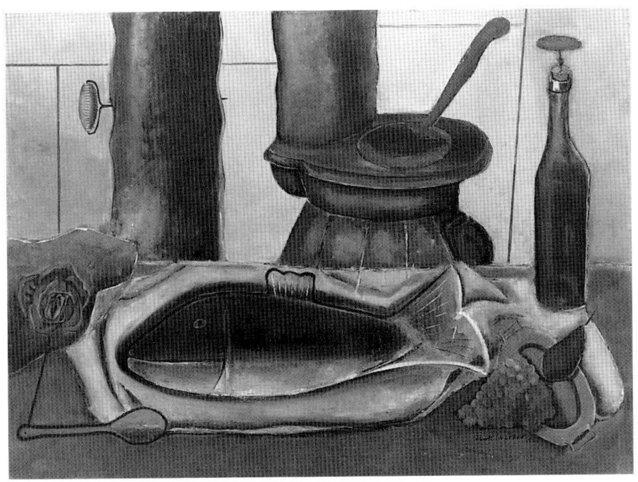

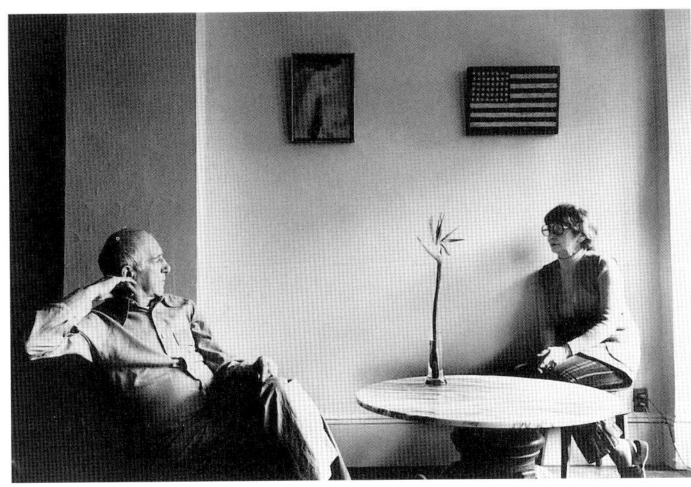

Fig. 14
Jack Tworkov
American, 1900–1982
Fish and Rose, 1928
oil on canvas, 25¼ × 34¼ (64.1 × 87)
Courtesy Mitchell-Innes & Nash, New York

Fig. 15
Jack and Wally Tworkov, ca. 1974–75
Photograph © Theo Westenberger 1975
Courtesy Estate of Jack Tworkov

National Academy of Design, and upon arriving in Provincetown, Jack aligned himself with Ross Moffett and Karl Knaths.[64] Dickinson, too, must have impressed him, because in 1928 Tworkov painted a still-life that can be seen as a kind of homage (fig. 14). Of a predominantly somber palette, with all the accoutrements—coal stove, large fish, spoon, uncorked bottle of wine, fruit on a tray—of an austere Provincetown existence, this otherwise Spartan spread has patched into it a brilliant red rose. Anyone who knew anything about Dickinson's work by this time knew about the rose, his signature motif. Jack and Biala became loyal friends and great admirers. Together they purchased one of Dickinson's nudes, painted in Buffalo in 1934, which eventually landed in Jack's New York loft, where it assumed a place of honor on the wall next to a small Jasper Johns *Flag* (fig. 15).

Biala and Jack were instrumental in fostering the relationship that developed between the Dickinsons and the de Koonings.[65] As early as February 1943, even before the family relocated to New York, Dickinson's journal records a dinner at Biala's and an evening spent with the de Koonings.[66] They would socialize throughout the forties and fifties, sharing a respectful rapport. In terms of studio practice and technique, Dickinson and Willem de Kooning shared a few traits, as well. Both courted a belabored process and the tendency to scrape and rework a canvas for years at a stretch. Both demonstrated impeccable draughtsmanship and understood that representation was a relative proposition. And both took liberty when painting the female nude, which they cropped, obscured, and abstracted to varying degrees (see cat. no. 32). Both of them honored painting's history and old masters, and both embraced the necessity for change.[67] Dickinson sensed de Kooning's remarkable potential when they first met in the fall of 1942, and their mutual admiration grew over time. During the sixties and seventies, Dickinson's work was frequently compared with that of de Kooning.[68] In the end, subjectivity, with its potential to transform otherwise recognizable subject matter, was their common ground (fig. 16).

Mutual admiration was one thing. Admiration through thoughtful prose another. After their introduction, Elaine de Kooning began tracking Dickinson's work and studio procedure, which eventually led to the publication, in 1949, of an article for *Art News*. As a critic, her career had been launched only a year before, through the encouragement of Edwin Denby, a personal friend and dance critic for the *New York Herald Tribune*. Her piece on Dickinson, part of an ongoing series of articles initiated by managing editor Thomas Hess about artists in their studios, and generically titled "so and so paints a picture or makes a sculpture," offered an insider's account of the artist's

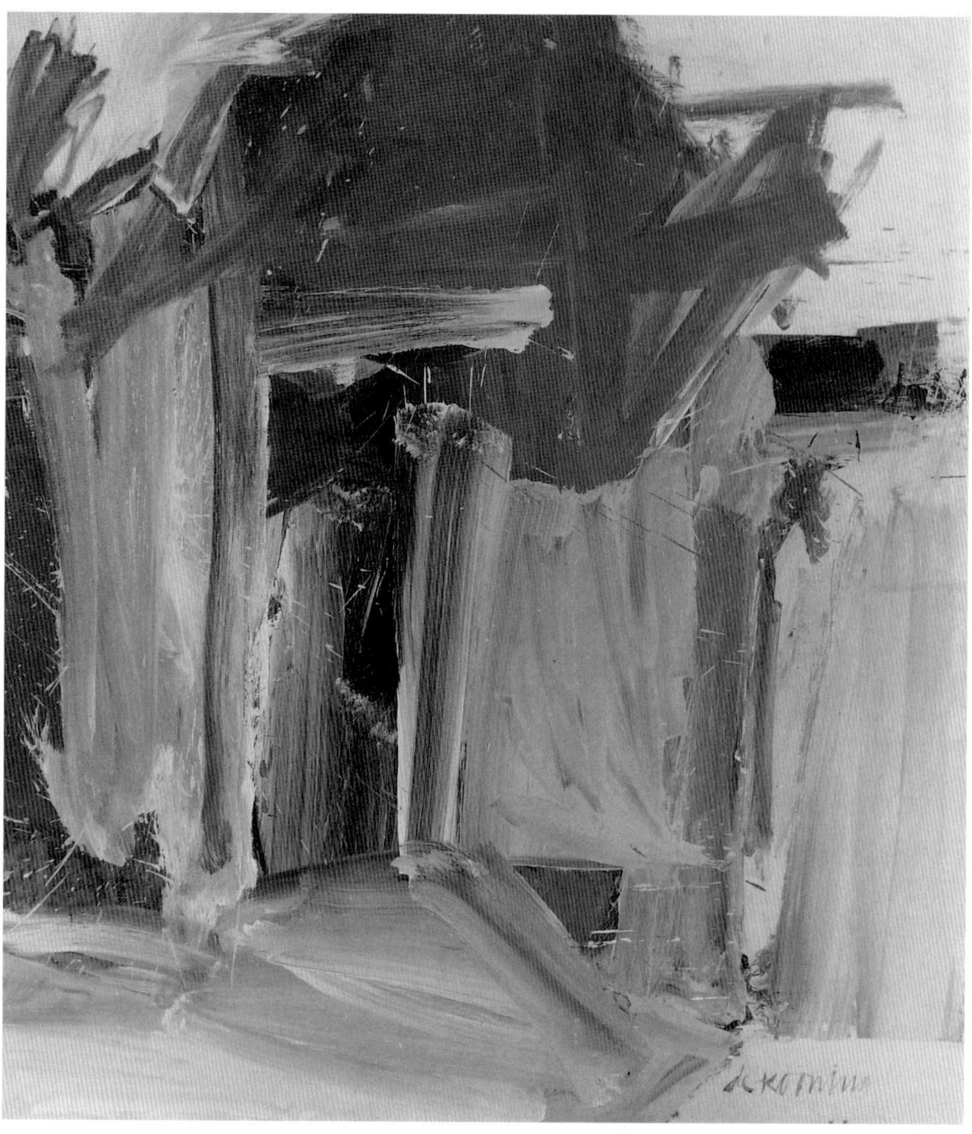

Fig. 16
Willem de Kooning
Door to the River, 1960
oil on canvas, 82¼ × 72 (208.9 × 182.9)
Collection Whitney Museum of American Art, New York
Purchase, with funds from the Friends of the Whitney Museum of American Art

pressed her most about Dickinson's work, in particular the *Ruin at Daphne*, was its poetic and mystical character and the way the painting defied completion. "The poetic content is an important part of the expression," she wrote, "but here [in *The Ruin*], as in his other work, by a curious reversal of the usual creative method, he does not start out with a fixed subject which he then describes or abstracts in paint, but rather he finds his subject through his method of composing. All of his past techniques; his life-long obsession with perspective; his sense of history, archaeology, architecture, poetry and nature seemed to lead him naturally to *The Ruin* as a theater of operations. *The Ruin*, as he presents it, is a dispassionate record of constantly changing possibilities in time, in place, in style and in design."[69] Photographed by Rudolph Burckhardt over the course of four years, in 1945 and 1949, for publication in *Art News*, by the time *Ruin at Daphne* appeared in *15 Americans*, it had already acquired a life of its own.

Dickinson's inclusion in *15 Americans* gave Elaine de Kooning another opportunity to write about him. Of the fifteen artists in the exhibition, many with well-established reputations by 1952, she chose to write about two underdogs pushing sixty—Dickinson and Frederick Kiesler. It was great press for both of them. Once again, in her discussion of Dickinson's *premier coups* and symbolical paintings, she stressed his process. "Any internal limitations," she wrote, "that his style presents in personal characteristics—the cold, dreamy greys, lavenders, greens and sandy tones of his palette, the smeary brush strokes, the alternate sharpening and blurring of detail and the sudden, hallucinatory changes of perspective in his large compositions—are the result of method not theory."[70]

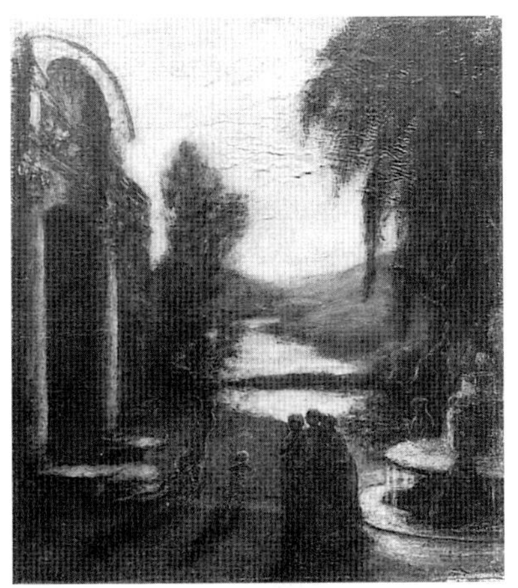

Fig. 17
Albert Pinkham Ryder
American, 1847–1917
The Temple of the Mind, ca. 1885
oil on wood, 17¾ × 16 (45.1 × 40.6)
Collection Albright-Knox Art Gallery, Buffalo, New York
Gift of R. B. Angus, 1918

On the heels of *15 Americans*, Dickinson's career took a noticeable upward swing. He seems to have reached an elevated level of recognition. His quasi-abstractions were singled out by a younger generation of painters, who saw in them a model for their own. Through his association with the de Koonings and Jack Tworkov, Dickinson found himself in an enviable position, lionized by a younger art crowd as a unique American phenomenon.

The history of modernism is punctuated by episodes of canonization, the adulation of older individuals who, through deed or personality, become the living incarnation of a vanguard ethos. Think of Henri Rousseau's banquet celebration hosted by Picasso and friends; the Surrealists' appropriation of Giorgio de Chirico in the twenties; and Albert Pinkham Ryder's posthumous celebration by the Stieglitz group. What Ryder was to Marsden Hartley and Paul Rosenfeld in the teens and twenties, Dickinson was to the Abstract Expressionists in the fifties: a role model for the visionary painter.[71] Dickinson's affinity with Ryder is apt (fig. 17). Even his Edwardian demeanor, so beautifully described by Elaine de Kooning in her recollection reprinted in this volume, reinforced the aura of someone from another time and place.[72]

Longevity pays off, especially if you end up, as Dickinson most certainly did, at the right place at the right time. His appearance in bohemian circles, even if sporadic, probably seemed like a breath of fresh air. By all accounts, he sparkled in company. Invited by Elaine de Kooning to sessions at the Club, he was also asked to submit *premier coups* to annual juried exhibitions at the Stable Gallery (cat. nos. 58–60).[73] Jack Tworkov, one of the Club's founding members and a Stable regular, continued to be ardently supportive.[74] To someone like Tworkov, and undoubtedly to others as well, Dickinson's refreshing authenticity and subjective tendencies reflected the contemporary mind-set of many downtown painters, summed up by John Ferren in 1958: "We faced the canvas with the Self, whatever that was, and we painted.... The only control was that of truth, intuitively felt. If it wasn't true to our feeling, according to protocol it had to be rubbed out. In fact, painters boasted of their painting as a tangible record of a series of errors."[75]

The fifties ushered in multiple exhibitions and numerous awards. Dickinson had finally arrived and was being recognized accordingly with full memberships at the National Academy of Design and National Institute of Arts and Letters, the American Academy of Arts and Letters, and awards from the Century Association, the Ford Foundation, and Brandeis University. In keeping with his life's philosophy, he never refused a show. Granted, some were more notable than others, especially between 1958 and 1959, when the Cushman Gallery in Houston, Texas, and the Art Gallery at Boston University sponsored substantive surveys. With all this action, there was no great urgency to find a dealer to represent him. This did not stop interested parties from approaching him with offers, and he heard from Eleanor Ward at the Stable Gallery, James Graham, and Philip Bruno at World House Galleries, where he exhibited selected paintings and drawings in June and July of 1960. By that time, he was ready to commit. So was James Graham & Sons, who signed him on for a retrospective the following year.

It was an eye-opening retrospective: 117 oils, beginning with the 1914 *Self-Portrait* (cat. no. 1) and ending with the *Chair* painting from 1956 (cat. no. 68), and 35 drawings spanning the years 1920 to 1959. Compared with the show's impressive contents,

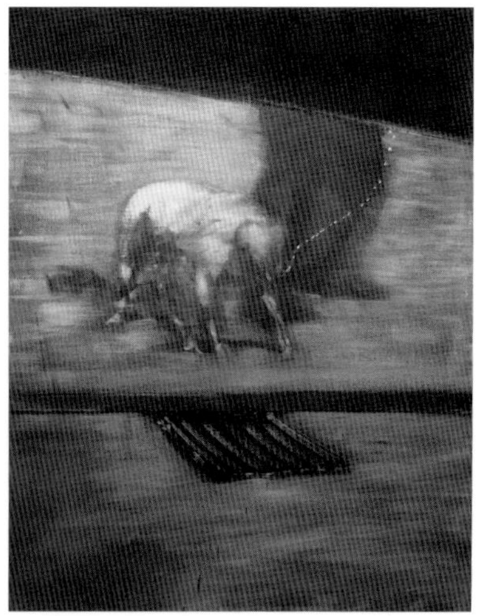

Fig. 18
Francis Bacon
English, 1909–1992
Man with Dog, 1953
oil on canvas, 60 × 46 (152.4 × 116.8)
Collection Albright-Knox Art Gallery, Buffalo, New York
Gift of Seymour H. Knox, Jr., 1955
© 2001 Estate of Francis Bacon/Artists Rights Society (ARS), New York

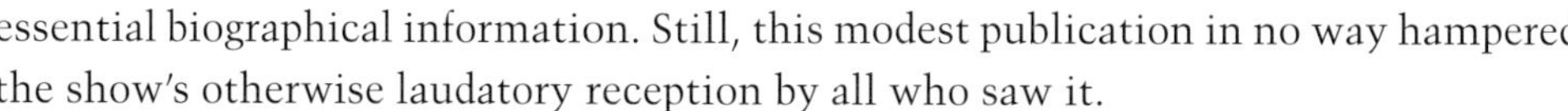

essential biographical information. Still, this modest publication in no way hampered the show's otherwise laudatory reception by all who saw it.

Even for those already acquainted with the work, the retrospective at Graham was revelatory, and its simultaneous run with other museum and gallery exhibitions—*The Precisionist View in American Art* at the Whitney, and shows of Yasuo Kuniyoshi at Edith Halpert's Downtown Gallery and O. Louis Guglielmi at Nordness—made for a constructive context. In such distinguished company, Dickinson's efforts stood out. "No American show this season," wrote Stuart Preston in the *New York Times*, "is likely to eclipse in all-around importance the retrospective of Edwin Dickinson's paintings and drawings at the Graham."[76] Of all the writers to review the show, Dore Ashton offered some of the most perceptive insights. She affirmed Dickinson's status among painters when she wrote, "For many years I have heard Edwin Dickinson discussed by other painters in tones of respect reserved usually for dead masters. The seventy-year-old New England eccentric—for that is his old-fashioned virtue—has exercised an unusual authority in the art world where the painter's painter becomes increasingly rare." She rightly observed that the luminous blurring in Dickinson's work related to that of other postwar figurative painters and sculptors—de Kooning, Francis Bacon, and Alberto Giacometti—who "have used the blurring and obscuring of features in a positive way to suggest the interplay of environment and personality" (fig. 18). And she encapsulated his distinct vision when she concluded, "Dickinson was instinctively aware . . . and repeatedly threw mystifying veils over the details of his subjects."[77]

The painter's fame, so well deserved by this late date, seemed assured. Three subsequent events would confirm it: Dorothy Miller's traveling survey, organized in 1961 through the Circulating Exhibitions Department at the Museum of Modern Art; the retrospective Lloyd Goodrich organized, with the artist's assistance, at the Whitney Museum of American Art in 1965; and Norman Geske's choice of him as principal painter at the American Pavilion at the XXXIV Venice Biennale in 1968.[78]

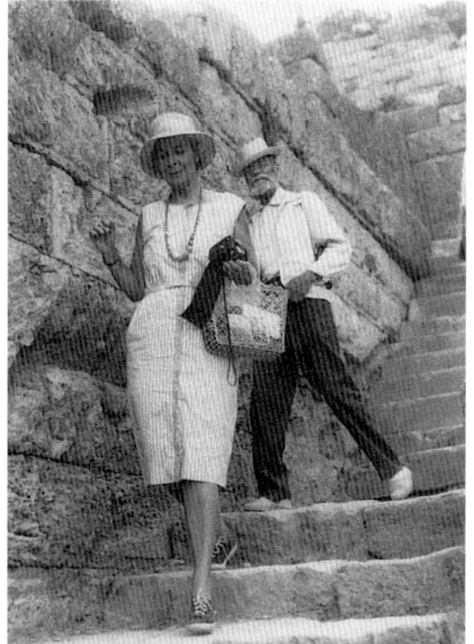

Fig. 19
Pat and Edwin at Delphi, Greece
Courtesy Dickinson Family Archive

MEMORY DISMANTLED

Dickinson's later years, though productive, seem tinged with sadness. He had achieved success and with it, a degree of financial security. His works were now in major collections, his reputation was secure, and he was finally free to paint. Throughout the sixties he was still able to paint, but painting did not figure largely in his daily routine. Instead, he sustained a rigorous commitment to teaching and gave generously of his time to various committees and panels. If painting fell by the way, he seemed to accept the situation with grace, even if he was at times frustrated by it.

In the twilight of life, traveling with Pat became a favorite pastime. Their trips abroad, to the Middle East and Greece (fig. 19), begun in 1959, became more frequent as time went on. He was never without his drawing kit and journal during these excursions, and the drawings from the early sixties are some of the most minimal and abstract he produced (cat. no. 93). Drawing persisted as his creative lifeline. His journals, too, continued to function as they always had, as a daily log. For someone so obsessed with memory, the sad irony is that by 1970 Dickinson had developed what was probably Alzheimer's disease, even though at the time no one knew what it was and what was happening to him. The journals document its onslaught as his writing becomes disjunctive and erratic. By this time, though he did want to paint, he could not. His memory had begun to dismantle. Had he been another kind of painter, he might have carried on, as de Kooning did during the eighties despite severe memory lapses.[79] But in this respect, Dickinson could not be de Kooning once the veil of forgetfulness lowered. His process required the motif, the site, to be primed. His was not de Kooning's broad gestural approach, where reliance on procedural memory might have compensated.

When all physiological systems began to shut down and his cognitive faculties failed him, Pat remained lovingly at his side. She was his constant companion until the end, even after his transfer from his Wellfleet home to a nearby nursing facility in Orleans, where she visited daily. And it was Jack and Wally Tworkov who brought him to their Provincetown home on October 11, 1978, to celebrate his eighty-seventh birthday. By then a shadow of his former self, he had slipped into another realm no one else could enter, a place devoid of memory but, for all we know, full of light.

Fig. 20
Edwin at Wellfleet, September 13, 1972
Photograph by Tom Breuer
Courtesy Dickinson Family Archive

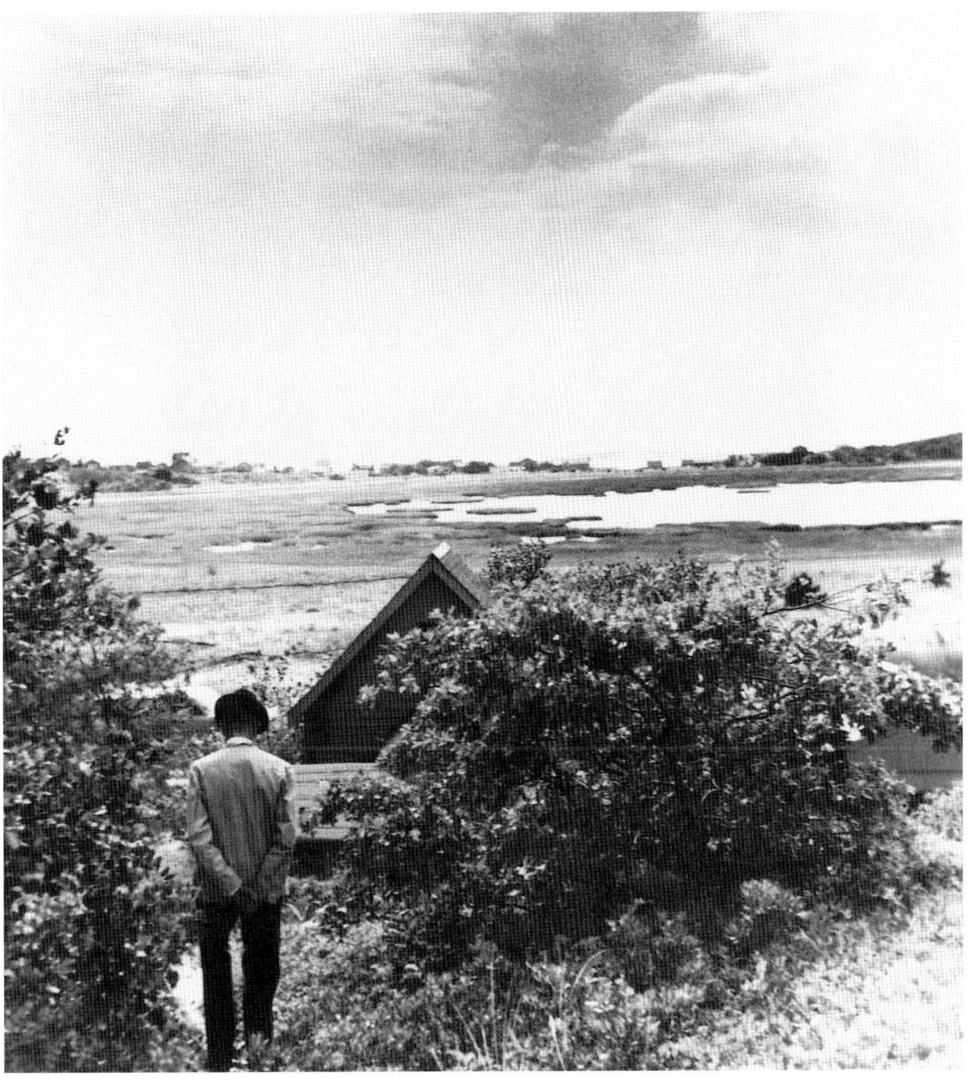

NOTES

1. Dorothy C. Miller and James Thrall Soby, *Romantic Painting in America* (New York: Museum of Modern Art, New York, 1943).

2. These included *Paintings by Nineteen Living Americans* (1929–30), *Painting and Sculpture by Living Americans* (1930–31), *Americans 1942* (1942), and *Fourteen Americans* (1946).

3. This description appeared in a letter Dickinson wrote from France to his longtime friend Esther Sawyer, in the midst of a prolific bout of painting; see Edwin Dickinson, letter to Esther Sawyer, Feb. 6, 1938, Archives of American Art, Washington, D.C. Unless otherwise noted, all Dickinson letters cited hereafter are housed at the Archives of American Art.

4. Elaine de Kooning, "Edwin Dickinson Paints a Picture," *Art News* (New York), Sept. 1949, p. 62. A painter in her own right and active in a burgeoning art scene south of Fourteenth Street, de Kooning's partisanship on behalf of Dickinson's work would play an important role in the way his career escalated in the late forties. They probably met through mutual friends Janice Tworkov and Jack Tworkov, both painters whose longtime friendship with the Dickinson family began in the small Cape Cod village of Provincetown, where Dickinson's own career had begun forty years earlier and where *Ruin at Daphne* was initiated January 1, 1943, less than a year before the entire family relocated to New York City.

5. For an insider's recollection of Provincetown during the early days, see Ross Moffett, *Art in Narrow Streets: The First Thirty-three Years of the Provincetown Art Association* (Falmouth, Mass.: Kendall Printing Co., 1964), and Mary Heaton Vorse, *Time and the Town: A Provincetown Chronicle* (New York: Dial Press, 1942; reprinted Rutgers University Press, 1991).

6. Robert Motherwell, "Provincetown and Days Lumberyard: A Memoir," *Days Lumberyard Studios, Provincetown 1914–1971* (Provincetown, Mass.: Provincetown Art Association and Museum, 1978), p. 16; reprinted in *The Collected Writings of Robert Motherwell* (New York: Oxford University Press, 1992), p. 226. Motherwell cited Provincetown as being on the forty-two–degree meridian. In actuality, it is on the forty-two–degree parallel.

7. Katharine Kuh, "Edwin Dickinson," in *The Artist's Voice: Talks with Seventeen Artists* (New York: Harper & Row, 1962), p. 77.

8. Helen Dickinson Baldwin, interview by author, Nashville, Tennessee, Sept. 22, 2000, audiocassette.

9. Dorothy Seckler, "Interview with Edwin Dickinson," Provincetown, Massachusetts, Aug. 22, 1962, transcribed manuscript, Oral History Collection, Archives of American Art, Washington, D.C., p. 2.

10. Carol S. Gruber, "The Reminiscences of Edwin Dickinson," transcribed manuscript (New York: Oral History Research Office, Columbia University, 1957–58), p. 23.

11. Dickinson's original journals, comprising forty-six volumes dated 1916 to 1971, are on deposit in the Special Collections Library at Syracuse University, New York. All entries quoted are taken from these journals. Thirty-six of the forty-six volumes of Dickinson's journal can also be consulted in the Archives of American Art, Washington, D.C., Reels D93–D96, 1916–61.

12. Gruber, "The Reminiscences of Edwin Dickinson," p. 25.

13. For a discussion of Dickinson's brief involvement with monotype, see Joann Moser, *Singular Impressions: The Monotype in America* (Washington, D.C.: Smithsonian Institution Press, 1997), pp. 116–17. The monotype, as it turned out, had a lot in common with the *premier coup* in that both were process driven. The monotype medium courted quick impressions, using brushes, rags, fingers, and whatever else could be appropriated. If the resulting image was unsatisfactory, the plate could be wiped and begun again. Each pull produced a unique image grounded in the circumstances of its making.

14. See Dickran Tashjian, "Broom and Secession," in *Skyscraper Primitives: Dada and the American Avant-Garde, 1910–1925* (Middletown, Conn.: Wesleyan University Press, 1975), pp. 116–42.

15. Lewis Mumford, "Regionalism and Irregionalism," *Sociological Review* (London), Oct. 1927, pp. 277–88; "The Theory and Practice of Regionalism," *Sociological Review* (London), Jan. and Apr. 1928, pp. 18–33, 131–40.

16. For a discussion of Stieglitz, Rosenfeld, and Frank, see Wanda M. Corn, "Apostles of the New American Art: Waldo Frank and Paul Rosenfeld," *Arts Magazine* (New York), Feb. 1980, pp. 159–63.

17. Henri's notions for an art of personal expression evolved into a bona fide credo, the stuff of ballyhoo, published in 1909 as an article for the *Craftsman*; see Robert Henri, "Progress in Our National Art Must Spring from the Development of Individuality of Ideas and Freedom of Expression: A Suggestion for a New Art School," *Craftsman* (New York), Jan. 1909, pp. 387–401. I want to thank Thomas Hill, Head Librarian at Vassar College, for so kindly forwarding a copy of this article to me in the eleventh hour.

18. The notion of radical painting in the United States before and after 1913 warrants clarification. In the wake of the Armory Show, Henri's proselytizing for a representational art responsive to all sectors of American society seemed hopelessly provincial. The transition escalated with unsettling speed, a surprisingly short span of about twenty years, if measured between the 1893 World's Columbian Exposition and opening night at the 69th Street Regiment Armory on February 17, 1913. What changed during these watershed years was not the desire to be modern, to explore the pictorial implications of a new age, but the means of expressing it. For artists trained in the academic fold—Henri, Dickinson and his teachers Chase and Hawthorne, and earlier generations of American students schooled in Munich, London, and Paris—the Armory Show challenged the rules of the game. Pointillism, Fauvism, Cubism, and Expressionism rendered time-honored precepts of representation and anatomy relative. Those who dismissed such innovations cast a conservative lot. It was inevitable that older artists would feel threatened.

Even through the forgiving lens of revisionist art history, Hawthorne's canvases from the teens and twenties display a strong academic bias, which had a considerable impact on Dickinson, who because of his brother's suicide missed the Armory Show's premiere in New York, as well as its equally controversial run in Boston. Regardless, noticeable repercussions would have infiltrated the sedate environs of Provincetown through experimental work by Karl Knaths, Ross Moffett, William and Marguerite Zorach, Blanche Lazzell, and others. And Dickinson surely would have encountered European modernism firsthand during his trip to France in 1919–20. In the end, he opted for a more traditional orientation, especially in his figurative compositions. But to these he brought a prescient, surreal edge, pushing academic constraints in unexpected ways to create bizarre narratives. In more spontaneous circumstances, particularly with the *premier coups*, a tendency to paint more abstractly evolved naturally, as subjectivity and the act of painting commingled.

19. For a recent study on improvisation's ubiquitous influence on postwar American art, see Daniel Belgrad, *The Culture of Spontaneity: Improvisation and the Arts in Postwar America* (Chicago: University of Chicago Press, 1998).

20. In their philosophical and aesthetic writings, Bergson and Croce stressed the virtues of intuition as a means of attaining knowledge. Change and movement, Bergson believed, were the basis of all reality. Time should not be measured scientifically or mechanically, since for the human being time operates as a continuous flow in which past and present are inseparable from consciousness and memory. This theory of time in relation to the human self figures prominently in Marcel Proust's *Remembrance of Things Past*, a book of great import to Dickinson and his wife Pat, who read all of it aloud to her husband. He, in turn, committed certain passages to memory.

21. Maurice Merleau-Ponty's essay on Cézanne, an extension of Bergson's phenomenological notions, is relevant to Dickinson's rapport with the landscape; see Merleau-Ponty, "Cézanne's Doubt," originally published as "Le Doute de Cézanne" in *Fontaine* (Paris), Dec. 1945; reprinted in translation by Hubert L. Dreyfus and Patricia Allen Dreyfus, *Sense and Non-Sense* (Chicago: Northwestern University Press, 1964), pp. 9–25.

22. It was not uncommon, for instance during the 1870s, for American students enrolled at the Ecole des Beaux-Arts to breathe a sigh of relief as summer approached and they anticipated fleeing to Barbizon, Fontainebleau, Grez, and Montigny-sur-Loing to set up their easels in fields,

described the stifling conditions at the Ecole des Beaux-Arts and the joy he felt when summer finally arrived and he and his classmates migrated north to paint outdoors; see Low, *A Chronicle of Friendships* (New York: Charles Scribner's Sons, 1908), pp. 123–39.

23. The *premier coup* had its musical analogue in jazz, a simultaneous development arising out of New Orleans at the turn of the last century. Here was an indigenous expression, American to the core, a music driven by improvisation and grounded in the art of survival; see Ken Burns, *Jazz*, Episode One, "Gumbo: Beginnings to 1917," aired January 8, 2001, on PBS.

24. Seckler, "Interview with Edwin Dickinson," p. 3.

25. Edwin Dickinson as quoted in Allen S. Weller, *Art USA Now*, ed. Lee Nordness (New York: Viking Press, 1963), p. 55.

26. Kuh, "Edwin Dickinson," in *The Artist's Voice*, p. 73.

27. Ibid.

28. Occasionally, a specific movie is noted, when for instance, on May 23 and November 21, 1917, he mentions seeing *Cleopatra* with Tibi and Caroline and *Common Clay* with Tibi.

29. The classic study on the movie industry in America is Robert Sklar's *Movie-Made America: A Cultural History of American Movies* (New York: Random House, 1975).

30. Herbert Groesbeck, a close friend and fellow painter, was killed near Verdun just ten days before the Armistice. They had planned to go to Europe together. Instead, Dickinson arrived in Verdun on March 28, 1920, and walked twelve kilometers in the moonlight to visit Herbert's grave.

31. The fact that *The Fossil Hunters* was mistakenly hung on its side at both the Carnegie and the National Academy of Design always rankled Dickinson, who was embarrassed by the sensational press.

32. Georgette Passedoit opened her gallery sometime around January 1932 in the La Salle Hotel. By the late thirties she had moved to 121 East Fifty-seventh Street and remained there until closing the gallery sometime around 1959.

33. There were short reviews in the *Art Digest*, *New York Herald Tribune*, and *New York Times*. A lengthier piece appeared in *Art News*; see Ann Hamilton Sayre, "Drawings by Four Artists: Iacovleff, Dickinson, Wortman, Kirby," *Art News* (New York), Feb. 15, 1936, p. 7.

34. Gruber, "The Reminiscences of Edwin Dickinson," p. 18.

35. Dickinson, letter to Esther and Ansley Sawyer, Dec. 17, 1937.

36. Frances Dickinson, letter to Esther and Ansley Sawyer, Feb. 9, 1938.

37. Dickinson, letter to Esther and Ansley Sawyer, Feb. 6, 1938.

38. Dickinson, letter to Esther Sawyer, Mar. 7, 1938.

39. "Metropolitan Buys Native Canvases," *New York Times*, July 17, 1938, p. 7.

40. Edward Alden Jewell, "Edwin Dickinson Exhibits Canvases," *New York Times*, Apr. 16, 1938, p. 14.

41. "The Visions of Dickinson, 'Lone Spirit,'" *Art Digest* (New York), Apr. 15, 1938, p. 13.

42. Helen Dickinson Baldwin, interview with author, Nashville, Tennessee, Sept. 23, 2000.

43. Helen Dickinson Baldwin, interview with author, Wellfleet, Massachusetts, Aug. 19, 2000, audiocassette.

44. Gruber, "The Reminiscences of Edwin Dickinson," p. 165.

45. Paul Bird, "Dickinson's Vapors," *Art Digest* (New York), Apr. 15, 1939, p. 19.

46. Howard Devree, "Works by Edwin Dickinson," *New York Times*, Apr. 11, 1939, p. 10.

47. Devree, "A Reviewer's Notebook," *New York Times*, December 17, 1939, p. 12.

48. "Review of Passedoit Show," *New York Times*, Apr. 14, 1940, p. 9.

49. The rose appears in numerous paintings and drawings, beginning in the twenties with *Two Figures*, 1922–24 (see fig. 5 of O'Connor essay in this book) and continuing into the thirties and forties with *The Cello Player, Esther Hill Sawyer, Woodland Scene, Composition with Still Life, Roses*, and *Rose and Sextant* (cat. nos. 8, 75, 16, 20, 84, 85), and others. Sometimes it appears on its own, other times associated with a female figure. Obviously the motif had a profound resonance for the artist. Perhaps it signified, as John Driscoll noted in his dissertation "Edwin Walter Dickinson: An Iconological Interpretation of the Major Symbolical Paintings" (Pennsylvania State University, 1985, p. 111), that which was sub rosa, the unknowable subtext of the image. Perhaps it came to symbolize the essential being of his deceased mother, the pain and beauty of her memory. When combined with a balloon, as in *The Finger Lakes*, maternal memory found an appropriate analog in the form of a lighter-than-air projection soaring heavenward—the spirit of exploration as a metaphysical soul unbound.

50. "Nostalgic Mysticism of Edwin Dickinson," *Art Digest* (New York), Apr. 1, 1941, p. 19.

51. Edward Alden Jewell, "Reviews," *New York Times*, Apr. 6, 1941, p. 9, and Mar. 15, 1942, p. 5.

52. Dickinson, letter to Esther Sawyer, Feb. 23, 1943.

53. Esther Sawyer initiated the Buffalo Association of Collectors and Artists in 1936–37 and made Dickinson her chief advisor. The Association's main objective was to organize exhibitions and to bring artists together with collectors in the hope of generating sales. It was through one such exhibition that Pollock sold his first painting, *Cotton Pickers*, now in the collection of the Albright-Knox Art Gallery. There is no indication in the Gallery's documentation files, however, that the Bairds ever owned the work. Pollock later wrote Dickinson to thank him for his help.

54. Dickinson, letter to Esther Sawyer, Feb. 23, 1943.

55. Dickinson, letter to Ansley and Esther Sawyer, June 9, 1943.

56. Dickinson, letter to Esther Sawyer, Sept. 2, 1943.

57. Dickinson, Journal, Feb. 2, 1944. Sid was Dickinson's cousin, the artist Sydney Dickinson. Mary was Sydney's wife, and Thorn was their son.

58. Dickinson, letter to Ansley Sawyer, Mar. 24, 1944.

59. Dickinson, letter to Esther and Ansley Sawyer, Aug. 12, 1944.

60. The portrait commission came through Grand Central Art Galleries, where Dickinson was a member. Catherine Hughes Waddell, the artist's cousin, purchased the suite of ten drawings originally intended for *Tricolor* and offered them as a gift to Harold Wolff, a renowned neurologist who was considered to have saved the life of her son, Theodore. Dr. Wolff was married to the painter Isabel Bishop, who bequeathed five of the drawings to the Metropolitan Museum of Art in 1988.

61. Dickinson, letter to Ansley Sawyer, Aug. 16, 1944.

62. Dickinson, letter to Esther Sawyer, Oct. 27, 1944.

63. Biala (1904–2000) later married the painter Daniel Brustlein, and together they moved to Paris where they lived most of their married life, making periodic trips to New York to see family and friends and to exhibit their work. Biala remained a close friend of the Dickinson family, and her Paris apartment was always available to them on their visits to France.

64. Still one of the best sources on Jack Tworkov's life (1900–1982) and career is Richard Armstrong's *Jack Tworkov: Paintings, 1928–1982* (Philadelphia: Pennsylvania Academy of the Fine Arts, 1987), with essays by Armstrong and Kenneth Baker.

65. By the early forties, Jack Tworkov and Willem de Kooning had become close friends, having met in 1935 through the New York division of the WPA Federal Arts Project.

67. Dickinson's pantheon of old masters included Velázquez, El Greco, Manet, and Cézanne.

68. Diane Waldman compared Dickinson with de Kooning when she wrote: "Dickinson . . . refuses to repeat an idea until it hardens into a formula or consciously to delimit the boundaries of his art. He will, instead like de Kooning, destroy entire paintings in search of resolutions without succumbing to the quickening pace of our machine milieu"; see Diane Waldman, "Dickinson: Reality of Reflection," *Art News* (New York), Nov. 1965, p. 31. So did James Schuyler: "Dickinson is decidedly a modern painter. His way of seeing and feeling are as particularly of our age as Willem de Kooning's or the late Florine Stettheimer's"; see James Schuyler, "U.S. Painters Today," *Art News Annual* (New York), 1960, p. 92; and Carter Ratcliff in his review "New York Letter," *Art International* (New York), Jan. 1973, p. 59.

69. Elaine de Kooning, "Edwin Dickinson Paints a Picture," p. 51.

70. Elaine de Kooning, "Dickinson and Kiesler," *Art News* (New York), Apr. 1952, p. 67.

71. For tributes to Ryder from two members of the Stieglitz group, see Marsden Hartley, "Albert Ryder," *Seven Arts* (New York), May 1917, pp. 93–96; and Paul Rosenfeld, "American Painting," *Dial* (New York), Dec. 1921, pp. 649–55; reprinted in Paul Rosenfeld, *Port of New York* (New York: Harcourt, Brace, and Co., 1924).

72. Both shared a love for nature, had eccentric habits, and walked in moonlight, and both kept certain paintings in a perpetual state of becoming. One of Ryder's confessions, published in 1905 twelve years before his death, suggests an uncanny affinity with Dickinson, in so many ways a kindred spirit: "The canvas I began ten years ago I shall perhaps complete to-day or to-morrow. It has been ripening under the sunlight for years that come and go. It is not that a canvas should be worked at. It is a wise artist who knows when to cry 'halt' in his composition, but it should be pondered over in his heart and worked out with prayer and fasting"; see Albert P. Ryder, "Paragraphs from the Studio of a Recluse," in *Broadway Magazine* (New York), Sept. 1905, p. 11.

73. The origins of the Club, its activities and duration, are recounted by Irving Sandler in "The Club," *Artforum* (New York), Sept. 1965, pp. 27–31. Dickinson exhibited *premier coup* landscapes at Eleanor Ward's Stable Gallery for two years, in 1953 and 1954. She signed him on for a one-artist show in 1954, from October to November. For a discussion of Ward and the Stable Gallery, see Paul Gardner, "The Stable Wasn't Just Another Gallery," *Art News* (New York), May 1982, pp. 108–13.

74. In a letter to Pat on the occasion of Dickinson's show at the National Academy of Design in 1982, five months before his own death, Jack Tworkov declared: "I'm certain that in spite of the fact that 'modern' art took over our miserable century, the time will come when Dick will be acclaimed not only as the great artist of his time but as one among the great artists since the renaissance. I truly believe it. There was no other artist working in the classic mode in this country or in Europe that was his equal. That's why I was in awe of him all my life." Tworkov, letter to Frances Dickinson, Apr. 22, 1982, Dickinson Family Archive.

75. John Ferren, "Epitaph for an Avant-Garde," *Arts* (New York), Nov. 1958, p. 25; quoted in Bruce Altshuler, *The Avant-Garde in Exhibition: New Art in the 20th Century* (New York: Harry N. Abrams, 1994), p. 162.

76. Stuart Preston, "Dickinson's Works Displayed," *New York Times*, Feb. 4, 1961, p. 16.

77. Dore Ashton, "Art," *Art and Architecture* (New York), Apr. 4, 1961, pp. 4–5. Dickinson greatly admired Bacon's work, especially *Man with Dog*, 1953, and used to say to his daughter, "Oh . . . that dog!"; Helen Dickinson Baldwin, interview with author, Nashville, Tennessee, Sept. 23, 2000, audiocassette.

78. Dorothy Miller's survey, consisting of about thirty-eight works (mostly *premier coups* and drawings, with only a few of the major symbolical paintings), traveled to eleven U.S. venues between 1961 and 1963; see Miller, letter to Lloyd Goodrich, Apr. 9, 1964, Goodrich files, Whitney Museum of American Art, New York.

The Goodrich project, Dickinson's swan song, was the most comprehensive retrospective ever mounted, with 104 oils, 2 early watercolors from the twenties, and 37 drawings. The show did not travel beyond the Whitney Museum; see Lloyd Goodrich, *Edwin Dickinson* (New York: Whitney Museum of American Art, 1965).

Norman Geske enlisted Dickinson, along with nine other artists, to represent the United States at the Venice Biennale in a thematic show titled *The Figurative Tradition in Recent American Art.* In the company of younger painters and sculptors—Richard Diebenkorn, Red Grooms, Frank Gallo, Fairfield Porter—Dickinson's figurative compositions and *premier coups* seemed entirely relevant and eccentric at the same time. Represented by twenty-one works, compared with five or six for each of the others, his preeminent senior status was obvious; see Norman Geske, *Venice 34: The Figurative Tradition in Recent American Art* (Washington, D.C.: Smithsonian Institution Press, 1968), pp. 43–70. After Venice, the exhibition traveled to the National Collection of Fine Arts, Washington, D.C., and the Sheldon Memorial Art Gallery, University of Nebraska–Lincoln.

79. Gary Garrels and Robert Storr have written about this period in de Kooning's life with great sensitivity. See Gary Garrels, "Three Toads in the Garden: Line, Color, and Form," and Robert Storr, "At Last Light," in *Willem de Kooning: The Late Paintings, The 1980s* (San Francisco: San Francisco Museum of Modern Art, 1995), pp. 9–37, 39–79.

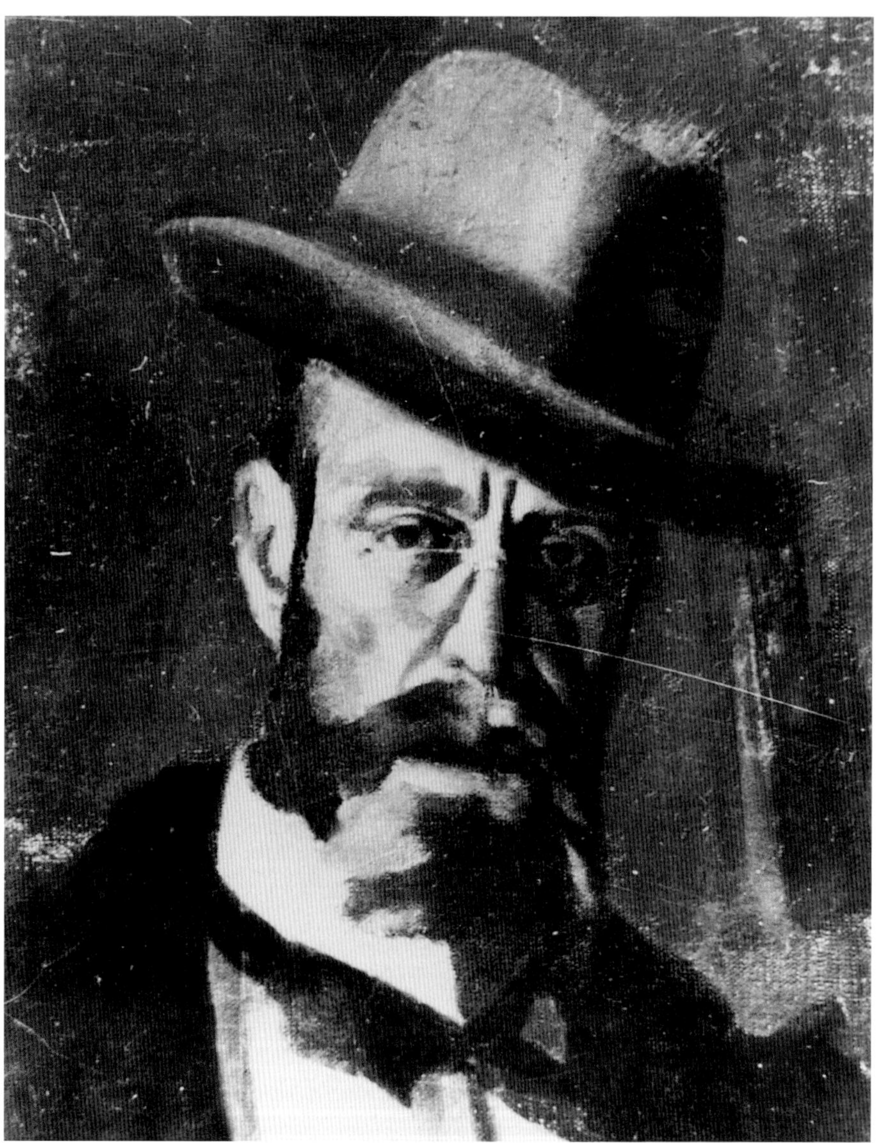

Fig. 1
Edwin Dickinson
Self-Portrait in Homburg Hat, 1947
oil on canvas, 15 × 12 (38.1 × 30.5)
Now lost
Courtesy Dickinson Family Archive

ALLEGORIES OF PATHOS AND PERSPECTIVE IN THE SYMBOLICAL PAINTINGS AND SELF-PORTRAITS OF EDWIN DICKINSON An Interpretive Essay

Francis V. O'Connor

INTRODUCTION

Interpreting Art

Oscar Wilde said that "all art is at once surface and symbol." The scholar as historian deals with the "what, when, and how" of the work of art; the scholar as interpreter engages the more difficult questions of "why does it look as it does?" and "does it means anything?" Indeed, Wilde went on to say that "those who go beneath the surface . . . [and] read the symbol do so at their peril."[1] The danger is that exposing art's origins may seem untoward or reductive to those who have made aesthetics a panacea. If the scholar-interpreter understands art as a human construct rooted in its creator's life and place in history, then the speculative enterprise is worth the risk. Kierkegaard, anticipating Freud, put the interpreter's challenge succinctly: "Life must be understood backward; [but] it must be lived forward."[2]

This is especially true with Edwin Dickinson, whose work is in transition between academic allegorizing and a modernist individualism that depends upon reduction to essentials. The opportunity afforded by such abstraction is the elimination of the superficial for the internally symbolic; the artist can no longer depend upon conventions, since only personal experience remains as subject. Dickinson's art is an allegorical self-portrait, and what we dare to speculate, linked with historical fact, sheds new light upon this marvelous artist's darkly numinous world.[3]

The Nature and Context of the Oeuvre

Edwin Dickinson's major oeuvre falls into four categories: large, semiabstract, darkly colored symbolical paintings that could take years to complete; a series of self-portraits concentrated in the second half of his life; directly observed and quickly achieved paintings known as *premier coups*; and numerous drawings. Stylistically, these range from careful realism to bravura painterliness. Formally, they demonstrate a taste for startling viewpoints. As such, the oeuvre displays a dialectic among an introverted sense of pathos, outdoor light and color, and a conspicuously askance perspective on both.

This essay offers an interpretation of the symbolical paintings and self-portraits. In these works, Dickinson's penchant for allegory—that is, for letting iconic images and formal structures *stand for*, rather than *describe*, experience—is most explicit.

The approach here owes a great debt to the first serious interpreter of Edwin Dickinson, Dr. John P. Driscoll, whose superb dissertation on the symbolical paintings, and his insight that their meaning was rooted in the artist's life events, has laid the foundation for interpretation of Dickinson's art.[4] The current study includes a wider range of work, however, and goes further in analyzing the artist's motifs and identifying their origins and meaning. But Driscoll well understood that art is self-portraiture. He used as the epigraph to his dissertation Dickinson's statement of 1952 that the interpreter cannot "be privy wholly to what the piece may mean to me. . . . " Indeed not, but given the key Driscoll provides, more can be unlocked in these self-consciously allegorical works.[5]

Dickinson's Need for an Allegory of Pathos

Edwin Dickinson was not a modernist by training or early inclination. His major teachers, William Merritt Chase, Frank Vincent DuMond, and Charles W. Hawthorne, were artists in the old, academic tradition, whose work reflected nothing more "modern" than Impressionism, nor later than *fin de siècle* romantic expressionism—and allegory.[6] Not surprisingly, aspects of twentieth-century modernism will be found in his work along with remnants of an academic culture that had begun to wane as he came of age. What is remarkable here is not the mixed influences upon him, but Dickinson's capacity to assimilate them all into a personal mode of perception and expression.

It is hard for our latent modernist sensibilities to grasp the need that an unpsychologized culture had for projecting meaning outside the self. For academically trained artists, this habit led them to personify abstract ideas as figures with identifying attributes or characteristics in allegorical narratives legible to the public. We must learn to respect this visual vocabulary if we are to understand an artist like Edwin Dickinson, who chose to allegorize his deepest sentiments.

At the heart of sentiment is memory. The memorial allays grief and meaninglessness with symbols of honor, continuity, and immortality. Dickinson never lost his capacity to memorialize human pathos—to empathize with the human realities of birth and death, love and relationship, joy and suffering, and humankind's eternal struggle with itself in warfare and with natural forces such as the sea.

Dickinson refused to explain his art, except in technical terms. So do many artists. Their feelings are focused on the emotion-laden process of creating, and they are more or less unconscious of their subject's import. Dickinson was also of a time when personal feelings were concealed. He nevertheless employed a free-associative technique that maintained art's capacity to induce feeling, while letting modernist irony arrange motifs. He let the emotions speak, with both drama and humor, in the allegories found in his large works and implied in his self-portraits.

Dickinson did not plan paintings in advance, but he did admit to using his imagination. As for belonging to a school of painting, he stated, "It never occurred to me to join a group which advocated a particular philosophy of art."[7] Yet he displays a deep understanding of abstraction when he says, "An abstract work of art and abstraction as a state of mind are different things."[8] He admits to an affinity with Surrealism. While denying that *Ruin at Daphne* (cat. no. 50) is surrealist, he does acknowledge the validity of his work being described as such, noting that he "did a lot of work around 1914, '15 that I think very possibly is in that vein, and I've heard it said that it was. It's nothing I would not be happy to acknowledge. I guess maybe it probably was."[9]

Here he is anachronistically referring to his painterly style seen in *House, Mozart Avenue* of 1913 (fig. 2) and his 1914 *Self-Portrait* (cat. no. 1), in which the painting process freely formed his images—a process he maintained in his *premier coups*.[10] But then, in the very next sentence he switches from discussing that form of painterly free-

Fig. 2
Edwin Dickinson
House, Mozart Avenue, 1913
oil on unknown support, 12 × 16 (30.5 × 40.6)
Scharf Family Collection
Courtesy Dickinson Family Archive

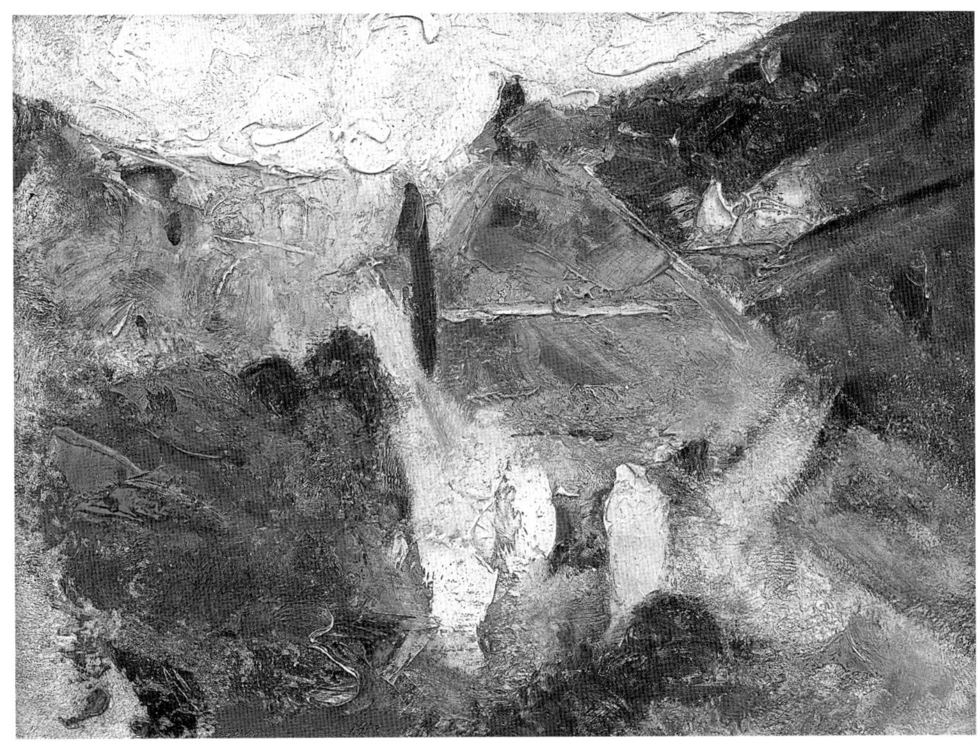

association to the juxtapositioning of disparate objects found in Surrealists such as Salvador Dalí when he says: "Consistency among objects as being the consistency of their ordinary use never fitted a painting of necessity to my mind. I've done . . . quite a number . . . [of paintings] with still life on the bottom that is of course heterogeneous—put in without regard to its being naturally so. More as you see things on a town dump, a . . . juxtaposition of objects completely unassociated in one's experience. . . ."[11] He then proceeds to explain:

Well, anyway, I'd look at them and . . . picture someone saying . . . "What would you say would be the most surprising thing to see next to such-and-such an object?" and he'd name the ones I was looking at. This is someone I was talking to in my imagination—I do it a good deal. . . . I'd pretend to try to think of some object that just looked ridiculous being with that one, and then the fellow points to what's the case, and it's always three or four jumps better than the one you could have thought of as being the most diametrically opposed in appropriateness. You see what I mean? . . . Of course that's what the surrealists do—put all kinds of things that haven't normal association, as has a kitchen knife with a kitchen spoon. That would look tiresome in a painting, I would think.[12]

Notice three important things: First, Dickinson claims conscious juxtapositions of objects that are "unassociated in one's experience" while not realizing that their "imaginative" selection is determined *by* unconscious experience. Second, he personifies his own imagination—"the fellow"—the better to distance himself from his unconscious. Finally, he correctly acknowledges that all this can be related to surrealist "psychic automatism"—or free association of disparate visual motifs prompted by the unconscious.[13]

Why did Dickinson need such a method of painting? To reimagine pathos, the artist must find surrogates for old emotions, the better to conform what cannot be spoken openly with what can be laid bare publicly with personifications and allegories.

Biographical Prefigurements

Four life events influenced the themes and form of Dickinson's art. The first of these was the death of his mother, Emma, from "tuberculosis of the bone" in 1903. She had taken ill about 1894 and was frequently placed in sanatoria. From 1899 on, Edwin often accompanied her to one of the three institutions where she sought treatment. In 1901 she went alone for about four months as an outpatient to a sanatorium in Saranac Lake, New York. She was in the care of Dr. Edward Livingston Trudeau, who had established a popular therapy that consisted of "taking the air" on the porch of a "cure cottage"[14] no matter what the temperature, reading uplifting books, keeping a journal, and meeting with him once a month.

Cure cottages (fig. 3) were boarding houses in the vicinity of Trudeau's sanatorium and were favored by patients wanting to avoid the stigma of tuberculosis associated with clinical facilities. One patient described life at Saranac Lake in 1893 as follows: "The climate was dismal and there was no escaping a 'consciousness of invalidism,' which made the place appear more desolate than ever. [There was a] crude barrack-like air about everything. . . . " Trudeau's success at "cures" was confined to patients who were in the very early stages of the disease; the rest were doomed, and he offered only a "more comfortable way of dying" based on hygiene, climate, and diet.[15]

Emma Dickinson's journal, which indicates that her own health deteriorated during her stay in 1901, documents that Edwin was her favorite child, and she often refers to him as her "dear One" or "my Baby"; he is recorded as sending her "dear little stories and drawings."[16] Through her death in 1903, he was almost always with her, and he later complained that his grades suffered because he had to change schools so many times. He was present with his family when she died, and said that the "emotional affect of my mother's death was great."[17]

Thus, between the tender ages of eight and twelve, Dickinson was placed in situations where he could observe the sufferings of his mother and her fellow patients under circumstances that deeply influenced him.[18] The oedipal situation here, not to mention

Fig. 3
Linwood Cottage, Main Street, Saranac Lake, New York, April 1897
Barbara Parnass, Photographer
Courtesy Adirondack Collection, Saranac Lake Free Library, New York

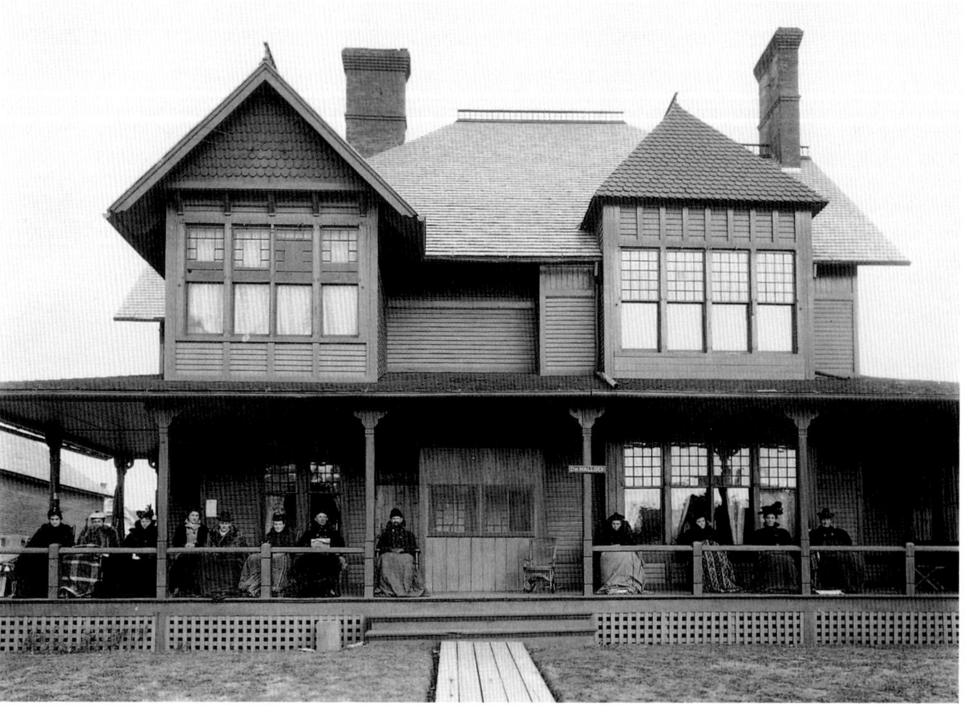

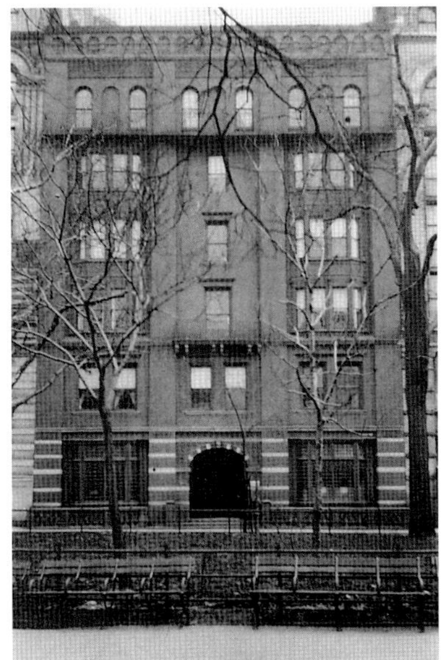

Fig. 4
Benedick Building, 80 Washington Square East, New York, ca. 1913
Photograph by Thomas T. Telor
Courtesy New York University Archives

the blame he would have taken on for the sufferings he was forced to observe, joined with other psychodynamic events in his young manhood, could not help but find expression in his later art.

The second event was the suicide of his brother, Burgess, an outdoorsman who had studied forestry at Yale and who was so talented in music that he was nicknamed "Beethoven." He was also a depressive and alcoholic, and his problems were readily apparent even in his early teens.[19] On the evening of January 28, 1913, after meeting with his three siblings in the apartment he shared with Edwin on Washington Square (fig. 4), and after the latter had walked his brother Howard and his sister Antoinette down to the door, Burgess jumped from the sixth-floor window. Edwin returned, found the apartment empty, and, fearing the worst, looked out the open window to see his brother's dead body in the courtyard below. Edwin was devastated and left New York.[20] He would say later, "Burgess was the chief influence in my entire life."[21]

The third event was the remarriage of his fifty-nine-year-old father to a thirty-eight-year-old woman on June 14, 1914, when Dickinson was twenty-three. An unmarried son is seldom unaffected by such a marriage. He sees the father both as betraying his mother and as a competitor for other women. The stepmother becomes an intruder in the family, and worse, is unconsciously associated with loss and mourning. As a result, the son tends to bond with his siblings in reaction to the threat the stepmother embodies. Further, the father can appear a different person to the son, since he will react to his new wife in a different way than he did to the son's mother. In short, such an intrusion into the "family romance" raises any number of oedipal conflicts.[22] While Dickinson's relationship to his stepmother was always proper, he and his sister kept their distance.[23] There is also ample evidence in his subsequent paintings that his father's irksome remarriage dominated his work until his own marriage in 1928 at the age of thirty-seven.

The fourth event was the death of one of his closest friends in the very last days of the First World War. On November 1, 1918, Herbert Groesbeck was killed at Verdun—a loss that deeply affected Dickinson. He found solace in Milton's famous elegy *Lycidas*, written when the poet was at Cambridge for a friend lost at sea. Dickinson memorized this work of some two hundred lines and is said to have recited it often.[24] This is a good example of Dickinson's taste for allegory.[25]

While Dickinson was of the old school, the polarity in his work between carefully construed allegories of personal experience and the immediate transcription of vision overtly represented the transition from tradition to modernity. But his exploitation of the free associative methods of the Surrealists helped to preserve his privacy covertly while permitting the enactment in visual terms of his own most resonant memories.[26] He understood that it is easier to be frank about mourning—be it mother, brother, father,[27] or friend—if it is represented indirectly within the conventions of modernism. This permitted him to make his own life events a personal tradition displaced upon symbolical juxtapositions of figures, furnishings, and viewpoints.

Note also that Dickinson memorialized the deaths of his mother, brother, and friend (but not the remarriage of his father[28]) in his diaries for the rest of his life—often indicating how old they would have been. And in these same pages he recorded the loss of ships at sea, the dates of famous battles from world history, and the deaths of symbolically resonant individuals such as Beethoven (a copy of whose death mask the artist owned).[29]

Dickinson had known suffering and death firsthand from the age of eight, and his empathetic temperament allowed him to take this inheritance of pathos upon himself. Understanding the utility of academic allegory when modernist tendencies were stressing individual self-expression, he chose to combine the two in his major symbolical paintings. He also inculcated his experience of the human condition into the formal structures of his creations.[30]

THE SYMBOLICAL PAINTINGS

Allegories of Everyday Life, 1915 to 1919

The Rival Beauties, 1915[31]

It is late afternoon. The viewer[32] stands to the west facing the rising crescent moon seen through the arch that dominates the scene (cat. no. 2). The sun still shines on the buildings outside. Inside, a café is coming to life. The tables to the right are already occupied, and musicians at the left are preparing to entertain. A line of women enters the space through an arch to the back left, and they look for places near the piano. Indeed, a young man with a cello, and wearing a bow tie, has leaned across the piano and has struck a note at the center of the keyboard—middle C[33]—giving a pitch for a singer, here standing with her score, in an elaborate hooded gown that obscures her face. A well-dressed gentleman seems to be making an announcement—perhaps the master of ceremonies introducing the singer. Almost everyone is looking toward, and listening to,[34] the sounds made by the piano and by the speaker. The two white-clad young women with parasols outside the arch seem oblivious, as do the beggar girl with her bowl to the lower right, a young man in a dark jacket who seems to be reclining, and one of the two women standing in front of the stage, who seems to be looking straight ahead at us while her companion turns to the singer. Most expectant of all is a little girl who stands upon the hindquarters of a horse that is sitting in front of the stage and who apes the pompous pose of the announcer. In front of this kid is a man in a dark jacket with stripes on its cuffs (a tipsy naval officer, perhaps?), who turns away from the stage and looks over his shoulder. The scene is charged with bustle and anticipation. And we, standing to the west, and well above the scene, viewing it perhaps from a window on the same level as the two women to the far upper left,[35] wonder what that shoe is doing in front of the beggar girl—or why there is an odd, seven-bladed fan—or is it an overturned table or umbrella?—at the singer's feet.

So located, where are we? The artist evokes a local café in the "West End" Portuguese quarter of Provincetown.[36] At the gate, two flags form the pinnacle of the triangular composition, although they do not help identify the site. One is red with a horizontal white stripe and the other bluish with a similar stripe. The latter suggests a naval signal flag—something Dickinson would have learned when preparing for his unsuccessful entrance exams for Annapolis in 1909—and it means "I am going to send a message by semaphore." When combined with another flag, as here, it would convey some degree of distress.[37] So we have an arcane yet legible signal to the viewer that more is going on than meets a cursory eye.

What rivalry, then, is implied in the title? One notes that the two most conspicuous figures, the two women at the lower center, are quite different. The one to the left is more abstract and featureless than her companion, who is wearing a belted smock and shoes and looks out at us. Perhaps there is a suggestion of the contention between artistic realism and abstraction that the Armory Show had set going just two years earlier.[38]

But the painting itself is literally about the two major, non-verbal art forms: music and painting, and it well demonstrates that while you cannot paint sound, you can paint the reaction to hearing it, and virtually define the note and voice in doing so. There is also the more abstract dichotomy to be found at dusk, watching night kill light in the west—where we stand in the painting—while looking east toward its waning glory.

The painting is a portrait of the human comedy as the young Dickinson knew it. The playerless piano can be seen to represent his musically inclined, dead brother. Perhaps the rivalry is simply between music and painting—that is, between the brothers themselves. It is normal to be in contention with the dead who have left you bereft, even as you mourn their absence. As Driscoll demonstrates, Burgess never really leaves these symbolical paintings, even as he never leaves his brother's memory. But Burgess's presence is displaced onto the rest of the world around the artist, and even the most commonplace events or things—such as what happens at the local café—can suddenly substitute themselves for what cannot be forgotten—so that this charming, almost rustic, allegory of ordinary life becomes the semaphore message of Dickinson's mixed emotions.

Interior, 1916

The viewer, looking head on at this triangular, and utterly unnatural, pile of figures, thinks at once of synthetic Cubism (cat. no. 4). While Dickinson was living in Buffalo and never saw the Armory Show, he most certainly by 1916 would have seen at least reproductions of the Cubist works and discussed their innovations with his artist friends. The overall pattern of forms suggests a conscious attempt to play with the new mode of vision—although he later felt *Interior* had not "come off too well."[39]

As in *The Rival Beauties*, the scene is a café. The location is outdoors with a plaza of sorts stretching out behind. In the immediate foreground is a vacant-eyed woman with her hair covering most of her face. Next to her is a white bowl set on a geometrically patterned cloth. Just above her, a young man plays a guitar and whistles, while a young girl peeks out at the viewer from behind his right leg. Above her is another, rather excited young man holding aloft a cat. Flanking this central heap, and extending the central triangle to the margins of the canvas, are two older women in profile staring impassively left and right, lending the group a heraldic air. All this is crowned by a radial-topped doorway, where a formally clad violinist plays while a few other figures go about their business on the plaza.

The title refers to Maurice Maeterlinck's one-act play *Interior*,[40] which was performed by the Washington Square Players in 1915 along with the playwright's *A Miracle of Saint Anthony*,[41] and deals with the death of a woman by drowning. It is unclear if Dickinson saw this production, since he was in Provincetown in 1915, but he owned copies of both plays.[42] *Interior* is a minor melodrama centered on the pathos of having to tell a family consisting of four women (a mother and three sisters) and two men (a father and a baby boy) that one of the daughters has died under ambiguous circumstances.

While Driscoll sees the painting as an allegory of the stages of life,[43] with the women representing the maiden, mother, matron, and crone, it seems more a reflection of the family in the play, with the dead older daughter represented by the disheveled "figure" in the right foreground who stares blankly, is all bundled up, and may well reflect memories of Dickinson's own mother before her death—or of her fellow patients. This disturbing figure recurs in other works.[44]

Inland Lake, 1919

Dickinson was discharged from the Navy on July 19, 1919, and began to paint again in his father's study at Sheldrake by July 26. Since he left for Europe in December, *Inland Lake* was created during this period and reflects his feelings at the time. He was twenty-eight, and his theme was sailors without women (cat. no. 5).[45]

It would seem to be late afternoon by the side of a windswept lake. The viewer looks down from across an inlet branching from the lake to the left that is bridged by a plank. To the right sit two women, one with her skirt pulled up to the knees, and another with her face hidden by her hair, who is watched by a child. Beyond them are three houses. At foreground center, three handsome women stand demurely, looking in different directions, while a fawn next to the nearest looks at the viewer. To their immediate left, a reclining girl sells flowers, while another huddles against a tree, hair hiding her face. Behind her, leaning against another tree, is a sailor; a woman behind him has her back turned. To his right another sailor talks to a man, while a woman in front of the first house to their right looks on with crossed arms. Another sailor at the edge of the lake has found a friend despite a frowning old man. Off in the distance, another has found two friends for the evening. But it is windy—there are broken twigs in the foreground, and the stylized whitecaps on the lake suggest wind gusts disproportionate to the unruffled appearance of the crowd. Everyone is arranged within a long triangle from the foreground to a tall, lighted arch on the horizon that invites them inside. The question is left open as to whether the café we saw in *The Rival Beauties* is their destination.

The invisible realities here are the sexual tension and the wind that touches the water (but not the crowd) in so abstract a fashion it seems copied from folk art. The diagonal crack in the plank that leads to the scene before the viewer points to the bare leg of the flower girl selling favors. The young deer that looks at the viewer fawns at its dear mistress's skirt while suggesting, if you consider its homonym *faun,* a certain goatish rut with which both artist and viewer are challenged to identify. The comedic pathos that inheres in this visual and verbal pun bespeaks the human lottery as only a lonely artist who failed as a midshipman for want of mathematics, and had just spent eighteen months as a naval telegrapher, could encode before walking that plank from a minister's study!

The Recurring Iconography of Pathos in the Symbolical Paintings

Dickinson's early symbolical paintings set out a catalogue of idiosyncratic motifs that he would repeat selectively in subsequent works. Although the artist refused to explain his paintings except as meaningless compositions and objects of craft, the meaning of these motifs can be deduced from the work. The motifs are:

> the viewer, the artist's surrogate, who is made complicit in the visual situation almost as much as that "fellow" his imagination—and who is left responsible for the interpretation of motifs;
>
> sites without a clearly defined location—although most are out of doors;
>
> events depicted more in shadow than in light—with gray tones predominating in later works;
>
> individual figures seemingly isolated from each other, yet involved together in some invisible relation—such as listening, sexual attraction, a windy dusk, or the sound of a cello;

faces that are partly or completely obscured;

faces looking straight out at the viewer to engage his or her complicity;

mechanisms or objects of various sorts divorced from their usual purpose and location, and often found in the foreground;

explicit signs—the signal flags or the cracked plank, or later a rose—placed somewhere in the painting to announce that this is more than just a "composition."

As we shall see below, this deliberate displacement of meaning onto such motifs is Dickinson's way of employing modernist irony to mask deeply personal tensions.

Allegories of Domestic Tension, 1920 to 1928

Dickinson created nearly all of his major symbolical canvases between 1920 and 1928—*An Anniversary* (cat. no. 6), *Two Figures* (fig. 5), *The Cello Player* (cat. no. 8), *The Fossil Hunters* (cat. no. 12)—and started *Woodland Scene* (cat. no. 16).

Having returned from the navy in 1919, and having just painted randy sailors while he visited his father and stepmother, it is not surprising that Dickinson's thoughts were turning to marriage. Indeed, in August 1921, he went all the way to Seattle to propose marriage, but was refused. He would not marry for seven more years.[46]

All these paintings contain variations on the recurring motif of an old man and a younger woman and can be related to his father's marriage to a woman twenty-one years his junior.[47] The dominant figure in each of these paintings is a withered old man, except in the last, where the central figure looks like an old man until one realizes it is an old woman.

It should be said that there was no overt animosity between Dickinson and his stepmother. Relations were always appropriate. Indeed, the only open annoyance seems to have been her asking for flower paintings—which might give an ironic origin to the overtly symbolic rose.[48] But none of this explains away the overriding theme of these paintings that parallels his last eight years as a bachelor and wanes after his own happy marriage in 1928.

An Anniversary, 1920–21

This work (cat. no. 6) was begun in August 1920. Dickinson said it was not about a specific event, but given his penchant for recording anniversaries, and the recurrence of old motifs, such as the triangular composition and the household items on the floor—not to mention his big family and the juxtaposition of an old man and a young woman—there is more happening than Dickinson's protestations would suggest.[49]

The model for the old man was a Provincetown fisherman, Ben Atkins, who posed for Dickinson's *Old Ben and Mrs. Marks* of 1916 (cat. no. 3). That work shows an elderly couple, the man behind the woman solicitously grasping her shoulders, the only symbolic commentary a withered tree to the upper right.

Here, the same old man dominates the left half, with an elegant young woman seated to his right with crossed legs. They are surrounded by a dozen introspective people, the most alive standing above the couple. He holds a cello and raises a hand with only four fingers, in a striking but unregarded gesture.[50] At the top is a wall of rocks and trees, placing the scene outdoors. A collection of crockery, sheet music (Mozart and Bach are visible), seashells, and comestibles is arranged on the ground.

The identification of the old man with Dickinson's minister father is established by two details. His left hand is raised in the gesture of a mock ecclesiastical blessing, and there is a large fish next to him between the feet of the stepmother surrogate—who, along with the fish, stares out at the viewer. The half lemon next to the fish (the other half of which is under the old man's chair), and the fact that the woman's foot rests on a china tureen, suggests she intends it for chowder—and that her ironic stepson may well feel himself, along with the "fisher of men"[51] next to her, in the same oedipal soup.

Two Figures, 1922–24

The viewer immediately notes that this work (fig. 5) seems to be seen by moonlight. The same old man dominates the scene. Above him to the right is a fashionably coifed young woman, posed for by a different, and slightly older, model. Both stare to the right beyond the picture space. The composition is divided diagonally, with these two figures filling the lower right. To the upper left, a glass-sided lantern stands upon a flat rock—where the artist had earlier painted a chessboard set up for an endgame, and then a red-haired girl's head and torso. There are two flowers set in front of it, as if before a

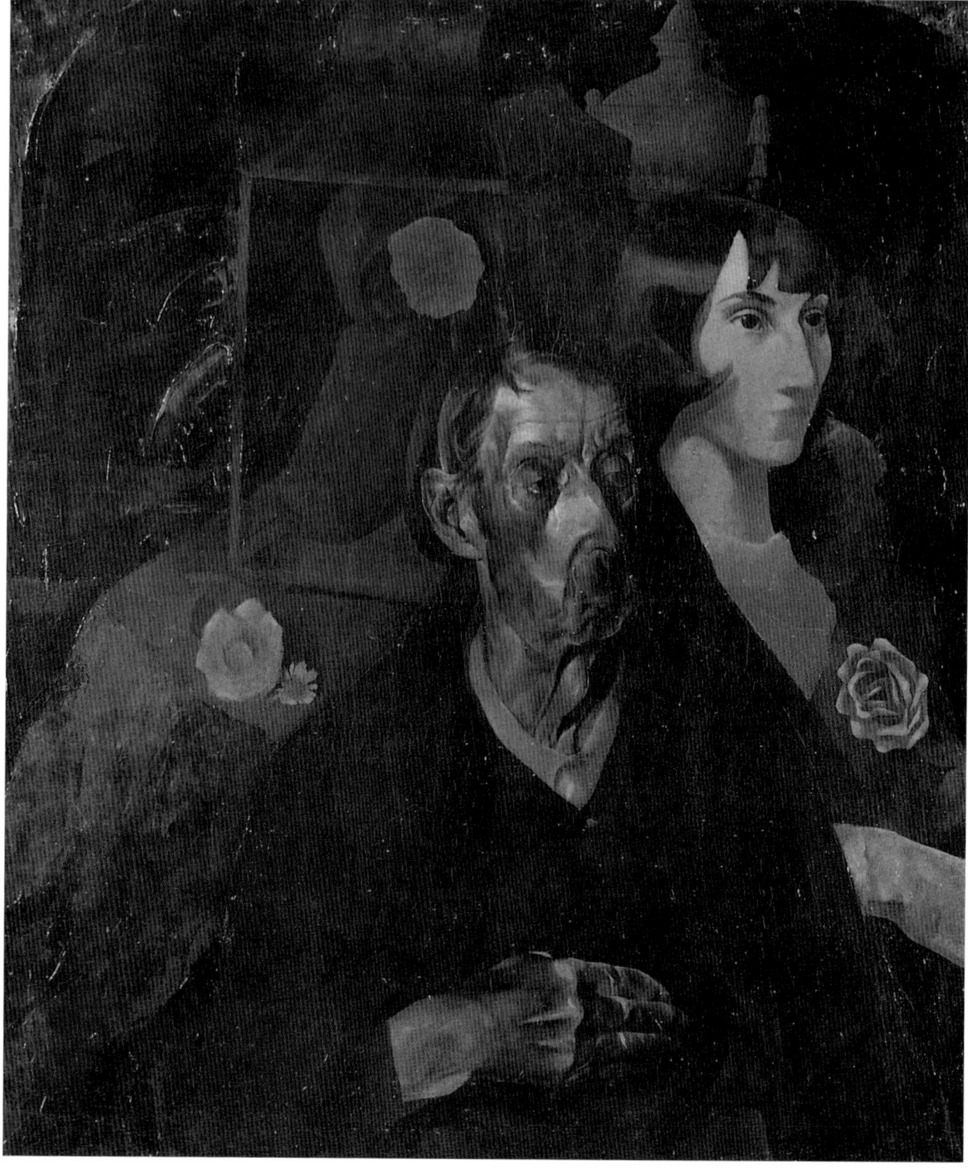

Fig. 5
Edwin Dickinson
Two Figures, 1922–24
oil on wood, 36 × 30 (91.4 × 76.2)
Collection The Metropolitan Museum of Art, New York
Hugo Kastor Fund, 1959

shrine. One is wilting. Inside the lantern is a Grand Banks fisherman's shoe Dickinson found in a dump and kept for years in the lantern.[52]

The key to this mysterious arrangement is to be found in the tension displayed in the old man's hands. At first glance, his right hand seems extended across his breast—another ecclesiastical gesture. But it is anatomically ambiguous, and the right hand can be read as a fist pressed against the fingers of the left. The woman's face is impassive. The old man's head is surrounded by a triangle formed by three flowers, the upper suspended in front of the lantern—a triangle being one form for God the Father's halo. Crowning the woman's head is a vessel resembling a funerary urn.[53]

The pale pink rose at her bosom—one of several artificial roses Dickinson kept about the studio—will appear in subsequent paintings. Like the signal flags, and the half lemons, it indicates, *sub rosa*, a point to be taken.[54] Here it would seem to be a son's conflicted libido. There is no light in the lantern, just an old shoe—something you call an old man. The couple look away from all this; the son faces it. Only the larger, fresh flower in front of the lantern looks out at the viewer.

The Cello Player, 1924–26

The viewer looks down upon an old man playing a cello (cat. no. 8). The model is now different, but it is hard to tell since the head is foreshortened. He is surrounded, according to Dickinson, by "14 books; 2 potatoes; 2 saucers; 3 sheets of music (Intermezzo for Cavaliera [*sic*] Rusticana, Marriage of Figaro, LVB[eethoven] quatuor [*sic*] 18 #3, 2nd violin, Allegro); 2 china pitchers (Sherman); 1 photograph; 7 shells; 1 trilobite; 3 kettles; 1 rose; 1 music stand; 1 chair; 1 organ; 1 piano; 1 cello; John Cordes. (45 [*sic*] pieces of still life)."[55] These objects fill the floor of a studio, and a wide-angle view leads from the lower right to the upper left.

As Driscoll points out, there is a shift here to a wider range of reference: the artist's hobbies, interests, and situation. The potatoes and shells refer to the meager diet of poor Provincetown artists. A book set on the organ is about Arctic exploration.[56] The "Sherman" teapot, from which General William Tecumseh Sherman was supposedly served, testifies to Dickinson's interest in the Civil War. The music can be related to the influence of Mozart on Beethoven, and since the latter's name was his brother's nickname, to the admitted influence of Burgess on Edwin.[57] One notices also that amid the musical instruments are many metal objects such as kettles and shells, all of which could be made to sound in sympathy with the cello's vibrations.[58]

Further, the theme of an old man in love is still the central motif, for Dickinson would have understood the long tradition going back at least to Vermeer, of the cello as a female symbol—the instrument's curvaceous shape, and the fact that it is held between the player's legs. But this indirect reference anticipates his next two works.

The Fossil Hunters, 1926–28

While painting *The Fossil Hunters* (cat. no. 12), Dickinson met and courted Frances [Pat] Foley—and put off his marriage until just after the work was completed. Indeed, one can see a certain falling off of tension over the relationship between his father and stepmother—and a rather public admission of what the work is about. The old man and young woman sleep together here head-to-head beneath blue drapery inscribed with the letters *F2* for his future wife's name, and *Sheldrake*, the name of their summer retreat. A rocky cliff typical of that place intrudes into the space of the painting, and a rivulet flows down toward the lower left corner. His sister Tibi posed for the sad-looking figure in the lower right. On the opposite side from her is a photograph of a fossil half covered with a copy of the death mask of Beethoven—inscribed with Burgess's initials, *BD*. Several other fossils are scattered about. A grindstone kept at Sheldrake occupies the lower left corner, and the old man's arm reaches across another fossil photograph and almost touches it with a twig. The old man is ground down now; the younger man has finally won out.

Shortly before finishing this work, the usually reticent artist wrote to his fiancée that the painting was a "source of satisfaction to me, and a rare experience, that as this canvas approaches the finish, interest increases; on previous things of size, their villanies [*sic*] grew and interest waned as they seemed not worth finishing."[59] Obviously something had happened: an old envy had been laid to rest by new love.

The painting's title can be read in several ways depending on who is hunting fossils—that is, old folk, old men in particular. Dickinson, a collector of actual fossils, no doubt once felt his stepmother the huntress—and had uneasily identified with the father, who caught her. But the son was now a successful hunter himself, and the recurrent theme of repressed jealousy, expressed in a displacement of the threatening relationship, was apparently resolved—since this theme did not work in the next painting in which he engaged it.

Allegories of Transition and Contentment, 1929 to 1937

Woodland Scene, 1929–35

The viewer, looking across a well-like abyss and the ruin of its curved brick wall, with an old plow to the left and a broken wheel to the right, finds in this painting (cat. no. 16) a scene not dissimilar to that in *The Fossil Hunters.* What appears to be the same old man, here bundled in a heavy coat and hood, looks out at the viewer. A woman, with a lilac rose at her bosom, lies head-on to the left, next to the central figure's shoulder. The right half of the work contains an amorphous, lighter area that vaguely resembles another inverted, reclining figure. There are flames below it, and to the right, blasted trees, the most prominent of which resembles that to the right of the figures in *Old Ben and Mrs. Marks* (cat. no. 3).

Indeed, we have come full circle in the series of symbolical works on the now-exhausted theme of his father's remarriage. The old man is really a woman modeled by the same Mrs. Marks.[60] The heavy coat and hood resemble what Dickinson would have seen when he stayed with his mother during a winter at Saranac Lake. The woman to the left perhaps still stands for his stepmother; the unresolved figure to the right is the remains of a nude modeled by his wife. It is obscured by an aura of eros. The old man of the previous works is gone; he is now androgynous—defeated in the oedipal battle waged and won in these paintings.

The work, as originally conceived, is unfinished, although it took six years, and three changes of size, to reach this unresolved state.[61] It is a classic example of an artist trying to achieve another success with a theme that has lost psychological resonance. As a result it regresses back to that dismal world of sick women Dickinson knew in his childhood, huddled outdoors in heavy coats, or glimpsed across their sickbeds, afflicted by inner fevers, fearing social ostracism, seeking a cure but knowing themselves doomed—and projecting their anguish onto a healthy little boy who thinks he is to blame for not being able to cure everybody—and onto the later artist who can barely cure himself with his painting.

Driscoll is thus correct when he sees this painting as an "emotional inventory" rather than the "object inventory" found in *The Cello Player*.[62] In the latter were numerous references to the artist's interests; here the references are to old oedipal states once powerful enough to unify a painting, but now dissipated by his own new and fruitful life.

During the years 1929 to 1933, while struggling with this now unnecessary work, Dickinson's two children were born, Helen in 1931 and his son, Constant, in 1933. In the latter year, frustrated by *Woodland Scene*, he did something he had never done before—started a new symbolical work before finishing the last.[63] This resulted, as he said, in an "improvement in physical & mental condition since I decided to put aside the old 'time-top-heavy' [*Woodland Scene*] & begun [*sic*] new work [*Composition with Still Life*] on which to express more advanced views."[64]

Dickinson, ever empathetic, turned from eight years of allegorizing personal frustrations to the pathos of one of his lifelong obsessions: the sea and its farers.

Composition with Still Life, 1933–37

The viewer stands at the top of a flight of stairs leading down into the dark hold of a sunken boat, the stern of which curves across the top of the canvas[65] (cat. no. 20). A blue rose hovers in this void. To the lower left is a mirror in a cracked gilded frame behind a broken banister. Water runs forward at the lower right, presumably from a water jack seen above two blue-and-white porcelain pitchers that seem set between a banister and the jack. Above this still-life configuration sprawl two life-size, headless, nude bodies of indeterminate sex, arranged head-to-head as were Dickinson's parent-surrogates in *The Fossil Hunters*—but here there is no need to show the heads. To the upper right are tree stumps; at the upper center draped sails. The overall tonality is gray, with the yellow and blue in the foreground balanced with a few reddish strokes toward the top. The entire work has an aura of desolation and tragedy about it prompted by his internalized sense of universal pathos.[66]

In this large painting, Driscoll correctly sees a summation of the artist's life-long fascination with storms, shipwrecks, salvage operations, lost mariners, and the emotional toll these events took on the local population of Cape Cod.[67] This fascination seems to have been an offshoot not only of his long residence in Provincetown, but of his failed career as a naval officer and his stint as a sailor during the war. The sea was something he knew intimately, and its capacity to induce pathos due to its scale, unpredictability, and overwhelmingness echoed the emotional impact of his own personal losses and frustrations. It was an apt conclusion to his series of symbolical paintings. Further, its emphasis on events exterior to himself presaged the subjects to be found in his art during the last thirty-odd years of his life.

Ruin at Daphne, 1943–53

Within fifteen days of the completion of *Composition with Still Life*, the Dickinsons left for Europe, where they stayed just under a year, returning because of the uneasy political situation. They lived for a while in France, traveled in Italy, and returned via Britain in September 1938. The next year they bought a house near Wellfleet, near Cape Cod. In the fall of 1940, Dickinson built a permanent studio nearby, which gave him great satisfaction. The years 1941 and 1942 were taken up with family and professional matters with less time devoted to art. On January 1, 1943, he began *Ruin at Daphne* (cat. no. 50) and a month later said: "I have begun a piece I have wanted to do for a long time—a good size piece.... The piece is entirely from imagination and should be a sweet piece being most cheerful in subject, & full of incident."[68]

Indeed, the viewer finds in this last large work a veritable sea-change from the symbolical canvases that preceded it. Gone are the lowering shadows, claustrophobic settings, clutters of still-life objects, hieratic figures precariously poised and posed in mysterious worlds and odd relationships.

Here we face a monumental classical ruin whose only inhabitants are birds. There are three great Roman arches, broken columns, Corinthian capitals, a relief of a rearing horse, and enough stairways going down into sepulchral grottoes to imply that something ought to be afoot—but is not. Also striking is the way the unfinished painting dissipates around the edges from grisaille to a reddish underpainting scored with perspectival directions.

Dickinson worked sporadically but happily on this canvas until 1953, for the most part keeping it as a large drawing on a reddish ground, adding and subtracting architectural elements, figures, and birds. He only started to paint in 1951. But in the end, and after the Metropolitan bought the unfinished work in 1954, he abandoned it, telling his sister Tibi: "I have not worked on the . . . ruin, etc. since November 1952. A piece of th[is] size and complexity is not re-attackable after so long a lapse, when it is already then 10 years old. Though I am disappointed in finding myself unable to carry out the piece of so much aspiring as I wanted to, I am adjusted to leaving it—as, indeed, in one measure or another, all my large pieces have been [left] since the An Anniversary of 1921–22. . . . I am to receive the price I asked. . . . The incompleteness of the piece to my mind is why I asked only three [thousand]. . . . I could not finish it; it has a good home, good indeed!"[69] His wife recalled that his private, "true" name for the *Ruin at Daphne* was "'Two Sisters in Syria.' One sister was the whole design; the other the elaboration."[70]

One cannot read through Dickinson's running commentary on the eleven-year development of this painting without feeling that, at least in the early years, for the first time in his life he was enjoying painting a picture—that the Muses left him in peace to create in complete emotional freedom, unhampered by lugubrious associations, free to elaborate or change it to his heart's content. This was partly because both theme and elaboration were exercises in unconscious archaeology—creating an ever-changing fantasy of antiquity on top of his own now-buried history.[71]

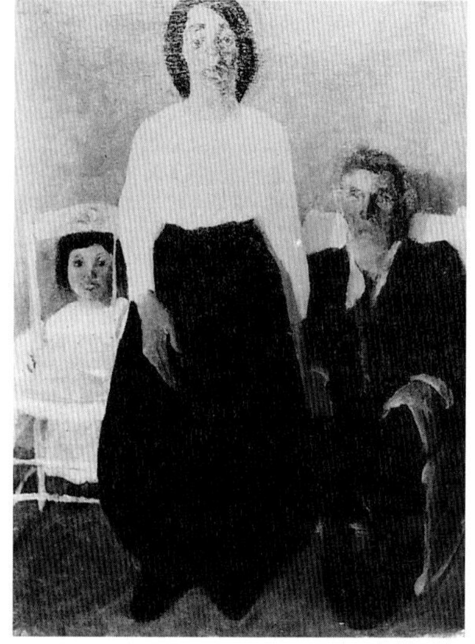

Fig. 6
Edwin Dickinson
Old Man Hines, Mayme Noons, Frances Silva, 1914–15
oil on canvas, 60 × 48 (152.4 × 121.9)
Now destroyed
Courtesy Dickinson Family Archive

Beneath *Ruin at Daphne* is first the remains of a *premier coup* of "Mayo's beach house," which he painted the day before and then obliterated the better to begin an "antique peristyle, villa of 1820 & pool."[72] Beneath the *premier coup* was once a full-length nude self-portrait he did in 1942 and felt to be a failure.[73] And the work's stretcher was taken from a painting he had done in 1914 titled *Old Man Hines, Mayme Noons, Frances Silva* (fig. 6).[74] Finally, as Driscoll points out, this painting was started in January 1943, exactly thirty years after Burgess's suicide. Dickinson inscribed his brother's initials, *BD,* on the painting (as he had on *The Fossil Hunters*), and they remained there for over a decade, until shortly before the work was sold.[75]

Ruin at Daphne had accumulated many elaborations[76] until the enthusiasms this last large-scale effort had generated over a decade waned. It stands today as a physical record of his artistic career and emotional evolution down to the year of his first self-portrait.

THE SELF-PORTRAITS

As we have just seen, the symbolical paintings between 1915 and 1953 were allegorical self-portrayals. It is time to discuss Dickinson's actual portraits of himself. While Dickinson said he created about twenty-eight of these,[77] not all have survived, and only about four were done between 1914 and the completion of *Composition with Still Life* in 1937. They are significant for their form more than their overt iconography.

About seventy-five percent are frontal, that is full face looking straight out from the canvas with planes of brow and shoulders usually parallel to the picture plane. Frontal self-portraits are distinct from oblique or profile views, since they are often painted at moments of trauma and transition in the life course. They indicate a recentered psyche and signify positive adjustments to change.[78]

Early Allegories of Self, 1914 to 1923

Self-Portrait, 1914

Dickinson's first self-portrait (cat. no. 1), not surprisingly, was frontal, and painted in the winter of 1913–14, a year after Burgess's death. It indicates a revived spirit in Dickinson, deep mourning having led to resignation and acceptance. This was also the year of his father's second marriage, to a younger woman, about which he was ambivalent. More positively, his brother Howard would make him an uncle. He could see life proceeding and himself, with it.

Of even greater significance, he ceased to be a student. Hawthorne would make him his class assistant that summer, and he would take no further formal instruction as an artist.

This self-portrayal sums up his situation. His frontal face is set in shadow against the light—suggesting latent sadness. His location in the portrait is ambiguous; is he viewing himself reflected in a window, or before his easel holding a maul stick?

He wears a fur cap that his father wore when he was a student at Amherst—thus identifying himself, perhaps ambivalently, with his parent. As for leaving studenthood, we find his "graduation gown," a blue artist's smock made for him by a fellow student, Esther Sawyer,[79] rolled up across the bottom of the painting. This anticipates his placement of symbolic images at the bottom of his paintings. Dickinson was now an artist in his own right and would soon paint his first major picture, *The Rival Beauties*.

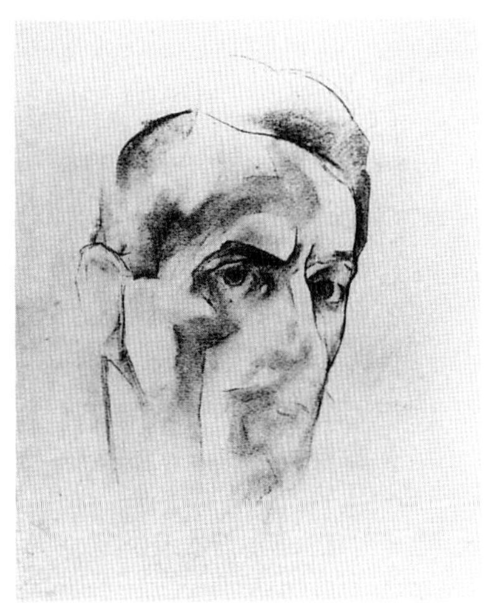

Fig. 7
Edwin Dickinson
Self-Portrait, 1923
charcoal on paper, 18 × 14½ (45.7 × 36.8)
Now lost
Courtesy Dickinson Family Archive

Dickinson made only three more self-portraits before 1940.[80] An oblique drawing of himself done in 1923 (fig. 7) is incomplete below the eyes—as are a number of portrait drawings of others he did over the years.[81]

Another frontal portrait, begun in 1932, is titled *Shiloh* (cat. no. 19). It shows him in a Civil War uniform[82] "lying on my back, evidently on a shield, with both my swords. I suppose I was simulating a casualty."[83] This was made at a time when he suffered from back pain and had grown increasingly troubled by progress with *Woodland Scene*—whose symbolical implications had worn thin—and worn him down. This enactment of inner feelings—the draperies suggest a sick bed more than a battlefield—may well indicate the growing need that led him, in 1933, to abandon *Woodland Scene* and begin *Composition with Still Life*.

Allegories of Contentment and Conflict, 1940 to 1954

In Dickinson's journal, between 1939 and 1940, he clipped the following quote from James Joyce's *Ulysses*: "Love loves to love love. . . . You love a certain person. And this person loves that other person because everybody loves somebody and God loves everybody."[84] This presages the years between his forty-ninth and fifty-sixth birthdays (1940 to 1947), which were a time of deep contentment. In September 1939, Dickinson bought a house near Wellfleet. By 1940, he had his own studio—the first of his own, having formerly rented or borrowed studios. This contentment was signaled by eight self-portraits, six frontal, and all but two created between 1940 and 1943—the year he began *Ruin at Daphne*.

He started off tentatively in March 1940 with a small portrait of himself against a blank wall, turned to the left, but glancing frontally, if warily, over his shoulder at the viewer (cat. no. 36). At the top is a light area balancing his collar and shoulders at the bottom—perhaps indicating his pleasure, as an artist, at having at last a roof over his head.

Indeed, 1941 began with a rare personal statement: "Note: I feel more contented, and in better health now that I have a studio. Am working, and not doing physical work. . . . Pat well, children well."[85] This was followed by three frontal self-portraits.

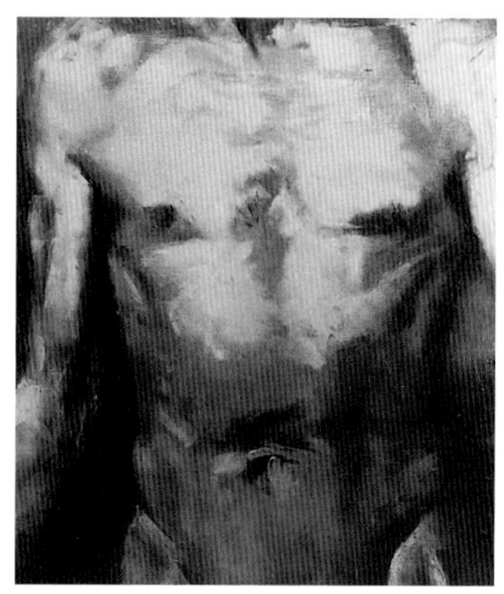

Fig. 8
Edwin Dickinson
Self-Portrait [Nude Torso], 1941
oil on canvas, 23 × 30 (58.4 × 76.2)
Now lost
Courtesy Dickinson Family Archive

The first was a frontal nude torso that is lost and known only from a photograph (fig. 8). Next in 1941 came a full frontal image of himself (cat. no. 40). His entire head is surrounded by a dark, halolike shadow that extends above his head to the top of the canvas. To the left is a house with a dormer window that attracted him when he was in St. Cyr, France.[86] The year's last frontal self-portrait has the facture of a *premier coup* and shows a landscape behind him (cat. no. 41).

Dickinson is centered in his life, has a studio of his own, is receiving honors (he had recently been elected to the Federation of Modern Painters and Sculptors), and by all outward signs, is deservedly content. Yet we must ask why he looks so troubled in his self-depictions.

Dickinson would always be vulnerable to the pathos of life. Recently escaped from war-threatened Europe, he notes in his 1941 *Journal*: the deaths of three persons, including James Joyce; "Schooner lost off Boston w. 18 men. Hard"; his contentment with his studio; the good news that former President Herbert Hoover had invited him to join a wartime commission and a friend had sent him a number of Native American stone axes, spearheads, and an arrowhead; Burgess's death (an annual entry)—"he is 50 years old"; the death of an Australian friend and of Beethoven; the sinking of the *Titanic* in 1912; the bombing of London (in several entries); another friend's death; the battle of Runneymede in 1215; the death of Herbert Groesbeck in 1918, commenting, "It now seems more tragic than ever"; "BURGESS' BIRTHDAY, 1884"; war with Japan; "Death toll at Pearl Harbor 2,897"; 500 dead in Honolulu; the battle of Fredericksburg 1862; concluding, "So ends this sad world year."[87]

So thinking, in January 1942, he donned the Civil War uniform he had last used at a moment of personal crisis in *Shiloh* and painted *Self-Portrait in Uniform* (cat. no. 46). Facing right, his cap at a rakish angle, a bugle over his shoulder, a flag to the lower left and a bomb approaching in the upper right,[88] he geared up—allegorically—for war. Later, in September 1942, he painted another frontal nude self-portrait that he rejected; it is now under *Ruin at Daphne*.[89]

In 1943, the year he began *Ruin at Daphne*, he did two more frontal self-renderings: *Self-Portrait in Gray Shirt* (cat. no. 49), which shows him in a French fisherman's shirt acquired at Sanary, France, where he had lived, and *Self-Portrait* (cat. no. 48). He was content—with a big new painting about archaeology founded upon his own archaeology. He would not do another self-portrait until 1947.

That year he painted the frontal *Self-Portrait in Homburg Hat* (fig. 1), which shows him the perfect gentleman about town—the very ape of his old dandy of a teacher, William Merritt Chase! Indeed, Dickinson, already respected by his peers for decades, was now being recognized by the art establishment. In 1948 he was elected an Associate of the National Academy of Design, and as part of his initiation, painted a required *Self-Portrait* (cat. no. 54). Here he wanted to present himself as the skilled artist he was. He stands in profile at his easel with an elaborate study in perspective on the wall behind him. It is a variation on an art-school exercise in drawing a cube in mechanical perspective—here, a rectangular solid, the lines at the top and bottom of this solid converging at "vanishing points" to the left and right of the object. The diagram is rendered itself in perspective on a wall in the painting not parallel to the picture plane.[90] This "sampler" of his skill can also be related to the almost endless process of perspectival readjustments that he was making in his ongoing *Ruin at Daphne*.

In 1950, elected to full membership in the National Academy of Design, he painted a frontal nude self-portrait that included a still life of pieces of blue-and-white porcelain. He later destroyed it, preserving as separate paintings the head (cat. no. 55)—which is "presented as though a shingle were blowing across the face in a high wind"[91]—the hands (now lost), and the porcelain, which he gave to the Academy as his "academician's diploma."

His last known frontal self-portrait (cat. no. 65) was done in 1954, the year he turned sixty-three. He had "finished" *Ruin at Daphne* by selling it to the Metropolitan Museum of Art. He looks distraught, with a heavy architectural element bearing down upon him.

While Dickinson received many honors for, and exhibitions of, his life's work in his last years, his health began to deteriorate, and his output declined. In 1958 he was diagnosed with tuberculosis, most probably contracted while attending his dying mother as a child, and part of his right lung was removed. Later, about 1970, he slipped away into Alzheimer's disease and died in 1978.[92]

Of his later works, perhaps the most surprising is *South Wellfleet Inn* of 1955–60 (cat. no. 67). Based on a drawing he made in 1939, it shows a cascade of dormer windows falling from the window at the upper right. It recalls the tentative attempt at Cubism in *Interior*, and more acutely, the circumstances of Burgess's death. It also alerts us to the many other images of windows—most often dormer windows—to be found in his life's experience, such as the cure cottages at Saranac Lake (fig. 3). It is also visible behind him in the 1941 *Self-Portrait* (cat. no. 40) and many of his *premier coups* and drawings. Indeed, *South Wellfleet Inn*, like the symbolical paintings, is an indirect instance of allegorical self-portraiture since it portrays a formal complex that informed much of his oeuvre.

CONCLUSION

Formal Allegories of Pathos and Perspective

So far, the symbology of Dickinson's works has been described in the context of his life events. It is time to conclude with some insights into the sources of his form—that is, the structural and spatial elements that appear in his art and their prefigurement in the sources of his symbolism.

Form is not the equivalent of style or shape. *Form is the style of the artist that shapes the characteristics and strategies that add up to a visual temperament.* The artist's form establishes early on an infrastructure that remains relatively constant and is later elaborated as the artist evolves. With Dickinson, we have seen that a tendency for oblique views evolved into a deep interest in the problems of mathematical perspective—with which he codified the earlier proclivities of his visual temperament.

Throughout Dickinson's work, four formal devices recur:

> First, as noted, he looks up at windows—often dormer windows such as those of the cure cottages at Saranac Lake that he saw as a child (fig. 3)—or places one behind his head as in the 1941 *Self-Portrait* (cat. no. 40). When discussing the optics of drawing dormer windows he free-associates with children: "From babyhood, the eye plays no tricks or we fall."[93]
>
> Second, he looks across an abyss of some sort—an inlet crossed by a plank, as in *Inland Lake* (cat. no. 5), or that ruined wall of a well in *Woodland Scene* (cat. no. 16).
>
> Third, and related to the last, he looks down upon his subject—as from the balcony in *The Rival Beauties* (cat. no. 2)—or into the ship's hold in *Composition with Still Life* (cat. no. 20), or into the crypts of *Ruin at Daphne* (cat. no. 50), or down into works like *The Cello Player* of 1924–26 (cat. no. 8), the *Two Brigantines in the Ice: Antarctica* of 1926 (fig. 9), *Andrée's Balloon* of 1929–30 (cat. no. 15), and *Ulysses, Oh Cissy!* of 1938 (cat. no. 28).
>
> Fourth, and most often with individual figures, he is looking across or up or down at them—as in *The Fossil Hunters* (cat. no. 12) and *Woodland Scene* (cat. no. 16)—including even the 1927 portrait of *Frances Foley* (fig. 10), in which his future wife lies in a fetal position—as well as in all of those drawings of women in bed.[94]

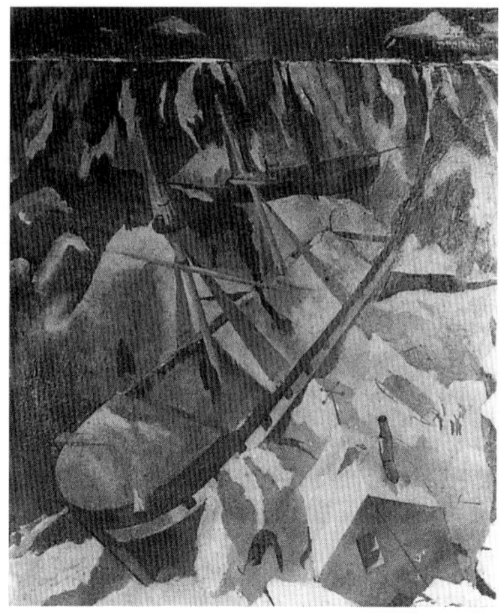

Fig. 9
Edwin Dickinson
Two Brigantines in the Ice, Antarctica, 1926
oil on composition board, 24 × 20 (61 × 50.8)
Collection Deborah and Joseph Goldyne
Courtesy Dickinson Family Archive

Indeed, one must ask why so many of his paintings, self-portraits, and sensitive figure drawings look so incomplete—have no mouths or chins—are so dead to the world—seem so quietly distraught—remain so sunken within themselves or amid unnatural accumulations of drapery—why everyone appears so sad?[95]

As with symbols, Dickinson's choice of such unexpected views and contexts is emotion-laden and thus meaningful. Deeply emotional situations with strong visual components—such as patients and his own mother seen across a bed, or sunken within bed clothes, or with disheveled hair, or bundled up to their ears on the freezing porches of cure cottages with dormer windows, with only their terrified eyes visible—or looking down in despair at his dead brother—were indelibly imprinted in memory and influenced his abstract formal structures for a lifetime. More emotionally distant situations, such as a mourned but unwitnessed death in battle or an annoying event in the "family romance," got displaced upon images of the Civil War or upon ironic exaggerations of his father's second marriage.

Fig. 10
Edwin Dickinson
Frances Foley, 1927
oil on canvas, 50 × 40 (127 × 101.6)
Collection Mr. and Mrs. N. J. Nicholas, Jr., New York
Courtesy Dickinson Family Archive

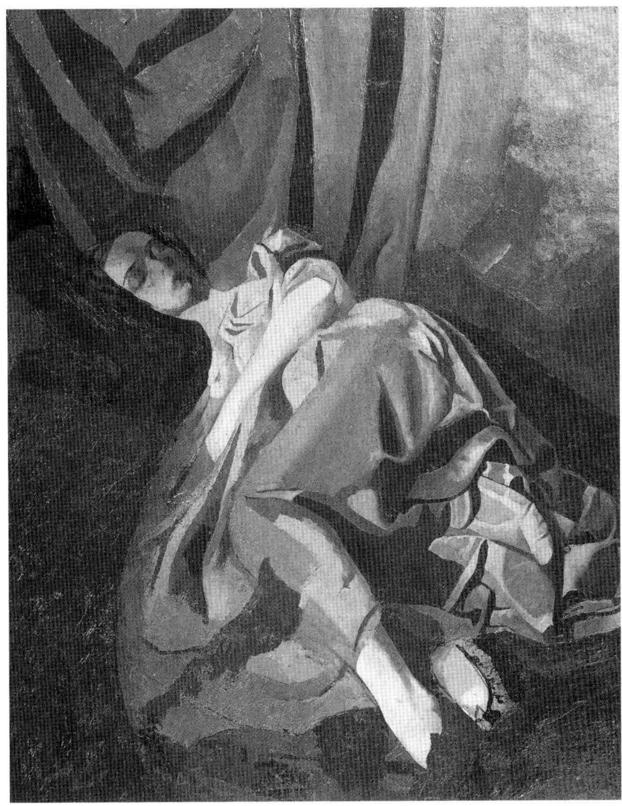

For Dickinson, the view up, aslant, across, or down, accompanied by his having taken upon himself the emotions of others and his own when he was young, became permanently etched upon his temperament as an artist and played a determining role in the form of his later art.

When he was asked about the oblique viewpoints so often found in his work, he replied that they made his work "livelier" than just looking straight on at vertical subjects,[96] and that indeed they did—especially for him as he felt their emotional resonance. But they also force the viewer, when looking head on at his work, to share the shifting perspectives of that allegorical world of pathos Dickinson first felt and later perceived as the human condition.

I am indebted to Edwin Dickinson's daughter, Helen Dickinson Baldwin, for sharing information collected for a catalogue raisonné of her father's work and for replying to numerous questions—and to her husband, Robert A. Baldwin. I am grateful for the assistance of Dr. Douglas Dreishpoon, the curator of this exhibition, and to the staff of the Albright-Knox Art Gallery, especially Ms. Karen Lee Spaulding and Ms. Laura Fleischmann. I am also indebted to Ms. Avis Berman, Professor Greta Berman, Mr. Tram Combs, Professor Beth Darlington, Dr. John P. Driscoll, the Drs. Mary and John Gedo, Professor Bruce Johnson, Dr. Stephen Poser, Mrs. Joan Washburn, and the staffs of the Archives of American Art, Washington, D.C.; the Twentieth-Century Department of the Metropolitan Museum of Art; the New York Academy of Medicine Library; the Brill Library of the New York Psychoanalytical Institute; the Frick Art Reference Library; and the Archives of New York University.

NOTES

1. Oscar Wilde, from "Preface" to *The Picture of Dorian Gray*, 1891.

2. Søren Kierkegaard, *Journal*, 1843.

3. Space limitations require that these interpretations concentrate on the sources of images and form. Physical data about specific works and information concerning artistic influences and stylistic development can be found elsewhere in this volume.

4. John Paul Driscoll, "Edwin Walter Dickinson: An Iconological Interpretation of the Major Symbolical Paintings" (Ph.D. diss., Pennsylvania State University, 1985; Ann Arbor, Mich.: UMI Research Press, 1985).

5. General information about Dickinson's life, unless otherwise referenced, is based on a chronology prepared by his daughter, Helen Dickinson Baldwin, and is cited hereafter as HDB. Edwin Dickinson's original Journals, comprising forty-six volumes dated 1916 to 1971, are on deposit in the Special Collections Library at Syracuse University, New York. Of these, thirty-six volumes can also be consulted in the Archives of American Art, Washington, D.C., Reels D93–D96, 1916–61.

6. See the Chronology in this volume for details of Dickinson's education as an artist between 1903 and 1914. DuMond employed allegorical personifications in his murals. See Jeffrey W. Anderson, "The Art and Life of Frank Vincent DuMond" in *DuMond: The Harmony of Nature* (Old Lyme, Conn.: Florence Griswold Museum, 1990), pp. 4–21.

7. Quoted from the transcript of Carol S. Gruber's interview, "The Reminiscences of Edwin Dickinson" (New York: Oral History Research Office, Columbia University, 1957–58), p. 106.

8. Gruber, "The Reminiscences of Edwin Dickinson," pp. 152–53. For Dickinson, abstraction is a reduction of visual perception to its essentials and its elaboration into a harmony. Here he reflects Charles Hawthorne's teaching that a picture's beauty is the result of spots of color brought together. See Mrs. Charles W. Hawthorne, comp., *Hawthorne on Painting* (New York and Chicago: Pitman Publishing Corporation, 1938, pp. 14ff; reprint, New York: Dover, 1960).

9. Gruber, "The Reminiscences of Edwin Dickinson," p. 105.

10. Ibid., p. 110.

11. Ibid., p. 105.

12. Ibid., p. 106.

13. Dickinson does not mention Freud even though Freud's theories were prevalent from about 1913, when his *Interpretation of Dreams* was translated. But then Dickinson ignored art magazines and did not read a newspaper until he married in 1928 (Gruber, "The Reminiscences of Edwin Dickinson," p. 204). Nonetheless, he used a free-associative method of painting that served his conscious and unconscious purposes.

14. See Philip L. Gallos, *Cure Cottages of Saranac Lake: Architecture and History of a Pioneer Health Resort* (Saranac Lake, N. Y.: Historic Saranac Lake, 1985) and Sheila M. Rothman, *Living in the Shadow of Death: Tuberculosis and the Social Experience of Illness in American History* (New York: Basic Books, 1994).

15. Quotes from Rothman, *Living in the Shadow of Death*, pp. 216–17, 223, 201–4 respectively.

16. Emma Dickinson, Journal, Jan. 29–May 27, 1901. Transcript courtesy of HDB, pp. 15 and 22–23.

17. Dickinson stayed with his mother in "rest homes" at Clifton Springs, New York, and Pinehurst, North Carolina, in addition to Saranac Lake.

18. Gruber, "The Reminiscences of Edwin Dickinson," pp. 10–11. Dickinson may well have been infected with tuberculosis at this time, since the disease can remain dormant for years until the immune system is weakened by illness or old age. He lost part of his right lung to the disease at sixty-seven, twenty years before his death in 1978.

19. HDB, correspondence to author, Dec. 18, 2000.

20. This event was reported on the front page of the *New York Times*, Wednesday, Jan. 29, 1913. Its prominence was no doubt because Burgess was a nephew by marriage of Charles Evans Hughes, a justice of the U.S. Supreme Court, and Howard Dickinson an assistant district attorney in New York City. See Gruber, "The Reminiscences of Edwin Dickinson," pp. 199ff. After leaving New York, Dickinson went first to his family in Buffalo, moving to Provincetown in the summer of 1914.

21. Gruber, "The Reminiscences of Edwin Dickinson," p. 19, and Driscoll, "Edwin Walter Dickinson," passim. Dickinson witnessed his father's grief when a close friend, the Reverend Dr. Maltbie Babcock, committed suicide in 1901. See Emma Dickinson, Journal, pp. 40–41, where she describes her husband as "crushed" and describes Babcock as "so talented, so consecrated, so useful." Children often have a way of taking such grief upon themselves, and it becomes a model for their reactions to similar circumstances later.

22. See E. P. Heilpern, "Psychological Problems of Stepchildren," *Psychoanalytic Review* (New York), 1943, vol. 30, p. 175, and Paul Bohannan, "Stepparenthood: A New and Old Experience," in Rebecca S. Cohen et al., eds., *Parenthood: A Psychodynamic Perspective* (New York: Guilford Press, 1984), pp. 211–13.

23. HDB, correspondence to author, Jan. 16, 2001: "My father and Tibi were certainly accepting of her—everyone was on very good terms, but it was more polite . . . they did not really feel warm or loving to her as I did. Tibi did everything she could to be away from her father and Luty." Further, HDB went on to say that shortly after Luty's marriage to their father in 1914, she asked Edwin and Tibi to call her "mother"—a request that angered them.

24. Driscoll, "Edwin Walter Dickinson," pp. 54–55. HDB, born in 1931, does not recall Dickinson quoting the poem. The influence of Milton's *Lycidas* remained with him, however, since its lines "So may some gentle muse / With lucky words favor my destined urn . . . " (lines 19–20) are most probably behind Dickinson's drawing *Young Man's Tombstone,* of 1962 (cat. no. 92), which was done after a photograph of its subject whose pathos obviously attracted the artist.

25. Milton's elegy centers on the conceit of the mourner as shepherd lamenting a fellow, and is dense with arcadian, classical, and Christian allusions, polemical asides, and complex personifications. The first two lines—"Yet once more, O ye laurels, and once more / Ye myrtles brown, with ivy never sere . . . "—demonstrate the poem's range of allegorical imagination. Laurel refers to honor and glory won, myrtle represents love, and ivy, fidelity or a force in need of protection. While the context implies that the grieving Milton is reassuming the poet's crown, which consisted of these three leaves, their symbolism sets the themes of the poem, which laments the death of a future poet. *The Victorian Language of Flowers.* Reprinted from *Collier's Cyclopedia of Commercial and Social Information,* Internet via Google: http://www.apocalypse.org/pub/u/hilda/flang.html.

26. Donald Kuspit's insight that Sophocles, in his play about Oedipus, was not himself able to articulate the child's conflict with his parents, "but had to symbolize and bury [the Oedipus Complex] in a dramatic fable, giving its rough edges and obscure aspects narrative smoothness and clarity," is highly pertinent to Dickinson's use of allegory. See Kuspit, "A Mighty Metaphor: The Analogy of Archeology and Psychoanalysis," in Lynn Gamwell and Richard Wells, eds., *Sigmund Freud and Art: His Personal Collection of Antiquities* (Binghamton: State University of New York; London: Freud Museum, 1989), p. 135.

27. Gruber's interview indicates that Dickinson's father "was an extremely sympathetic person" to his parishioners but was more or less dead for him emotionally: "I never took troubles . . . attached to the problems of adolescence to him because he never gave me any opening. He evi-

dently was too conventional to feel he could discuss things. . . . I was closer to [my mother] than I was to my father." ("The Reminiscences of Edwin Dickinson," pp. 9–10.)

28. Dickinson, Journal, July 25, 1942, notes his father's ordination sixty years before in 1882, as well as what would have been his mother's eighty-second birthday.

29. See examples from the 1941 Journal, p. 66.

30. In short, the content of his art, in Freudian terms, is "over-determined" and cannot be reduced to any single event. Rather, a wide range of emotional experiences and artistic permissions, accumulating and integrating over his life course, are factors in the content and structure of his work. Thus Driscoll's reduction of the meaning of the symbolical paintings primarily to Burgess's suicide did not do justice to the complexity of the relationship between Dickinson's experiences and his iconic imagery and formal structures.

31. This is the earliest extant symbolical painting. The first was *Old Man Hines, Mayme Noons, Frances Silva,* painted in Provincetown in 1914–15 and destroyed when Dickinson salvaged its stretcher in 1943 for what became *Ruin at Daphne.* See acquisition questionnaire for *Two Figures,* 1922–24, dated March 12, 1961, in the Metropolitan Museum of Art's archive. Its image survives in an old photograph (fig. 6).

32. For interpretive purposes both the reader and Dickinson are understood as the "viewer."

33. Dickinson to HDB, Jan. 29, 1965, ". . . of 'The Rival Beauties' a quite big one with a horse lying half under a gd. [grand] piano with a cellist by it, striking C."

34. This focus of attention explains the seeming psychological isolation of the figures that Driscoll emphasizes in "Edwin Walter Dickinson," p. 34.

35. Referring to the painting, Dickinson says "This is on [i.e., viewed from] the balcony, of course." Gruber, "The Reminiscences of Edwin Dickinson," p. 120.

36. Ibid., p. 119.

37. Professor Emeritus Bruce Johnson, U.S. Naval Academy, correspondence to author, Dec. 27, 2000; *Meanings of International Maritime Signal Flags,* Internet via Google: http://www.anbg.gov.au/flags/signal-meaning.html; *U.S. Navy Signal Flags,* Internet via Google: (http://www.chinfo.navy.mil/navpalib/communications/flags/ flags.html). These flags—the J Flag, with two blue stripes and one white stripe, meaning "I am going to send a message by semaphore," and the One and Seven flags, with two red stripes and one white or yellow stripe, along with combinations of them, can be used to signal, for instance, "man overboard."

38. Dickinson missed the Armory Show in 1913 because he left New York after Burgess's death. He felt its contribution was "greatly to the advantage of everybody." Gruber, "The Reminiscences of Edwin Dickinson," pp. 33–36.

39. Ibid., p. 123. In the years just after its completion, it came off well enough, perhaps due to its "modern" appropriation of Cubism, to be shown at the Pennsylvania Academy of the Fine Arts, the Corcoran Gallery of Art, and the National Academy of Design.

40. Driscoll, "Edwin Walter Dickinson," p. 44.

41. Daniel Blum, *A Pictorial History of the American Theatre: 1900–1956* (New York: Greenberg, 1956), p. 103.

42. HDB, correspondence to author, Jan. 28, 2001. It is interesting that lanterns appear in both *Interior* and *A Miracle of Saint Anthony* and that the lantern Dickinson kept around the studio for years is included in *Two Figures* (fig. 5). It is also notable that the woman resurrected by St. Anthony is declared "fresh as a rose"—a key symbol in Dickinson's later works.

43. Driscoll, "Edwin Walter Dickinson," p. 43.

44. In *Inland Lake, The Fossil Hunters* (in the figure of his sister to the lower right), and several drawings.

45. *Inland Lake* was first titled "Composition with Sailors." His patron, Esther Sawyer, used to tease him about its final title, asking, "What other kind of lake is there?" HDB, correspondence to author, Feb. 27, 2001. Indeed, from that perspective, the title emphasizes all the more the artist's ironic stance concerning his personal isolation.

46. Dickinson's relationships during this period remain undocumented, but his marriage prospects were clouded by his parlous economic situation as an artist. HDB, correspondence to author, Jan. 16, 2001.

47. His father and stepmother visited him in June 1921 while he was painting this work—as they did frequently during these years. It is notable that Dickinson selected a model much younger than his stepmother in all but the last of these paintings—*Woodland Scene*.

48. HDB, correspondence to author, Jan. 16, 2001, indicates that Dickinson did not like flowers—but kept a supply of artificial roses in his studio. This was most likely because his sense of pathos made dying flowers disturbing. In his dissertation, Driscoll best describes the rose as "a key which signals the viewer's attention to the fact that all the seemingly diverse objects and people that are brought together . . . are in fact a unified statement by Dickinson," p. 111. Driscoll to author, Feb. 15, 2001, recalls Dickinson, on seeing a rose in a painting by Hawthorne, saying it indicated a "shared confidence."

49. Katharine Kuh, "Edwin Dickinson," in *The Artist's Voice: Talks with Seventeen Artists* (New York: Harper & Row, 1962; reprint edition, Da Capo Press, 2000), p. 77. He tended to say the same thing about all of his symbolical paintings. See Gruber, "The Reminiscences of Edwin Dickinson," passim.

50. Regarding the gesture, I am grateful to Professor Greta Berman and her students at the Juilliard School of Music, New York, for the information that beginning cello students are taught to retract the middle finger and hold the bow with the other four. The gesture might also be an obscenity displaced upon negative space—or, given the overall situation of the artist, a sign of castration anxiety.

51. Dickinson's wife untenably denied that he knew anything about Christian iconography because he did not understand a chocolate fish he found being sold in Paris at Easter (Driscoll, "Edwin Walter Dickinson," p. 51). Aside from Americans expecting chocolate rabbits at Easter, Dickinson attended his father's daily Bible readings as a child (Gruber, "The Reminiscences of Edwin Dickinson," p. 3) and would certainly have heard Christ's charge to Peter to be a "fisher of men" read to him in three of the four Gospels, and perhaps even explained in the wider context of the Greek letters for "fish" being Christ's initials—or from seeing early Christian art. Further, he spent a good part of his life in Provincetown where the Portuguese fishermen worshiped at St. Peter's Roman Catholic Church, and where he occasionally participated in their festivals. HDB, correspondence to author, Mar. 4, 2001.

52. From Dickinson's description of the painting, and its earlier stages, for the Metropolitan Museum of Art's acquisition questionnaire, Mar. 12, 1961. The initials *A. D.*, for Dickinson's sister, were also inscribed at mid left, but are not now visible. HDB, correspondence to author, Dec. 19, 2000.

53. Could a miscarriage be memorialized here? The "shoe" looks more like a swaddled baby in some photographs, although it can barely be seen in the original. The flowers in front of it suggest one of those tombs to be seen in Montparnasse Cemetery in Paris, with displays of the deceased's effects inside and floral offerings outside. Also indicative is the change of images at the left, ending with the lantern, suggesting a radical revision of the work's meaning from games and sexual fantasy to mourning.

54. Driscoll, "Edwin Walter Dickinson," pp. 71–72.

55. Dickinson, Journal, Nov. 2, 1950. Dickinson is still bad at math; the actual count of objects comes to forty-one.

56. He would paint an imaginary scene about Antarctica in 1926 titled *Two Brigantines in the Ice, Antarctica.* It is unclear why the rose is set in front of the organ—which had been borrowed. Dickinson's sister, Tibi, played the organ in their father's church and also had cool but proper relations with their stepmother. HDB, correspondence to author, Jan. 16, 2001.

57. Driscoll, "Edwin Walter Dickinson," chap. 4, passim.

58. Professor Berman's cello students say a sympathetic resonance among the kettles, cups, and shells would be generated by the cello's resting on the floor.

59. Dickinson to Frances Foley, July 20, 1928. While Dickinson felt good about this work, it appears unresolved, with heavy demarcations between painted areas comparable to the jointures

in a fresco and noticeable disharmony between the grays and the blue of the drapery. Indeed, the drapery appears to be stark abstractions of black and blue—perhaps signs of a still-bruised psyche.

60. Driscoll, "Edwin Walter Dickinson," p. 126, note 80, indicates that a Mrs. Noones may also have modeled for the figure.

61. Ibid., pp. 94–95.

62. Ibid., p. 104.

63. He also did a portrait of himself as a dead Civil War soldier; see cat. no. 19.

64. Dickinson, letter to Esther Sawyer, Dec. 15, 1933, Archives of American Art, Washington, D.C.

65. Dickinson, Journal, Mar. 2, 1935, indicates that he used a whaleship as a model.

66. Its lugubrious aura no doubt reflects the mysterious murder of his brother Howard in Chicago on June 27, 1935, which received national publicity because he was the nephew by marriage of then Chief Justice Charles Evans Hughes.

67. Driscoll, "Edwin Walter Dickinson," pp. 112–16; see p. 66 for quotes from his journal.

68. Dickinson, letter to Esther Sawyer, Feb. 23, 1943. The first indication of the genesis of *Ruin at Daphne* is to be found in his Journal entry for May 4, 1941, where he quotes (with misspellings) an unknown source: "Les ruines majestueuses du monument de la Turbie, élevé il y a deux mille ans, à la Gloire de la 'paix romaine.'" (The majestic ruins of the monument to the Tribes, erected there two thousand years ago in honor of the *Pax Romana*.)

69. Dickinson to Tibi, 1954. This painting is signed and dated by the artist 1943–53.

70. Dickinson, Journal for 1947–48, indicates plans for two female nudes amid the ruins.

71. In 1937–38 he became fascinated with the Roman ruins at Arles, France, and later visited Rome. As with his love of fossils, the past emerging into the present out of the earth became a source of powerful, imaginative symbols. This recalls Freud's use of Rome's historical stratifications as metaphor for the unconscious. See Kuspit, "A Mighty Metaphor," passim; see note 26.

72. Dickinson, Journal, Jan. 1, 1943.

73. Gruber, "The Reminiscences of Edwin Dickinson," p. 91.

74. HDB, unpublished catalogue raisonné entry for 1942 *Self-Portrait*.

75. Dickinson removed the initials because he felt the painting "not good enough for Burgess." Driscoll, "Edwin Walter Dickinson," pp. 147–48.

76. For detailed discussions of the development of this work, see Driscoll, "Edwin Walter Dickinson," chap. 6, and Elaine de Kooning, "Dickinson Paints a Picture," *Art News* (New York), Sept. 1949, pp. 26–28 and 50–51.

77. Gruber, "The Reminiscences of Edwin Dickinson," p. 138. There seem to be fourteen extant self-portraits, of which eleven are frontal.

78. See Francis V. O'Connor, "The Psychodynamics of the Frontal Self-Portrait," *Psychoanalytic Perspectives on Art 1* (Hillsdale, N.J.: The Analytic Press, 1985), pp. 169–221, and also "True Grit: A Note on a Frontal Self-Portrait by Queen Victoria," *Psychoanalytic Perspectives on Art 2* (Hillsdale, N.J.: The Analytic Press, 1987), pp. 307–11. These essays interpret the concept of "centering," when distinguishing frontal from other self-portrait formats, using both Rudolf Arnheim's concept of centricity and C. G. Jung's symbology of the mandala; see *Psychoanalytic Perspectives on Art 1*, pp. 184–85. For an application of the theory here expounded, see Catherine C. Bock, Ph.D., "Henri Matisse's Self-Portraits: Presentation and Representation," *Psychoanalytic Perspectives on Art 3* (Hillsdale, N.J.: The Analytic Press, 1988), pp. 239–65.

79. She and her husband Ansley would later become his major patrons.

80. One, done in 1916, is lost.

81. See Lloyd Goodrich, *The Drawings of Edwin Dickinson* (New Haven: Yale University Press, in association with The Drawing Society, 1963), plates 7, 15, 36, and 51. See p. 62 for an interpretation of this incompleteness.

82. He would don this uniform again at the start of World War II; see p. 66 and cat. no. 46. It is of interest that he was given as a child a "West Point" jacket that his mother made for him. Emma Dickinson, Journal, p. 32. HDB, correspondence to author, Jan. 16, 2001.

83. Gruber, "The Reminiscences of Edwin Dickinson," p. 141.

84. He gives the page number as 327.

85. Dickinson, Journal, Jan. 21, 1941.

86. This painting, with its rather ominous symbolism, is perhaps best explained by the fact that Dickinson suffered from bouts of depression, as did his brother Burgess. His distressed expression, its dark context, and the dormer window will be discussed in the conclusion of this essay. The positive factor here is that he can face this head on.

87. These selected entries date from January to December 1941 and are typical of many others throughout his journal that record personal and historical disasters.

88. Gruber, "The Reminiscences of Edwin Dickinson," p. 140. He says "I guess it's a bomb, looks like a pterodactyl or whatever.... It's a bomb, I suppose, old fashioned bomb." The dark cartouche behind relates this work to a series of portraits of his children he had begun earlier.

89. It is of interest that Dickinson was a nudist (Nicolas Sperakis, a former student of Dickinson's, mentioned this in an interview with the author, Jan. 25, 2001), but a modest one, since only one of several nude self-portraits may survive. See fig. 8.

90. I am indebted to Robert A. Baldwin, Dickinson's son-in-law, for explaining this in a communication of Jan. 4, 2001.

91. HDB, unpublished entry for catalogue raisonné for this work.

92. Given his own burden of mortality, he was a man of exemplary empathy for others. His daughter recalls that Dickinson "was very alertly sensitive; one case illustrates this best I think: he had very long subway rides to his evening classes at the Brooklyn Museum. He noticed that no one ever spoke to the blind, that they traveled in isolation. So he made it his business on buses, subways, anywhere, to sit next to the blind and strike up conversations. He was always rewarded by their pleasure." HDB, correspondence to author, Dec. 27, 2000. Driscoll (correspondence to author, Mar. 5, 2001) recalls being told that Dickinson would destroy glasses he used at parties lest he spread his tuberculosis. He also recalled that later, about 1977, just before Dickinson died, he told him about a trip he had made to Cambodia. He had, of course, never been there, but seems, even in his decline, to have empathized with the victims of the "killing fields," just as he did earlier with those of the Civil War—or of shipwrecks.

93. For dormer windows, see Goodrich, *The Drawings of Edwin Dickinson,* plates 11, 14, 32, 41, 45, 47, 58—the last being a tomb. For quote, see Gruber, "The Reminiscences of Edwin Dickinson," p. 191.

94. See also a 1927 portrait of Frances Foley seen from above and behind that is similar in structure to *Ulysses, Oh! Cissy,* of 1938. For women in bed, see Goodrich, *The Drawings of Edwin Dickinson,* plates 7, 15, 26, 28, 56, 49. In most of these images, the pathos is palpable.

95. For figure studies, see ibid., plates 4, 7, 15, 28, 36, and 49.

96. Gruber, "The Reminiscences of Edwin Dickinson," pp. 159–60.

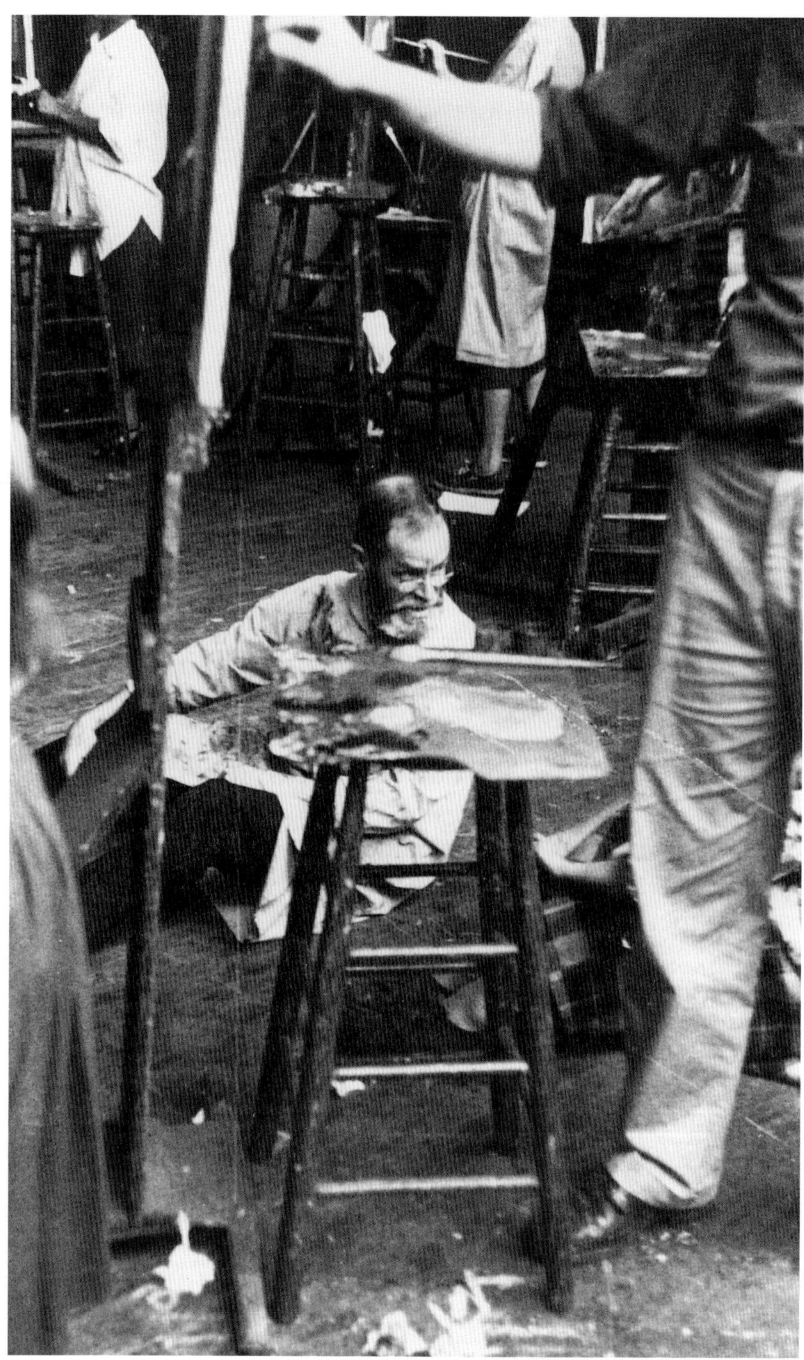

Edwin Dickinson teaching at the Art Students League, New York, 1954.
Photograph by Denver Lindley. Courtesy Dickinson Family Archive

"SEEING EVERYTHING FOR THE FIRST TIME"
The Teaching and Aesthetic Philosophy of Edwin Dickinson

Mary Ellen Abell

Elaine de Kooning once wrote that Edwin Dickinson "puts as much of life into his art as it will absorb" and concluded that "one might say that Dickinson has been painting a lifetime to present ultimately, in the bulk of his work, a defined philosophy of art."[1] De Kooning's statement is quite apt. Dickinson's works emerged from the fiber of his life and, equally if not more importantly, his direct engagement with the complexities of the artistic process. In response to the art historian Katharine Kuh's question as to his "influences," Dickinson quipped "I suppose being alive and awake."[2] Fortunately, Dickinson's philosophy of art is manifested not only in his oeuvre, but also in the legacy that he passed on to his many admiring students—for the artist was a renowned and gifted teacher. Dickinson taught intermittently from 1916 until 1944, but from 1945 to 1966 he taught continuously, predominantly at the Art Students League (ASL).[3] The recollections of his students provide rich insights into Dickinson's aesthetic philosophy, his character, and his personality. They also confirm the fusion of his classroom approach with his studio and field practices.[4]

Dickinson impressed many students as an example of an artist who had wholly integrated his art with his life. "I've never met a man in my life who was more involved with living and less involved with theoretical philosophy. Dickinson didn't think independently of his life and what happened on the canvas or the drawing paper—they were exactly identically one and the same thing," said Francis Cunningham, a student from the ASL.[5] The artist Donald Smith spoke about the "moral weight" in a Dickinson painting because the man's life and his work were "totally homogenous."[6] Dickinson could be formidable to a beginning student, according to Denver Lindley, another ASL student, because "his thinking and feeling were so integrated that it was almost overwhelming for someone whose own aesthetic was just forming."[7]

Dickinson's philosophy of art was acquired from years of working in relative isolation in the small towns of Provincetown and Wellfleet on Cape Cod (1913–44). Though his approach to art was influenced by his primary teachers William Merritt Chase and Charles W. Hawthorne, Dickinson always maintained that his pedagogical techniques came predominantly from his own experiences and experiments in resolving aesthetic problems. "I'm not aware of consciously teaching like my teachers taught me," he once explained. "My own development has been not as much through association with my teachers, molding and important and indispensable as it was [because] it was so short compared to the amount of time I worked by myself."[8]

THE HERITAGE OF EDWIN DICKINSON

Edwin Dickinson represents a strain of American modernism that reaches back through his most influential teachers Chase and Hawthorne[9] to both the Munich School's painterly realist orientation[10] and French and Italian Impressionism.[11] These European schools, in turn, can trace their ancestry to artists such as Manet, Delacroix, Hals, Velázquez, El Greco, and Titian.

Normally contemporary audiences do not view Chase and Hawthorne as modernists, yet during their own times both men were antiacademic in their orientations. They favored a realistic, yet untraditional, portrayal of their motifs based on direct observation and emphasized that the significance of a work was determined not by the subject matter, but rather by how it was painted. Both maintained that a genuine artist could find beauty in what was ordinarily considered commonplace. They warned against formulaic techniques of making art and believed in the central role of inspiration rather than method. Moreover, they held fast to the tenet that the individual soul of the artist would be present in the completed work. Students were taught to paint with a loaded brush and vibrant colorations. Hawthorne even favored the palette knife as the best means to teach his technique based on opaque color patches.

Though there were variations in the teaching legacy passed from Chase to Hawthorne and then to Dickinson, many of their ideas were similar. Among these were the importance of capturing in pigment the true hues in nature, the importance of pleasure in the art-making process, an emphasis on everyday-life themes, a stress on discovering unusual approaches to subject matter, and the idea of painting as problem solving. Also important was the idea of maintaining an objective stance toward the object. Taken together these approaches constitute both a definite and definitive aesthetic orientation. In the hands of someone like Edwin Dickinson, this orientation paved the way for a distinctive, open-ended modernist approach to art-making.

From the beginning of his exhibition career in the teens, Edwin Dickinson was perceived as a modernist. Though his work was based on things seen, his interest in finding unexpected approaches to his subjects produced an art in which the common became uncommon. Dickinson enjoyed employing oblique angles, rendering one detail or section of an object rather than the whole, or juxtaposing a variety of unexpected common objects. He blurred some forms and presented others in sharp focus. Dickinson's method of painting landscapes *premier coup* (meaning "first strike" or done in one sitting) on site produced forms that seem disembodied and vaporous, bordering on the abstract. His figurative compositions that combined the real with the remembered tend to be mysterious and sometimes even disquieting. He liked viewers to wonder "what is it?" when they perceived his work for the first time.[12]

THE AESTHETIC PHILOSOPHY OF EDWIN DICKINSON

Dickinson once defined a work of art as something that "moves the spirit through the eye."[13] He considered that the root of extraordinary art was "a very high endowment of one person" that went beyond technical skills.[14] Because of these convictions, the painter believed that he could instruct his students in the "how" of producing technically proficient paintings and drawings, but not "the art of it." He used to say that he was not teaching "art" because that was something that students would discover themselves with time.[15] The artist was scrupulous about not overriding what a particular individual wanted to do. He was respectful of the intangible quality of "rightness" that many people feel in front of a work of art. If "it felt right" to the student, then "it was right."[16] Though Dickinson was leery about imposing his ideas on the more intimate aspects of his students' art-making, he felt he could introduce them to important tools and techniques that would enable them to develop their capacity to "see" the sensory world. He claimed that in a few weeks of instruction he could save a student more than a year's worth of time in terms of trial and error in acquiring good

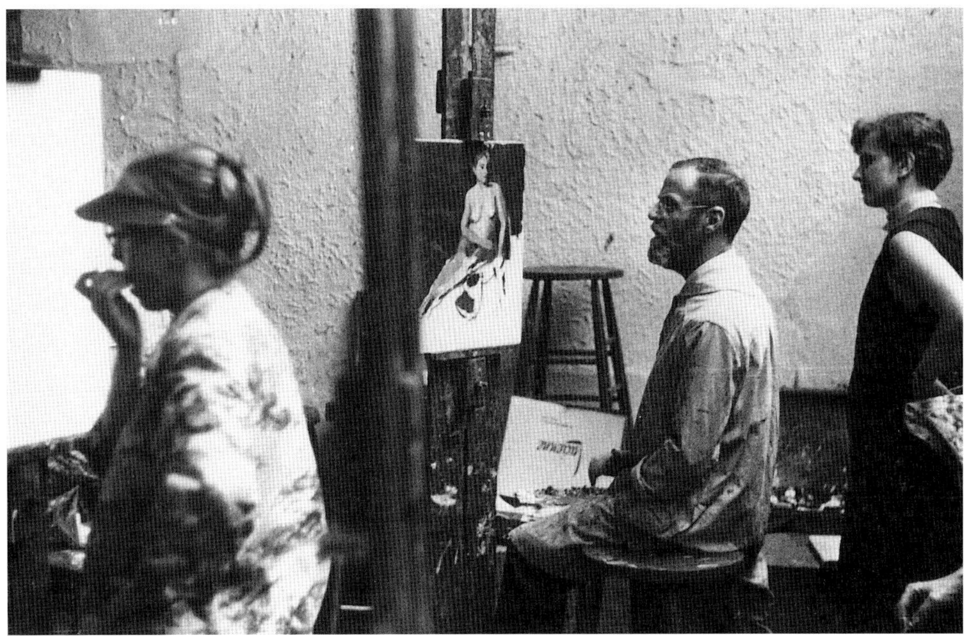

Fig. 1
Edwin Dickinson teaching at the Art Students League, New York, 1954
Photograph by Denver Lindley
Courtesy Dickinson Family Archive

painting habits. "The number of unnecessary blind alleys one has to climb through alone is wasteful," he told Katharine Kuh in explaining the usefulness of his own training under Chase and Hawthorne.[17]

In his pedagogical approach, Dickinson strenuously avoided any kind of systematic doctrines, which would have been inconsistent with his empirical, intensely personal approach to art. All of Dickinson's instruction was oriented around individual student critiques. There were no class lectures or group evaluation sessions. He did not believe in acerbic critiques, stating that pupils learned best through positive reinforcement. "I have never as a teacher used one word in sarcasm, and I don't in any other department of my life," he told the historian Carol Gruber.[18] Much of Dickinson's emphasis on maintaining a positive attitude stemmed from his conviction that quality paintings and drawings were produced by functioning at the height of one's enthusiasm. He often spoke to his students of the "joy in working." There was "no need to work without it," he said.[19] If students lost their zeal for a particular painting, he recommended that they scrape their canvases and begin anew. The artist, he maintained, should only initiate a work of art with the very highest ambitions, and during the process, bring every fiber of his being into play. This kind of physical and mental alertness he called being on the *"qui vive."*[20] Several students have related that Dickinson instructed them to paint "as though you're jumping on a moving train."[21] Dickinson admonished his students not to slump while working, but to "sit as if you are the first violin."[22] He preferred students to stand. Isabel Bishop recorded that Dickinson "believed that an artist should be aware of his precise relation to the physical world."[23]

Dickinson explained to his students that there were three ways that painters approached art-making: they could work strictly from nature; they could work creatively from nature (taking aspects of it but also deviating from it), or they could work solely from their imaginations.[24] Overall, the artist preferred students in his classes to work from nature.[25] In Dickinson's technique, there was no distinction between painting and drawing with the exception of the black-and-white limitation of graphic materials (he used to say that the "painter had the joy of color").[26] Students could work in either medium in his class.

The Key to Originality

One of the key aspects of the aesthetic experience in the Dickinson class was its stress on seeing things freshly, with no preconceived expectations. All of his devices—unusual poses, "unnameable color," "interstices," "angular" perspective, unusual angles—were about setting aside one's preconceptions and learning to look meticulously at something as if one were encountering it "for the first time" as he told his student Merrill Wagner.[27] The goal was to complete a more honest likeness or more authentic kind of work that was fresh and original. "If you do not bring anticipations to the sight of an object when drawing it, anticipations which are connected with its association in your lay life, it's easier to get it right than to get it wrong," he explained.[28] What Dickinson taught was not a style of painting or drawing, but a process whereby his followers could discover new color harmonies, new "marriages" or relationships between forms, new spatial constructions, new perspectives. As such, his training remained valid for a student's entire art career. The artist was led by the demands of the plastic elements in a process of continual discovery and fresh surprises, and each student ended up with a very individual work that was not based on clichés. What is remarkable is the range of idiosyncratic expressions that his students developed, from abstract to figurative modes.

THE CHARACTER AND DEPORTMENT OF EDWIN DICKINSON

Student Perspectives

The qualities most often mentioned by students regarding Edwin Dickinson were his respect for each pupil, his idealistic confidence in the importance of the artist, and his great love for the artistic process. His individualistic manner of speech and dress also impressed them, as did his integrity and wisdom.

Salvatore Del Deo, who studied with Dickinson at the ASL and knew him from Provincetown, admired his nondoctrinaire approach and the personal relationship that he forged with each student.[29] Many of Dickinson's students appreciated his absolute conviction that to be an artist was "a high calling."[30] Susan Smith, who studied with Dickinson at the ASL, believed that one of the reasons Dickinson's students respected him was because "he gave you so much to go into life with. . . . It wasn't just about painting, but it was also a professional attitude."[31] Arthur Cohen, who studied with Dickinson at the Cooper Union and never liked school or "being told things," believed that Dickinson was an exceptional teacher because "he showed wonder and a sort of innocence," but that the essence of his teaching lay in "the spirit of the thing," which is "what painting is about."[32] Ruth Hatch, another ASL student, also stressed Dickinson's "openness" and that he could be "euphoric like a child."[33]

Dickinson was a short man, about 5′ 6″ in height and weighing around 130 pounds. For most of his life he was in good physical condition and maintained a slim physique. Arthur Cohen remembered the first time that he saw Dickinson at the Cooper Union:

> He stood in the class doorway and looked to me as if he belonged to another time (in '47, few men had beards). His half glasses added to the picture, but mainly it was his face and bearing. . . . I was awed then without knowing anything about him, certainly not his work. The face can be seen in paintings and photographs, the presence and posture and movement can't. And when he spoke the impression of anomaly increased. I could hardly respond to him. He spoke as if he'd heard/read only Henry James and Shakespeare, in convoluted sentences with modifying clauses that stopped you in your

Fig. 2
Edwin Dickinson drawing the George Washington Bridge from Riverside Park, New York, spring 1963
Photograph by Kate Robinson
Courtesy Dickinson Family Archive

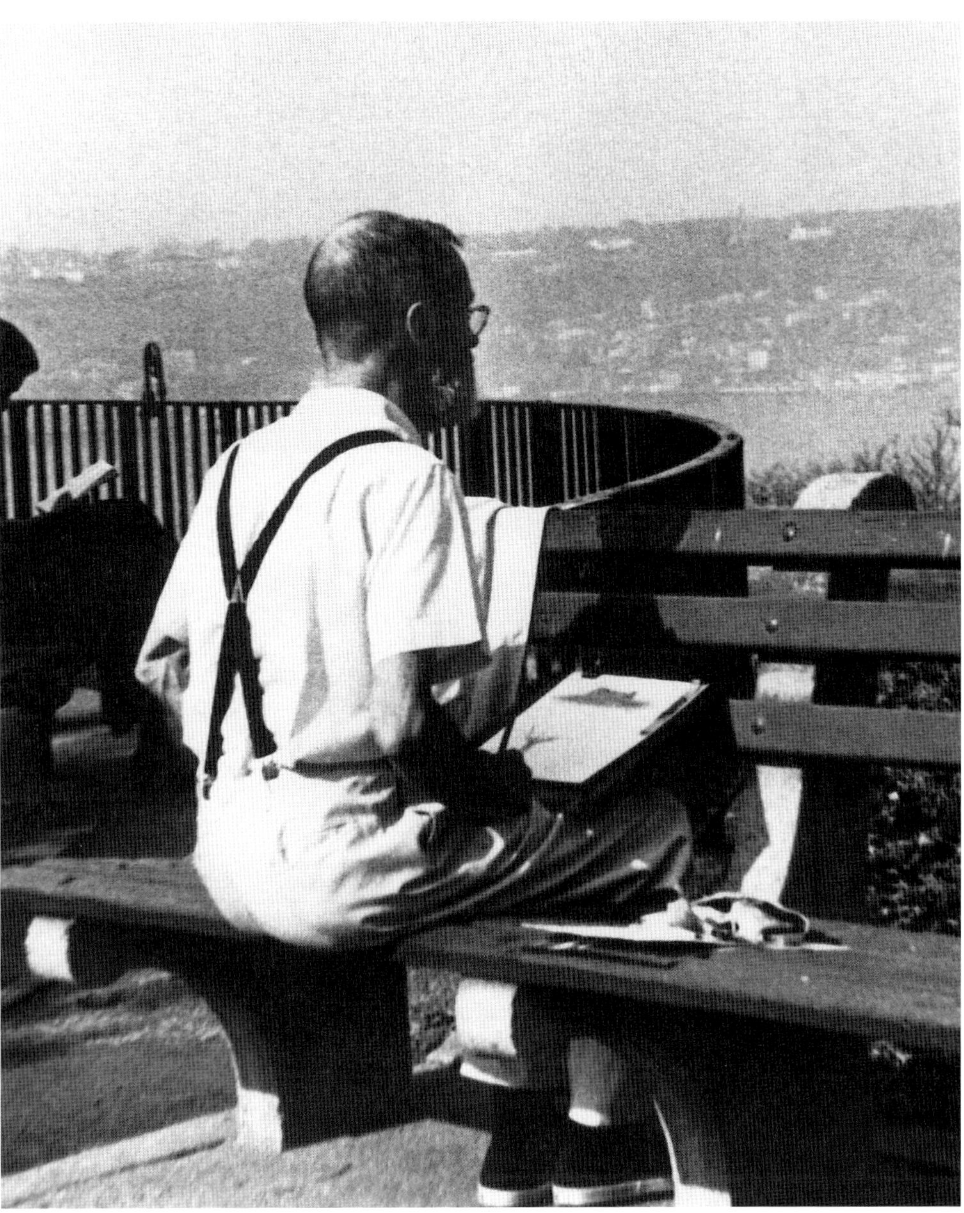

> tracks. I could only think of the nineteenth century and certain novels, and, of course, Shakespeare. But there was no pretension! He loved Shakespeare, I later learned.[34]

Many students proclaimed themselves delighted with Dickinson's unconventional appearance and decorum. Cohen wrote that Dickinson embodied "all that an adolescent wants out of an admired elder, including eccentricities and mannerisms you'd been taught to avoid in 'getting ahead.'"[35] Lennart Anderson, another student at the ASL, recalled how "impressive" Dickinson was with his "enormously deep voice" and "Edwardian attire." "You couldn't have an exchange with him without coming away with some kind of story," he said. One of Anderson's favorite reminiscences was how Dickinson once wore a windbreaker under a dinner jacket to have the effect of a light Edwardian waistcoat and knotted the widest end of a necktie, stuffing the long narrow end under his shirt, to simulate an early twentieth-century gentleman's cravat."[36]

Despite his eccentricities, Dickinson displayed humor and warmth and had a way of saying things that broke the ice with students; he treated them as budding professionals. Women in his classes never felt that he regarded them in a lesser light than their male counterparts, nor did older students feel neglected. Jean Buckley recalled that many of Dickinson's answers to student questions were "very hard to follow" because his language was so precise and he normally did not use colloquialisms.[37] Dickinson's exact use of language reflected a quality of discrimination that permeated his entire character. Ruth Hatch has expressed this as his abhorrence of the "dishonesty of inexactitude."[38] Thus, the artist was tidy in his personal attire, his manners were genteel, his painterly practices were acquired from years of disciplined and creative problem solving. When Dickinson used the word *mediocre,* he meant average.

Dickinson approached his chosen vocation with a dedication that extended even to details. He liked to say, "You tie your shoes as a professional."[39] Francis Cunningham said: "The economy of the professional artist in which every move is calculated to an end is something we learned in the Dickinson class. He never spoke of it as such, he never lectured or moralized on the subject. It was just there, in his teaching, in his conduct, and in his painting."[40]

When asked once what conditions he believed were necessary for the artist to produce quality work, Dickinson responded, financial security and sound physical health. The more important of these was "being physically up to the mark." Of maintaining one's health and fitness, he said, "That's part of one's professionalism. You're not less professional if you can't do it, but it's a character reflection."[41] Dickinson had enormous physical vitality, even later in his life. Denver Lindley remembered him at sixty-five vaulting over the rail in the lunchroom at the Art Students League.[42] Walter Prochownik, another ASL student who also knew Dickinson from Buffalo, recorded an anecdote about his interaction with students in 1947–48 [the artist would have been about fifty-seven at the time]: "Dickinson was a small man but athletic, like a bantam rooster. Some students were standing on their hands and he happened to walk in the room and saw them. He said that he could do the same. Tried but didn't quite make it. Some students helped him by straightening his legs. He kept all sorts of things in his pockets and everything fell out. He was very angry that they had helped straighten his legs. He tried again without help and succeeded."[43]

Everyone who knew him spoke of Dickinson's "principles," from which he seldom wavered. They were adhered to in his own art practice, his teaching, and in his personal conduct. Roger Van Damme recorded that Dickinson "had a wonderful sensitivity on top of a strong inner morality. He was the complete opposite of a man who would pursue a fad or a mode."[44] The artist was careful not to "criticize an institution which pays me a salary," as he phrased it to his friend and student Philip Malicoat.[45] Nor did he believe, as an educator, that it was appropriate to critique a student's work done in another teacher's class. Dickinson was scrupulous about not speaking in disparaging terms about contemporary artists because he did not want in any way to hinder the career of what he called a "fellow practitioner." As a humorous aside, he would sometimes say, "after all, there are plenty of dead ones to speak about."[46] Another of Dickinson's strongly held principles was his aversion to color reproductions. He abhorred them because of the inaccuracy of the resultant hues and preferred his work to appear in black and white. "You've everything to lose in taking a photograph of something that's beautiful and having it come out ugly. That's my point, and I feel very strongly about it," he told Carol Gruber.[47] He also was opposed to having his work profiled in non-art publications, acquiescing only on rare occasions.[48]

Ruth Hatch remembered Dickinson's scorn for anything "aesthetically dishonest,"as she phrased it; this extended to collectors who would purchase his work for speculation rather than sincere appreciation.[49] In the same vein, Dickinson was suspicious of work that showed a high level of technical finesse but that he perceived as having little genuine feeling. When he told students that they had produced a "non-commercial" work, it was high praise.[50] In 1963 he wrote on a blackboard at the ASL, "taste is the enemy of art."[51]

Dickinson's students have spoken of the enormous respect that they had for him not only as a teacher but also as a human being. Edward Denyer, who studied with Dickinson at the ASL, said:

> There was a magic that came from Mr. Dickinson. There was a quality which was beyond what he said.... One always acts with the greatest respect towards him. You would not think of saying to him what you may have said to someone else. It was unthinkable.... The influence he had on me was somehow far beyond what I actually got in any kind of tangible way from his work as a teacher. It was more the experience of being with a very rare, a very special human being.... There was a richness about him that seemed to come from his very special insight into many, many things about life. I guess that he was probably one of the few people that I would have wanted so much to be a friend of.[52]

Edwin Dickinson considered the profession of artist to be one of the most honorable to which a person could aspire. He believed deeply that one was called to it out of love. Thus, he respected all artists—including art students of any level of talent or skill—as friends and valued them as colleagues. In return, he was accorded their highest esteem.

> One very valuable aspect of Edwin Dickinson—something almost lost now—when he walked into a classroom—everyone knew that the master walked in. They looked at him, listened to him and respected him ... he had something about him as unique as his painting was.... There's no man about whom I can speak with greater admiration and respect than Edwin Dickinson.[53]

NOTES

1. Elaine de Kooning, "The Modern Museum's Fifteen: Dickinson and Kiesler," *Art News* (New York), Apr. 1952, p. 23.

2. Katharine Kuh, "Edwin Dickinson," in *The Artist's Voice: Talks with Seventeen Artists* (New York: Harper & Row, 1962; reprint Da Capo Press, 2000), p. 77.

3. Among the institutions where Dickinson taught were the Buffalo Fine Arts Academy (summer 1916) and Art Institute of Buffalo, New York (spring 1939); Art School of the Brooklyn Museum, New York (1949–ca. 1957); The Art Students League, New York (1922–23, 1945–66 [on leave 1961–62]); Association for Music and Art, Centerville, Massachusetts (1940); The Cooper Union, New York (1945–49); Midtown School of Art, New York (1945–47); Pratt Institute, Brooklyn (1950–51); Provincetown Art Association, Massachusetts (drawing classes 1929–32); The Raymond Moore Foundation, Dennis, Massachusetts (summer 1951); Skowhegan School of Painting and Sculpture, Maine (one month each summer in 1956 and 1958); Stuart School of Design, Boston (1941–42); and Wellesley College, Massachusetts (two weeks in 1940). In addition, he was a visiting instructor at such institutions as Cornell University, Ithaca, New York (1957); Columbia University, New York (spring semester 1957); Boston University (1961); and Yale University, New Haven, Connecticut (1963).

4. The material on Dickinson's pedagogical approach was gathered from students, from their notes, and from their reminiscences. Students who studied with Dickinson at the Art Students League supplied the bulk of the material relating to Dickinson's classroom instruction. Foremost among these are Lennart Anderson (enrolled 1954); Jean Buckley (enrolled 1963–65); Francis Cunningham (enrolled 1958–59); Salvatore Del Deo (enrolled 1949); Edward Denyer (enrolled ca. 1945–46); Ruth Hatch (enrolled 1950s); Denver Lindley (enrolled mid-1950s); Walter Pro-

chownik (enrolled 1947–48); Susan Smith (enrolled 1955–57; 1958–59); Roger Van Damme (enrolled 1960–61); Merrill Wagner (enrolled late 1950s). Arthur Cohen studied with Dickinson at the Cooper Union in 1947.

5. Francis Cunningham, interview by Donald Smith, Nov. 1981, audiocassette 1, Oral History Collection, Archives of American Art, Washington, D.C. Donald Smith, though not a Dickinson student himself, studied with Edward Denyer, who had been. Smith was intrigued by Dickinson's teaching methodology and interviewed many of his students.

6. Ibid.

7. Denver Lindley, interview by Donald Smith, Jan. 14, 1984, audiocassette 1, Oral History Collection, Archives of American Art, Washington, D.C.

8. Carol S. Gruber, "The Reminiscences of Edwin Dickinson" (New York: Oral History Research Office, Columbia University, 1957–58), pp. 50–51.

9. Dickinson studied with Chase at the Art Students League from the fall of 1911 to late January 1913 and with Hawthorne at his Cape Cod School of Art in Provincetown, Massachusetts, summers, 1912–14.

10. The Munich Royal Academy, where Chase studied, emphasized a realistic portrayal of everyday subjects with bravura brushwork and a limited tonal range. See Eberhard Ruhmer and Michael Quick, *Munich and American Realism in the 19th Century* (Sacramento, Calif.: E. B. Crocker Art Gallery, 1978). William H. Gerdts claims that during the period that Chase trained there (1972–78), the modernist concept of "the primacy of method and technique over subject matter began to be stressed" instead of traditional approaches to art. William H. Gerdts, "Munich School Modernism," paper presented at "Radical Departures: Aspects of the Modern in American Painting, 1876–1939" (conference held at New York University, May 7–9, 1998).

11. In its stress on the use of color patches in the direct study of nature and the emphasis on immediate observation without embellishment (which excluded as nearly as possible all preconceptions as well as literary allusions), the color-spot orientation espoused by Hawthorne and Dickinson is clearly indebted to French Impressionism, immensely popular during the late nineteenth and early twentieth century in both Europe and the United States. Claude Monet once told a student: "When you go out to paint, try to forget what objects you have before you, a tree, a house, a field or whatever. Merely think, here is a little square of blue, here an oblong of pink, here a streak of yellow, and paint it just as it looks to you, the exact color and shape, until it gives your own naive impression of the scene before you." Linda Nochlin, *Impressionism and Post-Impressionism, 1874–1904: Sources and Documents* (Englewood Cliffs, N. J.: Prentice-Hall, 1966), p. 35. Such a statement is reminiscent of Hawthorne, who once said, "Don't think of things as objects, think of them as spots of color coming one against another." See Mrs. Charles W. Hawthorne, comp., *Hawthorne on Painting* (New York and Chicago: Pitman Publishing Corporation, 1938; reprint, New York: Dover, 1960, p. 47).

12. Lindley, interview by Donald Smith, audiocassette 1.

13. Cunningham, interview by Donald Smith, audiocassette 2.

14. Gruber, "The Reminiscences of Edwin Dickinson," p.185.

15. Roger Van Damme, "Conversations with Edwin Dickinson,"1960–61, at the Art Students League, in files of Roger Van Damme, Woodmont, Connecticut, p. 5.

16. Lindley, interview by Donald Smith, audiocassette 1.

17. Kuh, "Edwin Dickinson," in *The Artist's Voice*, p. 78.

18. Gruber, "The Reminiscences of Edwin Dickinson," pp. 28–29.

19. Jean Buckley, "Notes on Studio Instruction with Edwin Dickinson," Feb. 1963–May 1965, typed manuscript in files of Jean Buckley, Basking Ridge, New Jersey, p. 24.

20. Francis Cunningham, interview by author, May 27, 1999, audiocassette.

21. Quote by Ruth Hatch from Nathan Halper, *Edwin Dickinson* (Provincetown, Mass.: Provincetown Art Association, 1976), n.p.

22. Lindley, interview by Donald Smith, audiocassette 1.

23. Isabel Bishop, "Commemorative Tribute: Edwin Dickinson (1891–1978)," *American Institute of Arts and Letters* (New York), no. 30, 1969, p. 48.

24. Francis Cunningham, "Dickinson's Practice," Aug. 1999, typed notes in files of Francis Cunningham, New York, p. 19.

25. Susan Smith, telephone interview by author, June 15, 1999, typed transcript, p. 2.

26. Cunningham, interview by Donald Smith, audiocassette 2.

27. Merrill Wagner, interview by author, June 18, 1999, typed transcript, p. 28.

28. Gruber, "The Reminiscences of Edwin Dickinson," p. 162.

29. Salvatore Del Deo, interview by author, Provincetown, Mass., Aug. 23, 1999, audiocassette.

30. Lindley, interview by Donald Smith, audiocassette 1.

31. Susan Smith, telephone interview by author, June 15, 1999, typed transcript, p. 24.

32. Arthur Cohen, letter to author, Aug. 24, 1997.

33. Ruth Hatch, interview by author and Douglas Dreishpoon, Wellfleet, Mass., Aug. 20, 2000, audiocassette.

34. Cohen, letter to author, August 24. 1997.

35. Ibid.

36. Lennart Anderson, interview by author, Mar. 31, 2001, audiocassette.

37. Jean Buckley, interview by author, May 30, 1999, audiocassette.

38. Ruth Hatch, interview by author and Dreishpoon.

39. Lindley, interview by Donald Smith, audiocassette 1.

40. Cunningham, "Dickinson's Practice," p. 7.

41. Gruber, "The Reminiscences of Edwin Dickinson," p. 72. In this same passage, Dickinson admitted that other artists were able to produce quality art under conditions of poor health, but acknowledged that he could not.

42. Lindley, interview by Donald Smith, audiocassette 1.

43. Walter Prochownik, letter to Frances Dickinson, June 22, 1977, page 2. Dickinson Family Archives.

44. Roger Van Damme, class notes taken at Art Students League, New York, 1960–61, in files of Roger Van Damme, p. 2.

45. Edwin Dickinson, letter to Philip Malicoat, Nov. 21, 1950, Archives of American Art, Washington, D.C. Malicoat was a Dickinson student who attended classes at the Provincetown Art Association.

46. Jack Hall, interview by author, Aug. 14, 1997, audiocassette. The only contemporary artist that he ever publicly criticized was Salvador Dalí, who he felt made the artistic profession look ridiculous in the eyes of the public.

47. Gruber, "The Reminiscences of Edwin Dickinson," p. 98. During his life, Dickinson's work was reproduced in color on only a few occasions: when it appeared in *Time*, Feb. 10, 1968, and when *The Fossil Hunters* was printed on the cover of *Art News*, Jan. 1959.

48. Helen Dickinson Baldwin mentioned that on several occasions (one being Mar. 10, 1961) her father was approached by *Life* for a feature article. He consistently refused. It was only in 1961 that he finally agreed to allow *Time* to cover his work on the occasion of his retrospective at James Graham & Sons. He told her that the only reason that he did it was "for my family." Helen Dickinson Baldwin, interview by author, Truro, Mass., July 9, 1999.

49. Ruth Hatch, interview by author and Dreishpoon.

50. Cunningham, interview by Donald Smith, audiocassette 1.

51. Buckley, "Notes on Studio Instruction with Edwin Dickinson," p. 4.

52. Edward Denyer, interview by Donald Smith, Feb. 10, 1984, Oral History Collection, Archives of American Art, Washington, D.C., audiocassettes 1 and 2.

53. Prochownik, letter to Frances Dickinson.

THE TEACHING OF EDWIN DICKINSON
An Overview and Glossary

Mary Ellen Abell

Edwin Dickinson once told a group of students: "If we don't continue to use painter's terms, the art world will inherit only writers' terms." Dickinson's terminology is used here to introduce aspects of his teaching methodology. The bulk of the material contained herein, grouped according to main subject areas, comes from interviews conducted by Mary Ellen Abell (1997–2001) and Donald Smith (1981–1986) with students of Edwin Dickinson.

COLOR

Color-Spots

A focus on color masses, called *color-spots,* was the central component of Dickinson's approach. Representational art had always rested on conventional ways of registering visual material, never with the raw data of sight. Drawing on the teaching of Hawthorne and Impressionism, Dickinson understood that sight consists of a patchwork of light and color and from this awareness, he came to depend on the color-spot. The mind interprets light and color sensations as objects in space, which the artist, working abstractly without a priori ideas, emulates. If a painter could capture the correct hue, mixed carefully after nature, then space and values as well as the illusion of light would be truthfully recorded.

The shape of the color-spot was not a systematized pointillist dot or the divided touch of the Impressionists, nor did its shape describe the customary forms with which objects are identified. Instead, the form of the color-spots related to how areas of color in nature stood out as abstract forms that could be captured on a two-dimensional surface. The color-spot aesthetic mixed during the direct observation of nature comprised hundreds of color-spots, which varied considerably in area, with delicate modulations from one to another. It was an extremely subtle and refined use of color.

Students were advised to begin a painting with only a scant drawing that laid out the main arcs and angles of their composition. Dickinson felt that line imposed an artificial "wire" around objects and that "relationships of one thing to another could only be shown truly in value [lightness or darkness of a color]."

Unnameable Color

Whenever there were references to color in the Dickinson class, the terms *unnameable color* or *no-color color* were used. In their study of hue, as in their study of shapes, Dickinson wanted students to rid their minds of conventional knowledge and, instead, attune themselves to an intense scrutiny of the various color-spots in their subjects, most of which were difficult to name.

Color-Value

Dickinson always applied the term *color-value* rather than *color* or *value.* The artist strongly believed that one could not separate the value of a color from its two other properties of hue and intensity because there was no such thing as a pure value, except in the case of monochromes. Mixing the truest color from nature meant finding value. Hence, by using the term *color-value,* this idea was promoted more forcibly in the mind of the student.

Color-Value Relationships

Because there is a much wider variance of colors in nature than the oil painter is capable of capturing and because all colors exist in harmonious relationships, Dickinson recommended that his students set up *color-value relationships.* So, after students had mixed their initial color-spot, based on the observed hues in nature, they immediately blended another color-spot and placed it next to the first. A third spot would next be associated with the other two. It was imperative that the spots be placed adjacent to one another so that their relationship could be better appraised against the white canvas ground. Dickinson used the analogy "like moss grows" to explain this outward expansion of the color-spots. During this crucial, formative stage of building up the color-spots, the students' work appeared quite abstract.

Strike the Note

Dickinson often used musical analogies in his teaching. The idioms *strike the note* and *hit the note* referred to the importance of learning to mix each observed color-spot accurately at the outset. If students did not strike the notes carefully as they proceeded, they would have to go back and remix color-spots. This would not only slow them down and ruin the delicate color-value relationships already established but would also produce a negative mental attitude.

Premising the Color-Spots

The initial color-values established the key to the entire painting, which is why it was important that these color-spots be scrupulously considered. Dickinson used to speak of students *premising their initial color-spots,* meaning that the selection of a particular color-spot bound the student to an array of colors. He stressed the importance of remaining steadfast with one's initial color decisions, even if fluctuating lighting conditions changed the color-values in nature.

Transposition: Mixing Refined Colors

Dickinson would often talk about making a *transposition* from the color-value perceived in nature to the color-value on the canvas by transforming the two hues in another key and color. He believed that his students could arrive at a closer approximation of the natural color if they began their mixing process with a hue very different from the one that they thought they saw, such as its complement. Through the procedure of mixing, the pupil would end up with a *refined* color relationship close to that perceived in nature.

Work Large and Take Less

Students were instructed to work life-size and to take only a section of the figure, not the whole. The purpose was to get them to study color-values more intensely. If they worked under life-size, they would have to rely more on imagination than on careful observation since they would be unable to see clearly the subtle color-value changes. The same thing was true if they worked over life-size. A student might focus on a portion of the torso near the armpit, or a section of the right arm and part of the torso. Dickinson did not want beginners to paint or draw the head because, in his opinion, most artists had too many assumptions about what it should look like. He tellingly said, "One learns to do faces better by painting torsos."

PERSPECTIVE

Angular Perspective

Angular perspective refers to how an object actually appears from an unexpected viewing position, such as close-up, canted at an odd angle, or from a bird's-eye or worm's-eye vantage point. In a classical study, perspectival distortion would be avoided by moving the cube further away from the viewer's eye and conforming the image to an ideal in which all verticals are vertical and all horizontals, horizontal. A Dickinson student, however, would record the irregularity of the object exactly as he or she saw it.

THE HOUSEKEEPING OF THE PALETTE

The tools of the painter's craft that Dickinson recommended were the plumb line, the finder, the eye shade, the squint, the palette knife, and the little finger. The use of many of these tools as well as advice on handling the palette were covered in what Dickinson termed *the housekeeping of the palette.*

The Plumb Line and the Finder

Dickinson encouraged the use of the plumb line and the finder to measure the world. The plumb line was made from a piece of No. 2 carpet thread with a nail or plumb bob used as a weight on the end. Its purpose was to determine verticality through the force of gravity. It was effective for accurately measuring arcs, angles, and *how high for how wide* (or proportion). The length was approximately twenty inches so that the student could hold it up and observe a model from head to toe. The finder was a device made from two adjustable L-shaped pieces of cardboard that were held together with paper clips to form a viewfinder from which to look out at an aspect of nature. It assisted students with composition and echoed the horizontal/vertical planes of the canvas or drawing paper. The end result of such optical devices was to train the eye to see the world from a particular vantage point.

The Eye Shade

Dickinson recommended the use of an eye shade because it eliminated overhead and peripheral light and increased visibility by 15 to 20 percent, thus enabling the student to see substantially more in terms of color-values.

The Squint

In the initial planning stages for a painting or drawing, a Dickinson student would pull out his or her finder and plumb line and then squint to perceive the main shapes, select the appropriate color-spots, and determine the lightest lights and the darkest darks of his or her subject. The basic drawing was established in about five minutes.

The Palette Knife and the Little Finger

Dickinson preferred that his students apply the pigment with palette knives or the outer edges of their little fingers. Color was mixed with putty or palette knives and applied opaquely, its viscous state enabling the student to judge better the color relationships on the canvas than would thinner paint. This approach also guided students away from drawing contour lines and thus kept them focused on large masses of color. The little finger was a useful tool enabling the artist to spread pigment easily, blur edges, make a delicate line, or remove excess paint.

FURTHER PEDAGOGICAL APPROACHES

The Site Taken as Seen

Edwin Dickinson's style of teaching involved training the eye to experience the visual without preconceived ideas. A favorite Dickinson challenge, *the site taken as seen,* meant that students should paint or draw what they actually saw, not what they thought they saw.

The Nature

When he used the term *the nature,* Dickinson was referring to the model or principal subject. As we have seen, he was trying to train his students to rely on visual perception rather than mental preconception. In order to reinforce this, he would not identify, by name, the object to which he was referring. Instead, he preferred to say "the nature, "this," or "the appearance," probably as a distancing device.

Painting Must Be Experimenting

Dickinson repeatedly spoke of his approach to his art as problem solving and experimentation. Dickinson challenged his students with set-ups and poses so unusual that they had to resolve them in unexpected ways. He advised them to create complicated compositions or color-value problems for themselves so that they could encounter resistance in their work. If they became too adept with their right hands, he recommended working with their left. Through this experimental approach, Dickinson hoped that his students would find their own originality.

Strikes

Strikes were quick, two-minute drawing exercises utilizing charcoal that Dickinson had devised to train his students' eyes to capture quickly and accurately the postures of their subjects by focusing on concise edges and judging angles correctly in relation to the vertical world. This was all done with the plumb line.

Interstices

Sometimes students would focus on the *interstices,* or negative space. For example, the interstice might be described as the triangle that is formed by a model sitting with his or her legs apart when viewed from the front. Dickinson believed that students would get a much closer likeness if they drew this triangular space rather than concentrating on the limbs.

The training in strikes and interstices enabled students to capture more successfully the underlying geometry of their subjects. Once the geometry of the figure was established, then the student could either leave it as an abstract design or incorporate anatomical elements onto the geometric scaffold.

Love Will Find a Way

Dickinson always said that he loved to teach and that he would stop the moment this was no longer true, but it is likely that he would not have taught as much if it were not for economic concerns. "I loved teaching very much but somewhat regretted the time away from painting," he once said. Throughout his lifetime, and in all his work, though, he believed pleasure was a great motivator. When students were feeling stymied in their work, he would simply say "Love will find a way."

A RECOLLECTION

Elaine de Kooning

"It's wonderful to hear young people talk about their art," said Edwin Dickinson in 1951 as he discreetly slipped out of the door of the Artists' Club where a panel of painters from the Tibor de Nagy Gallery was involved in a heated discussion, "but I don't have to listen to them."

He didn't have to listen to their elders—the founders of the Abstract Expressionist movement—either.

Walt Whitman wrote: "The soul has that immeasurable pride which accepts no deductions or conclusions but its own." This observation applies to Dickinson as it does to very few artists. Fiercely autocratic, he resisted the prevailing trends and pursued his own cryptic rules and regulations as though he were alone in a private dream world where imagination has as much authority as the floor under one's feet.

Although he worked in the center of the American art world with a studio in New York City and, in the summers, near an artists' colony at Wellfleet, Massachusetts, he didn't respond to the concepts of the painters around him as he did to those of Cézanne or El Greco. "When I saw *The Burial of Count Orgaz*, I knew where my aspirations lay." El Greco was a lifelong devotion. As a highly accomplished artist with a large body of work behind him, Dickinson went back to this source in the early 1940's, spending long months at the Metropolitan Museum copying the *View of Toledo*—a passionate investigation that yielded a taut, fresh commentary on that sublime painting. Dickinson could aptly join Willem de Kooning in a sly self-appraisal: "The more I'm influenced, the more original I get."

The Abstract Expressionist painters around Dickinson recognized his originality, and if he didn't respond to them, they responded to *him* with great enthusiasm and reverence, and he was included every year in their artist-juried show at the Stable Gallery in the early 1950's.

Contemplating Dickinson's large-scale "salon" paintings with their hallucinatory content—the haunted landscapes and interiors, the brooding, shadowy forms, the unearthly atmosphere and light, the pervading sense of tragedy—one might think of writers rather than painters, nineteenth century writers in particular—Edgar Allan Poe, Nathaniel Hawthorne, Ambrose Bierce, Stephen Crane. And Dickinson himself could have stepped out of one of their stories.

A tiny, immaculate, perfectly proportioned man, all edges, corners, contours, he seemed to belong to another period, an impression he cultivated in his elegant Edwardian attire—narrow trousers, high-buttoned jackets and beautifully groomed beard (which he was in the habit of combing when one's back was turned).

Witty, erudite, opinionated, Dickinson sparkled in company. But most of the time, he was isolated with his work, spending years on a single canvas, inventing, destroying, rebuilding, struggling with his complex frameworks of multiple perspectives. This excruciating conscientiousness can be dangerous for an artist as it was for some remarkable nineteenth century American painters, finally leading to constraint, timidity and provincialism. Dickinson, always daring, escaped to the grand manner. Through all of his rigorous control, his fanatic concentration on every element of his large compositions, he kept the spontaneity that characterizes the dazzling little paintings made from life that he would finish in one day at Wellfleet.

First published in *Edwin Dickinson: Draftsman/Painter* (New York: National Academy of Design, 1982), pp. 17–18. Reprinted courtesy National Academy of Design and Salander-O'Reilly Galleries, New York.

EDWIN DICKINSON

John Ashbery

"Among contemporary American artists few of our younger men are more gifted and their ability less appreciated, than is Edwin Dickinson. An excellent draftsman, he could easily have steered his course as to become not only a popular, but a successful portrait painter. Nature, however, does not seem to have destined this artist for a popular career. In recent years he has listened to the whisperings of strange muses, and has followed untrodden paths which inspired a mind austere to the point of forbidding. . . . "[1]

The comment above was made by William B. Hekking, director of the Albright Art Gallery in Buffalo, in the catalogue of Edwin Dickinson's first exhibition, which was held there in 1927. Unfortunately, until now, time appears to have proved Mr. Hekking right on most counts. Again and again Dickinson's reputation has seemed on the point of blossoming into that of a mainstream artist such as Edward Hopper. In 1961, at the time of the Graham Gallery's large retrospective, *Time*'s critic thought that the show "should help in making Dickinson's name as familiar to the public as it has long been within the profession,"[2] and other reviewers concurred. Yet this seems not to have happened, either then or after the Whitney Museum's retrospective in 1965, or the Hirshhorn Museum's show of Dickinson's "premier coup" paintings in 1980. Reviewing that show, which coincided with the Whitney's big Hopper exhibition, I mentioned certain similarities between the two painters so as to contrast them, and then wondered "if we really know who our greatest painters are."[3] I'm not sure we do—yet—but it does seem that the stepped-up pace of Dickinson exhibitions and the augmenting ground-swell of critical opinion may well be on the verge of bringing him to the attention of the same national consciousness that now embraces Hopper. Dickinson did indeed listen to the whisperings of strange muses and follow untrodden paths, but so, increasingly, do we all. Our collective sensibility has never seemed closer to catching up with the work of this mysterious genius who was so far ahead of his time, and who is only the latest in a series of eccentric American geniuses to be recognized posthumously.

Though not usually given to quoting myself, I am again reminded of a remark I made in a review, this one of two books of poetry—one by the late John Wheelwright, the other by A. R. Ammons. I suggested that the mainstream of American poetry "seems to be peopled by cranks (Emerson, Whitman, Pound, Stevens), while certified major poets (Frost, Eliot) somehow end up on the sidelines."[4] One could extend the comparison to our fiction, from Poe to Pynchon, to music (Ives, Varèse) and finally to the visual arts. The major Abstract Expressionist painters have been canonized to the point where no one considers them the least bit odd, yet it would be hard to find a more eccentric bunch of artists in history. Similarly, Dickinson's impending (I feel) assimilation will not be impeded by the "academic" aspect of his work which even now allows a general public to accept what in the work of a less competent artist might be found unacceptable.

It's strange, this weirdness which seems to be a main ingredient in the greatest works of the American imagination. How can it be that *Moby Dick* and *Leaves of Grass* and the *Fourth Symphony* of Ives are simultaneously so universal and so confoundedly bizarre? In other cultures the latter quality occurs chiefly in secondary practitioners—

William Beckford, Achim von Arnim, Barbey d'Aurevilly—and this seems a normal state of affairs. We, however, do not possess a Mozart or a Dickens—artists whose genius is both canonical and beyond dispute. Our major statements almost always come tinged with strangeness. Is it because our traditions are more recent and that therefore we are more suspicious of them, and consequently are always falling through them into a world behind the prosaic, reassuring one our landscapes try so hard to conjure up? It may be that the very banality of the American scene, as perceived by us who inhabit it, is the reason. Try looking at it a little closer and see what you come up with. Even artists who, like Dickinson, imagined that they were merely recording it with respectful fidelity, end up evoking phantoms. Witness what Charles Ives thought the Housatonic at Stockbridge sounded like. Or take an example of Dickinson at his most literal, the beautiful 1927 drawing of a New England clapboard house called *Souvenir of the Fossil Hunters*. No spectres are clustered at the windows as in Rodolphe Bresdin's etching *Maison Hantée*, which Dickinson's drawing somewhat reminds me of. The sky isn't peopled by strange flying creatures as in Charles Meryon's etched view of Paris, to cite another brilliant French eccentric whose work has never gained more than a cult following. The windows of Dickinson's house are blank, the sky behind pierced by a few bare branches whose somewhat irregular outlines nonetheless look perfectly natural. And the house is your basic American house, a "nice" one with shutters and a screen porch and a dormer window, and it is drawn with the utmost attention to detail to the way it must have looked. True, a few details are omitted, including some of the balusters in the porch railing; or left somewhat vague, such as the downstairs window in contrast to the one just above it, but there are none of the distortions we have come to take for granted in modern art. Yet the almost sinister strangeness of the drawing is overpowering, far more so than in the Bresdin and Meryon works mentioned above. Despite its apparent straightforwardness, it is as though the house were being looked at and recorded by a visitor from another planet.

Although he was sometimes reserved, Dickinson was at other times perfectly willing to discuss his work. Yet when he does so, the peculiarity is something he avoids or minimizes, so that one sometimes wonders if he was aware of it. The curious concatenations of objects that appear in his larger, more complex pictures like *The Cello Player* [cat. no. 8] and *Composition with Still Life* [cat. no. 20] are an element of his work that has puzzled and fascinated his audience. But Dickinson's typical reaction was to play them down. Although he went so far as to use the term "Surrealism" while discussing his work with an interviewer in 1958, one feels that he did so out of politeness to a public that was always trying to attach that label to him. (The present-day consensus seems to be that, however singular his work may be, it has little in common with Surrealism.) "Still life is also of use to the painter who is interested in Surrealism," he remarked, before proceeding to deflate any expectations this beginning might have aroused in the interviewer. "The layman is used to seeing the kitchen knife next to the kitchen fork. There's a relevancy that's ordinary. Very often the painter will put things together that are rather surprising and it's diverting, without being a tremendous thing in itself—but it's pleasing."[5] Back to square one.

Questions about his oneiric landscape called *The Finger Lakes* [cat. no. 34], which has a mysterious balloon hovering over a wooded cape in the background, while in the foreground a rose surges toward the viewer as though out of a tide of dreams, elicited a small response:

Interviewer: Why did you include the balloon?

Dickinson: The reason I put in the balloon was just a little capriciousness. I was born at the head of this lake in Seneca Falls. When I was five, I had been taken down to a recreation park . . . and once a year there was a balloon ascension there. A fellow in tights went up on a trapeze under a balloon. I guess he jumped off in a parachute, with an American flag in his hand. It was a regular 1890's fair. The balloon ascension I associated with the lake, and since this was the lake . . . I put the balloon in.

Interviewer: What was the reason for painting the rose in?

Dickinson: I suppose I thought it would look better.[6]

On the face of it, an evasive and even exasperating reply. But the question, albeit a natural one, is even more exasperating. Why do we persist in asking our artists to explain their work, *when that work is itself the answer to a question or questions that preceded it*? In this case, that question might have been: "What is this strangeness I feel connected with an event from the distant past?" Small wonder that interviewers are frequently unable to dredge up anything more illuminating than "I thought it looked better." Yet the answer, like Cordelia's reply to Lear, was obviously the correct one.

Dickinson's nostalgic recollection of the carnival balloon ascension is interesting because, like the Bible camp meetings and long-ago holiday celebrations that inspired Ives, it seems to have resulted in a work of art that has little to do with the original point of departure. Ives' *Decoration Day* sounds more like a Walpurgisnacht, though the composer evidently felt he was conveying the good-natured merry making of middle America when he was a child. Dickinson's phantom balloon and blue rose make as beautiful and deeply disturbing an image as any Surrealist painting, though the juxtaposition is less obviously disconcerting than Lautréamont's "encounter between a sewing machine and an umbrella on a dissecting table." Yet for the painter they were part of a happy childhood memory on one hand, and of a concern for the painting to "look right" on the other. I am inclined to trust the painter's explanation in this and in most other cases. Dickinson was a naturalist rather than a Surrealist, but the world he observed was not the one we think we see but one just beyond it, a little out of focus sometimes, but also painfully, astonishingly real.

The problem of painting "from life" with total accuracy and honesty involves lies and distortions, and Dickinson was well aware of this paradox, judging from his statement. Explaining why he never painted objects in the normal posture, he said: "I learned early that the assumption of verticality was going to get me in trouble. . . . Flagpoles are straight up and down and beds are sideways. I was very young when I discovered that you couldn't assume these things, because verticality and the appearance of the vertical object, when on a picture plane, is a very different thing."[7] He elaborates on this in a discussion of *Quarry, Riverdale* [cat. no. 63], which is, after the hide-and-seek game of multiple vanishing points in *Ruin at Daphne* [cat. no. 50], perhaps his most difficult-to-decipher composition. "What the sight appeared to be in the squint is what the painting is, and it's just like it in the squint. And if you look at the scene without squinting, you will know what it is, do you understand. Think of the leaves that might have been six feet from you, immediately beyond which was a piece of rock forty yards away. You just can't do it leaf by leaf. It's got to be taken in its large groupings. They will be found by the painter to be interesting compositionally. That's why he looked in that place instead of some other one . . . People assume that that was done with thoughts other than representation in mind. Honorable as that would be, it was not the case. It's exactly like it, to the extent that I could make it like it in six weeks."[8]

After the recent revelation at the Hirshhorn [1980] of the "premier coup" paintings: limpid, lightning-like spearings of a single object or a moment of landscape, the present exhibition [*Edwin Dickinson: Draftsman/Painter* at the National Academy of Design, New York, 1982] turns—and it is again time to do so—to the works of medium elaboration and beyond them to the vast compositions on which he worked for years, sometimes, as was the case with *Ruin at Daphne*, wiping out two years' work and beginning again. It is hard to think of other works of art that are as complicated and exalted at the same time. Perhaps Bach's *Art of the Fugue* would be one. In these, Dickinson's masterpieces, that which once seemed a paradox, (slow, labyrinthine plottings by a painter who was also obsessed with getting a finished image onto canvas in as short a time as possible) now seems merely heightened realism—but a realism attentive to *every* nuance of light, line, tone, and atmosphere, and which therefore looks somewhat odd. Nevertheless, "if you look at the scene without squinting, you will know what it is, do you understand."[9]

First published in *Edwin Dickinson: Draftsman/Painter* (New York: National Academy of Design, 1982), pp. 11–15. Reprinted courtesy National Academy of Design and by permission of Georges Borchardt, Inc., for the author.

NOTES

1. Edna M. Lindemann, *Edwin Dickinson Tribute Exhibition* (Buffalo: Burchfield Center, State University College at Buffalo, New York, 1977), p. 4.

2. *Time* (New York), Feb. 10, 1961, n.p.

3. John Ashbery, "Coups de Grace," *New York* (New York), Oct. 13, 1980, p. 51.

4. John Ashbery, "Collected Poems of John Wheelwright; Collected Poems 1951–1971; Collected Poems of A. R. Ammons," *New York Review of Books* (New York), Feb. 22, 1973, p. 3.

5. Interview with Carol S. Gruber, "The Reminiscences of Edwin Dickinson" (New York: Oral History Research Office, Columbia University, 1957–58), p. 150.

6. Ibid., pp. 166–67.

7. Ibid., p. 159.

8. Ibid., pp. 174–75.

9. Ibid., p. 175.

EDWIN DICKINSON A Self-Sustained Ego

Norman A. Geske

In 1967, I was invited to submit a proposal for the exhibition in the American Pavilion at the XXXIV Venice Biennale, to take place the following year. The proposed theme was "The Figurative Tradition in Recent American Art." It seemed to me that a somewhat different stance with regard to what was happening in American art would be appropriate, especially following the themes of several of the exhibitions of preceding Biennales. Something in the nature of a backing off from the art scene as defined in the art press of the moment—taking a wider view of the scene as a national phenomenon—might be in order. Although the development of Abstract Expressionism had achieved an international predominance for American art, it appeared to me that there were signs of an emergence of a new interest in figuration that deserved some attention.

Speaking only of the five painters involved: Byron Burford was, and is, a painter deeply imbued with a peculiarly American imagination; Richard Diebenkorn, although at first an initiate of Abstract Expressionism, had completed a decade or more of figurative painting that was the product of that initiation; Fairfield Porter throughout his career a true independent, a kind of shadow presence, devotedly figurative, but transcendently abstract; James McGarrell, the most sophisticated of painters, taking figuration to new levels of poetic intellection; and, Edwin Dickinson, not merely a precursor but, in fact, the guarantor of the tradition.

Edwin Dickinson was certainly not without recognition at home. The Museum of Modern Art, Whitney Museum of American Art, and the Pennsylvania Academy of the Fine Arts had all presented his work in one-artist exhibitions in the immediately preceding years. Venice was an opportunity to bring the work of a major American artist to the attention of an international audience. With all due respect to the other artists in the exhibition, it was my conviction that Dickinson's presence could hardly be argued.

In 1968, Dickinson's seventy-seventh year, he had achieved a body of work that includes some of the most mysterious and challenging images of our time: *The Rival Beauties*, 1915; *An Anniversary*, 1920–21; *The Cello Player*, 1924–26; *The Fossil Hunters*, 1926–28; *Composition with Still Life*, 1933–37; *Ruin at Daphne*, 1943–53 (cat. nos. 2, 6, 8, 12, 20, 50). As a kind of reverse side of the coin of his art, there are the landscapes and drawings that have received a somewhat belated recognition. Generally modest in scale, filled with light and space and wind and water, they are, even now, in advance of our ability to understand them. He is the master, nearly unique among American artists, of the *premier coup*, which (if I may repeat myself) embodies a kind of surreality that is essentially speculative and ambiguous. The added dimension is something more than convention ordinarily allows and represents his dogged insistence that appearances are not only transitory but also subject to any number of interpretations.

To have known the man, even as little as the organization of the Venice exhibition required, is a permanent treasure of my experience. At a dinner, I heard, unbelieving, a flowing quotation from Proust, not from the page, but from the mind of this extraordinary artist. A wonderful, self-sustained ego, filled with the real and imagined experience of history, literature, and music, he was a wonder to behold.

COAXING A PALPABLE MYSTERY An Appreciation

Michael Mazur

In 1965, a friend suggested that I see an Edwin Dickinson retrospective at the Whitney Museum of American Art in New York. He had shown me a reproduction of a self-portrait from 1949, in the collection of New York's National Academy of Design. Dickinson is in profile, in a shallow space below a skylight. Behind him is a geometric plan drawn in two-point perspective, and he reaches out beyond the frame in the act of painting or drawing. He has a graying beard, sharp nose, and high forehead. As I saw it for the first time, knowing nothing about this artist, I thought... a teacher at middle age, wearing his tan painter's smock. His demeanor is one of authority—nineteenth-century portraits of clerical or military subjects came to mind. In an interview that I heard much later,[1] he enunciated with clipped precision that had he done better in math, he might have been accepted to Annapolis and received a naval commission instead of becoming an artist.

At first, this Dickinson self-portrait seemed, to me, to have been painted by a contemporary of Degas or Eakins. Like them, he was a psychological realist as well as a disciplined academician. But when I saw his retrospective, I found a more "quixotic" painter, tilting toward reality at a slant. His surprising, small interiors with their abstract passages of thick paint and his eerily light-suffused landscapes could have been made only in the twentieth century. His large *grisaille* figure compositions, mysteriously lit scenes with skewed perspectives from some Gothic novel or film noir, were painted with the mastery of Zurbarán and the mystery of Magritte.

Like Edward Hopper, his contemporary and Cape Cod neighbor in South Truro, Dickinson worked mainly in New York and on the Cape. Both experienced European modernism but were contrarians, reluctant realists, turning toward the American scene in different ways. Hopper painted a view of urbanized figures solitary in their detachment. Dickinson often dealt with the dysfunction (or loss) of academic virtues such as perspective and tonal modeling. His work is literally darker and more dreamlike, even nostalgic, in an unsentimental way. His space is deeper and shifting, his light more romantic than Hopper's, whose light is sharp and whose space is flat and modern. Perhaps this is why Hopper produced images that were to become icons of their era, while Dickinson's paintings, harder to remember, have not fared nearly as well.

The merely great are served well in our culture. Their work appears with deserved regularity in museum surveys and college courses. There are far fewer opportunities for artists whose work eschews the going paradigm. Outside the canon, they emerge and depart from generation to generation, lost then found again, often only through word of mouth, artist to artist.

Dickinson's work meant a great deal to me in the lean "post painterly" sixties. He became even more meaningful in the seventies when an emerging realism needed a fertile and formal imagination to save it from a tedious naturalism.

Unfortunately I never met him, but on two occasions I came very close. Once, in the sixties, on a long train ride returning from a college in western Pennsylvania, I watched a man enter our car who, I thought, was the same man I had seen in the 1949 self-portrait. He was alone. While I wanted to approach him, I was shy and further discouraged by an older friend who insisted knowingly that he was, instead, "Sidney of course!" (Sidney Dickinson was a cousin who was also teaching at the Art Students League.) After the six-hour ride to New York, we left the car together and I noticed the initials *E. D.* on his luggage. I will never know how much I might have learned from him had I followed my instinct.

The second time I saw him he was entering the Museum of Fine Arts in Boston, a year or so before he died. Crippled by age, he was being carried up those daunting steps in that era of inaccessibility. My wife, Gail, and I were passing in a car. I thought how we always need, at whatever age, to renew our sources of inspiration, and I said something to her like "I understand that—one more time to the well."

In the mid-nineties I was lucky to obtain his painting, *Atlantic Fleet*, dated 1934.[2] The grand fleet is curiously diminished and is represented simply as a few tiny smudges of ships that hardly disturb the strict stripelike division of white sky and steel-gray sea. The painting is very "slow," imparting its message of the eternal and the temporal in the quiet unfolding, below the ships, of a subtle sea swell. No other event, neither cloud, land, nor pier—nor bravura passage of paint—impedes the quiet, nearly abstract scene. The painting is remarkable in its prescient relationship to the restrained devices of American minimalism, which arrived thirty years later.

The late Louis Finkelstein, the thoughtful and voluble painter, once described to me a conversation he had with Dickinson when he complimented him on his small *premier coup* landscapes. "They are not art," Dickinson was quoted as saying. When asked why, he responded something like "When I work outside, I am as out of control as if I were a drunken man!"

Anyone who has painted out of doors knows what Dickinson meant. As you work, the moving sun changes the shadows, or the wind shifts your easel or moves the trees and you struggle to keep the scene unified. Even on gray Cape days, the view is likely to darken or lighten during the very instant that you are looking at your canvas. This must have frustrated Dickinson's need for order. Even keeping a conceptual focus in the midst of all of nature's movements is a trial for any artist. "The seen distortion is what the thought did to the sight,"[3] he is quoted as saying in another interview. What continues to fascinate me about these works, however, is precisely this *giving in* to the momentary—not so much the "impression" of the scene, but the "expression" of the painter's quandary before the ever-changing light. This inevitable disturbance, this movement that Cézanne could celebrate in paint as his "little sensation," was dramatized by Dickinson's characteristic blur and scumble, as if a small storm had disturbed the focus of his attention.

But if there is a distinction between outside—"drunken"—work, and "controlled" studio painting, it is often belied by the same painterly abandon I see in his still lifes or portraits. He at once seems to reveal and hide the object of his desire (much as he admitted in a taped interview that he never wrote in his diaries about his personal life except in a "secret code").[4]

Dickinson could easily destroy the coherence of a straightforward subject like the side of a house, as in his *Stone Tower* of 1941 (Private Collection), with a smeared patch of paint that might stand for a tree or simply for itself. Only in the paintings and drawings of de Kooning have I seen such spontaneous disregard *of* coherence within the struggle *for* coherence. Even in his oddly erotic narratives, carefully painted in beautiful grays and rich blacks, objects shift into peculiar perspective and emerge, irrationally, out of a tonal fog. Like that of the British eccentric Stanley Spencer, Dickinson's work is at that admirable and frightening edge of the "normal," where it falls away into an abyss. He does not back away from it, but instead fills this void with his painterly imagination and coaxes palpable mystery from its depth.

Dickinson seems to accept reality and the subconscious in nearly equal portions and does not cancel out fantasy in the face of what might seem, for others, unnecessary risk. His treatment of this surreal paradox—the chaotic within the rational and the rational within the chaotic—may finally be his legacy for those of us who recognize and admire his work.

NOTES

1. Edwin Dickinson, interview by Karl Fortess, Aug. 5, 1970, audiocassette, Oral History Collection, Archives of American Art, Washington, D.C.

2. Previously in the collection of Ives Gamell, a painter friend of Dickinson.

3. Carol S. Gruber, "The Reminiscences of Edwin Dickinson" (New York: Oral History Research Office, Columbia University, 1957–58).

4. Dickinson, interview by Karl Fortess.

CATALOGUE OF THE EXHIBITION

Works are listed chronologically by year and then sequentially within the year.
Dimensions are given in inches, followed by centimeters in parentheses. Height precedes width.

PAINTINGS

1 *Self-Portrait*, 1914
oil on composition board
21¾ × 19⅝ (55.3 × 49.9)
Collection John O'Connor

2 *The Rival Beauties*, 1915
oil on canvas
46 × 38 (116.8 × 96.5)
Courtesy Curtis Galleries, Minneapolis, Minnesota

3 *Old Ben and Mrs. Marks*, 1916
oil on board
36 × 29½ (91.4 × 74.9)
Collection Middlebury College Museum of Art, Vermont
Gift of Robert C. Graham, Jr., '63
1991.001

4 *Interior*, 1916
oil on beaverboard
84 × 48 (213.4 × 121.9)
Collection Mr. and Mrs. Daniel W. Dietrich II

5 *Inland Lake*, 1919
oil on canvas
40 × 40 (101.6 × 101.6)
Courtesy Curtis Galleries, Minneapolis, Minnesota

6 *An Anniversary*, 1920–21
oil on canvas
72 × 60 (182.9 × 152.4)
Collection Albright-Knox Art Gallery, Buffalo, New York
Gift of Mr. and Mrs. Ansley W. Sawyer, 1927

7 *View from 46 Pearl Street*, 1923
oil on canvas
15 × 18 (38.1 × 45.7)
Private Collection

8 *The Cello Player*, 1924–26
oil on canvas
60 × 48½ (152.4 × 123.2)
Collection Fine Arts Museums of San Francisco
Museum Purchase, Roscoe and Margaret Oakes Income Fund, 1988.5
Buffalo only

9 *Helen Souza*, 1925
oil on composition board
36 × 30 (91.4 × 76.2)
Courtesy Curtis Galleries, Minneapolis, Minnesota

10 *X-Cliff, Great Night Rain*, 1926
oil on composition board
22¾ × 18½ (57.8 × 47)
Scharf Family Collection

11 *Girl on Tennis Court*, 1926
oil on panel
36 × 30 (91.4 × 76.2)
Collection Sheldon Memorial Art Gallery and Sculpture Garden,
University of Nebraska–Lincoln
Nebraska Art Association Collection, Gift of Olga N. Sheldon

12 *The Fossil Hunters*, 1926–28
oil on canvas
96½ × 73¾ (245.1 × 187.3)
Collection Whitney Museum of American Art, New York
Purchase, 58.29
Buffalo, Philadelphia, New York only

13 *Toward Mrs. Driscoll's*, 1928
oil on canvas
50 × 40 (127 × 101.6)
Collection Maurice and Margery Katz

14 *Sheldrake Winter*, 1929
oil on composition board
29⅞ × 24⅞ (75.9 × 63.2)
Collection Peter A. Baldwin and Robert A. Baldwin
Courtesy Babcock Galleries, New York

15 *Andrée's Balloon*, 1929–30
oil on canvas
30¼ × 25³⁄₁₆ (76.8 × 64)
Collection The Pennsylvania Academy of the Fine Arts, Philadelphia
Funds provided by the National Endowment for the Arts, Sponsors of the
Fine Arts Ball and Discotheque, and Daniel W. Dietrich Foundation

16 *Woodland Scene*, 1929–35
oil on canvas
71⅜ × 68½ (181.3 × 174)
Collection Herbert F. Johnson Museum of Art, Cornell University, Ithaca, New York
Gift of Esther Hoyt Sawyer in memory of her father, William Ballard Hoyt,
Class of 1881 and trustee of Cornell, 1895–1900

17 *Coast at Wellfleet with a Wreck*, 1930
oil on canvas
25 × 30 (63.5 × 76.2)
Private Collection

18 *Cottage Porch, Peaked Hill*, 1932
oil on canvas
26⅛ × 30⅛ (66.4 × 76.5)
Collection The Museum of Modern Art, New York
Grace Rainey Rogers Fund, 1961
Buffalo, Philadelphia, New York only

19 *Shiloh*, 1932–33 and 1940
oil on canvas
36 × 32 (91.4 × 81.3)
Collection The Nelson-Atkins Museum of Art, Kansas City, Missouri
(Lent by Commerce Bancshares, Inc.) 6–1991

20 *Composition with Still Life*, 1933–37
oil on canvas
97 × 77¾ (246.4 × 197.5)
Collection The Museum of Modern Art, New York
Gift of Mr. and Mrs. Ansley W. Sawyer, 1952
Buffalo, Philadelphia, New York only

21 *Stranded Brig*, 1934
oil on canvas nailed to board
40 × 50 (101.6 × 127)
Collection Museum of Fine Arts, Springfield, Massachusetts
Presented to the Museum by the Government, October 1934

22 *Laboratory Beach*, 1935
oil on canvas
30 × 36 (76.2 × 91.4)
Collection AXA Financial, Inc., through its subsidiary
The Equitable Life Assurance Society of the United States

23 *Gas Tank*, 1937
oil on canvas
25¼ × 30¼ (64.1 × 76.8)
Collection The Art Students League of New York

24 *Nude, Jean*, 1937
oil on canvas
30 × 25 (76.2 × 63.5)
Private Collection

25 *Villa Zingarella*, 1938
oil on canvas
23½ × 28½ (59.7 × 72.4)
Private Collection
Courtesy Babcock Galleries, New York

26 *Sanary Bay*, 1938
oil on canvas
23 × 28 (58.4 × 71.1)
Collection Gilbert and Ruth Scharf

27 *Rock of Port Issol, West Side*, 1938
oil on canvas
23¾ × 28¾ (60.3 × 73)
Collection Addison Gallery of American Art, Phillips Academy, Andover, Massachusetts
Museum Purchase, 1991.2

28 *Ulysses, Oh Cissy!*, 1938
oil on canvas
23 × 28 (58.4 × 71.1)
Scharf Family Collection

29 *Orchard*, 1938
oil on canvas
23½ × 28½ (59.7 × 72.4)
Collection AXA Financial, Inc., through its subsidiary The Equitable Life Assurance Society of the United States

30 *Still Life with Flowers*, 1938
oil on canvas
32 × 28 (81.3 × 71.1)
Scharf Family Collection

31 *Nude with Pine Cones, Marie*, 1939
oil on canvas
29 × 21 (73.7 × 53.3)
Collection Hirshhorn Museum and Sculpture Garden, Smithsonian Institution
Gift of the Joseph H. Hirshhorn Foundation, 1966

32 *Nude Figure, Marie*, 1939
oil on canvas
20 × 23 (50.8 × 58.4)
Collection Gilbert and Ruth Scharf

33 *Sandy's Yard*, 1939
oil on canvas
15 × 19 (38.1 × 48.3)
Courtesy James Graham & Sons, New York

34 *The Finger Lakes*, 1940
oil on canvas
23¾ × 29 (60.3 × 73.7)
Collection Theodore and Eleanor Waddell

35 *Artist's Hand Holding Children's Drawings*, 1940
oil on canvas
23 × 20 (58.4 × 50.8)
Collection Mr. and Mrs. Daniel W. Dietrich II

36 *Self-Portrait*, 1940
oil on canvas
20 × 15 (50.8 × 38.1)
Collection Philadelphia Museum of Art
Bequest of T. Edward Hanley

37 *Janice at the Beach*, 1940
oil on canvas
19 × 15 (48.3 × 38.1)
Courtesy Michael Rosenfeld Gallery, New York

38 *View of Great Island*, 1940
oil on canvas
15¼ × 19⅛ (38.7 × 48.6)
Collection Brooklyn Museum of Art
Gift of John R. H. Blum, 61.32

39 *Constant*, 1940–41 and 1944
oil on canvas
23⅞ × 29 (60.7 × 73.7)
Private Collection
Courtesy Babcock Galleries, New York

40 *Self-Portrait*, 1941
oil on canvas
19½ × 22½ (49.5 × 57.2)
Collection The David and Alfred Smart Museum of Art, The University of Chicago
The Mary and Earle Ludgin Collection

41 *Self-Portrait with Landscape*, 1941
oil on canvas
29 × 24 (73.7 × 60.9)
Collection Gilbert and Ruth Scharf

42 *Villa and Alice*, 1941
oil on canvas
24 × 29 (61 × 73.7)
Collection Mr. and Mrs. Daniel W. Dietrich II

43 *Sunflower*, 1941
oil on canvas
14 × 20 (35.6 × 50.8)
Collection Dr. and Mrs. Arthur E. Kahn

44 *Cap Fréhel, La Fauconnière, C. du N.*, 1941 and 1945
oil on canvas
20 × 23 (50.8 × 58.4)
Courtesy Estate of Janice Brustlein

45 *Still Life, Rotting Squash*, 1941–42
oil on canvas
30 × 36 (76.2 × 91.4)
Private Collection
Courtesy Babcock Galleries, New York

46 *Self-Portrait in Uniform*, 1942
oil on canvas
$24\frac{1}{8}$ × $29\frac{1}{2}$ (61.3 × 74.9)
Collection AXA Financial, Inc., through its subsidiary
The Equitable Life Assurance Society of the United States

47 *Evangeline*, 1942
oil on canvas
$19\frac{3}{4}$ × $22\frac{11}{16}$ (50.2 × 57.6)
Collection John O'Connor

48 *Self-Portrait*, 1943
oil on canvas
$11\frac{1}{2}$ × $8\frac{3}{4}$ (29.2 × 22.2)
Private Collection

49 *Self-Portrait in Gray Shirt*, 1943
oil on canvas
24 × 19 (61 × 48.2)
Collection Smithsonian American Art Museum
Gift of S. C. Johnson & Son, Inc.

50 *Ruin at Daphne*, 1943–53
oil on canvas
48 × 60 (121.9 × 152.4)
Collection The Metropolitan Museum of Art, New York
The Edward J. Gallagher III Memorial Collection, 1955
Buffalo, Philadelphia, New York only

51 *Cove, Wellfleet*, 1946
oil on panel
10 × 12 (25.4 × 30.5)
Private Collection
Courtesy Babcock Galleries, New York

52 *The Flag, Frazier's House*, 1947
oil on canvas
$11\frac{9}{16}$ × $9\frac{5}{8}$ (29.4 × 24.5)
Collection John O'Connor

53 *Through Two Cottage Windows*, 1948
oil on panel
$9\frac{3}{4}$ × $11\frac{1}{2}$ (24.8 × 29.2)
Private Collection
Courtesy Babcock Galleries, New York

54 *Self-Portrait*, 1949
oil on canvas
23 × 20⅛ (58.4 × 51.1)
Collection National Academy of Design, New York

55 *Self-Portrait*, 1950
oil on canvas
11½ × 9⅝ (29.2 × 24.5)
Private Collection
Courtesy Babcock Galleries, New York

56 *Rock, Cape Poge*, 1950
oil on Masonite
12 × 14½ (30.5 × 36.8)
Collection Mr. and Mrs. Daniel W. Dietrich II

57 *Gonzalez Studio*, 1950
oil on panel
12 × 16 (30.5 × 40.6)
Collection Gilbert and Ruth Scharf

58 *Mayo's Beach from Indian Neck*, 1951
oil on panel
12½ × 16⅛ (31.8 × 41)
Collection Philadelphia Museum of Art
Albert M. Greenfield and Elizabeth M. Greenfield Collection

59 *Paris Windows*, 1952
oil on panel
12 × 14½ (30.5 × 36.8)
Private Collection

60 *Carrousel Bridge, Paris*, 1952
oil on panel
12 × 14½ (30.5 × 36.8)
Collection Smithsonian American Art Museum
Bequest of Henry Ward Ranger through the National Academy of Design

61 *Still Life, Lascaux*, 1953
oil on canvas
37⅛ × 30¼ (94.3 × 76.8)
Collection Philadelphia Museum of Art
Albert M. Greenfield and Elizabeth M. Greenfield Collection

62 *Surf, Point Lookout*, 1953
oil on canvas
20 × 23 (50.8 × 58.4)
Collection Burchfield-Penney Art Center, Buffalo, New York
Purchased with funds from the National Endowment for the Arts and Friends of the Center

63 *Quarry, Riverdale*, 1953
oil on canvas
16⅛ × 21⅜ (41 × 54.3)
Collection Hirshhorn Museum and Sculpture Garden, Smithsonian Institution
Gift of Joseph H. Hirshhorn, 1966

64 *Jetty, Point Lookout*, 1953
oil on canvas
20¼ × 23¼ (51.4 × 59.1)
Collection Theodore and Eleanor Waddell

65 *Self-Portrait*, 1954
oil on canvas
26¼ × 24⅜ (66.7 × 61.9)
Collection Hirshhorn Museum and Sculpture Garden, Smithsonian Institution
Gift of the Joseph H. Hirshhorn Foundation, 1966

66 *Window and Oar*, 1955
oil on composition board
12 × 18 (30.5 × 45.7)
Collection Whitney Museum of American Art, New York
Purchase, 61.4

67 *South Wellfleet Inn*, 1955–60
oil on canvas
33¼ × 43⅝ (84.5 × 110.8)
Shein Collection
Buffalo, Philadelphia, New York only

68 *Chair, Skowhegan I*, 1956
oil on panel
14⅝ × 12⅜ (37.2 × 31.4)
Collection John O'Connor

WORKS ON PAPER

69 *Nude (Standing Nude, Hips and Legs)*, 1920
graphite on paper
13 × 10 (33 × 25.4)
Collection Sheldon Memorial Art Gallery and Sculpture Garden,
University of Nebraska–Lincoln
Gift of Mary Riepma Ross, 1965. U-477

70 *St. Tropez Yacht Basin in Winter*, 1920
watercolor and graphite on paper
9¾ × 13½ (24.8 × 34.3)
Collection Herbert F. Johnson Museum of Art, Cornell University, Ithaca, New York
Gift of Mr. and Mrs. Ferdinand Davis

71 *Propeller and Dory*, 1921
graphite on paper
13⅛ × 10¼ (33.3 × 26)
Collection Robert C. Graham, Jr.

72 *Nude, Helen Souza*, 1925
graphite on paper
21½ × 17 (54.6 × 43.2)
Collection Mr. and Mrs. Daniel W. Dietrich II

73 *Beach House*, 1926
graphite on paper
10 × 8 (25.4 × 20.3)
Morris Collection

74 *Staircase, The Manse at Ulysses*, 1928
graphite on paper
10 × 7¾ (25.4 × 19.7)
Collection Robert C. Graham, Jr.

75 *Esther Hill Sawyer*, 1931
graphite on paper
12½ × 9¼ (31.8 × 23.5)
Collection Esther Ewing

76 *Long Point Light, Provincetown*, 1933
graphite on wove paper
9¼ × 12½ (23.5 × 31.8)
Collection Fine Arts Museums of San Francisco
Achenbach Foundation for Graphic Arts purchase, 1986.2.39

77 *Pat's Studio, Provincetown*, 1933
graphite on paper
7 1/16 × 4 11/16 (17.9 × 11.9)
Collection Hirshhorn Museum and Sculpture Garden, Smithsonian Institution
Gift of Joseph H. Hirshhorn, 1966

78 *Roofs and Harbor, Provincetown*, 1933
graphite on paper
9¼ × 12⅜ (23.5 × 31.4)
Collection Julie Heller Gallery, Provincetown, Massachusetts

79 *Summer Morning, Beach Point*, 1934
graphite on paper
9⅜ × 12¼ (23.9 × 31.1)
Collection The Arkansas Arts Center
Foundation Purchase: Memorial Fund, 1933

80 *Nude #3*, 1936
graphite on paper
13 × 10 (33 × 25.4)
Collection Merrill Wagner and Robert Ryman

81 *View from a Window at Wellfleet*, 1939
graphite on paper
10¾ × 12¾ (27.3 × 32.4)
Collection Theodore and Eleanor Waddell

82 *Cottage Window*, 1939
graphite on paper
10⅞ × 12⅞ (27.6 × 32.7)
Collection Clark Atlanta University Art Galleries
Gift of Chauncey and Catherine Waddell

83 *South Wellfleet Inn*, 1939
graphite on paper
8⅝ × 11⅞ (21.9 × 30.2)
Collection Clark Atlanta University Art Galleries
Gift of Chauncey and Catherine Waddell

84 *Roses*, 1939
graphite on paper
10¾ × 12¾ (27.3 × 32.4)
Collection Whitney Museum of American Art, New York
Gift of Mrs. Robert M. Benjamin in honor of Flora Biddle

85 *Rose and Sextant*, 1943
graphite on paper
8¼ × 11½ (21 × 29.2)
Private Collection

86 *Boathouse, Wellfleet*, 1943
graphite on paper
5½ × 10½ (14 × 26.7)
Sweet Briar College Collection, Virginia
Gift of Fay Martin Chandler

87 *Bear, Sculpture Fragments*, 1944
graphite and charcoal on paper
12½ × 10 (31.8 × 25.4)
Collection The Metropolitan Museum of Art, New York
Bequest of Isabel Bishop Wolff, 1988
Buffalo, Philadelphia, New York only

88 *Bryant Park*, 1944
graphite on paper
12½ × 9 (31.8 × 22.9)
Collection The Metropolitan Museum of Art, New York
Bequest of Isabel Bishop Wolff, 1988
Buffalo, Philadelphia, New York only

89 *Hampshire House, Central Park South*, 1944
graphite and charcoal on paper
12½ × 10 (31.8 × 25.4)
Collection The Metropolitan Museum of Art, New York
Bequest of Isabel Bishop Wolff, 1988
Buffalo, Philadelphia, New York only

90 *Fallen Tree*, 1946
graphite on paper
11½ × 9⅜ (29.2 × 23.8)
Private Collection

91 *Tekla Torm, Off Algiers*, 1959
graphite on paper
9 × 11½ (22.9 × 29.2)
Collection Mr. and Mrs. W. Thomas Gossett

92 *Young Man's Tombstone*, 1962
graphite on paper
11 × 9½ (27.9 × 24.1)
Collection Dr. and Mrs. Philip L. Brewer

93 *Olympia*, 1962
graphite on paper
11½ × 9½ (29.2 × 24.1)
Collection Harvey and Deborah Breverman

94 *Nude, Breast and Shoulder*, 1964
graphite on paper
9⅜ × 11⅜ (23.9 × 28.9)
Collection Emerson Gallery, Hamilton College
Gift of Mr. and Mrs. Ferdinand H. Davis, in memory of Edward H. Dwight

95 *Lion*, 1964
graphite on paper
8⅞ × 11½ (22.5 × 29.2)
Collection The Metropolitan Museum of Art, New York
Friends of The Department Gifts and Matching Funds from The National Endowment for the Arts, 1978
Buffalo, Philadelphia, New York only

PLATES Paintings

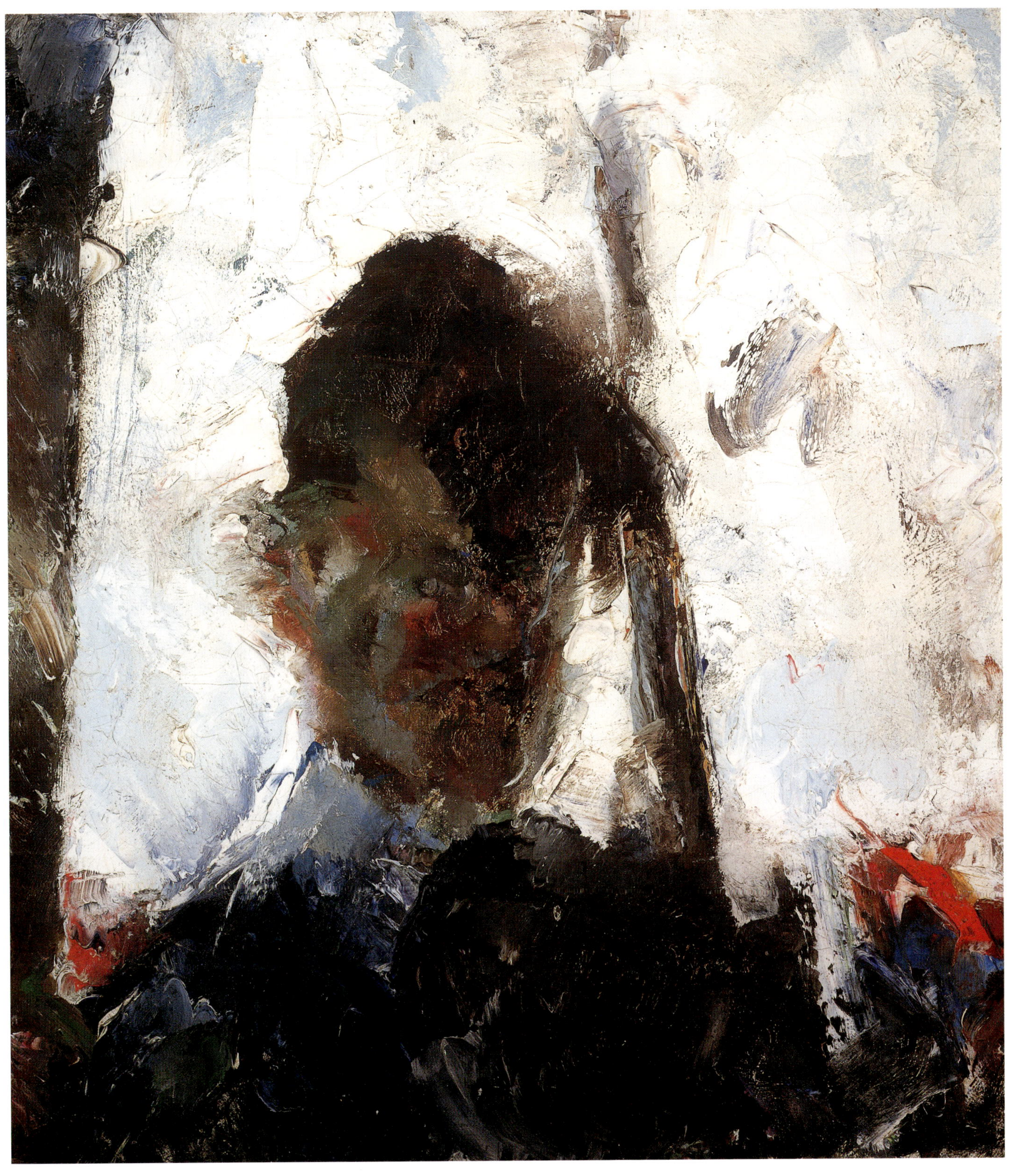

1 *Self-Portrait*, 1914

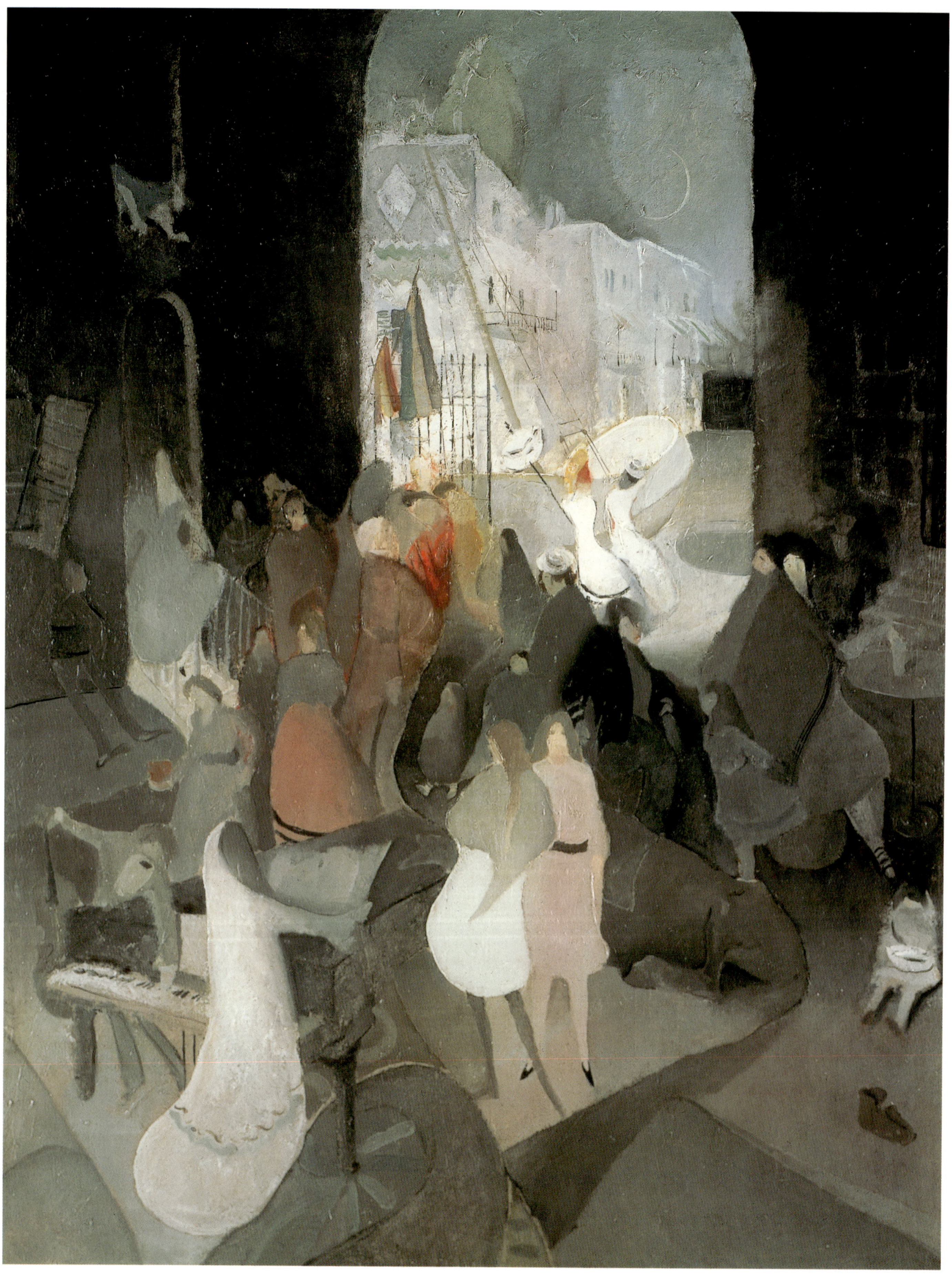

2 *The Rival Beauties*, 1915

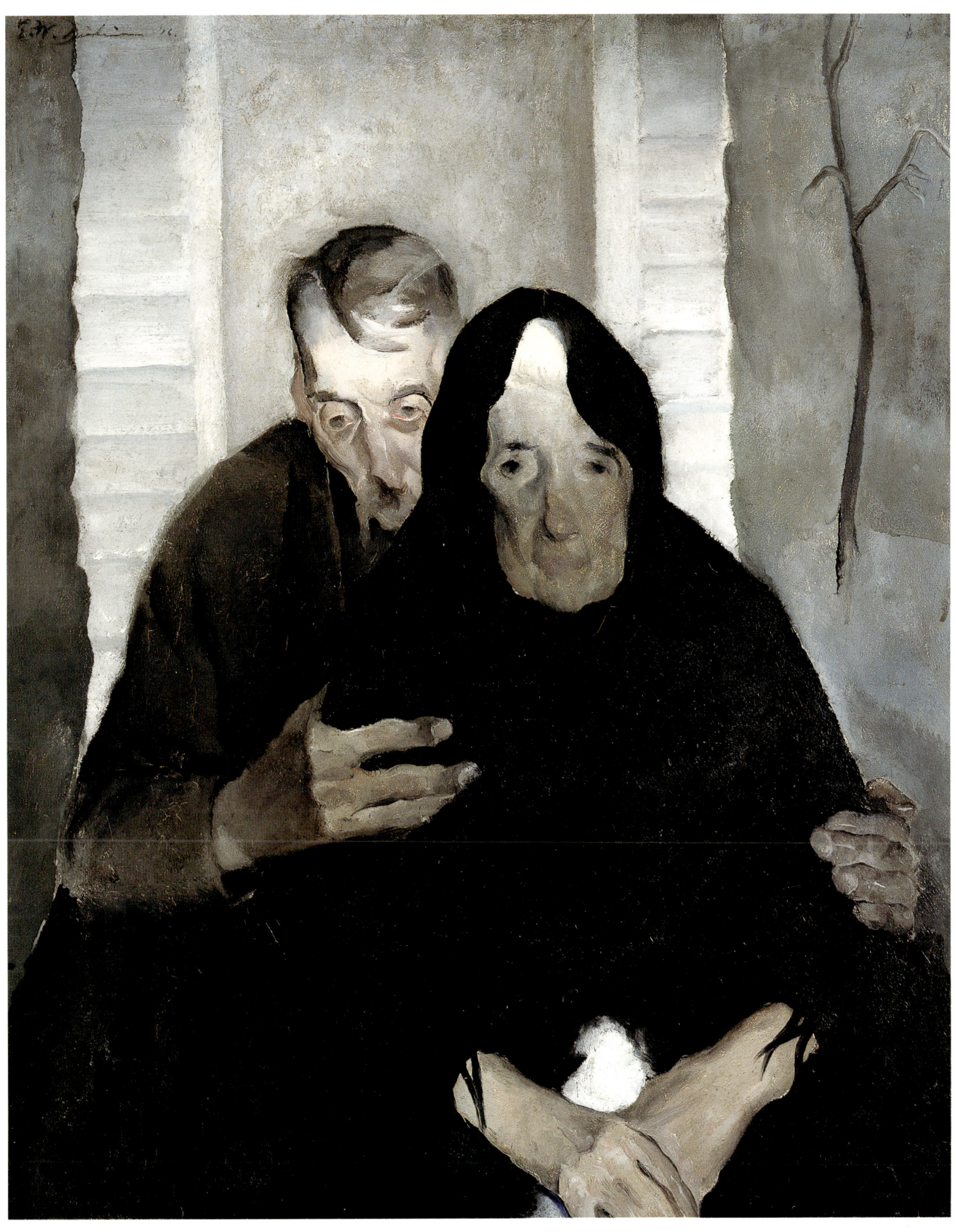

3 *Old Ben and Mrs. Marks*, 1916

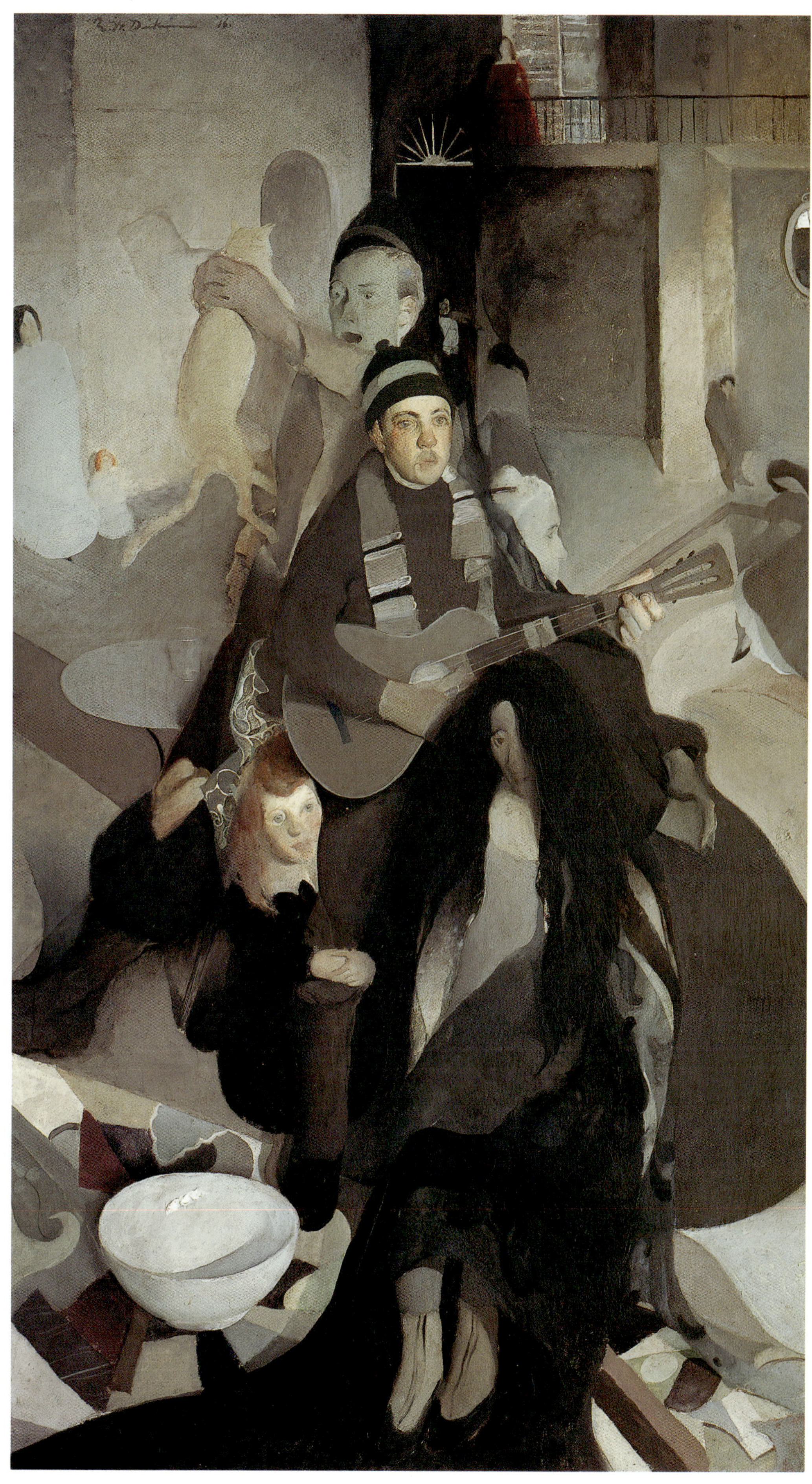

4 *Interior*, 1916

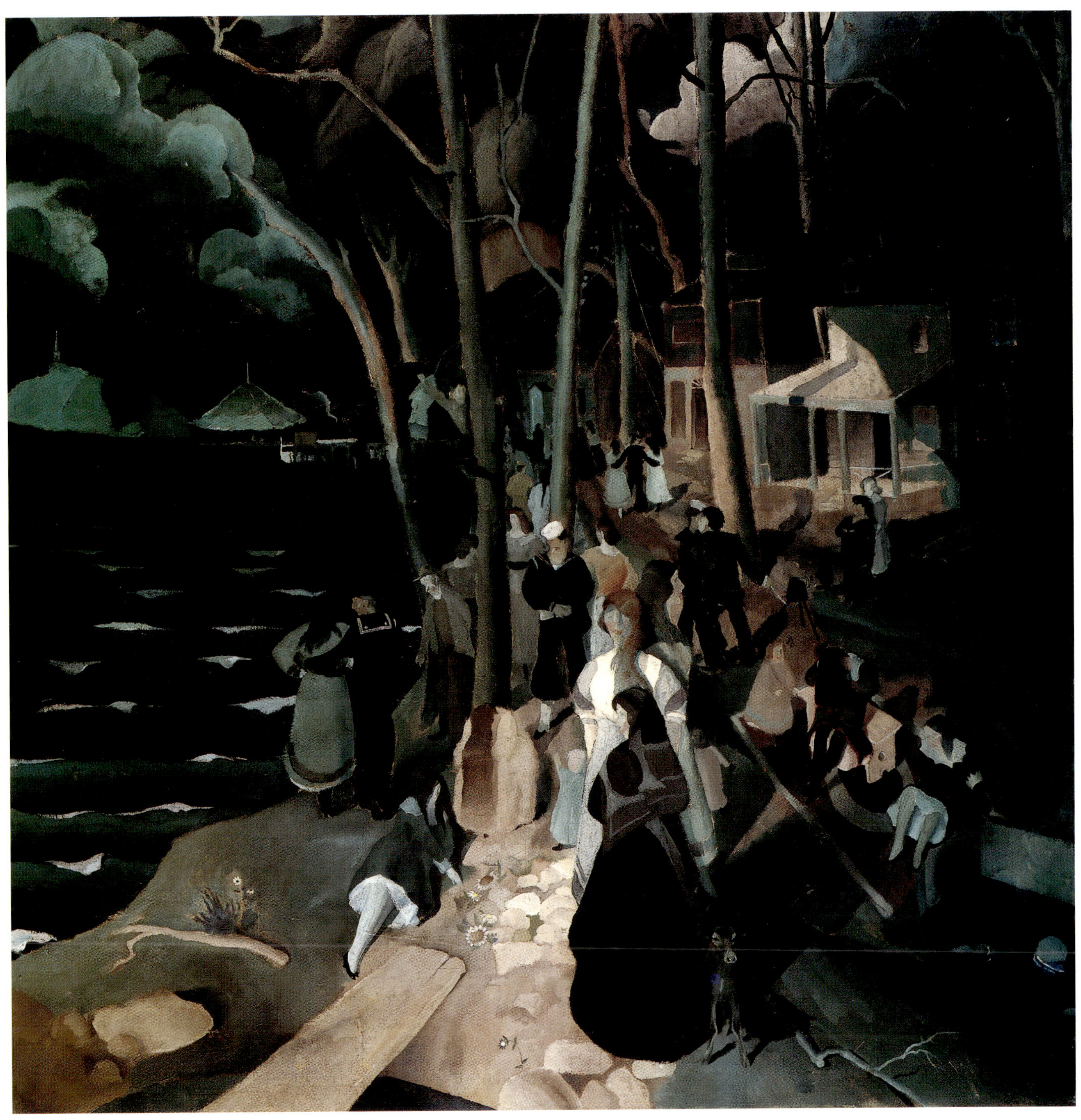

5 *Inland Lake*, 1919

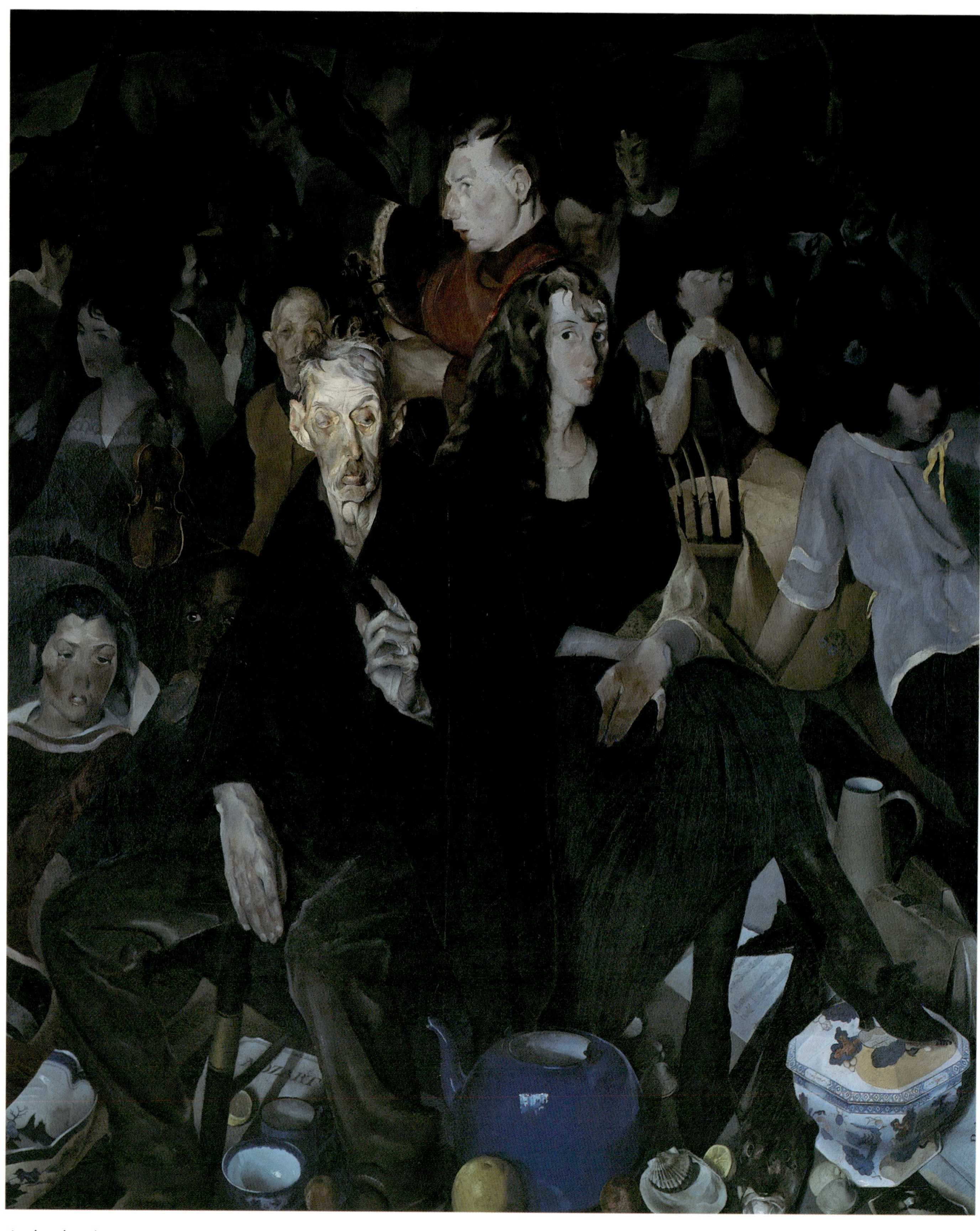

6 *An Anniversary*, 1920–21

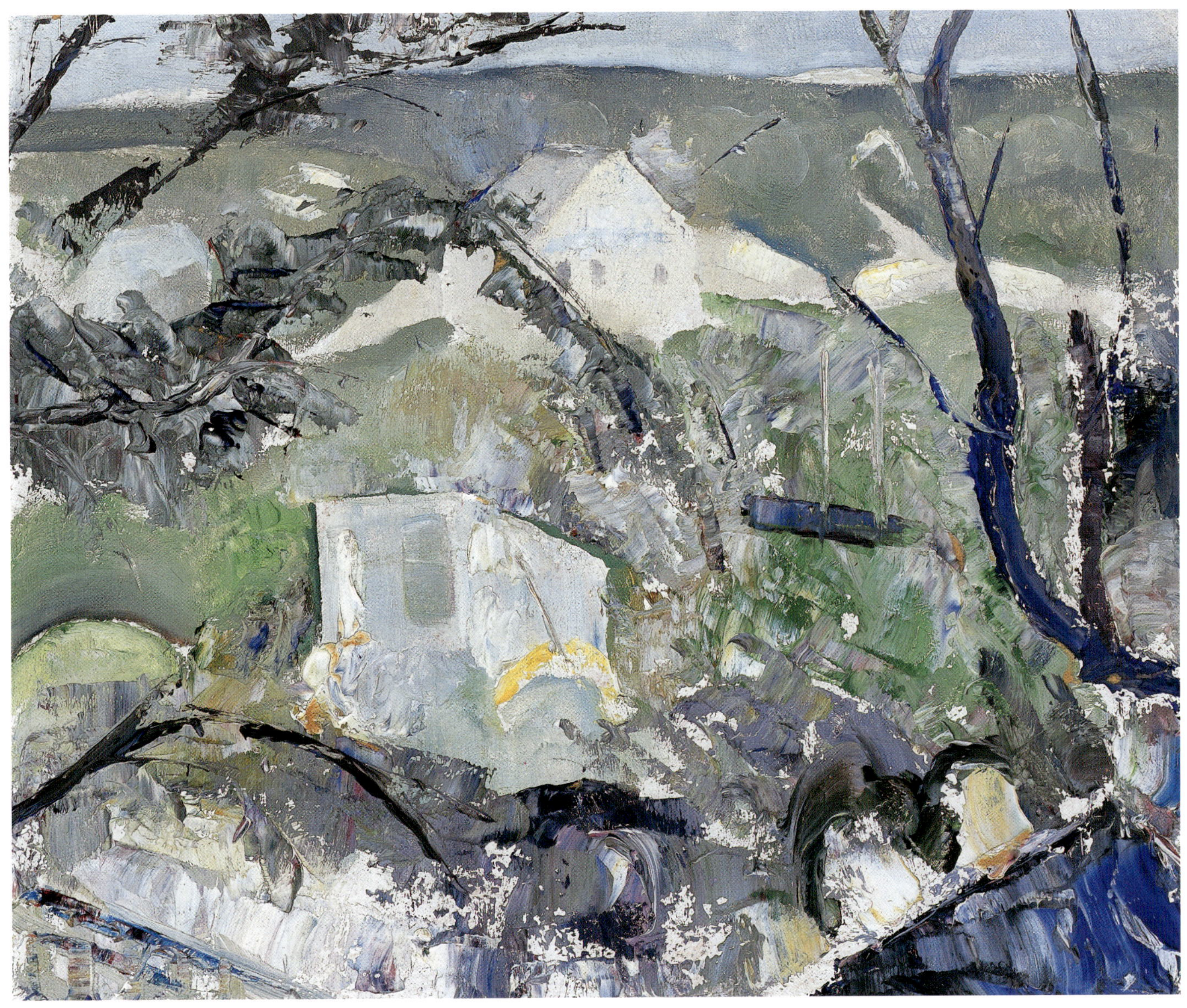

7 *View from 46 Pearl Street*, 1923

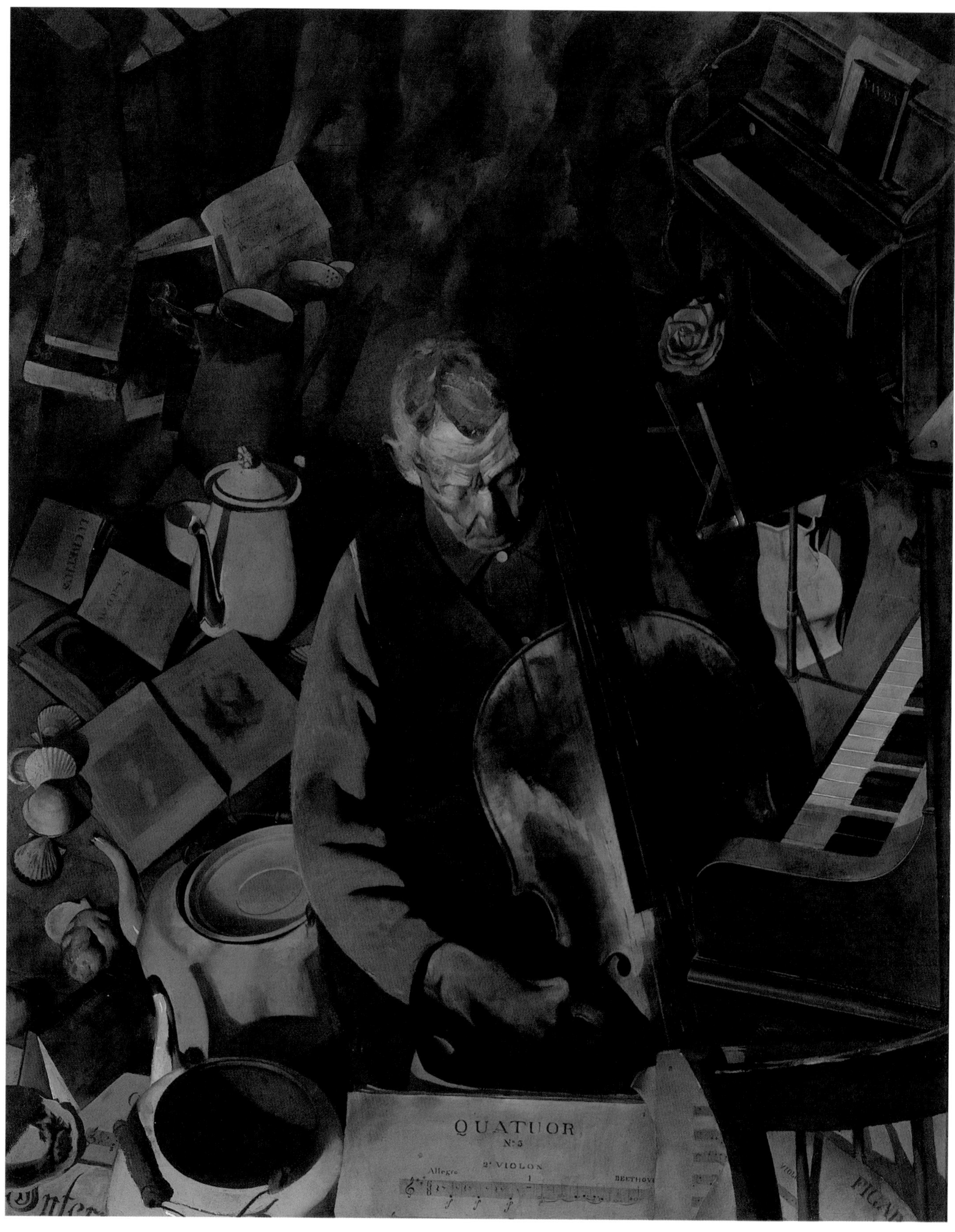

8 *The Cello Player*, 1924–26

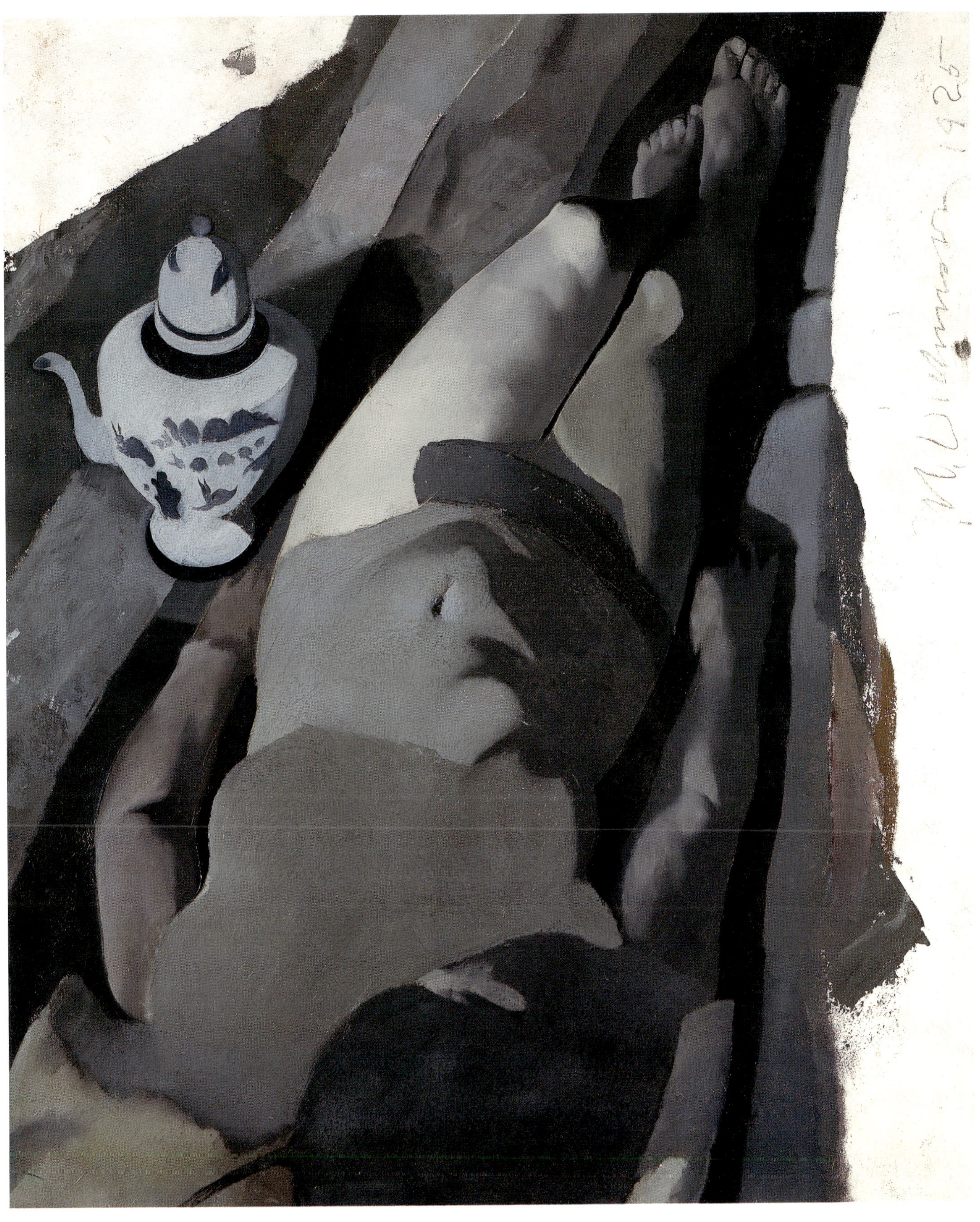

9 *Helen Souza*, 1925

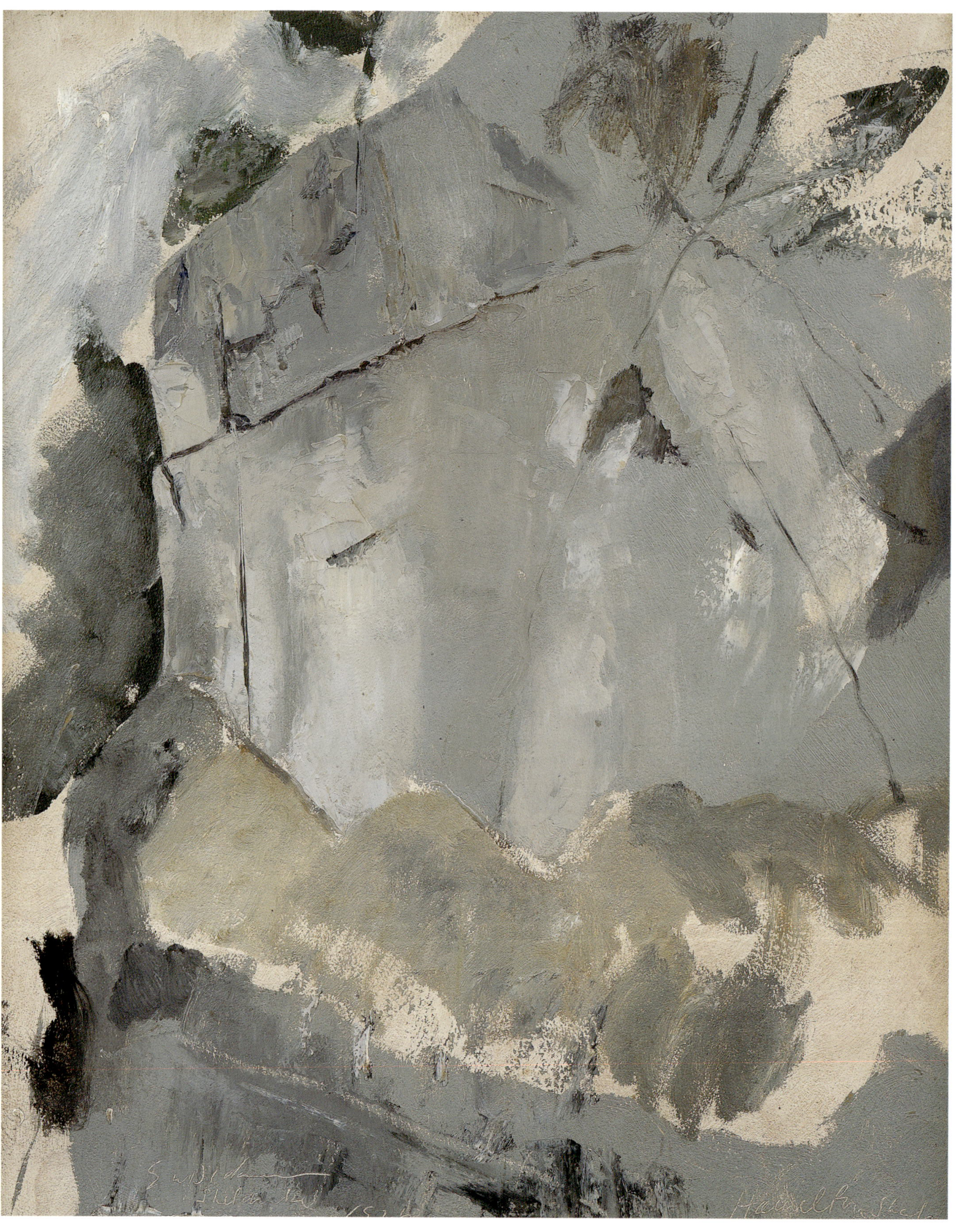

10 *X-Cliff, Great Night Rain*, 1926

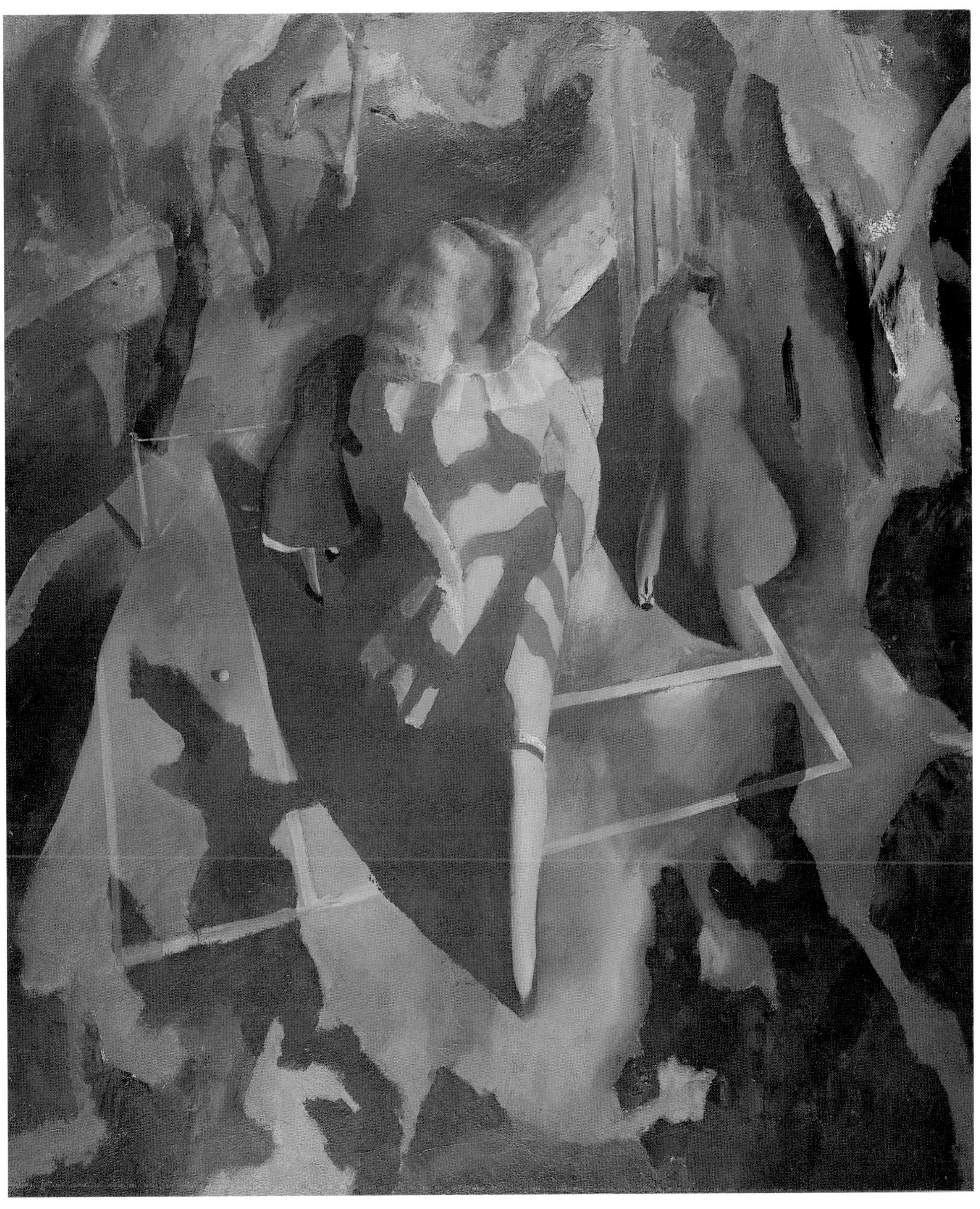

11 *Girl on Tennis Court*, 1926

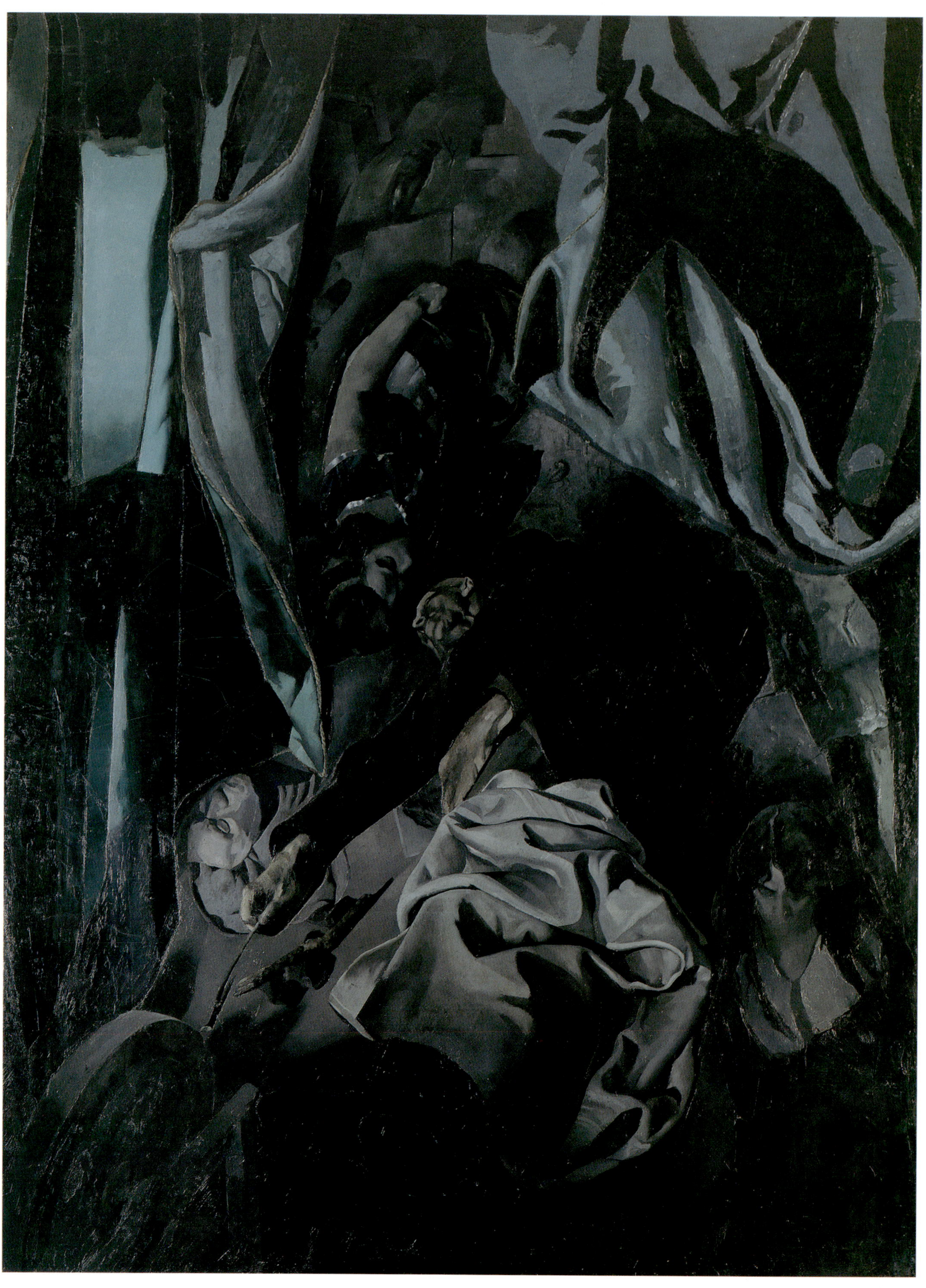

12 *The Fossil Hunters*, 1926–28

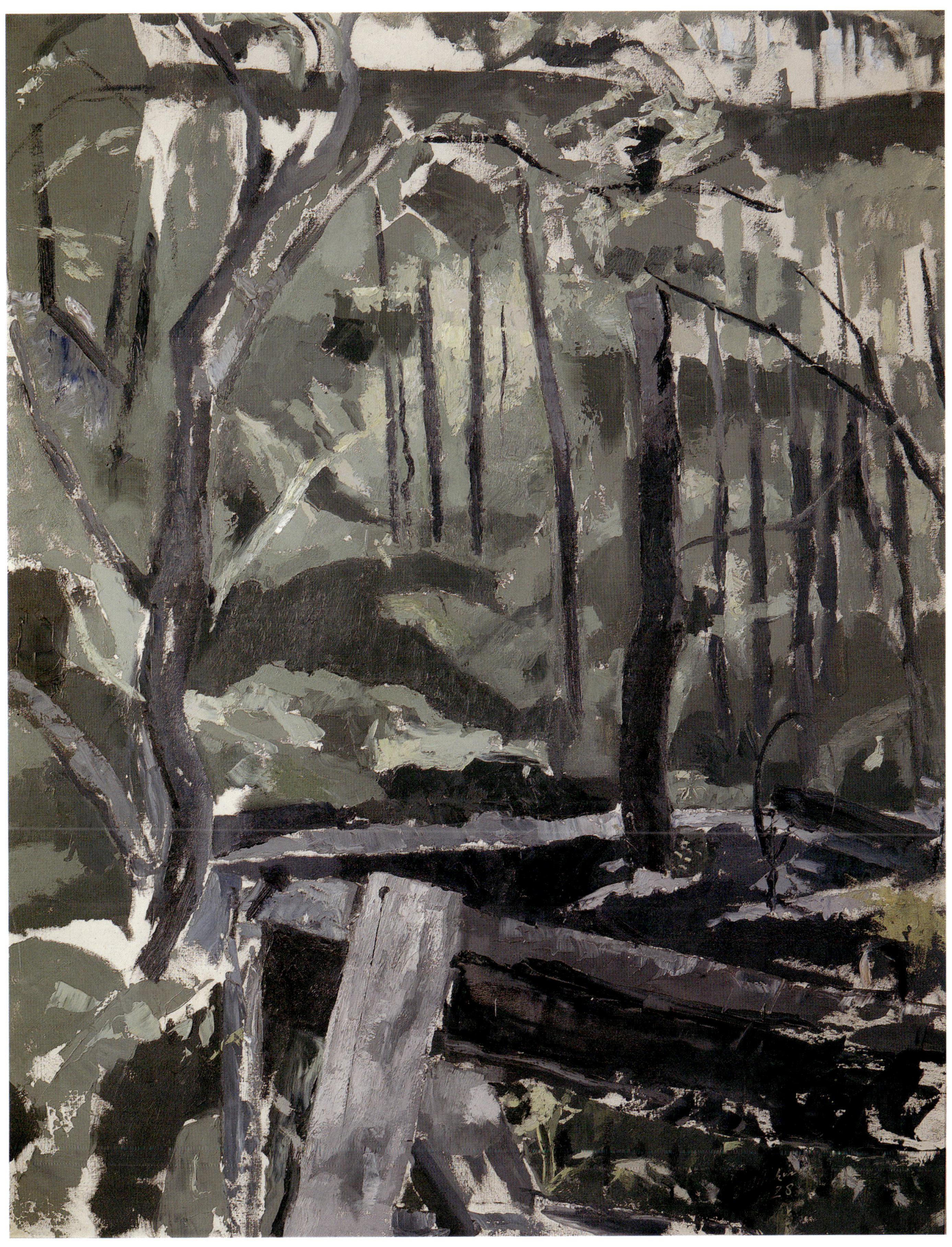

13 *Toward Mrs. Driscoll's*, 1928

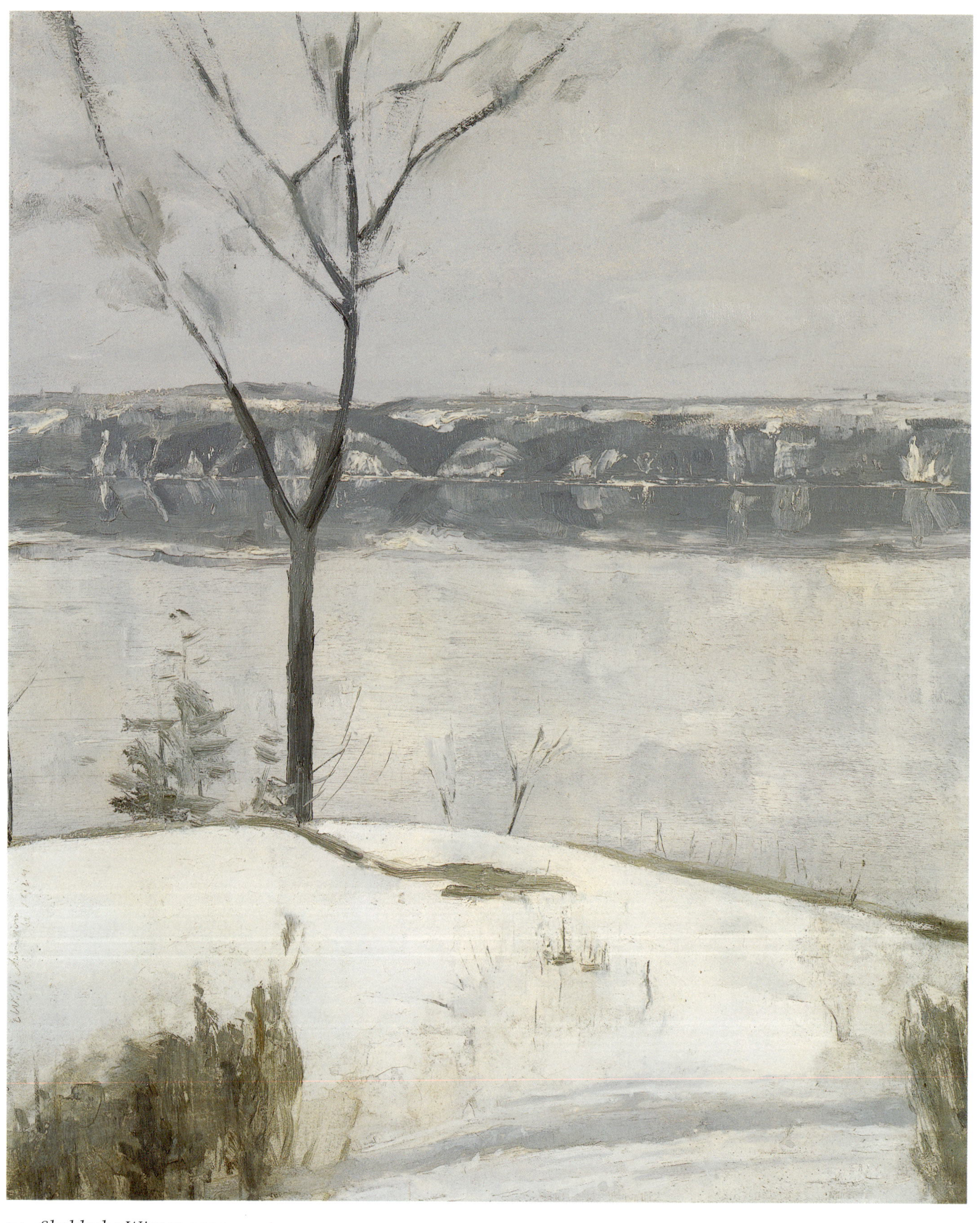

14 *Sheldrake Winter*, 1929

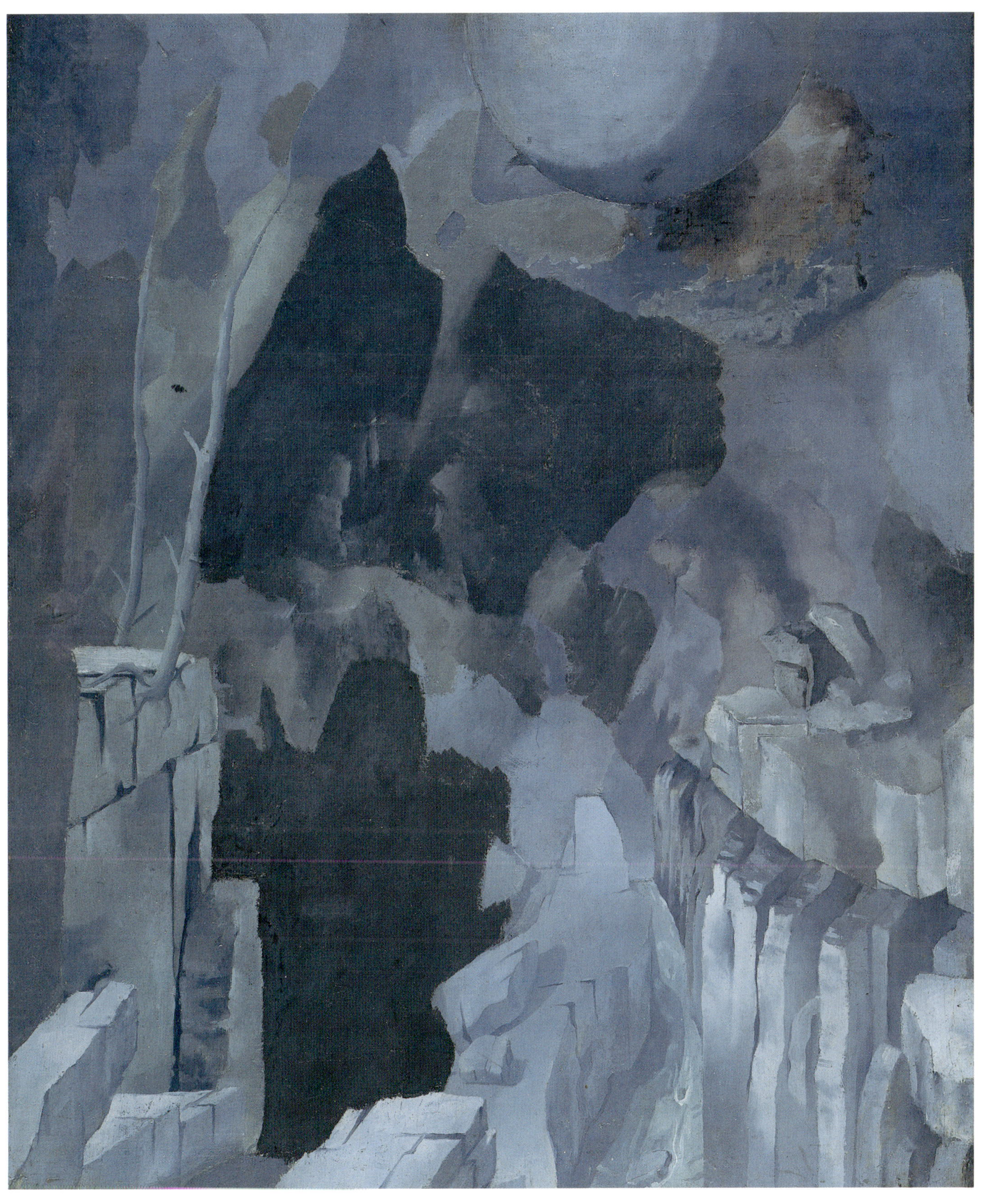

15 *Andrée's Balloon*, 1929–30

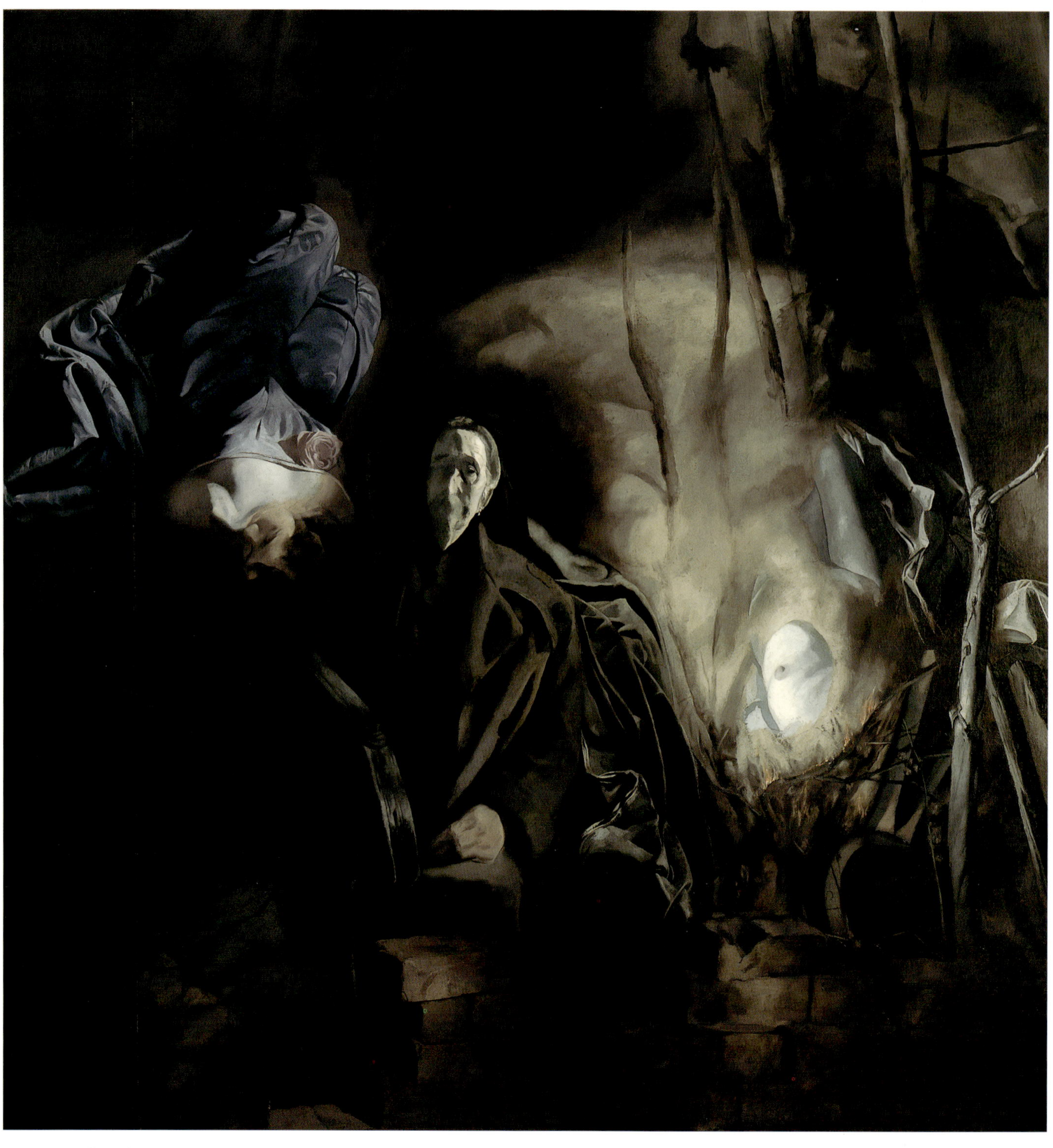

16 *Woodland Scene*, 1929–35

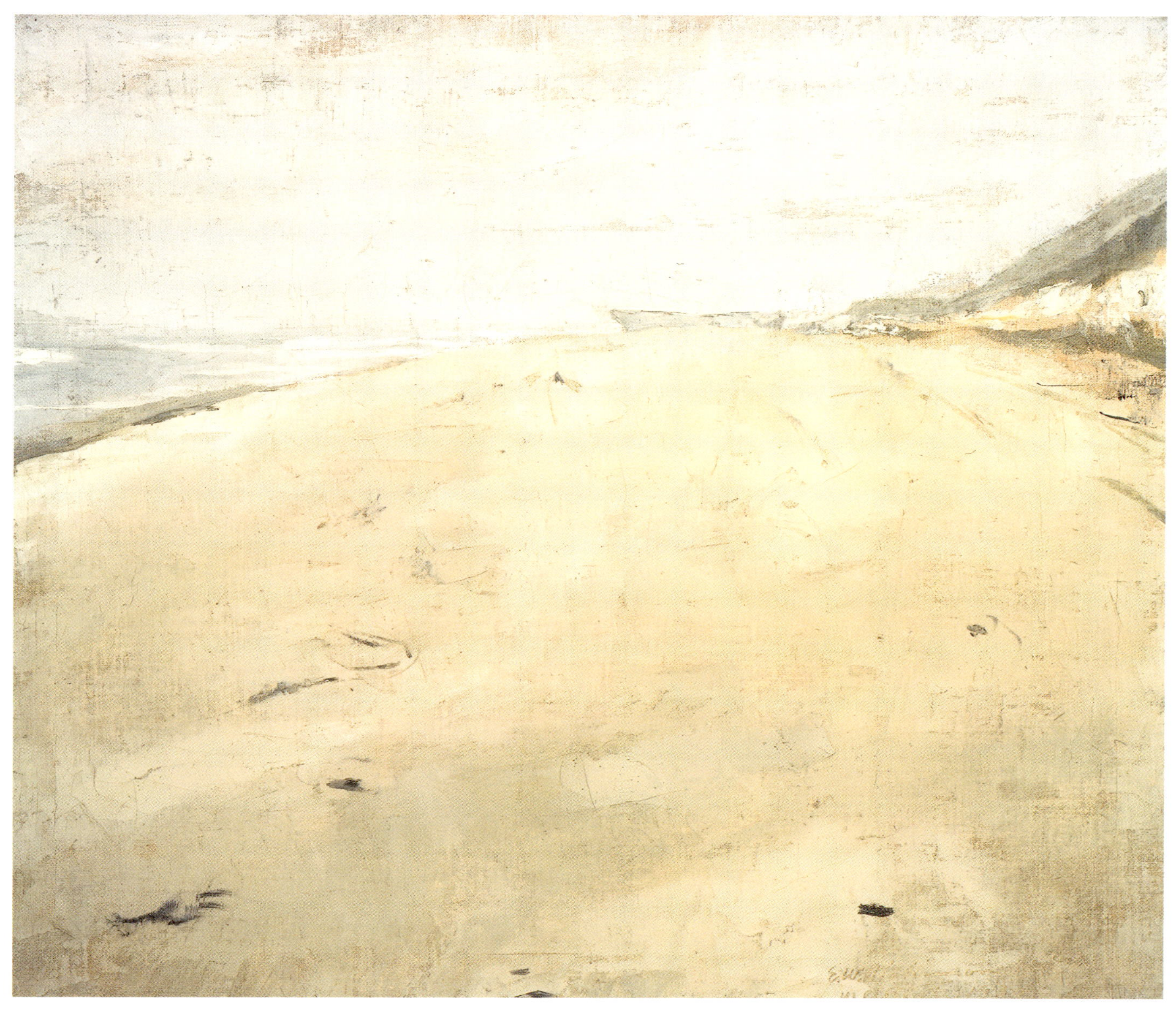

17 *Coast at Wellfleet with a Wreck*, 1930

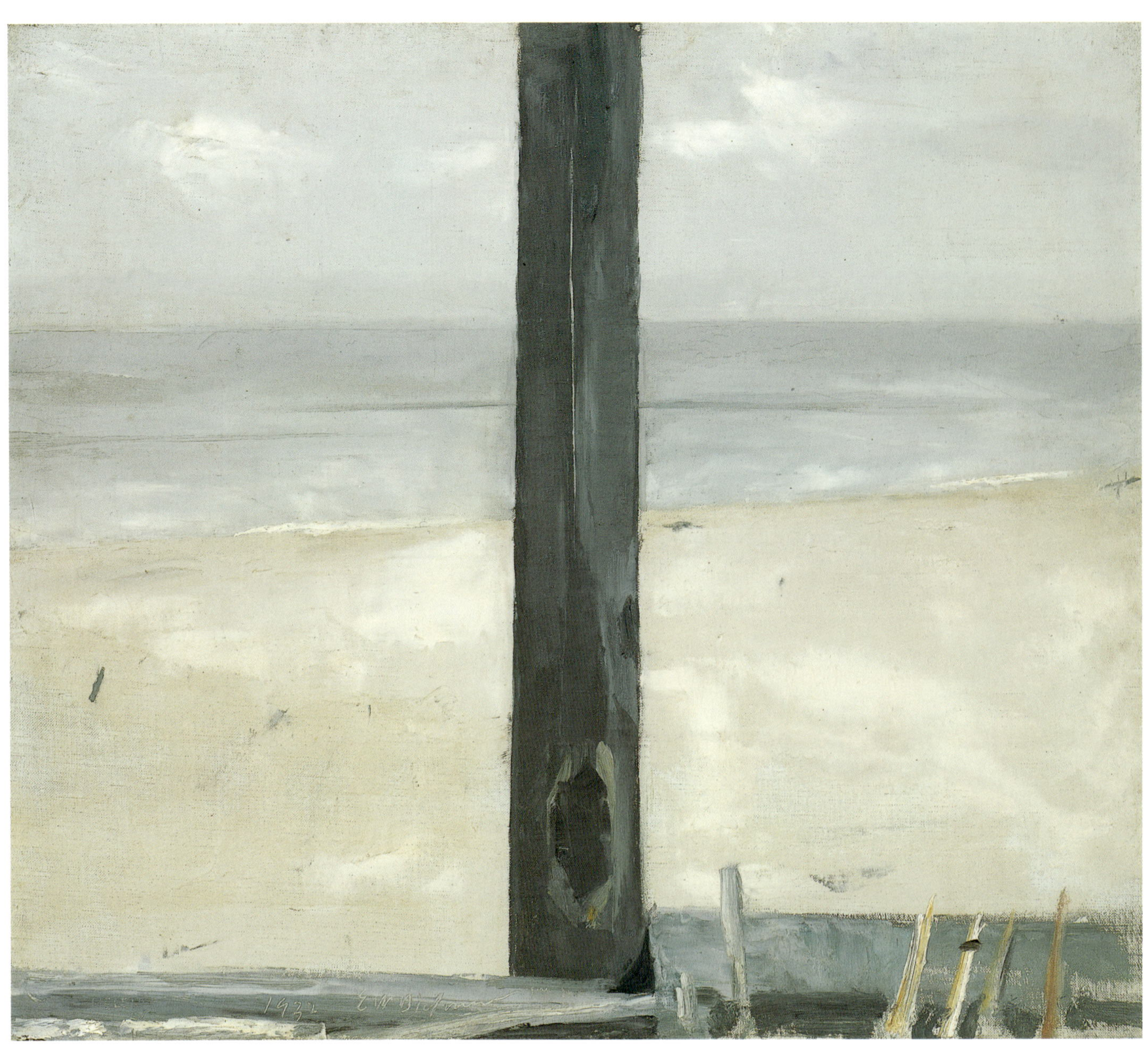

18 *Cottage Porch, Peaked Hill*, 1932

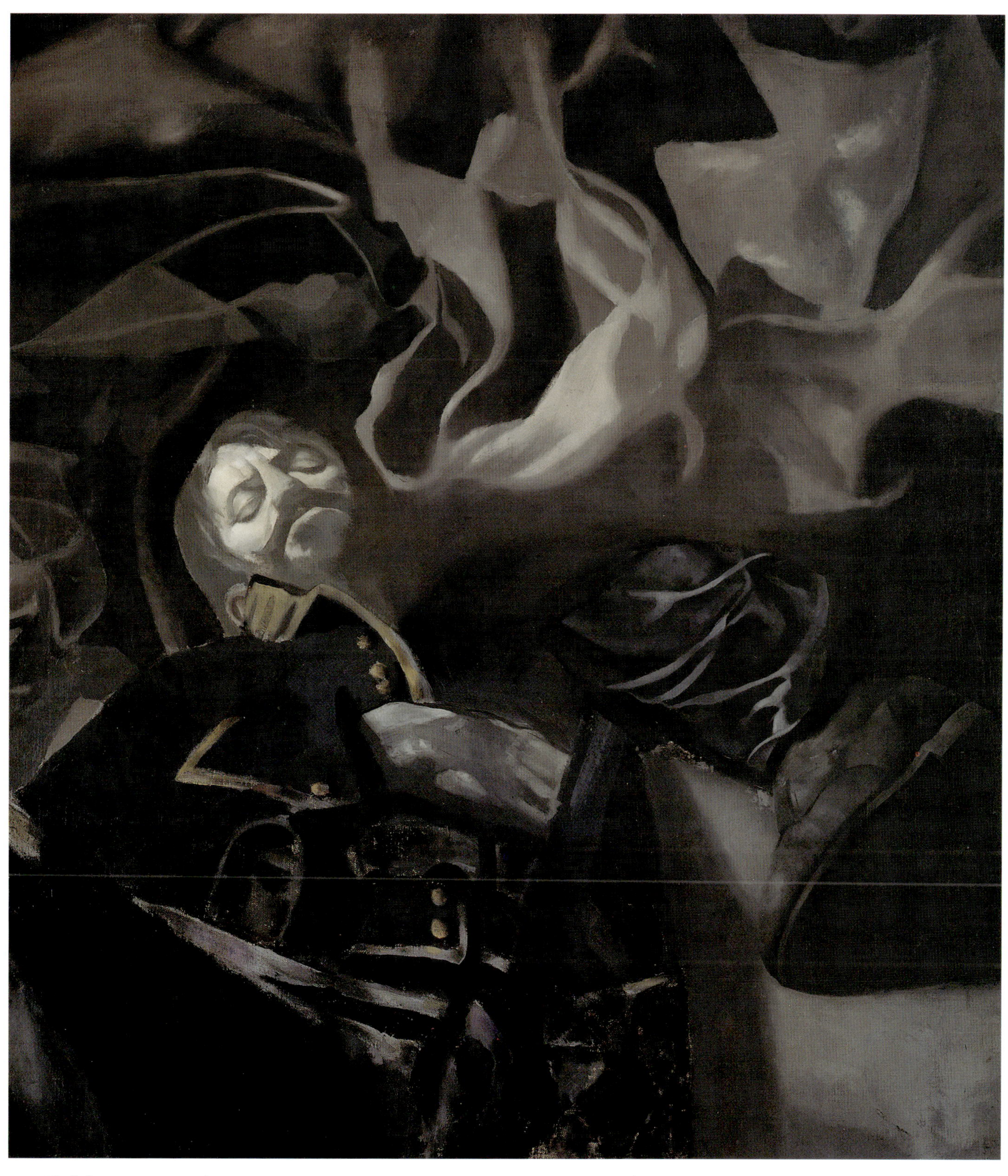

19 *Shiloh,* 1932–33 and 1940

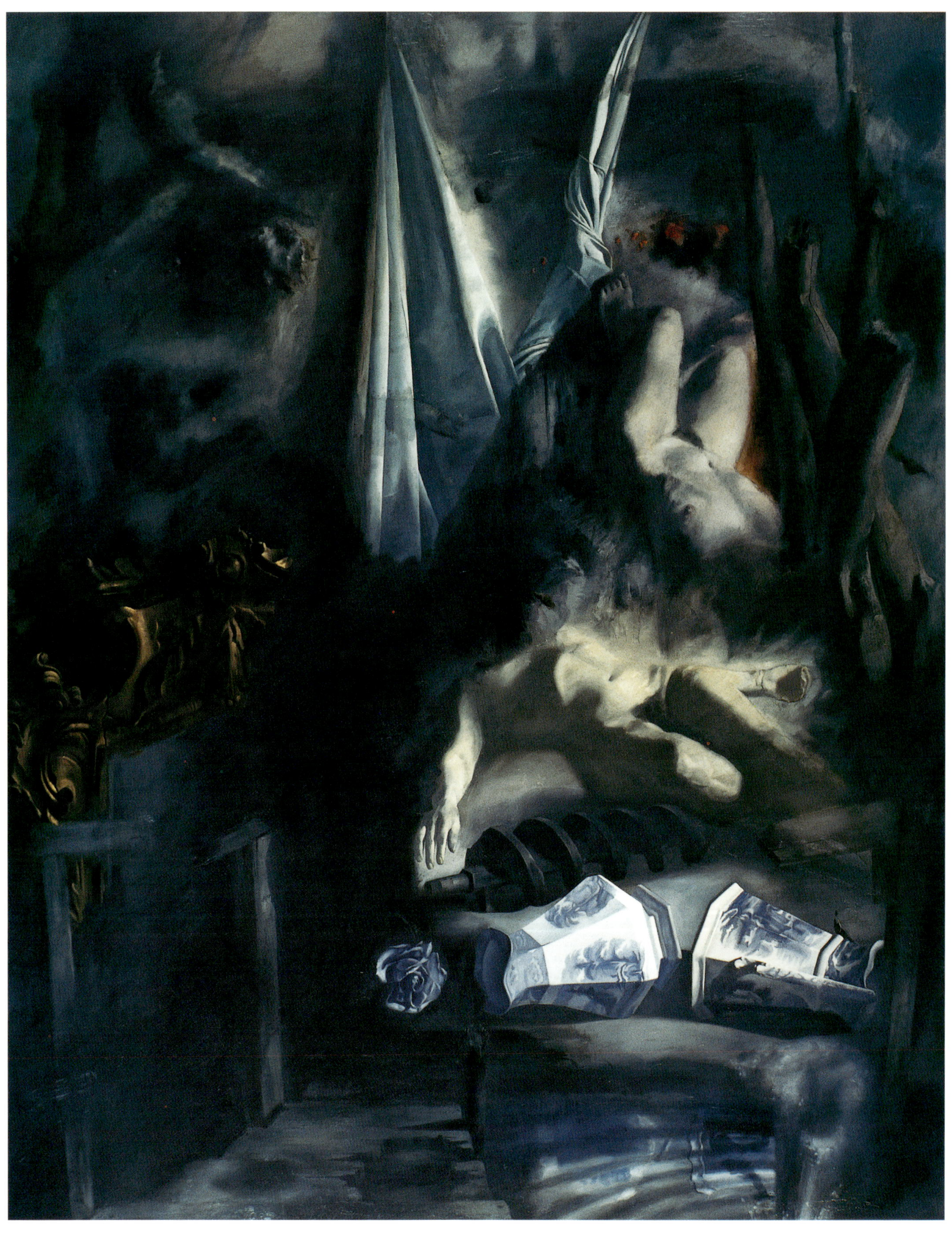

20 *Composition with Still Life*, 1933–37

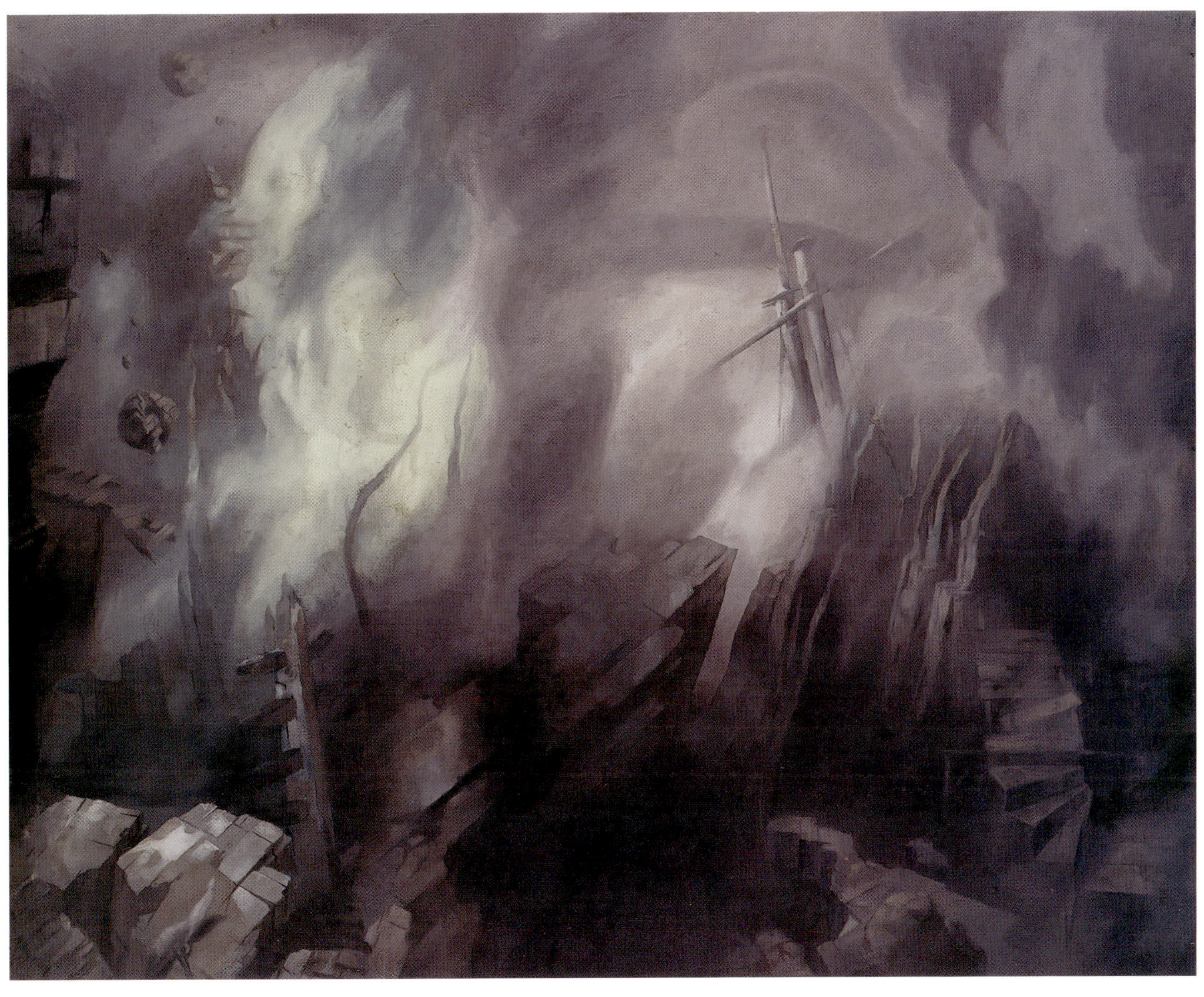

21 *Stranded Brig*, 1934

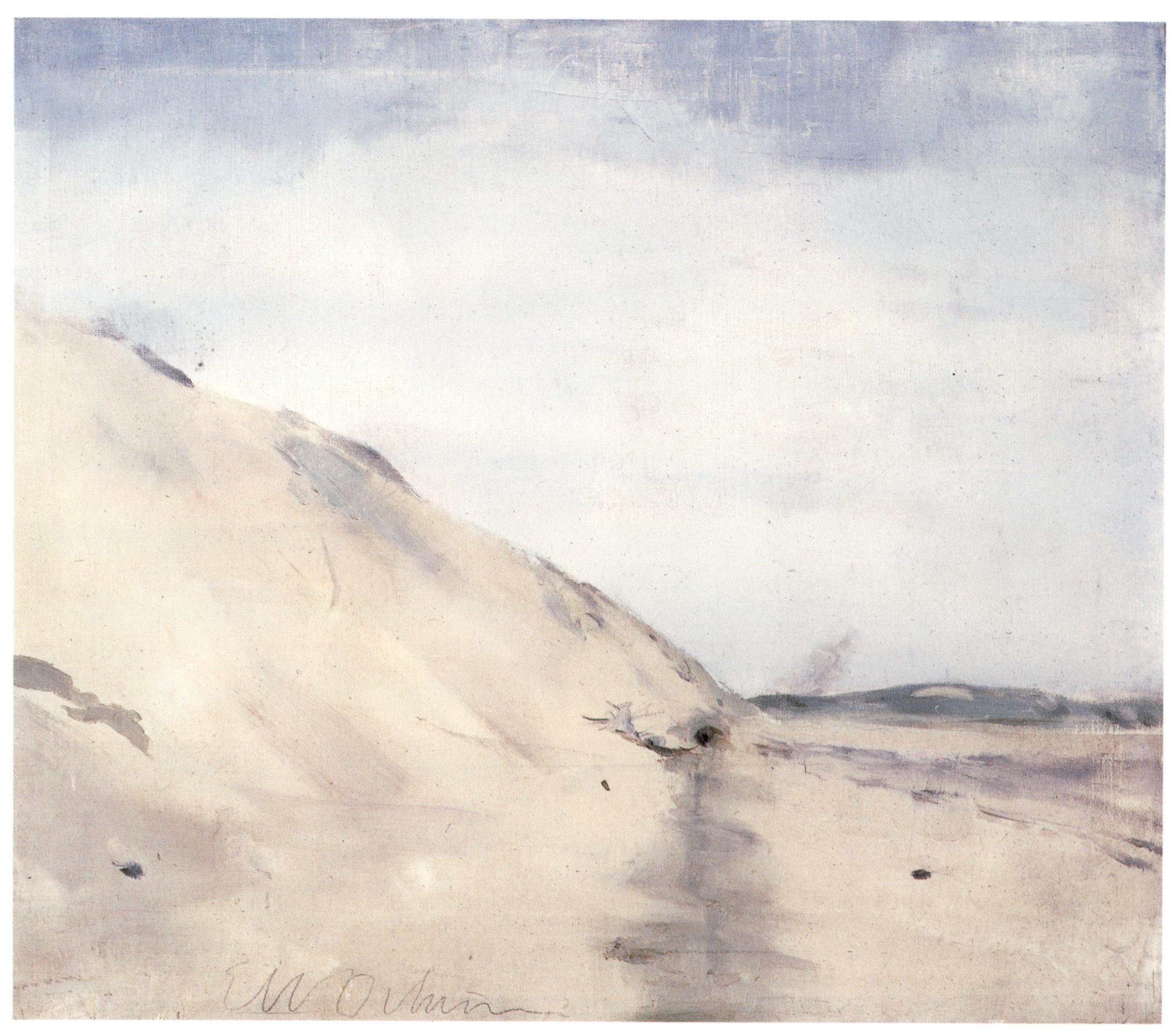

22 *Laboratory Beach*, 1935

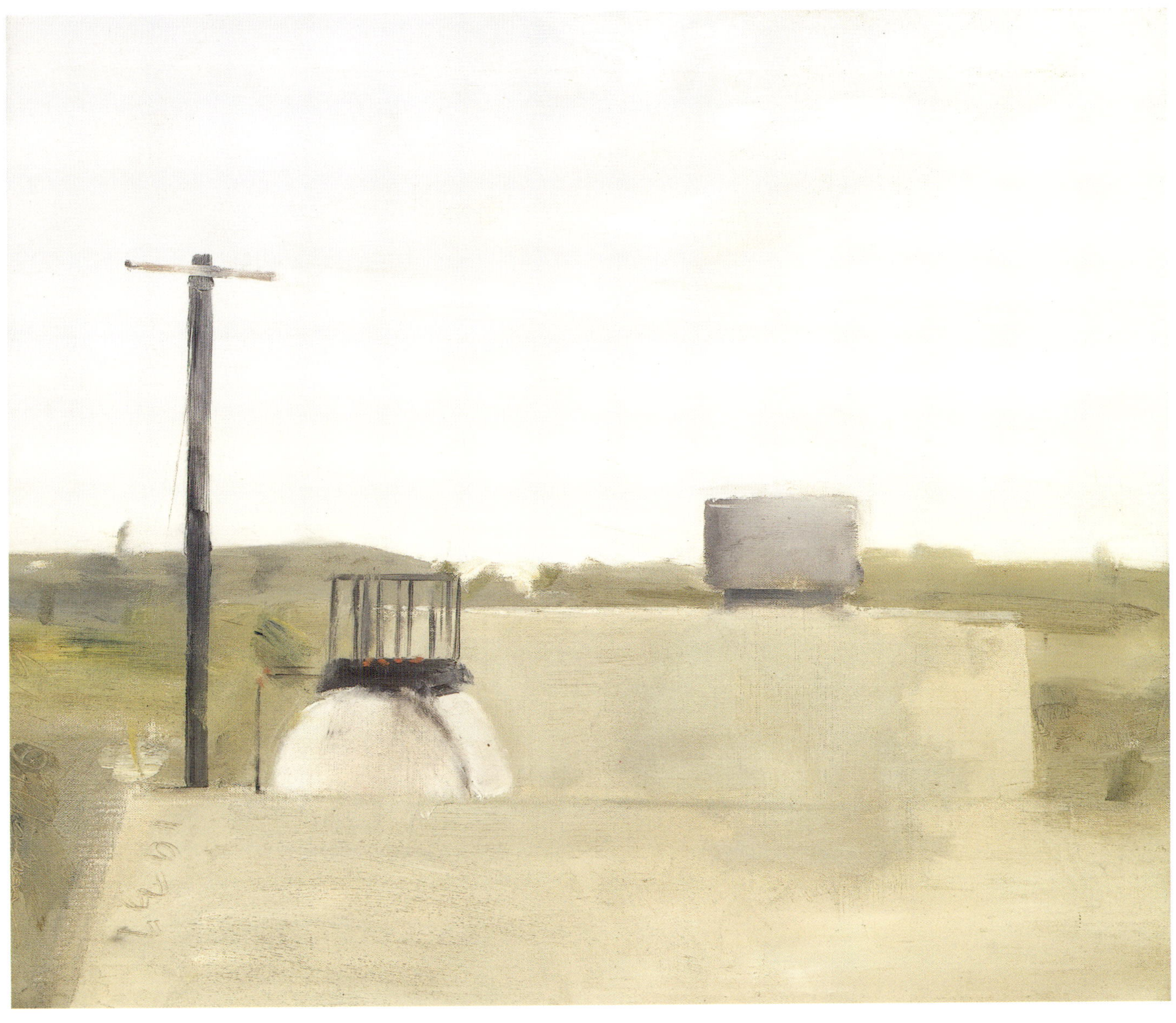

23 *Gas Tank*, 1937

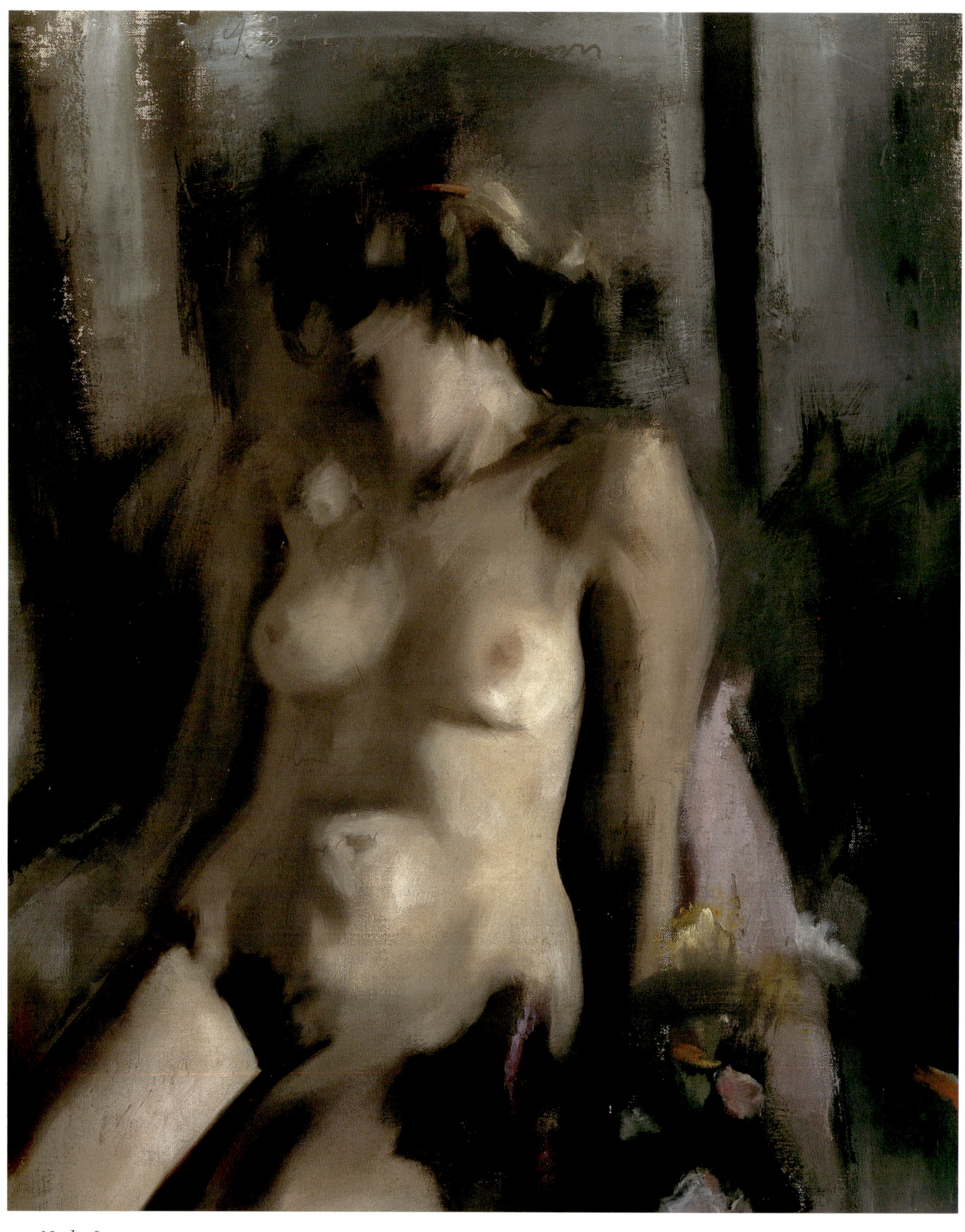

24 *Nude, Jean*, 1937

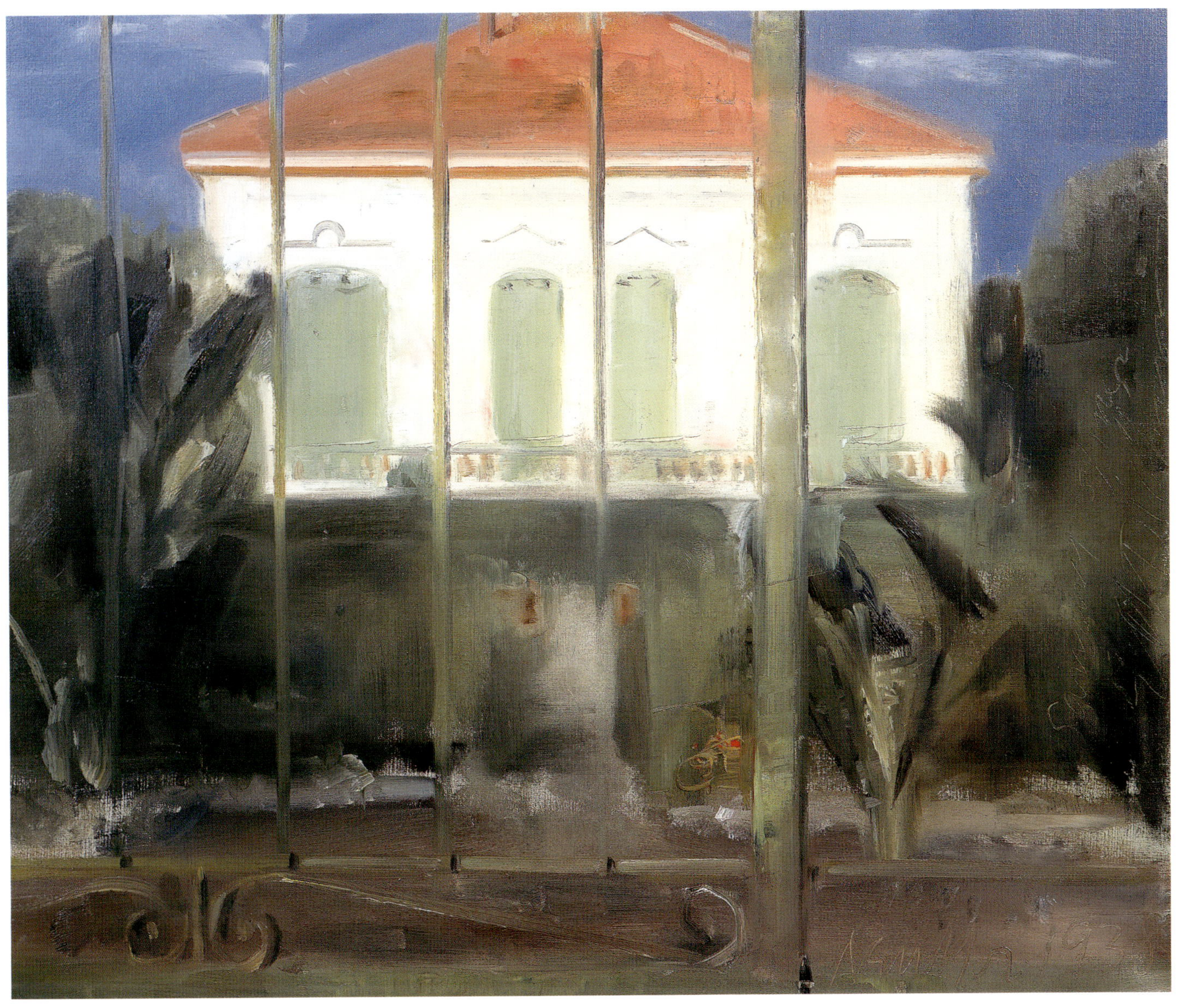

25 *Villa Zingarella*, 1938

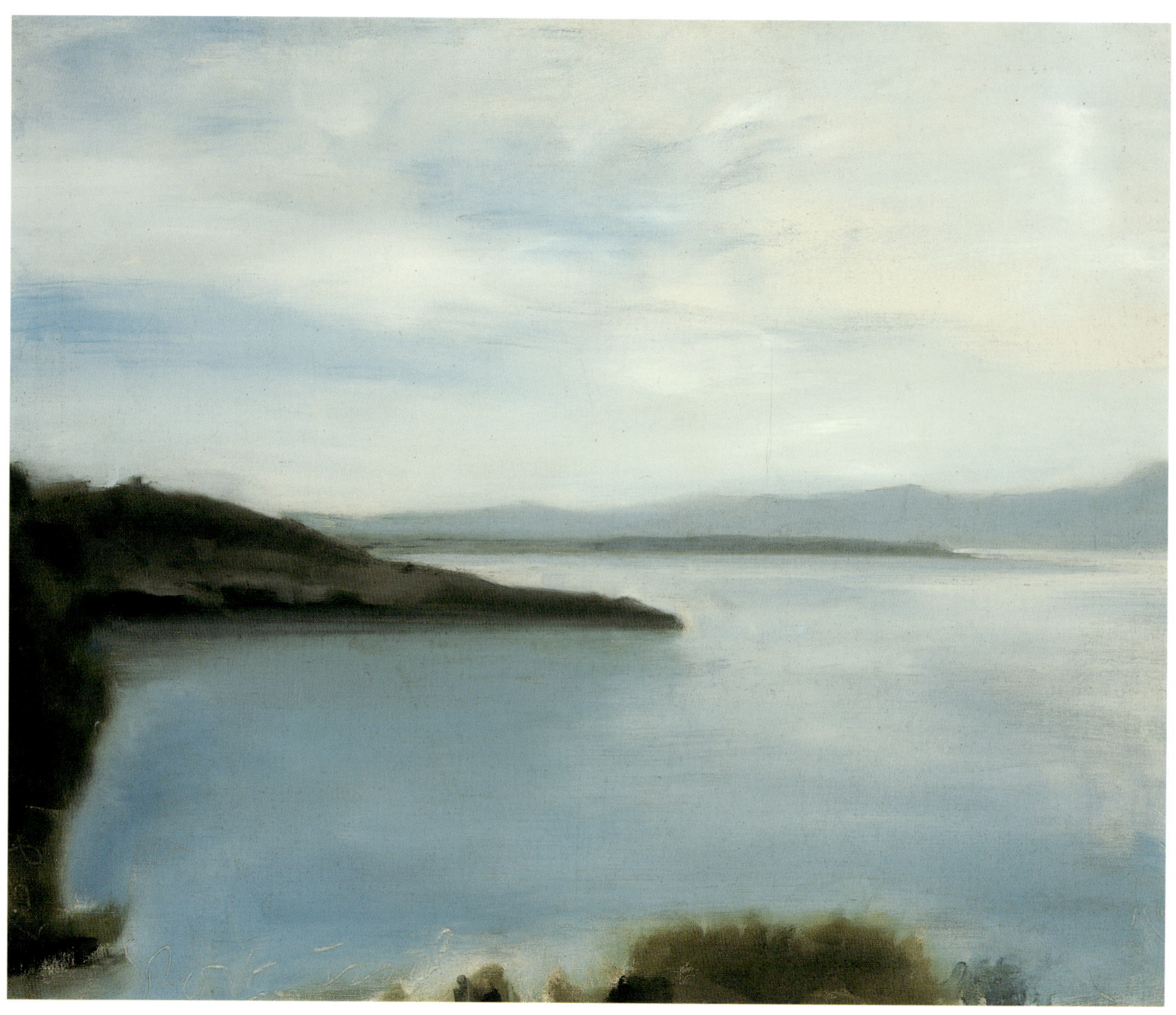

26 *Sanary Bay*, 1938

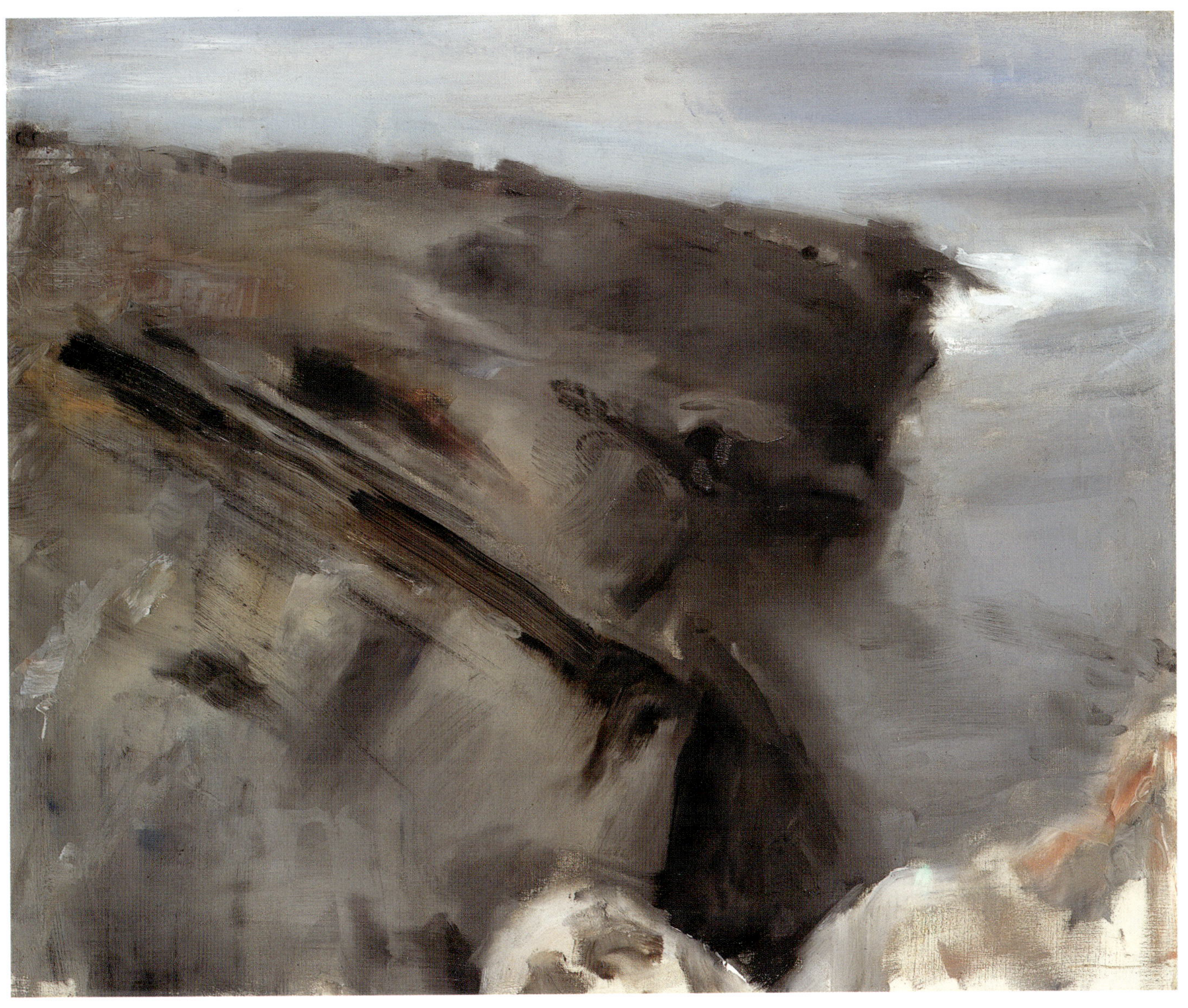

27 *Rock of Port Issol, West Side*, 1938

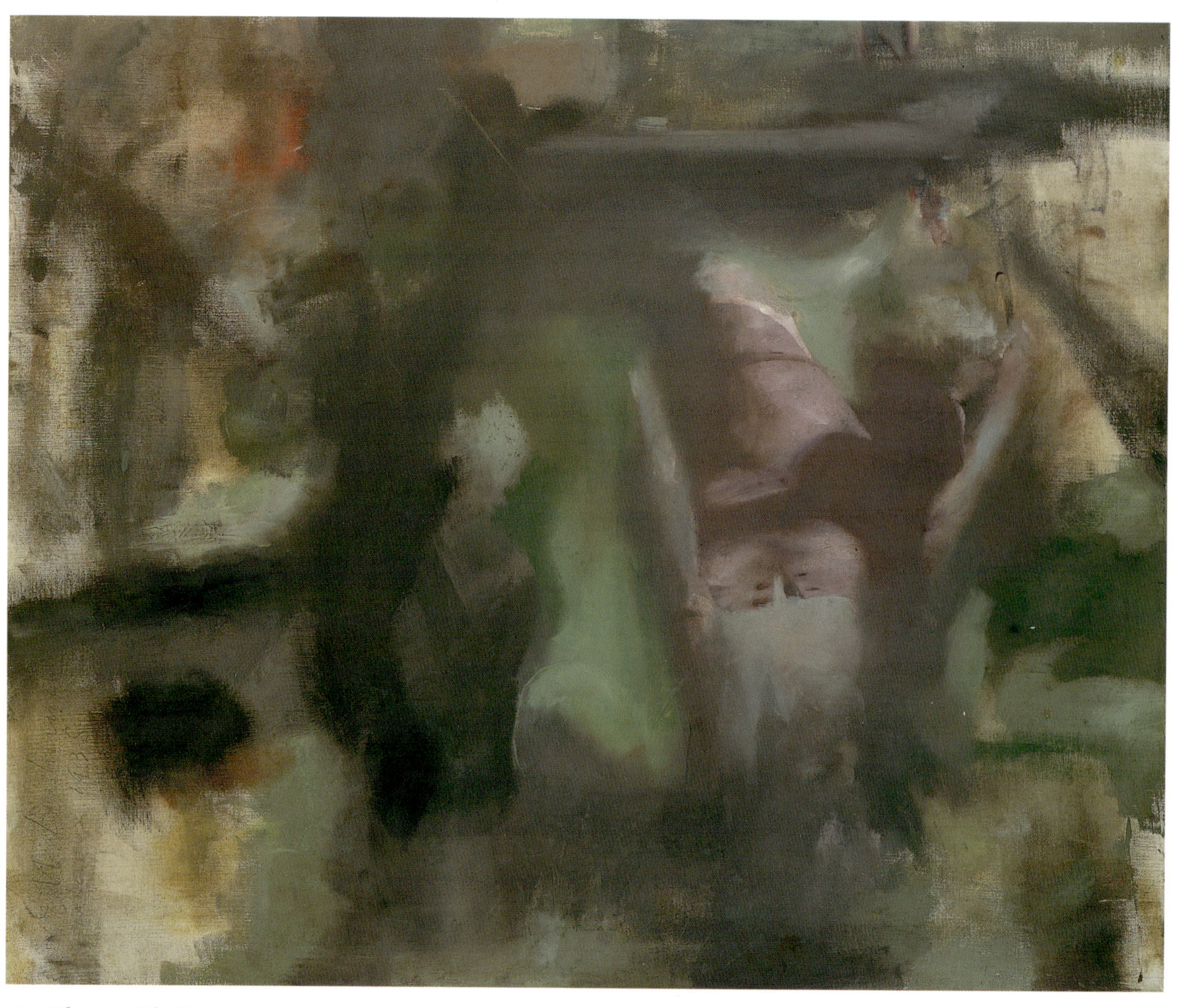

28 *Ulysses, Oh Cissy!*, 1938

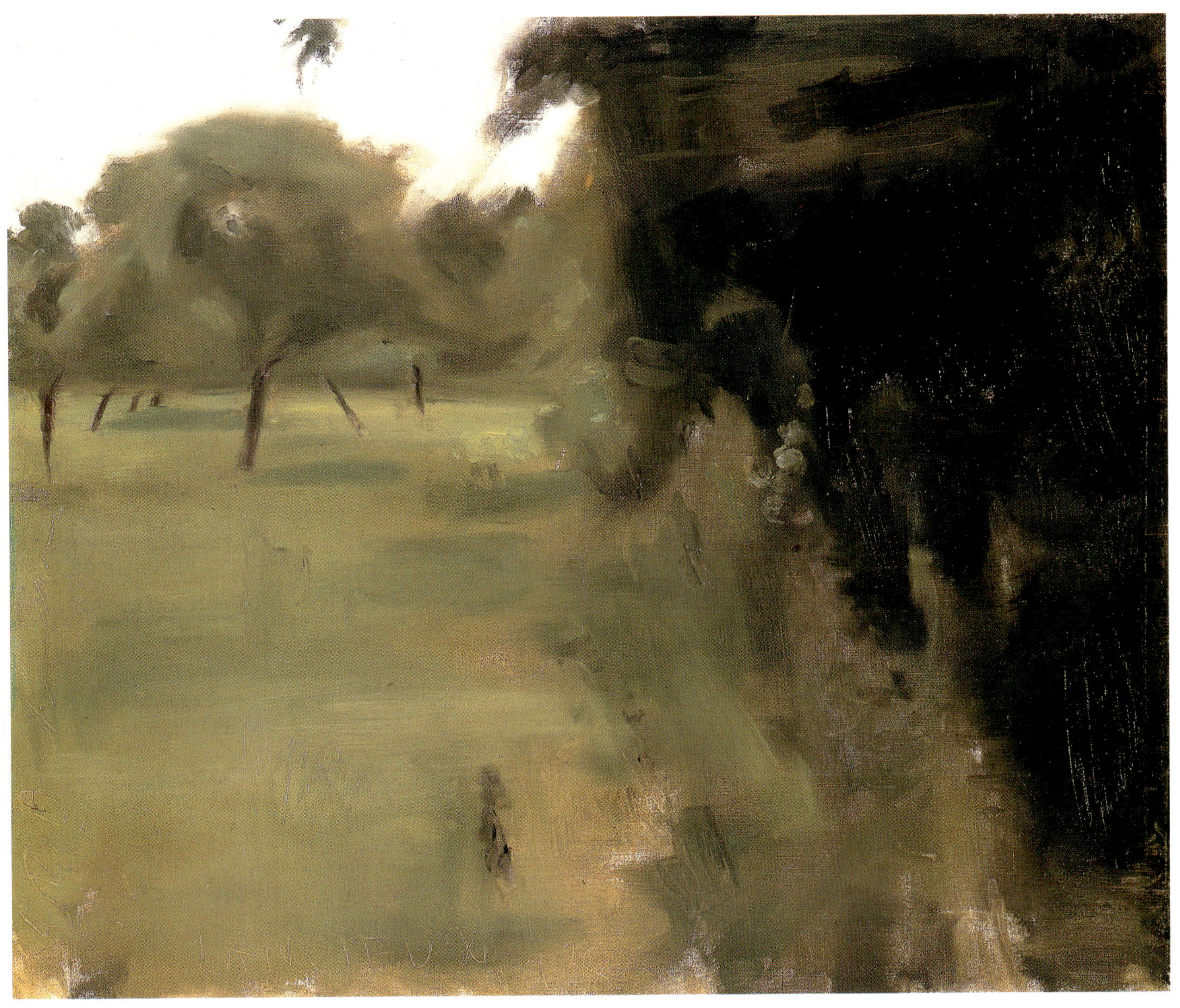

29 *Orchard*, 1938

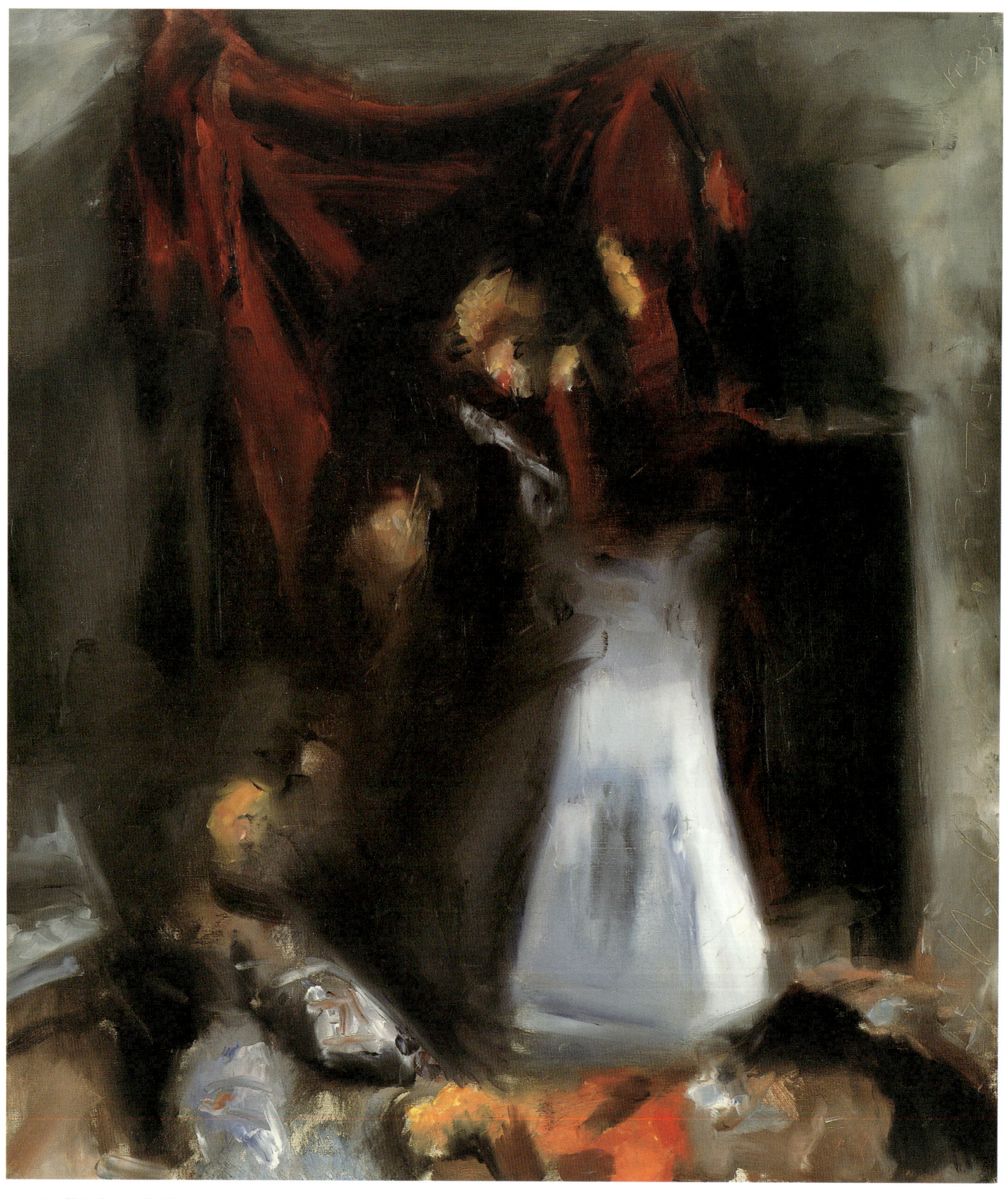

30 *Still Life with Flowers*, 1938

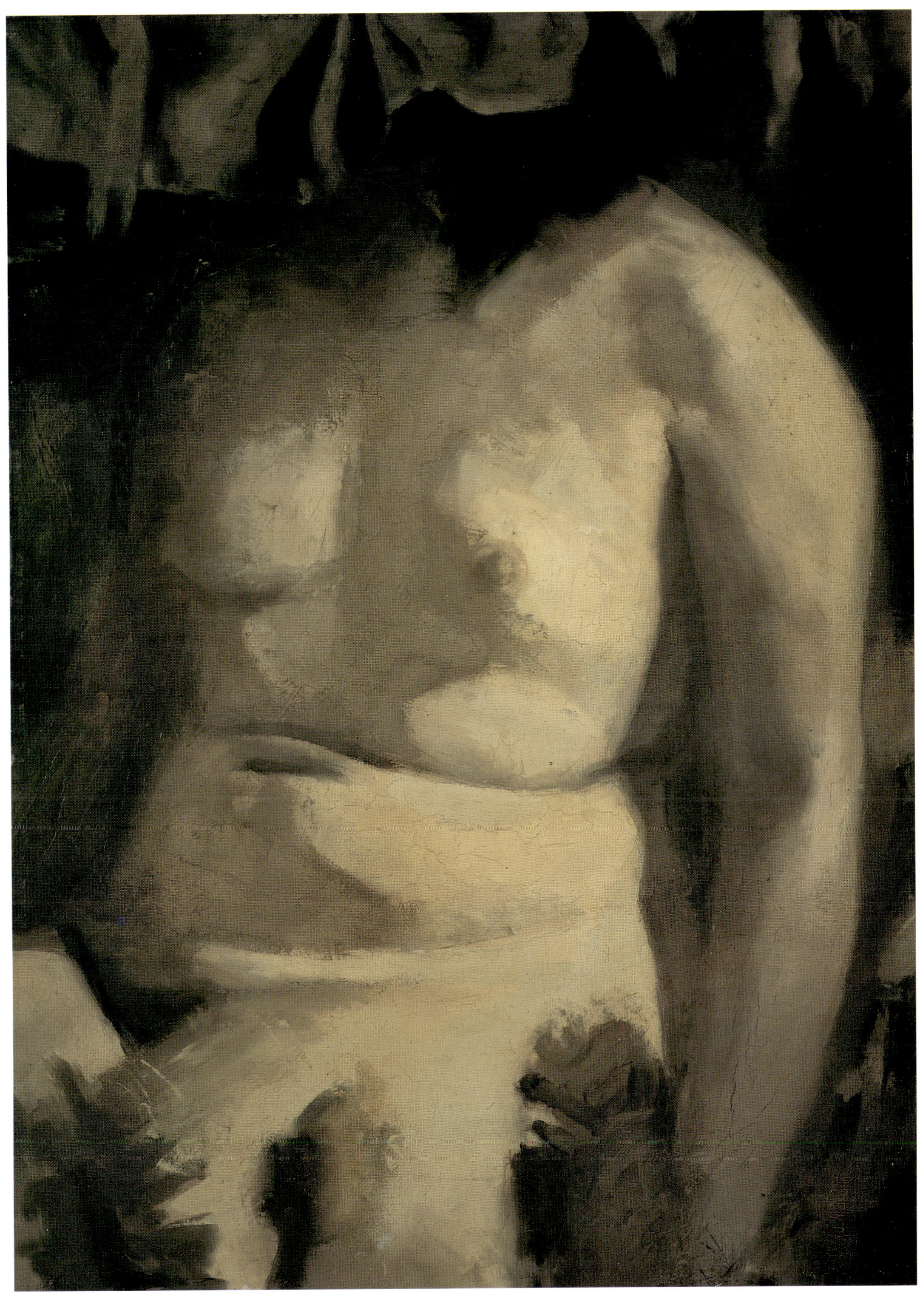

31 *Nude with Pine Cones, Marie*, 1939

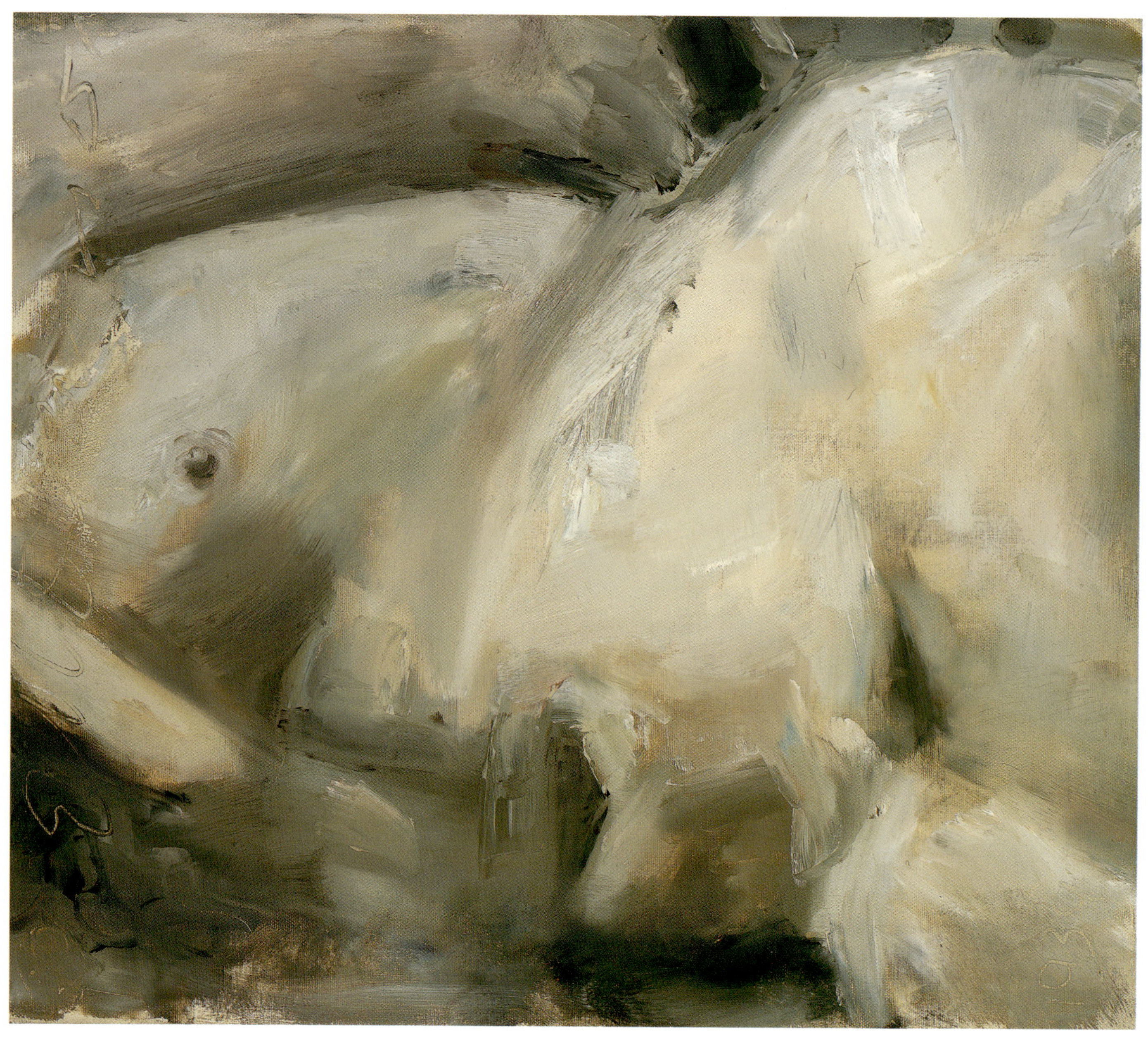

32 *Nude Figure, Marie*, 1939

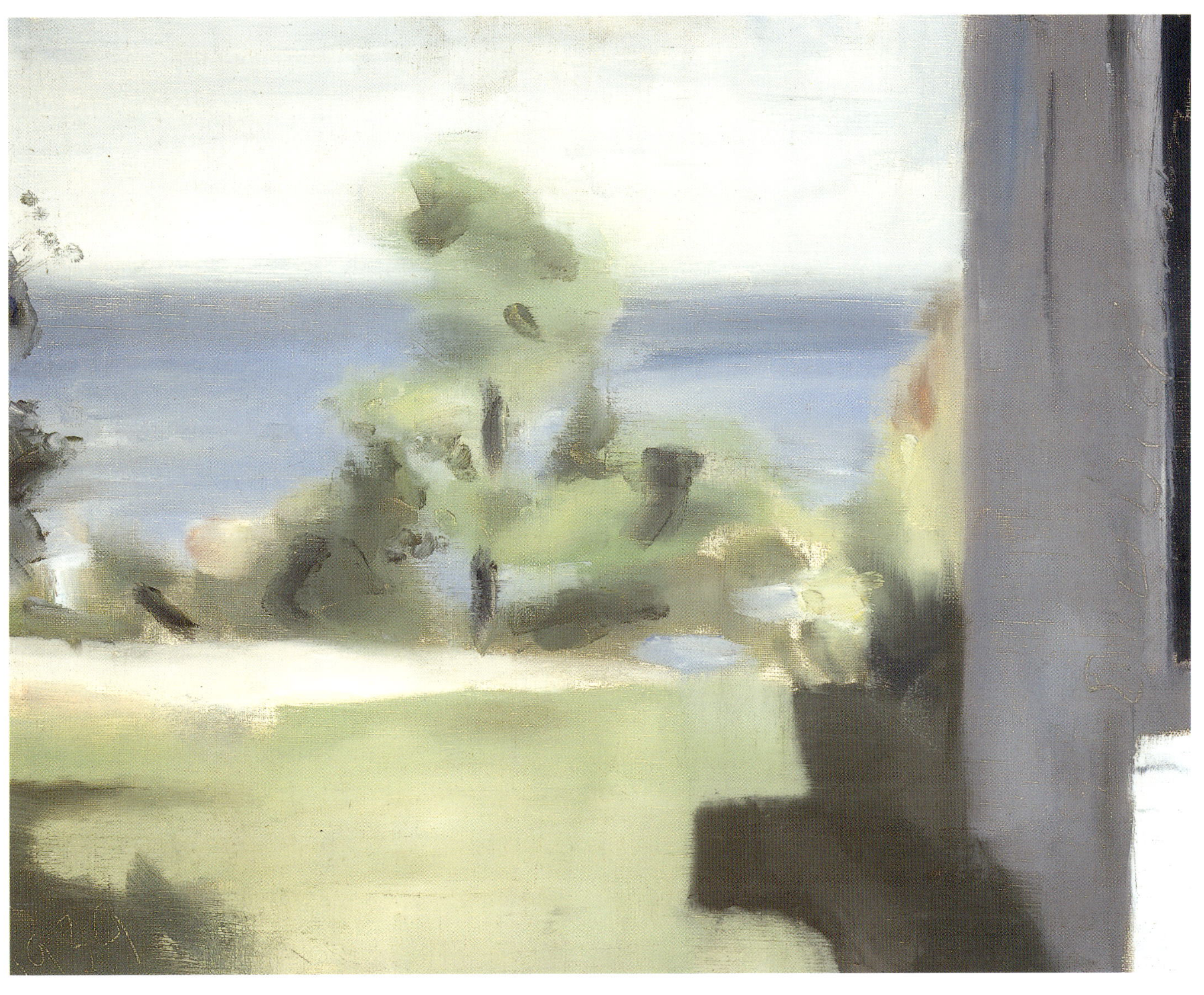

33 *Sandy's Yard*, 1939

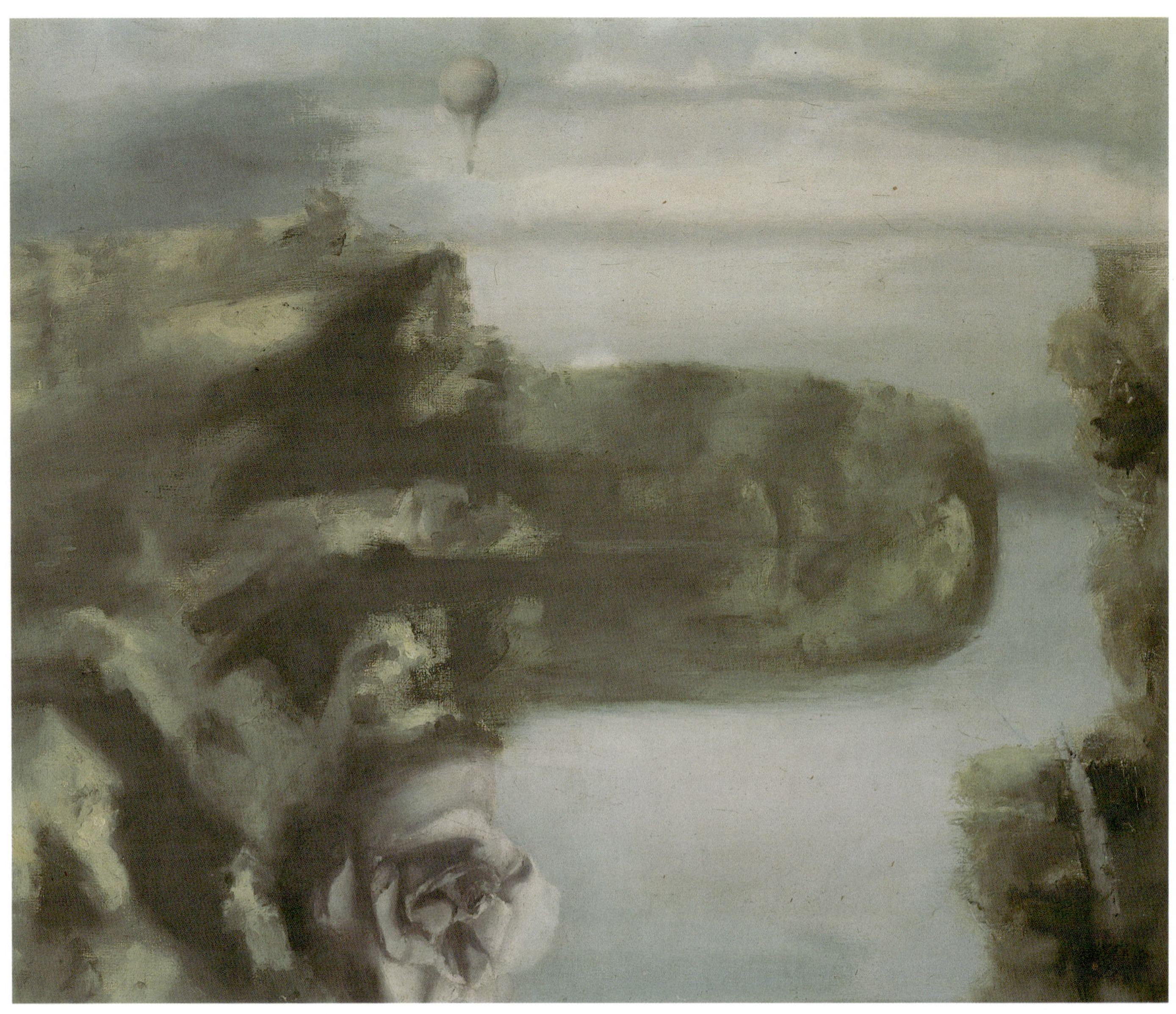

34 *The Finger Lakes*, 1940

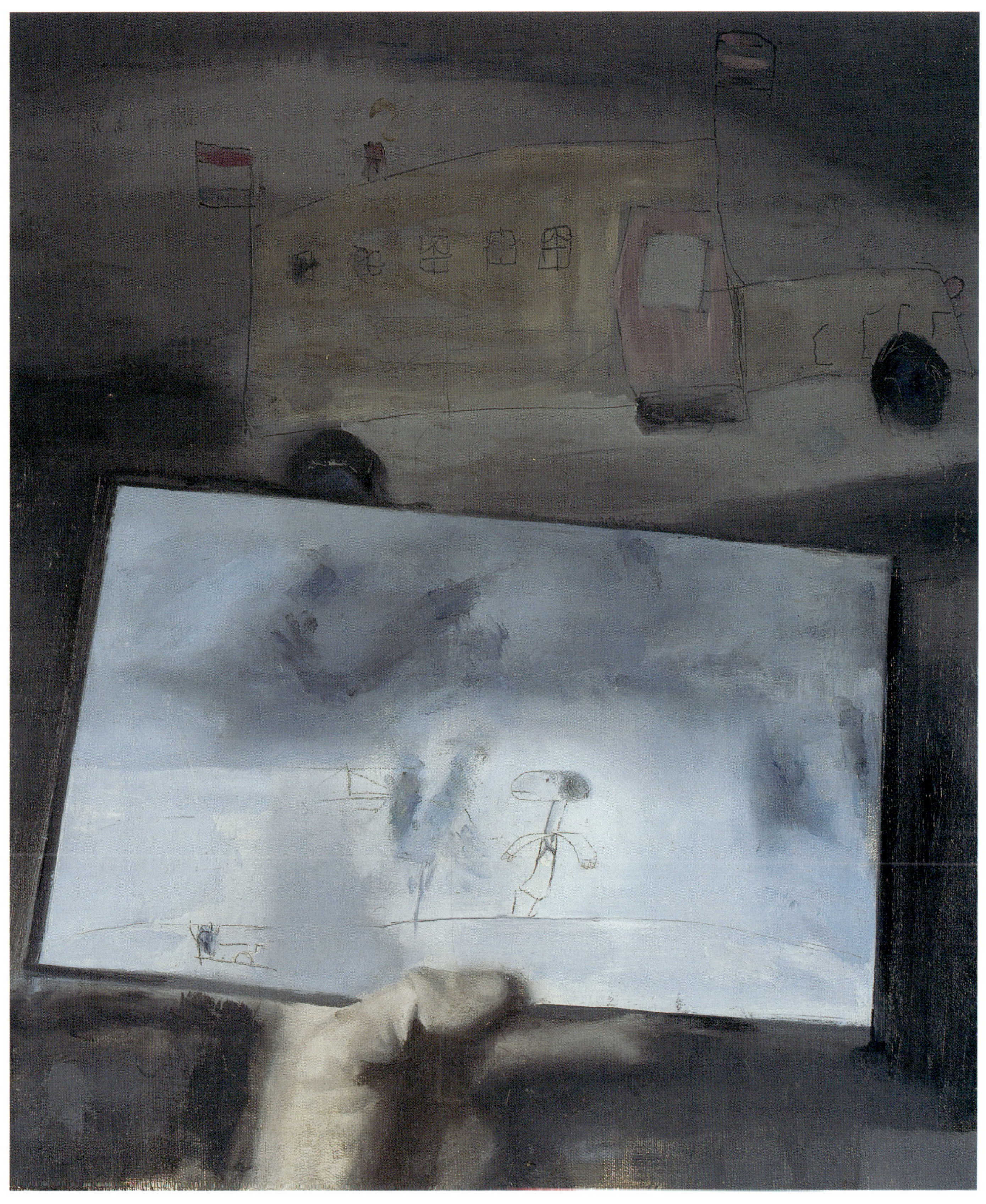

35 *Artist's Hand Holding Children's Drawings*, 1940

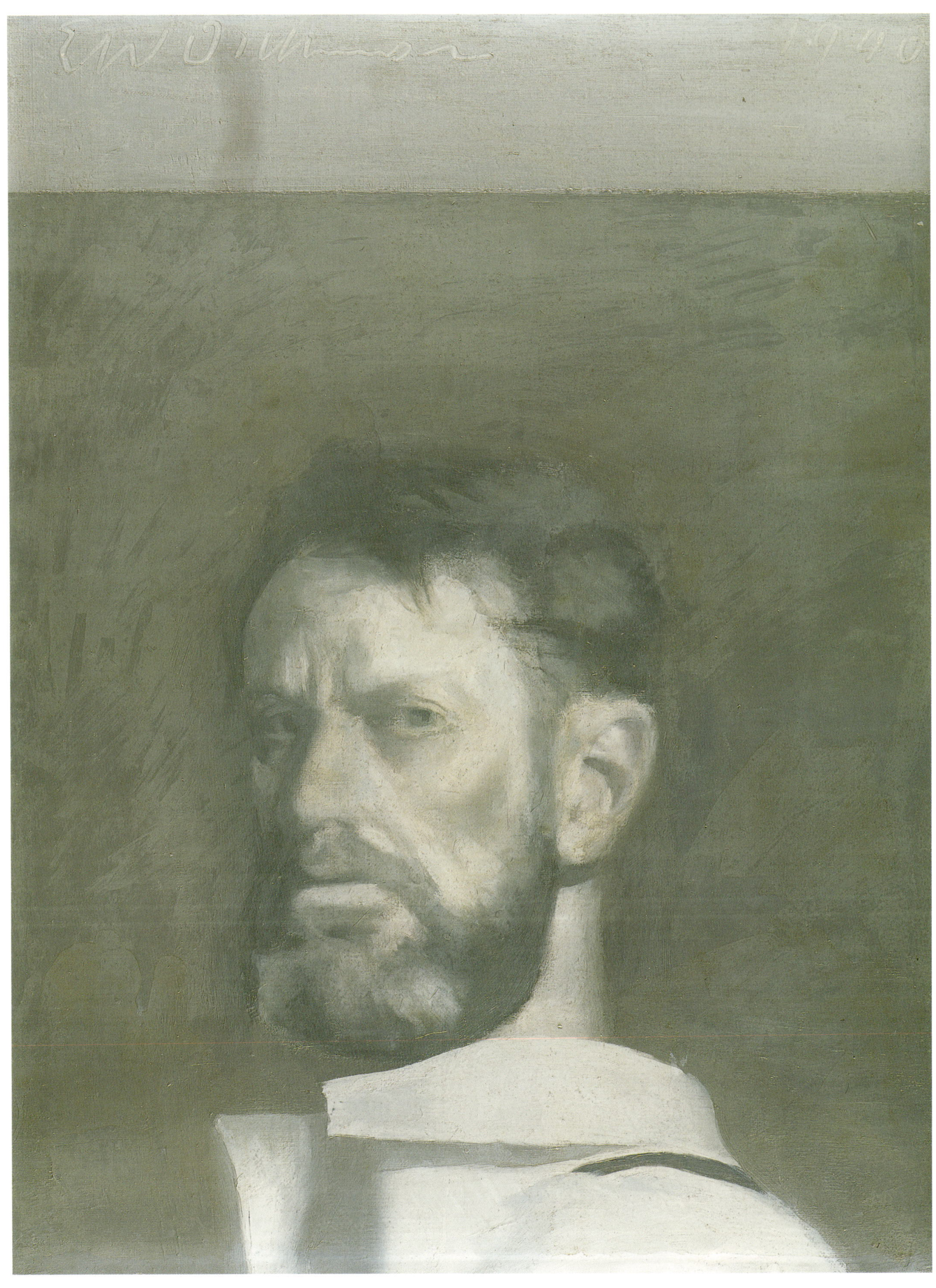

36 *Self-Portrait*, 1940

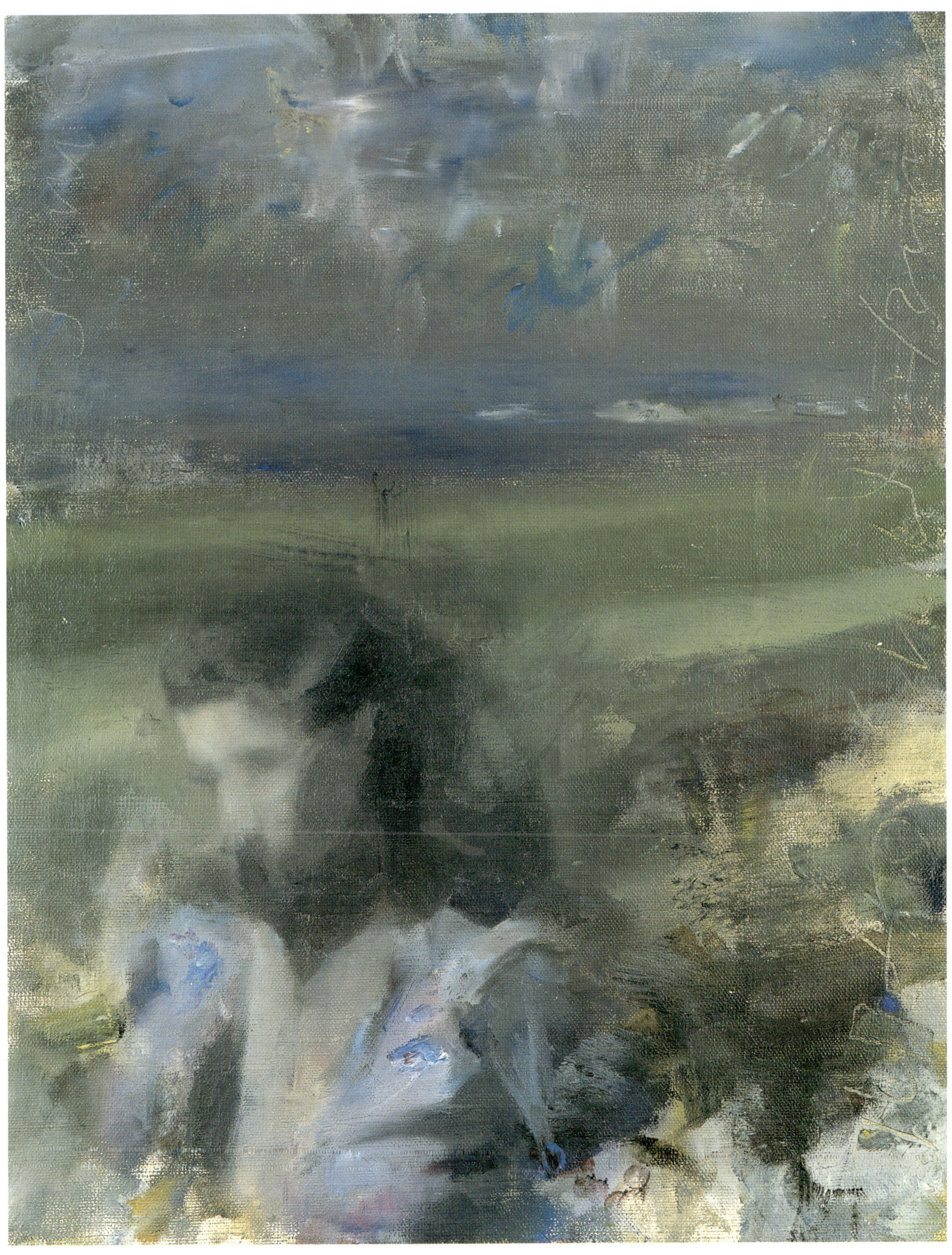

37 *Janice at the Beach*, 1940

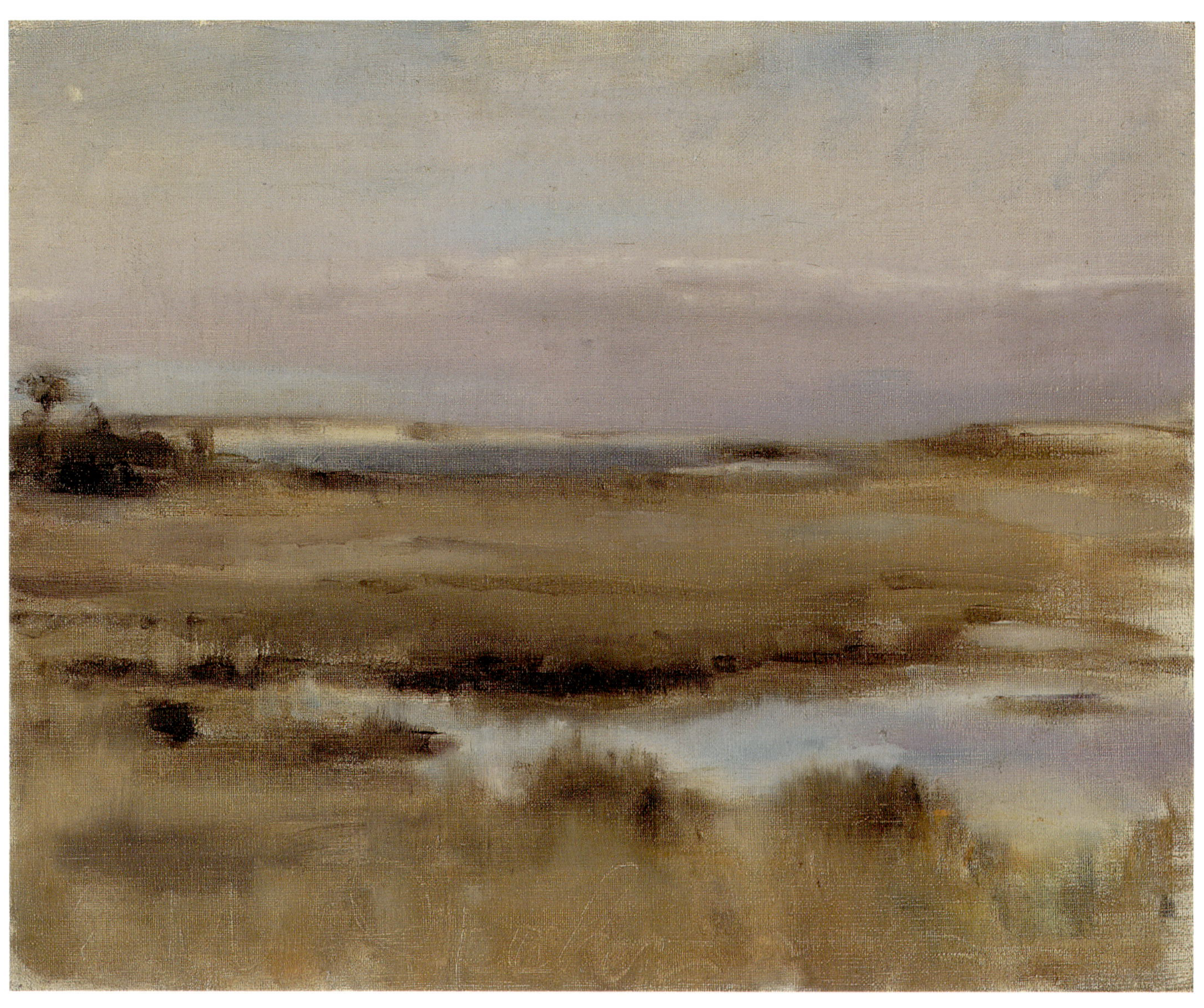

38 *View of Great Island*, 1940

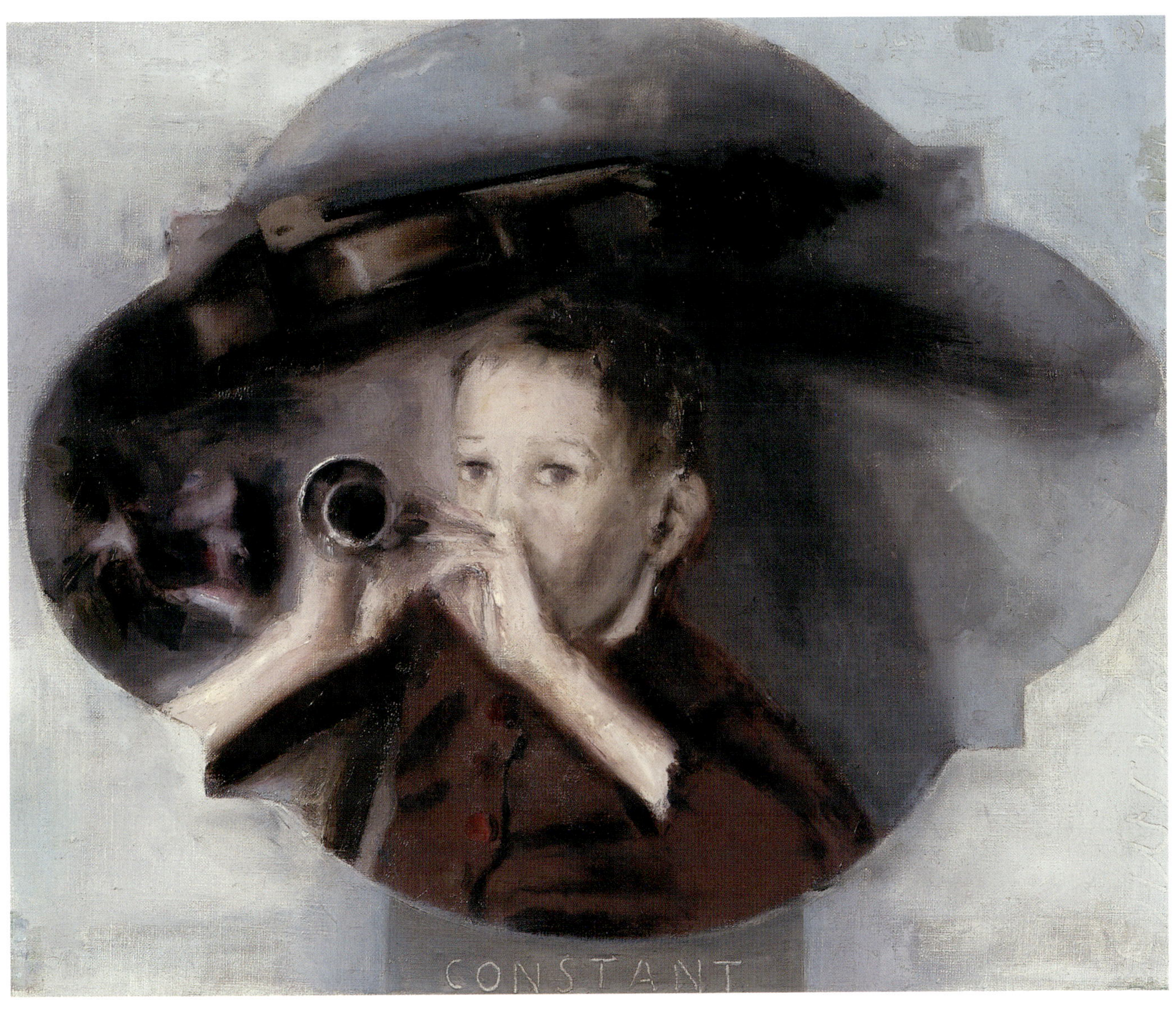

39 *Constant*, 1940–41 and 1944

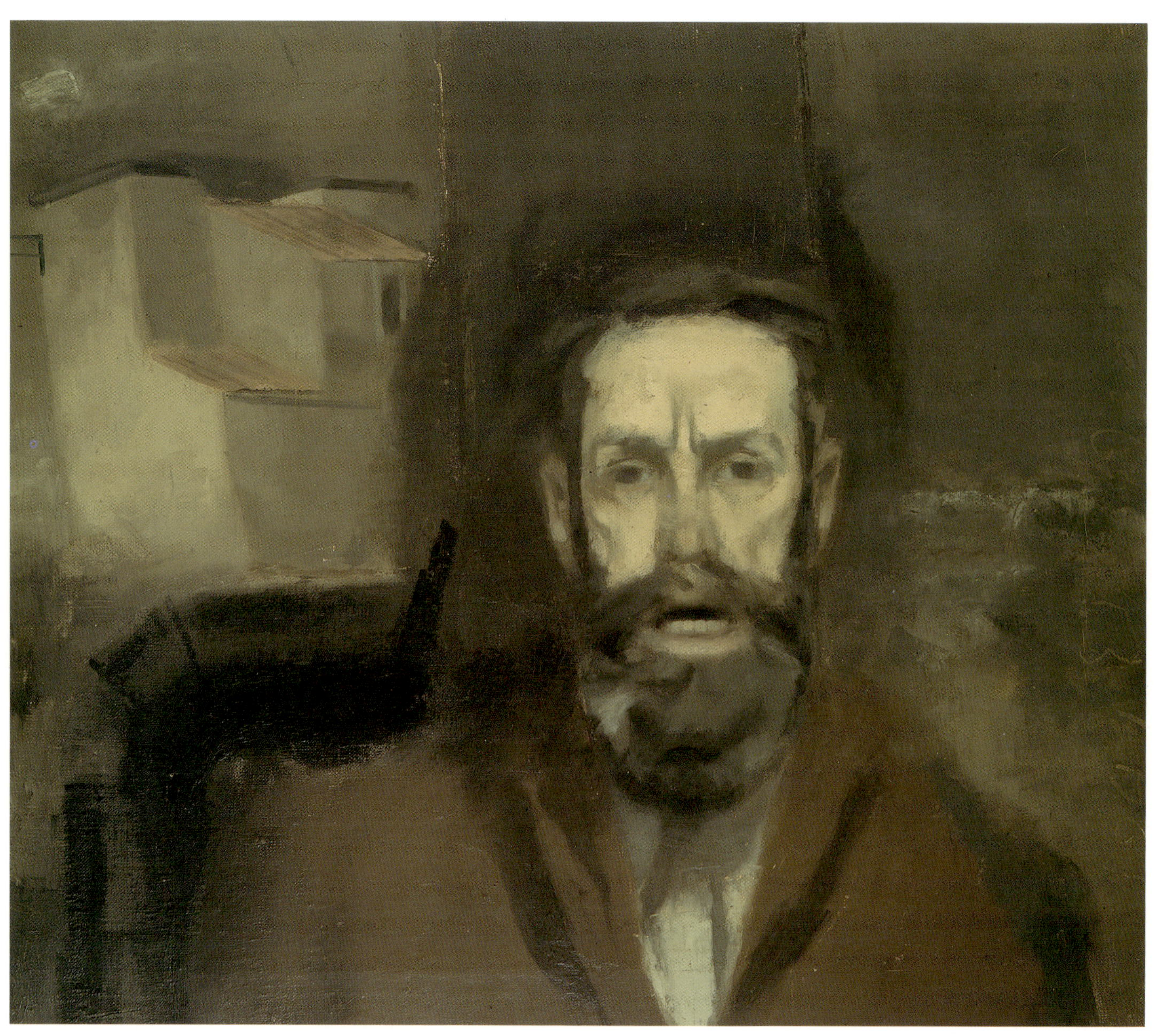

40 *Self-Portrait*, 1941

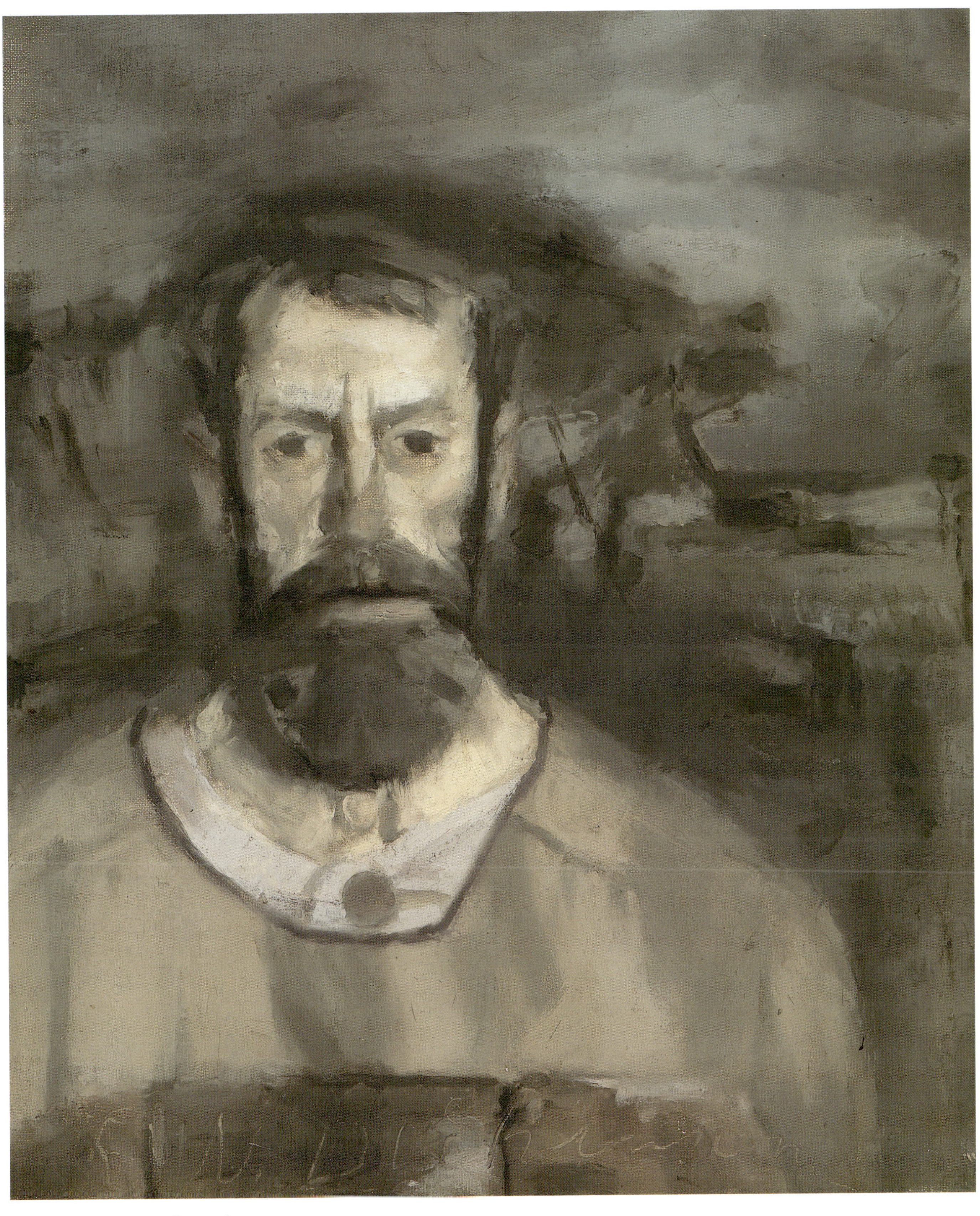

41 *Self-Portrait with Landscape*, 1941

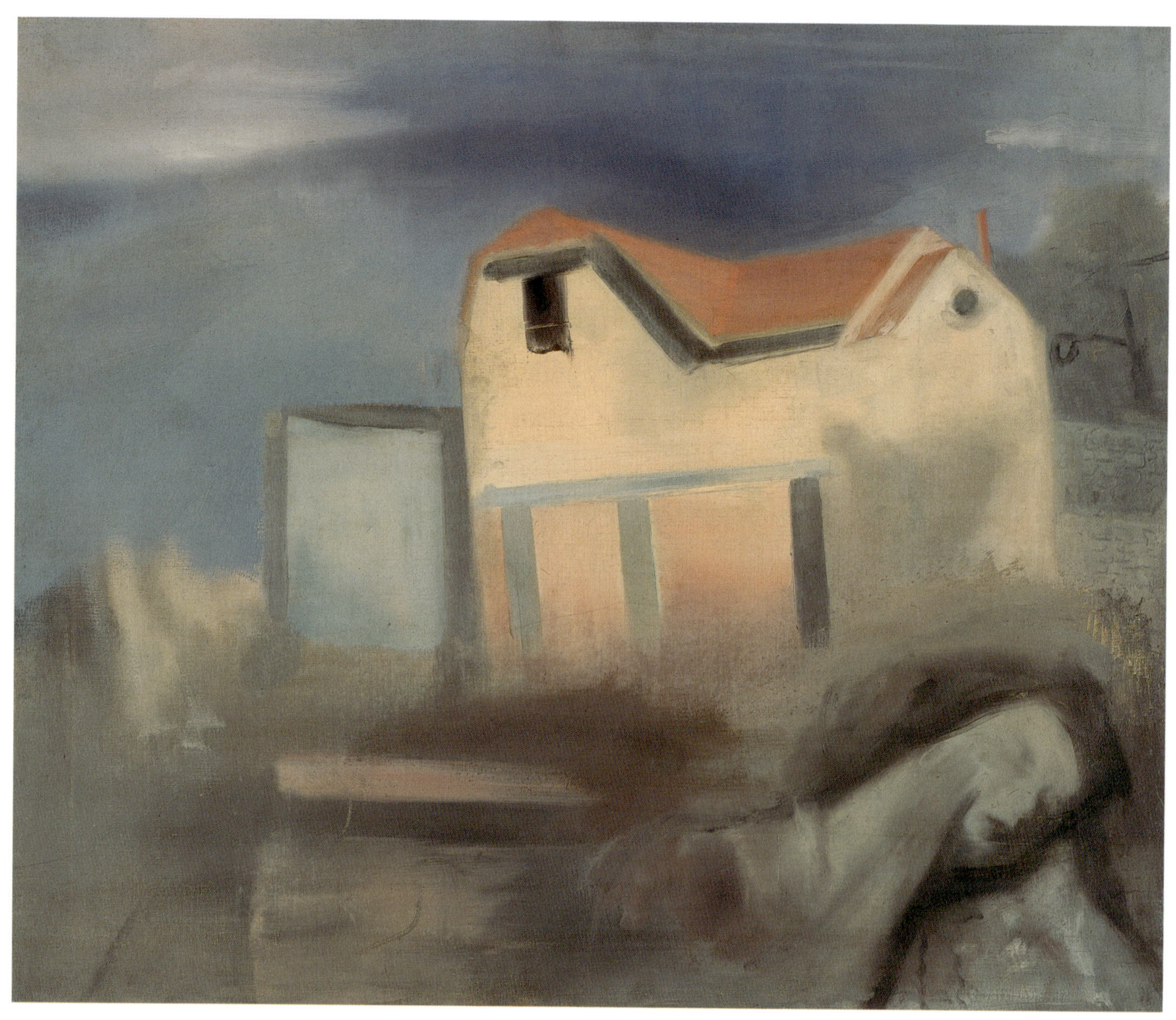

42 *Villa and Alice*, 1941

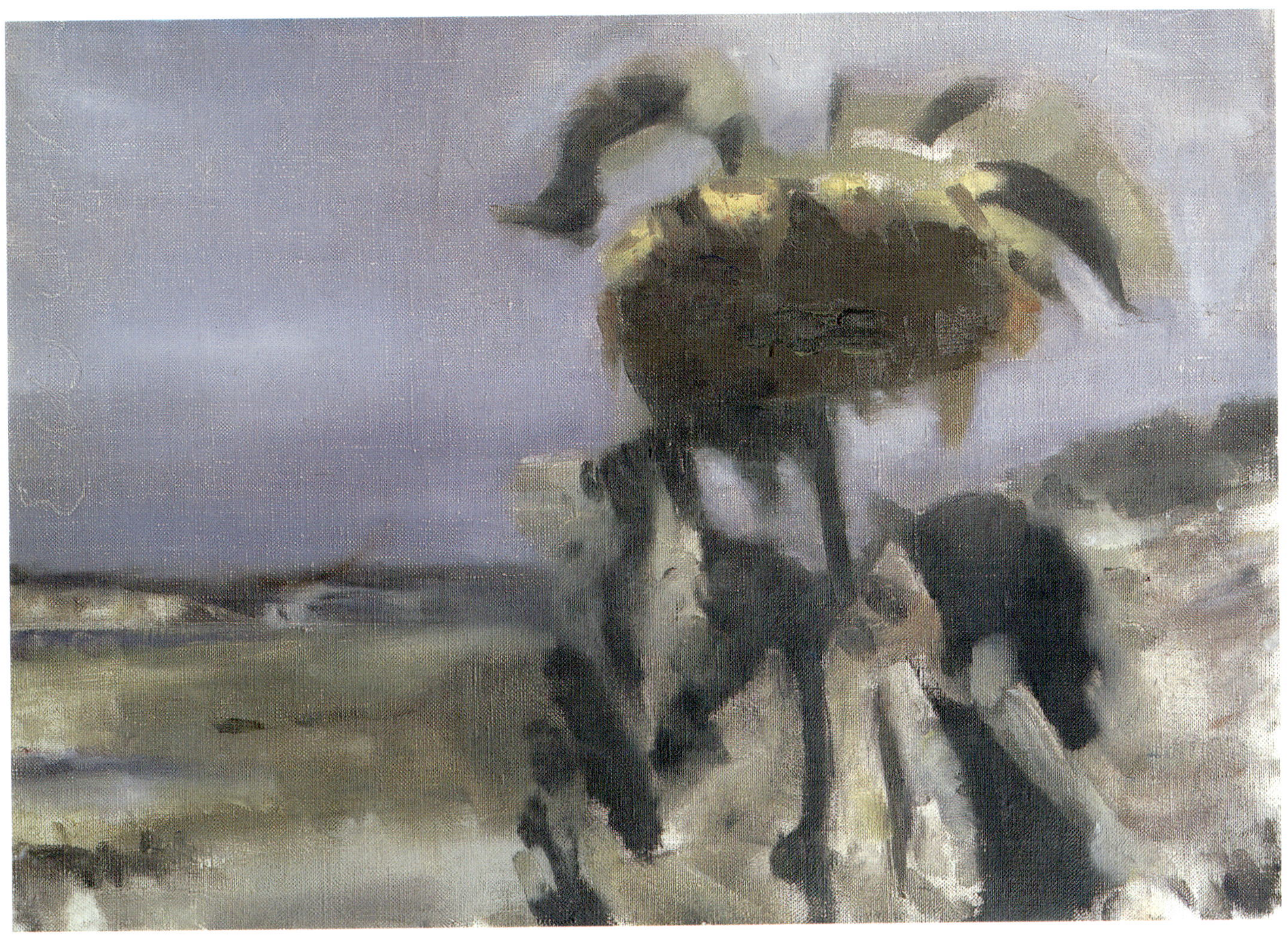

43 *Sunflower*, 1941

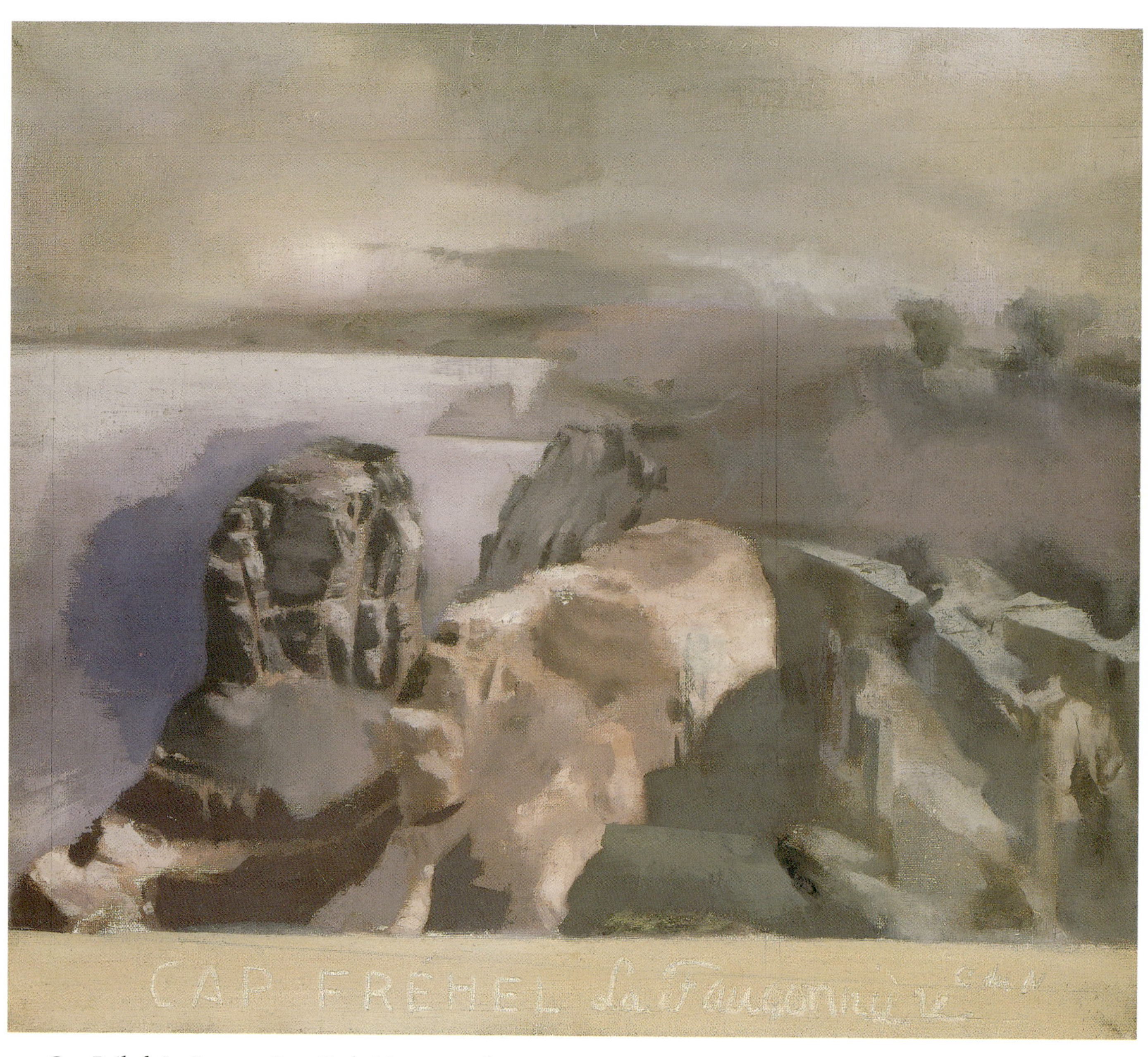

44 *Cap Fréhel, La Fauconnière, C. du N.*, 1941 and 1945

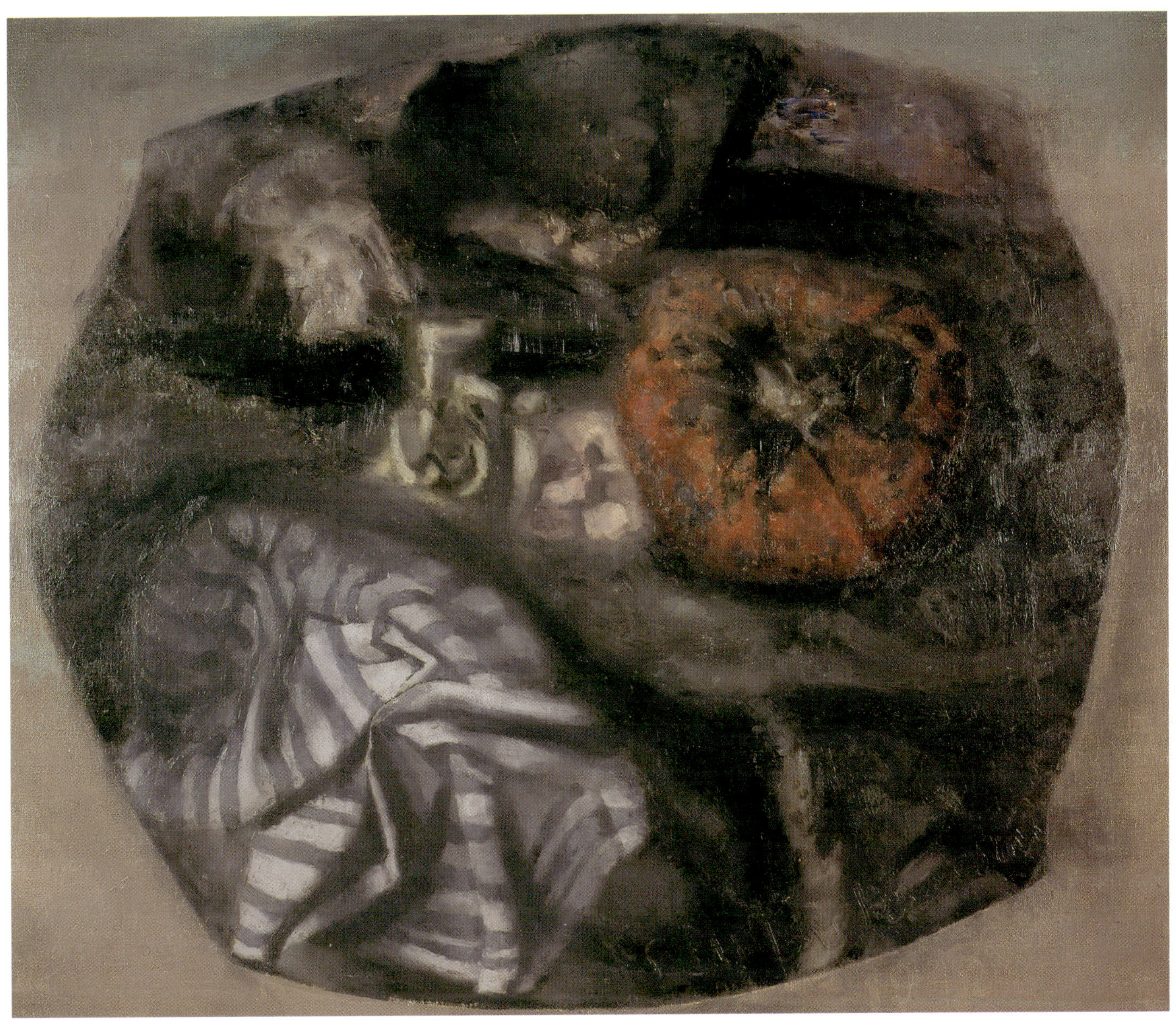

45 *Still Life, Rotting Squash,* 1941–42

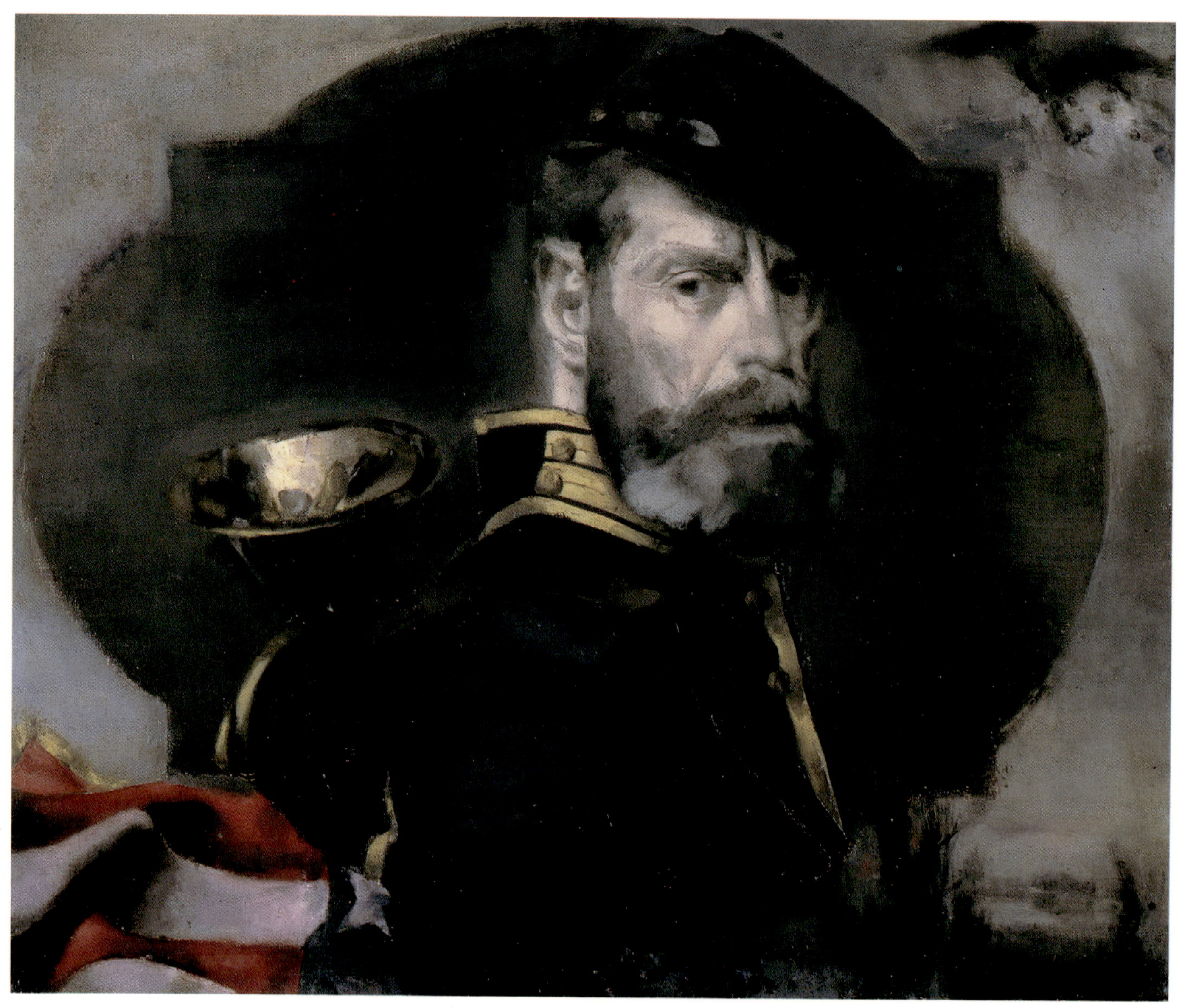

46 *Self-Portrait in Uniform*, 1942

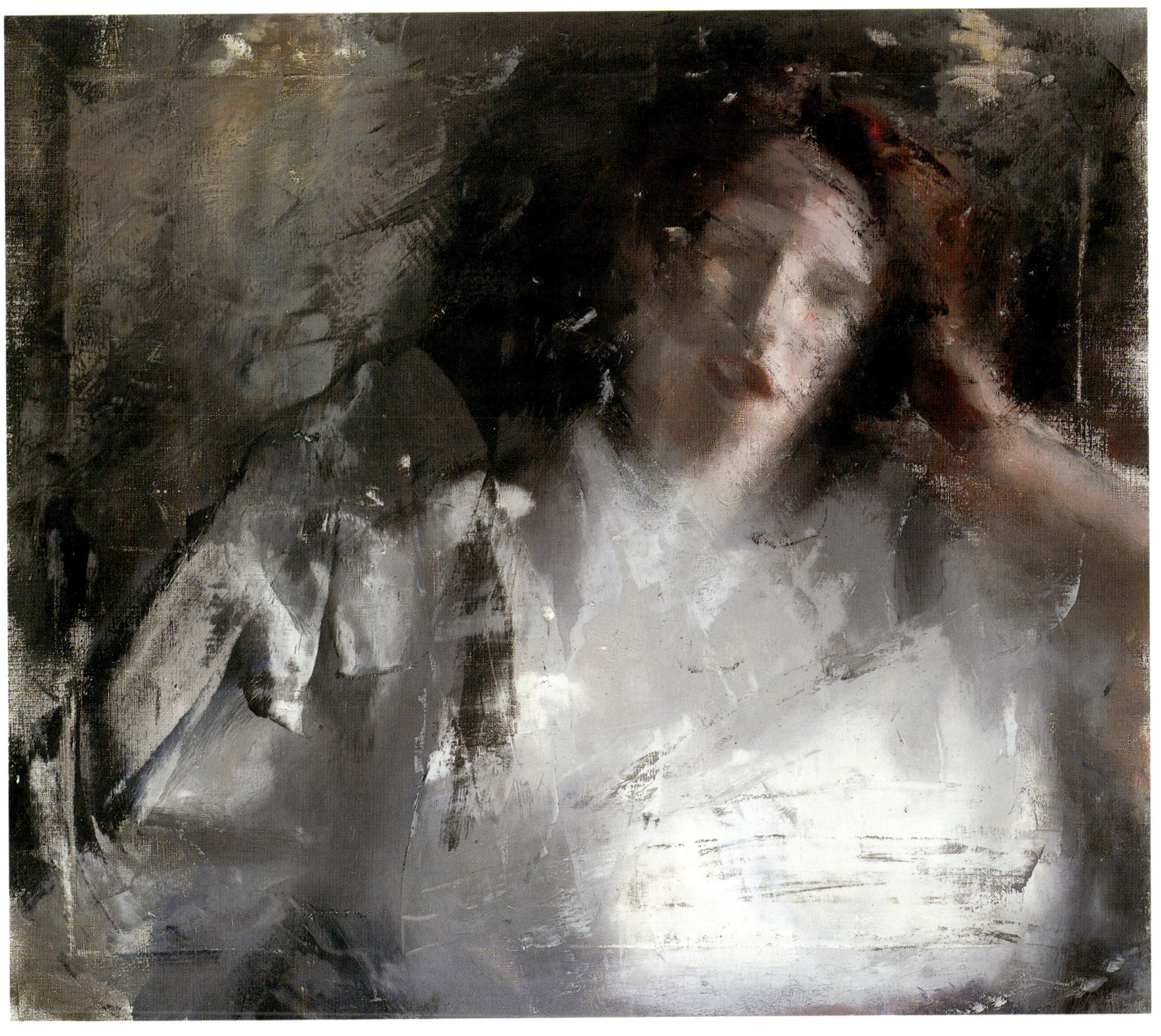

47 *Evangeline*, 1942

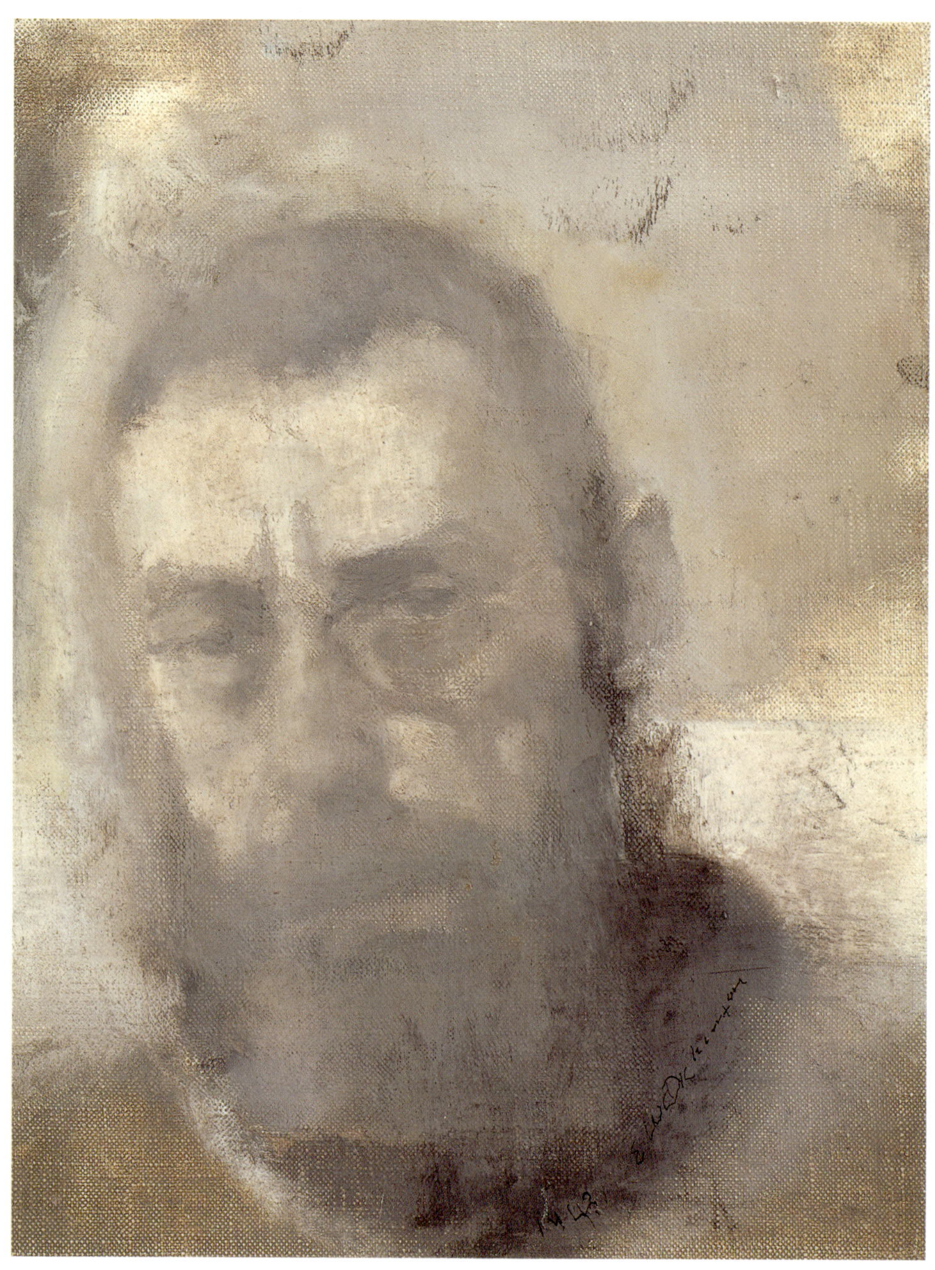

48 *Self-Portrait* [with Tilted Head], 1943

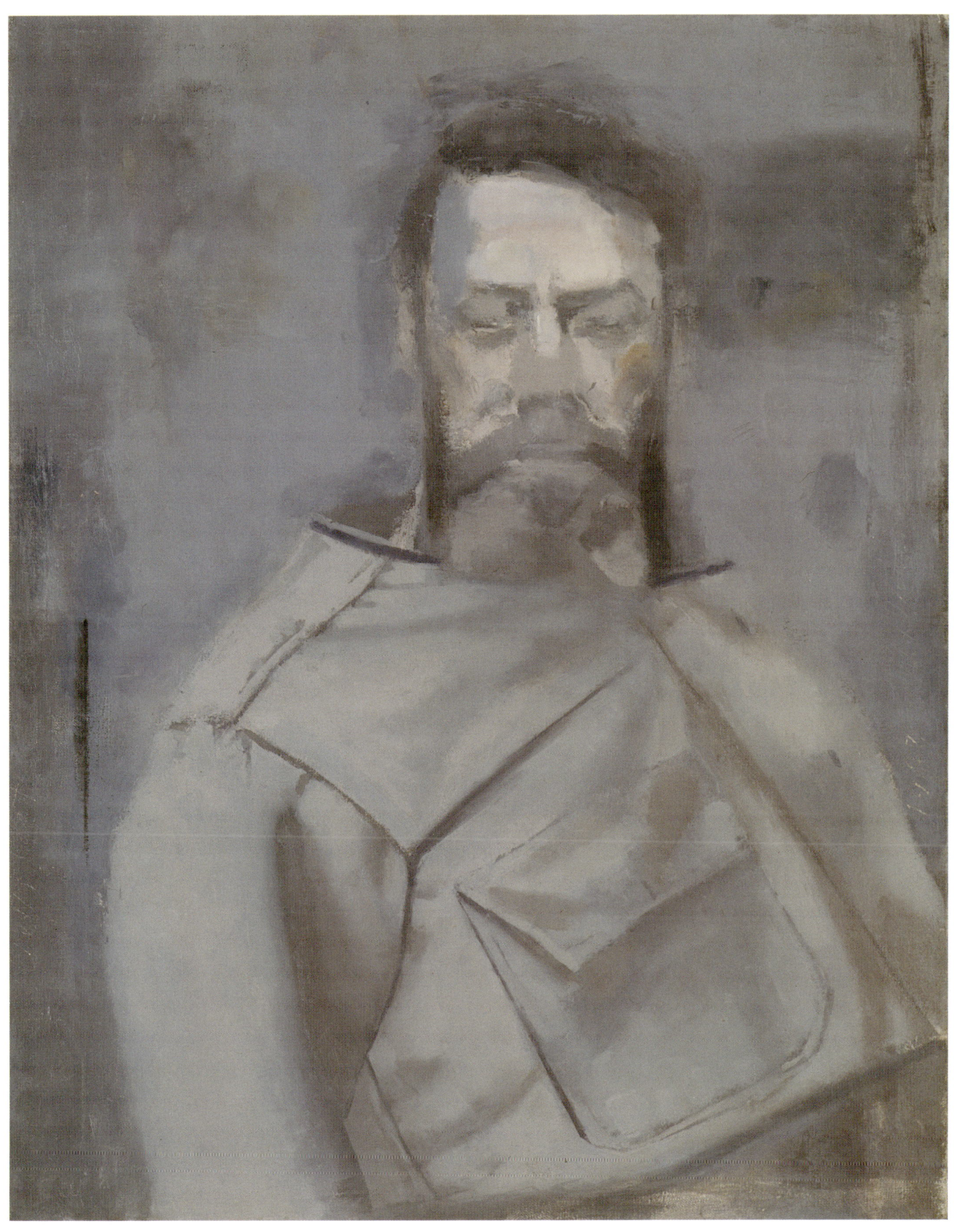

49 *Self-Portrait in Gray Shirt*, 1943

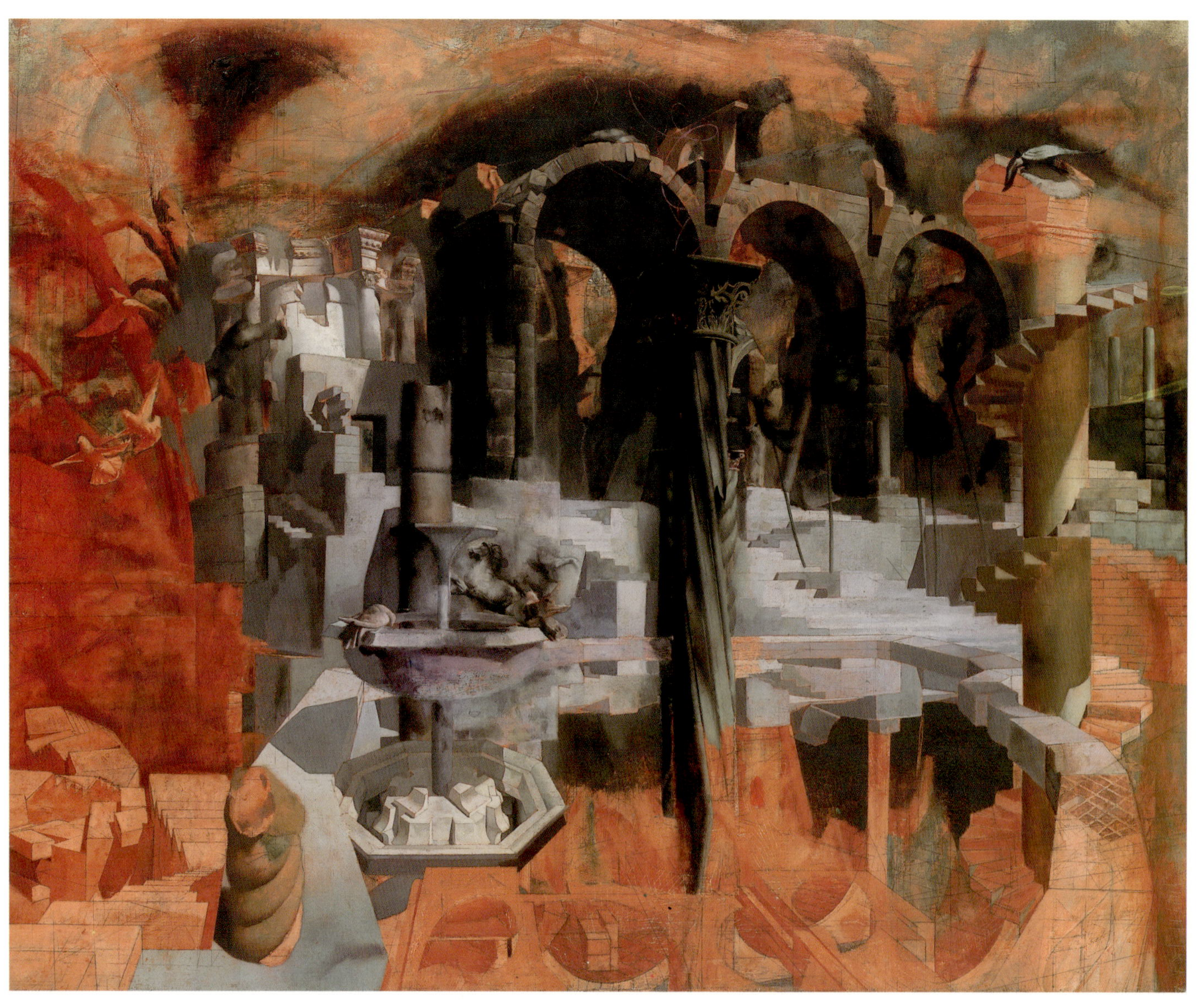

50 *Ruin at Daphne*, 1943–53

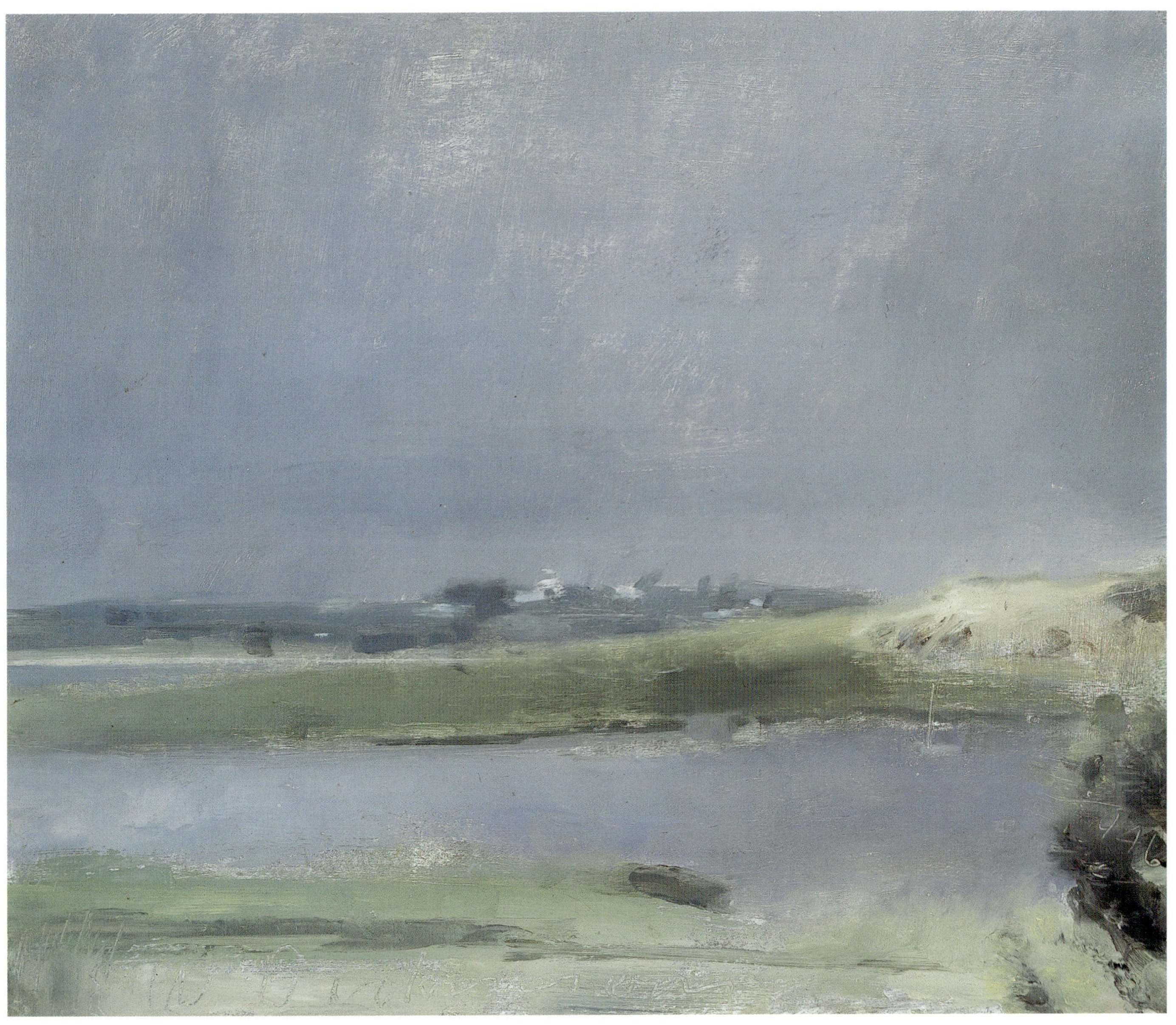

51 *Cove, Wellfleet*, 1946

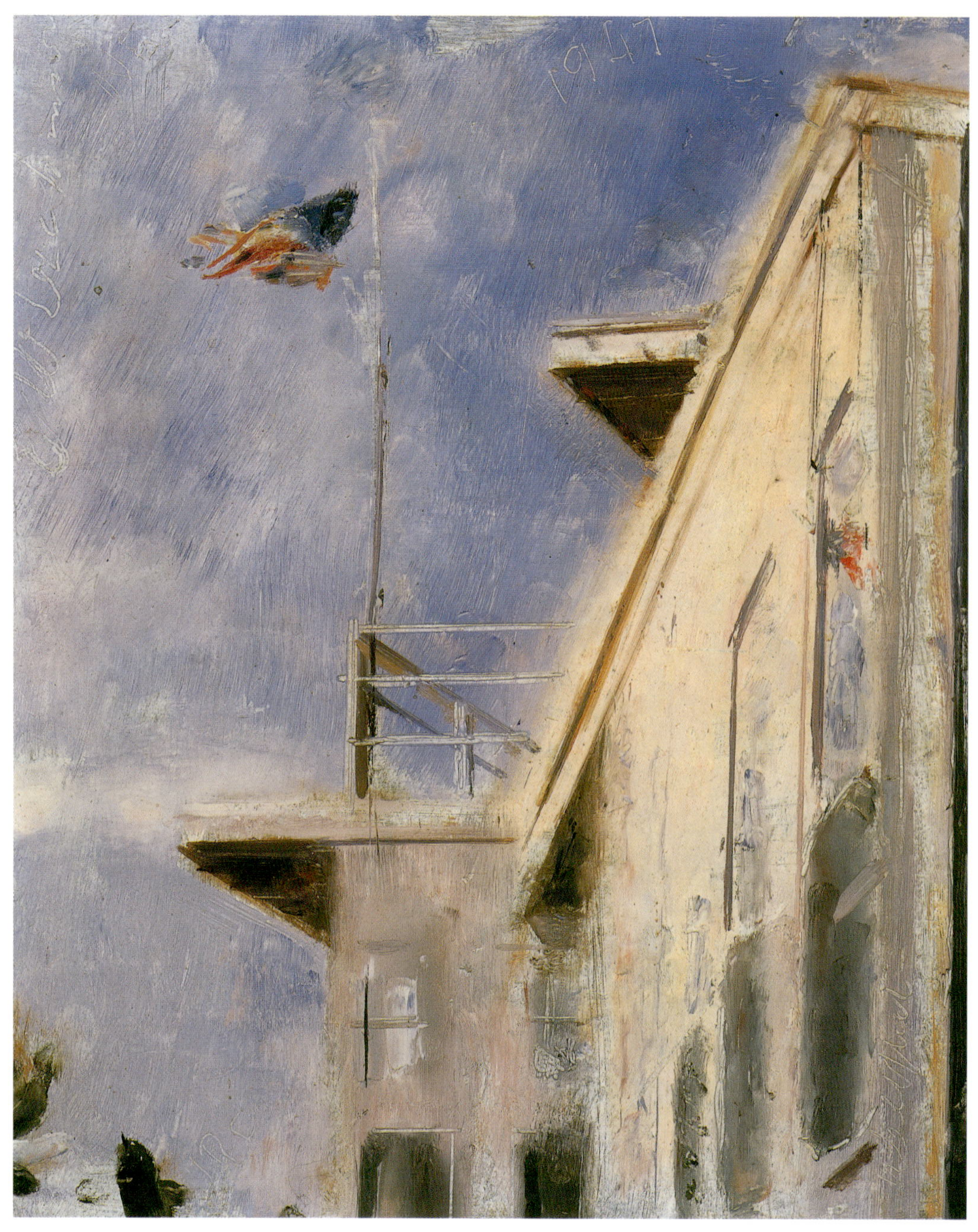

52 *The Flag, Frazier's House*, 1947

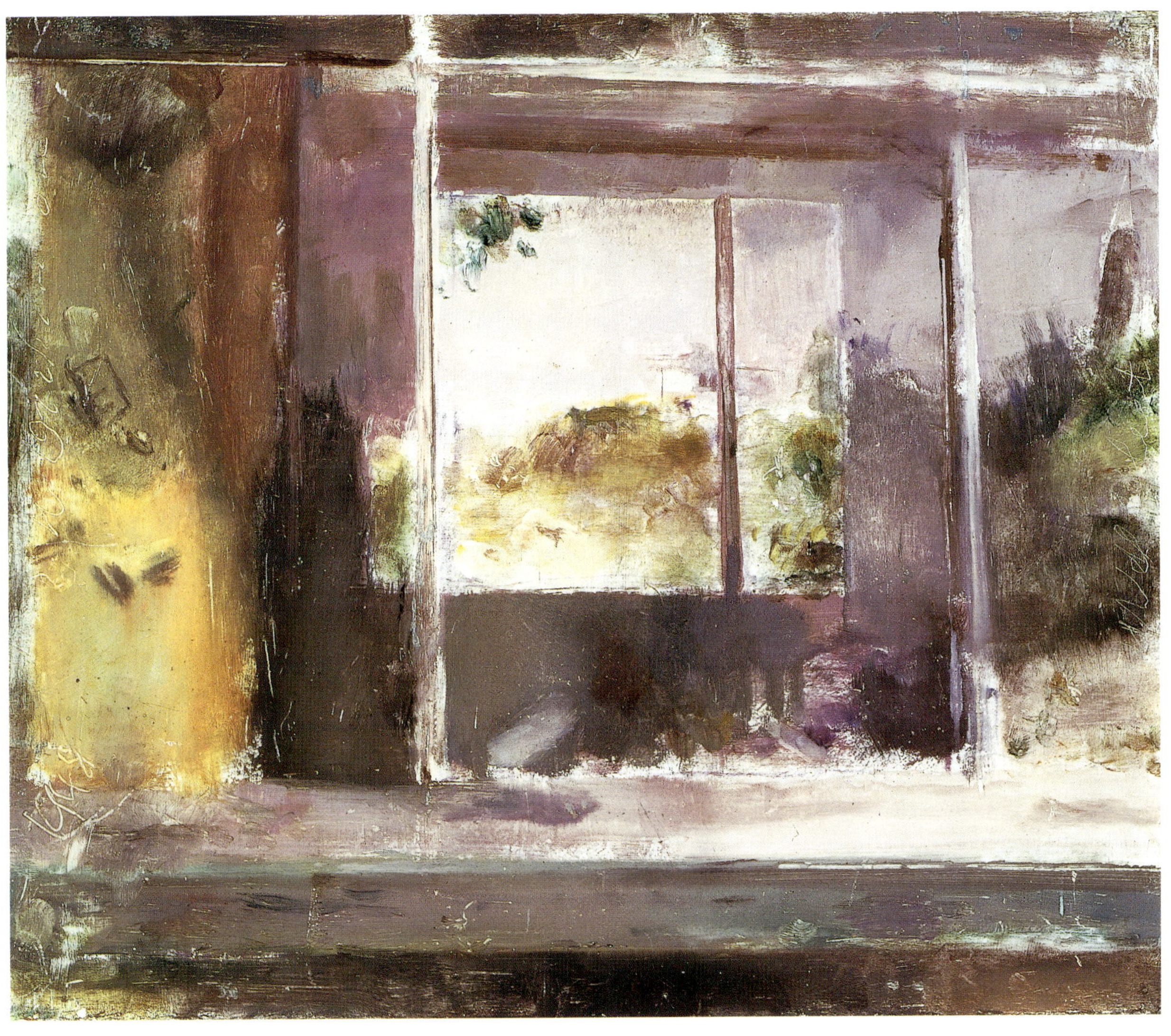

53 *Through Two Cottage Windows*, 1948

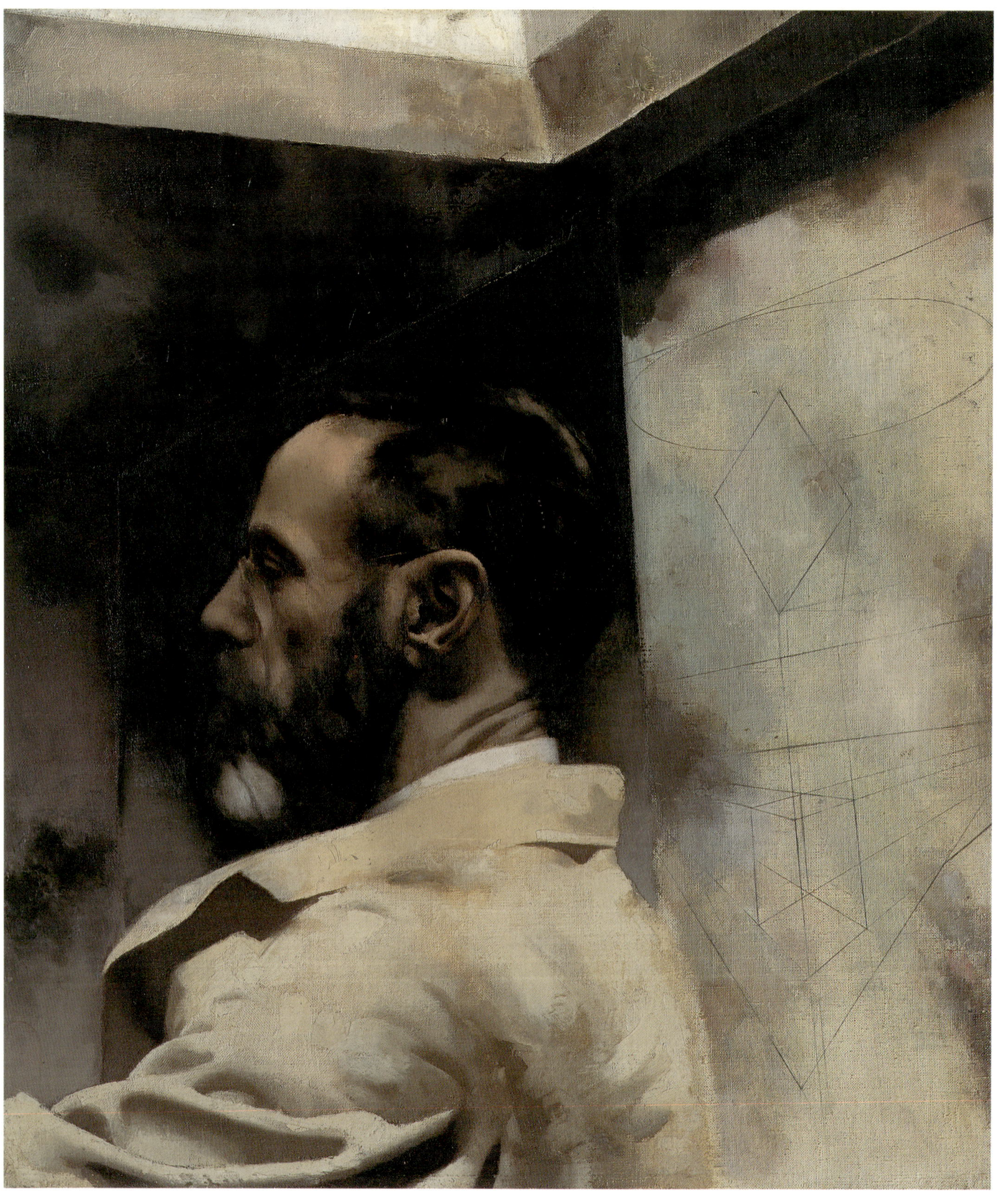

54 *Self-Portrait*, 1949

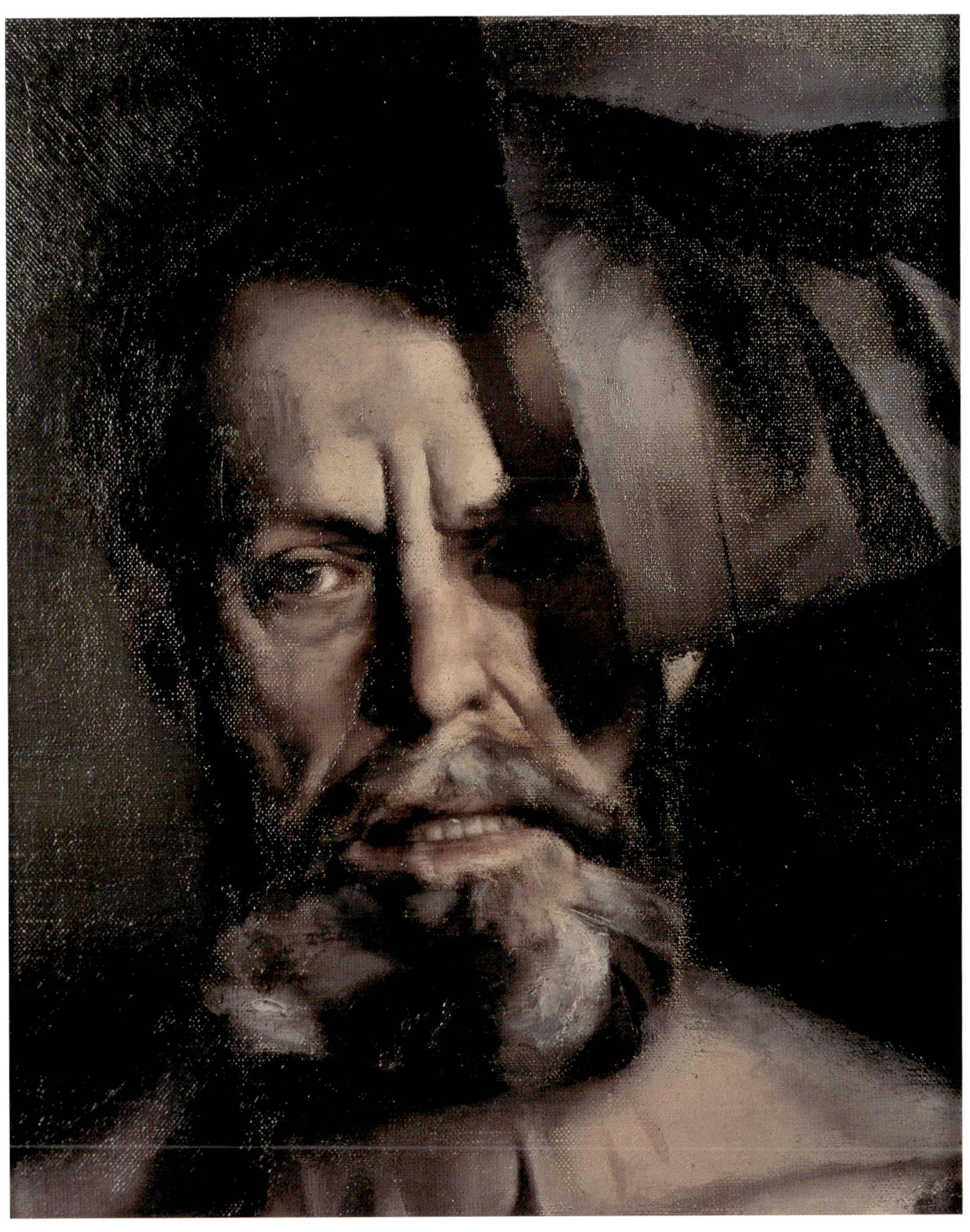

55 *Self-Portrait*, 1950

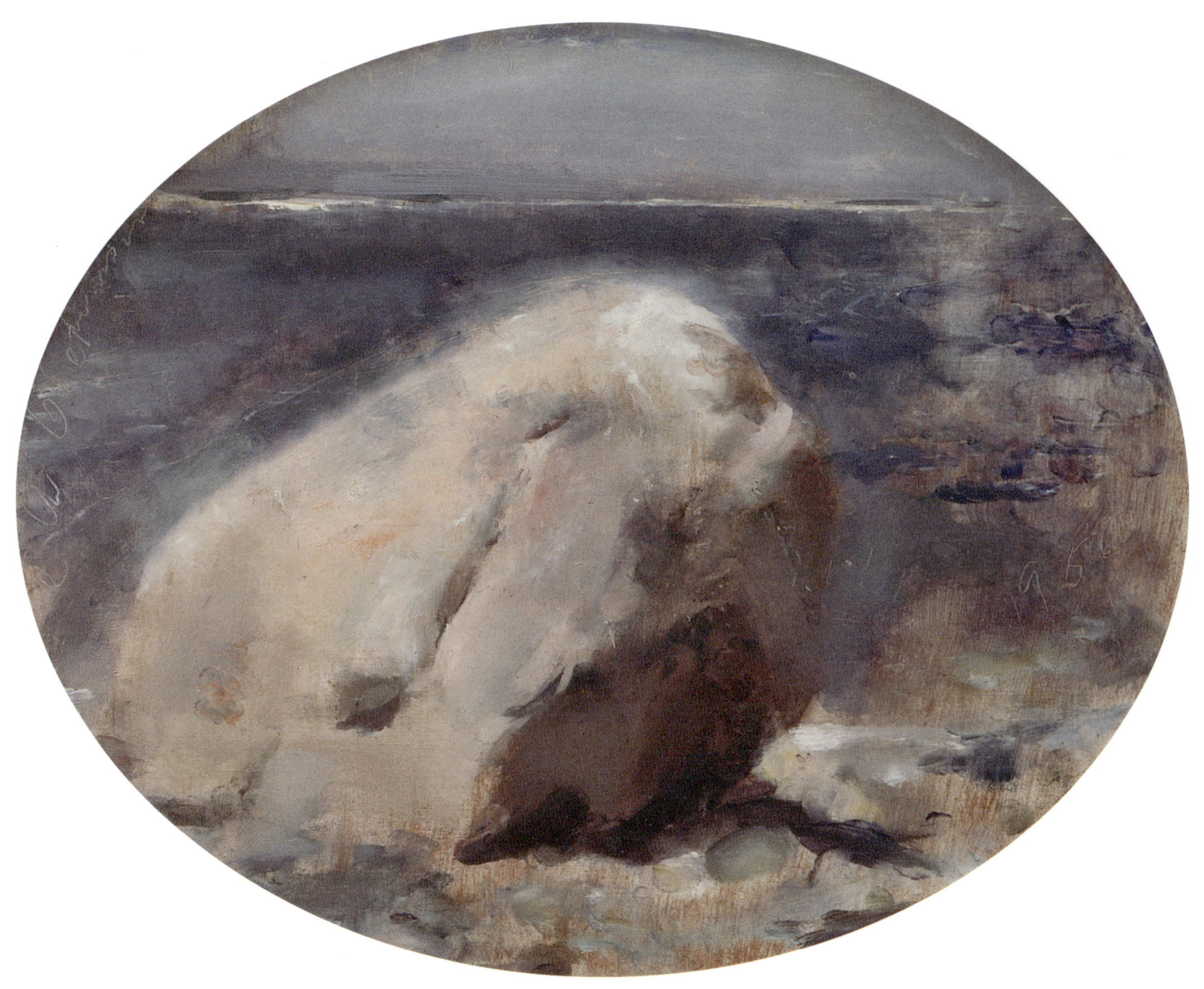

56 *Rock, Cape Poge*, 1950

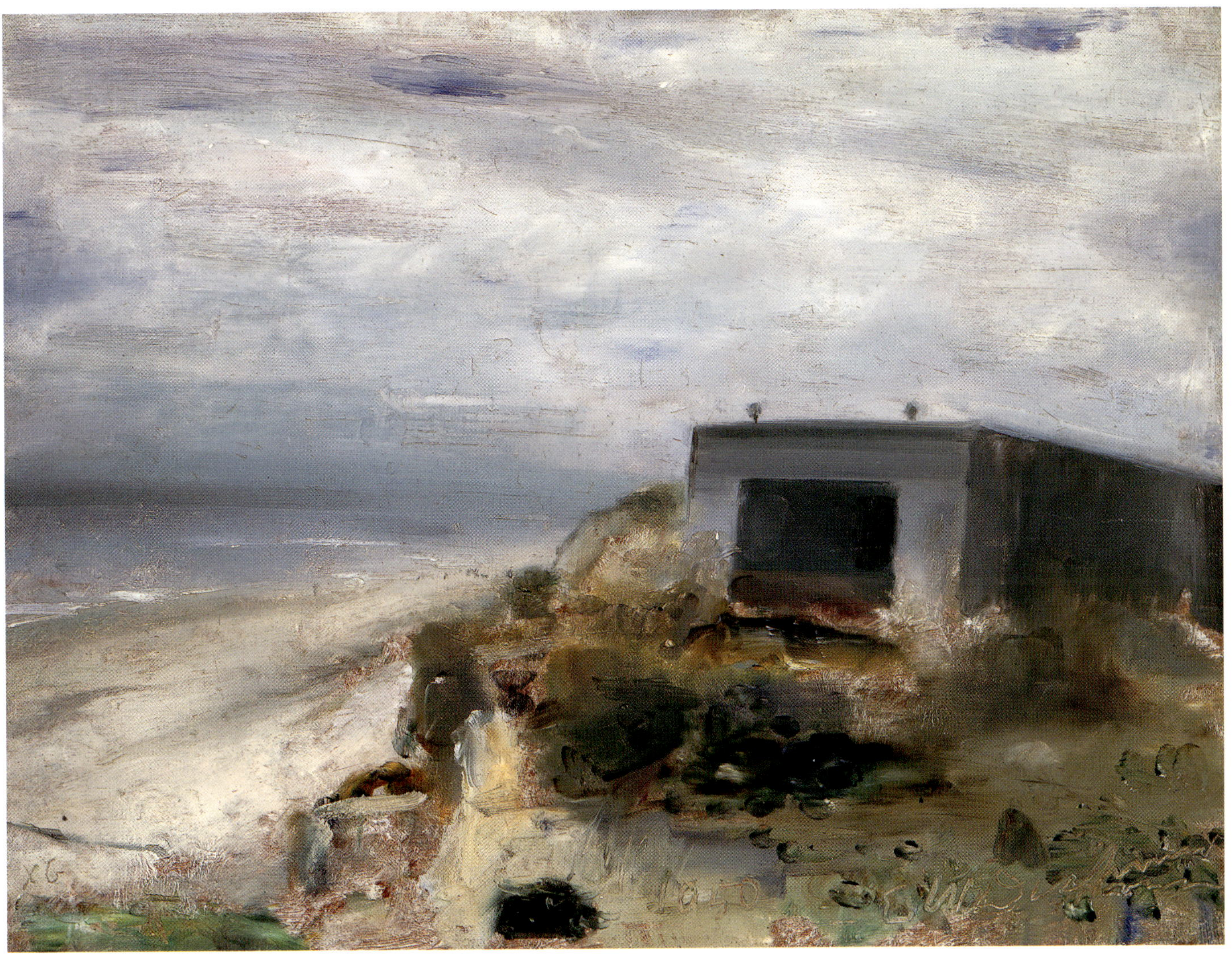

57 *Gonzalez Studio*, 1950

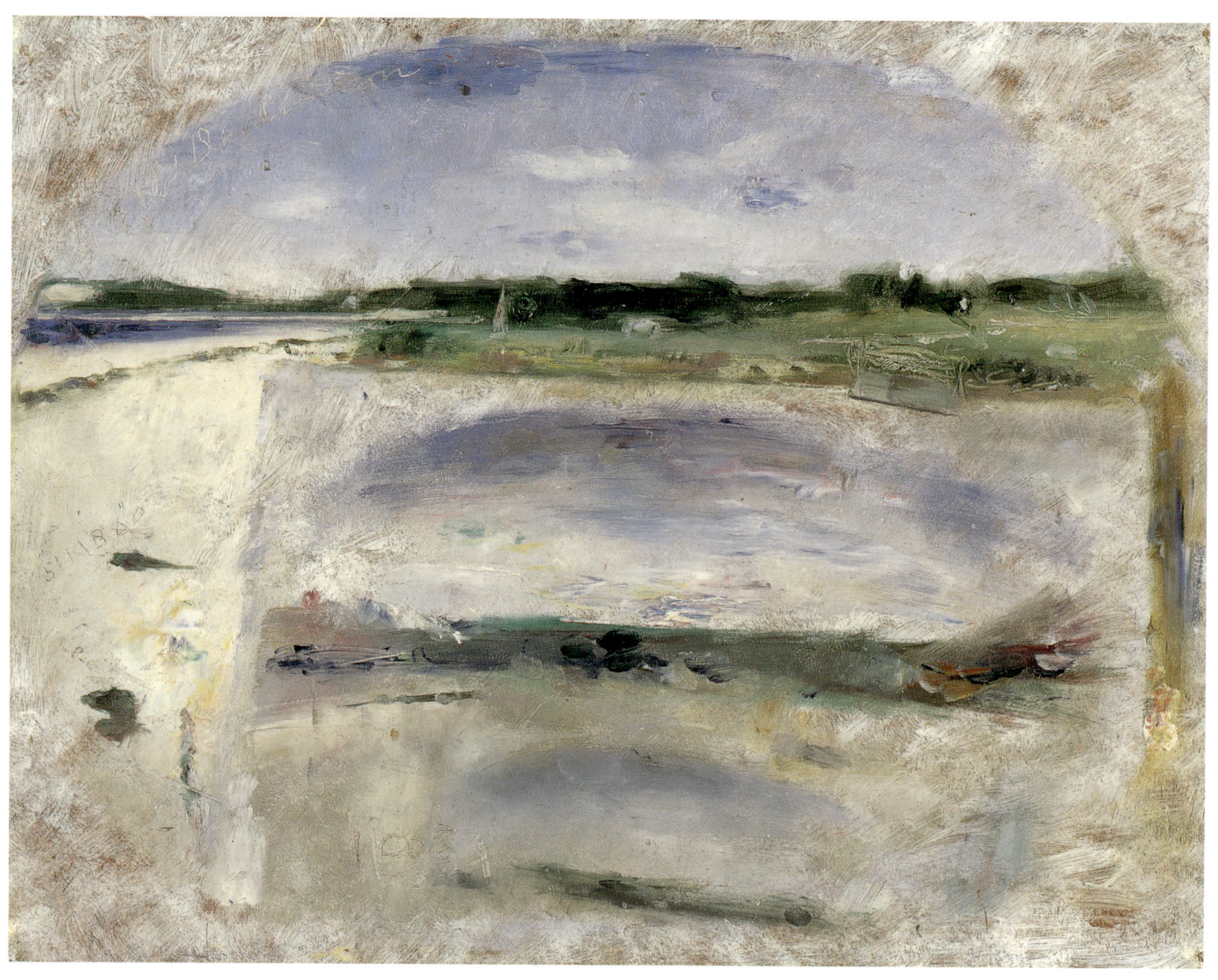

58 *Mayo's Beach from Indian Neck*, 1951

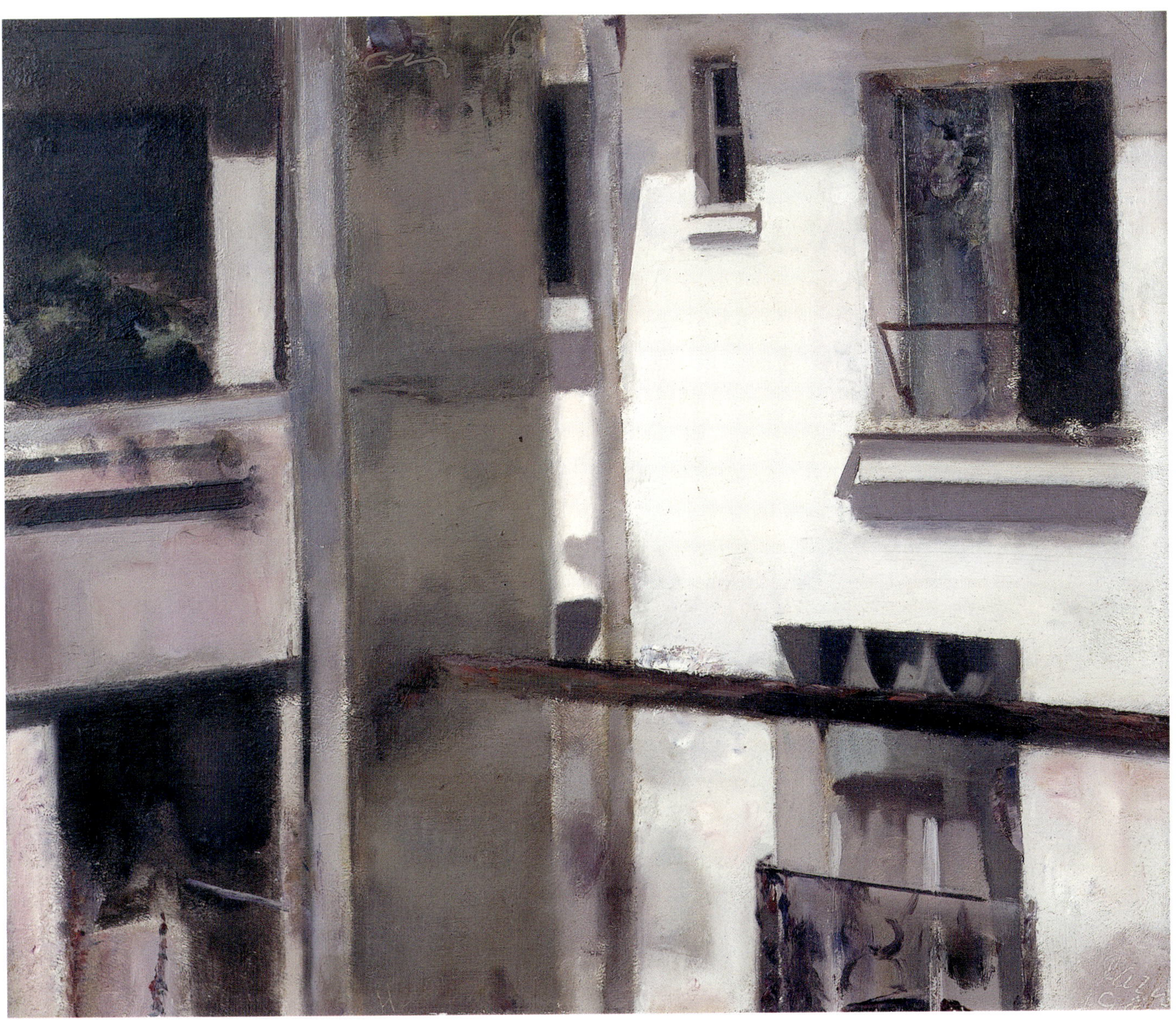

59 *Paris Windows*, 1952

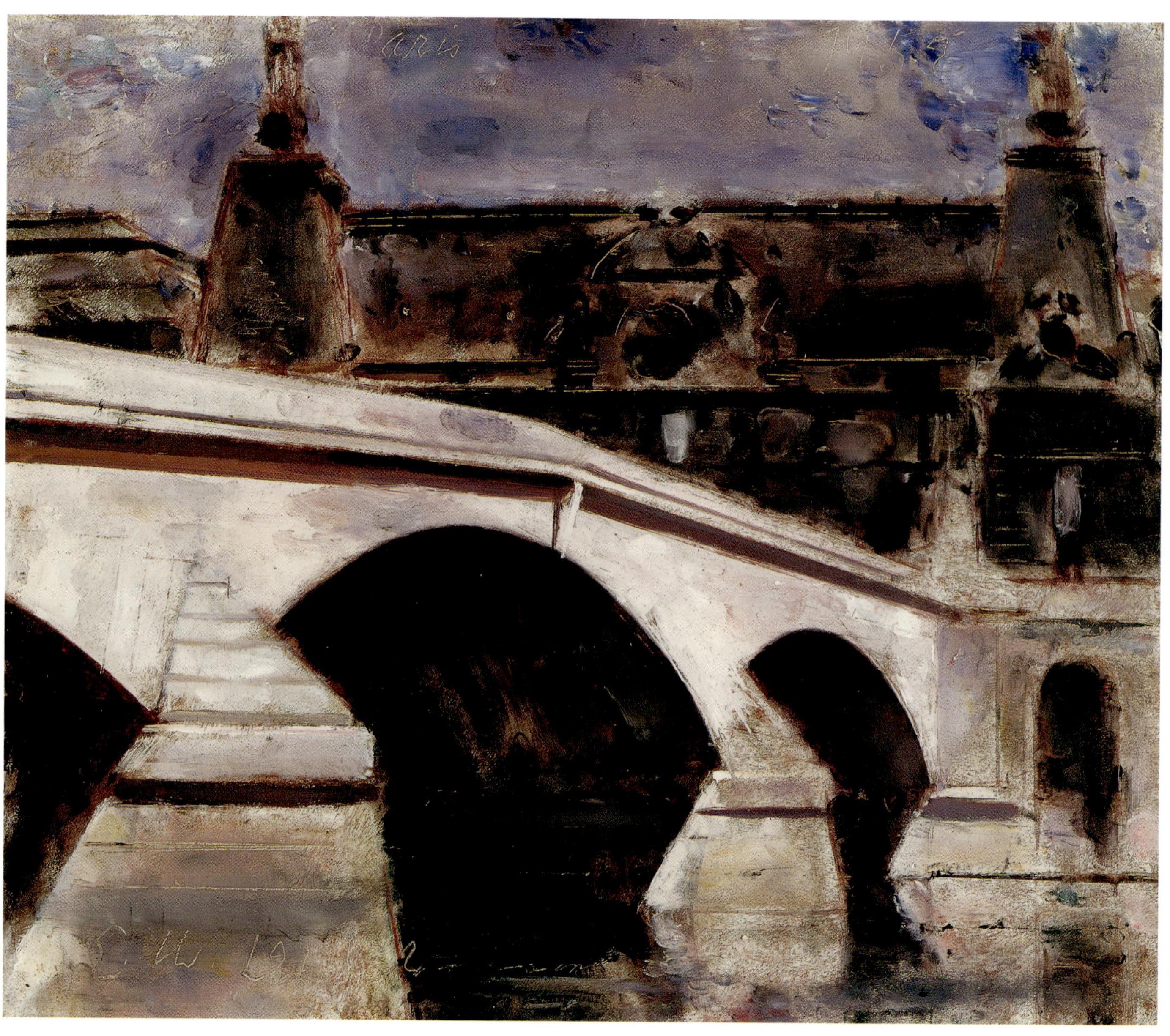

60 *Carrousel Bridge, Paris,* 1952

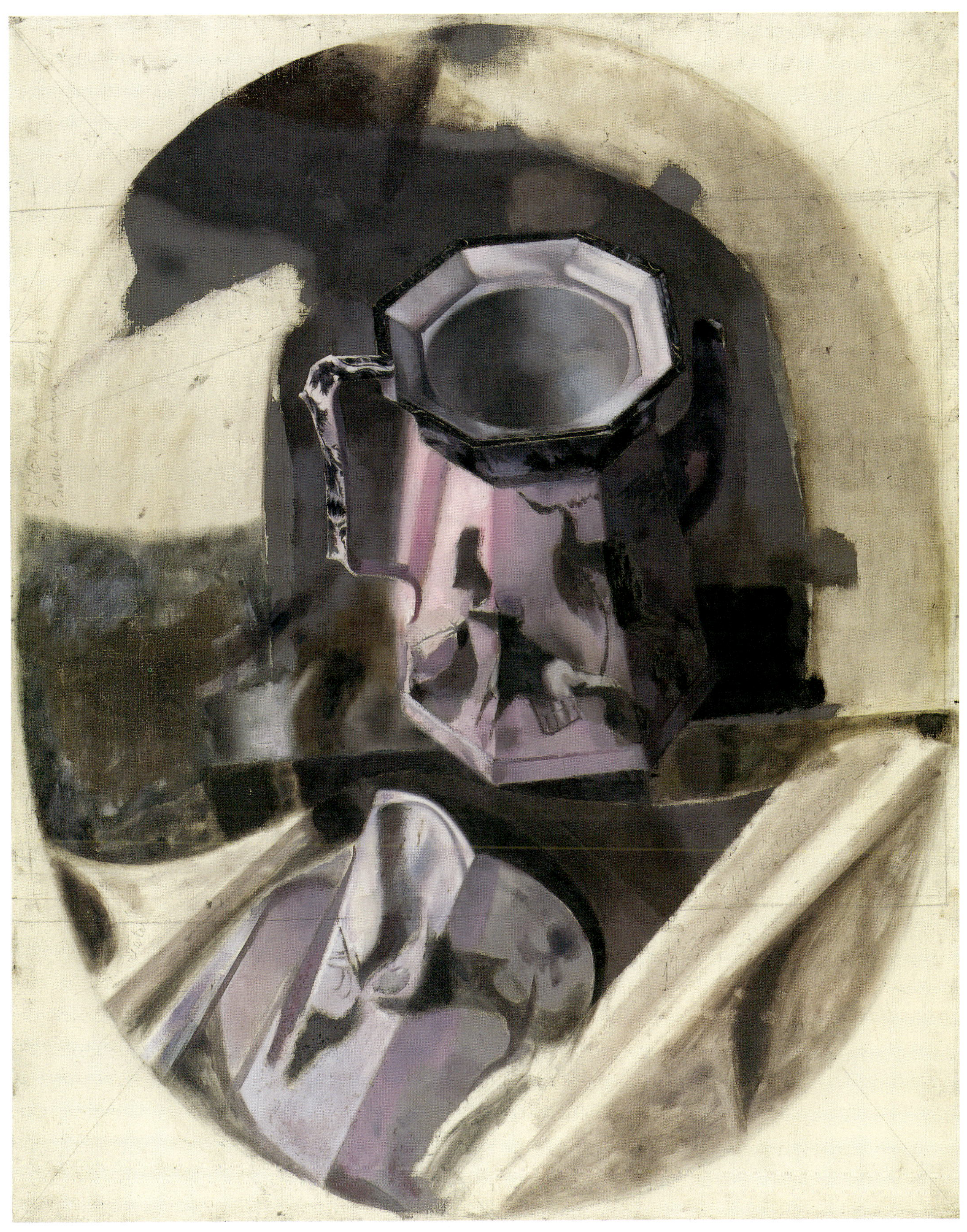

61 *Still Life, Lascaux,* 1953

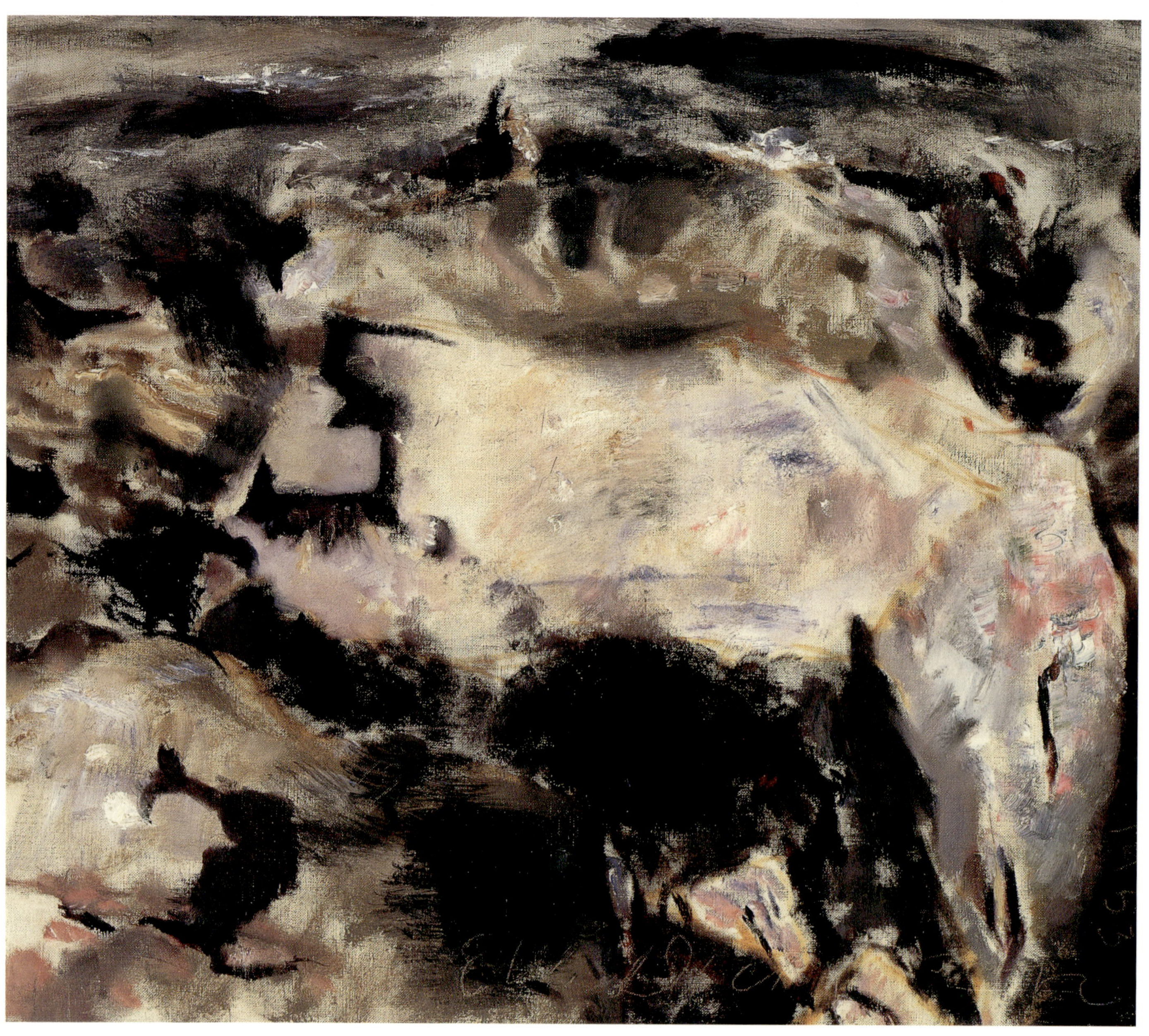

62 *Surf, Point Lookout*, 1953

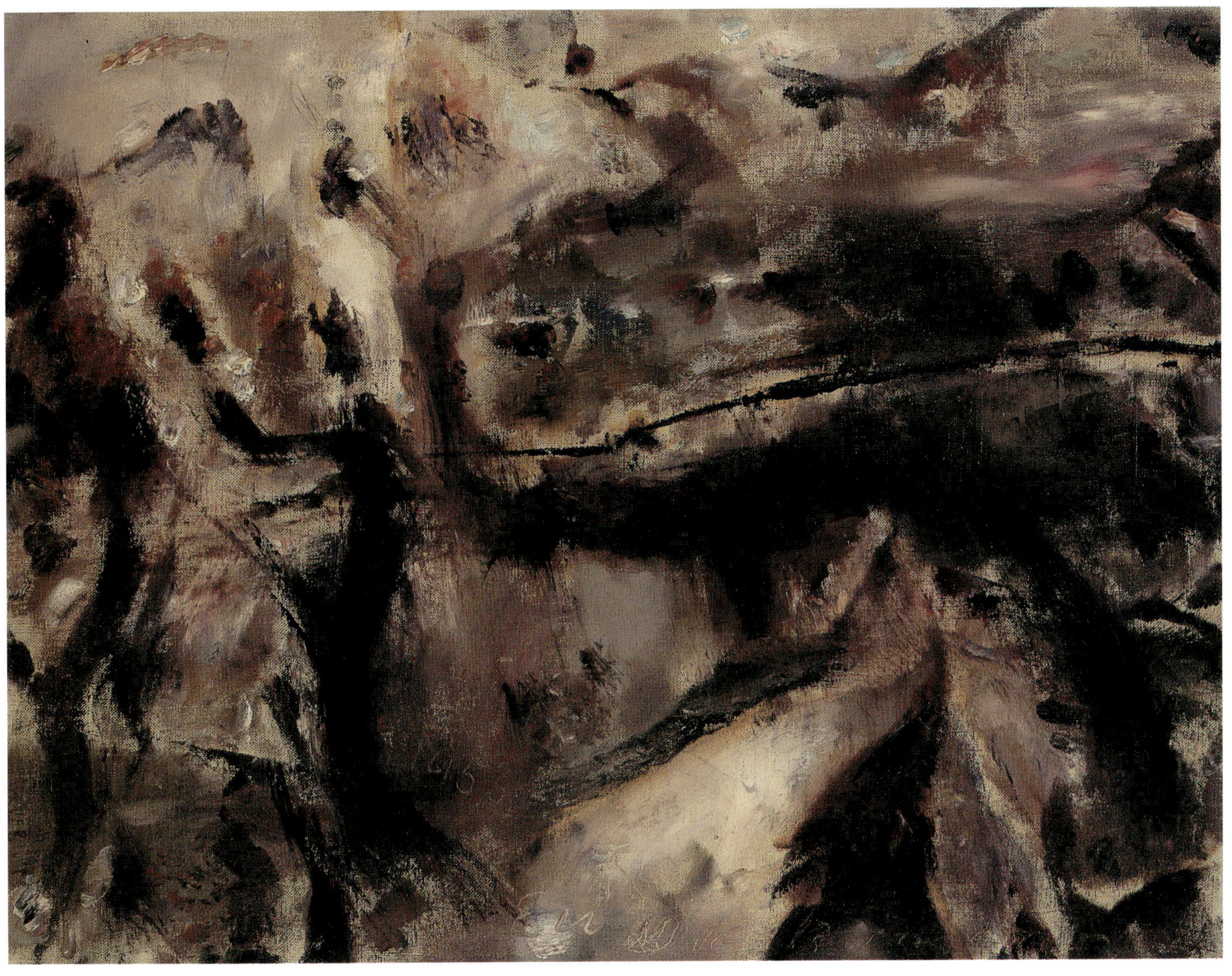

63 *Quarry, Riverdale*, 1953

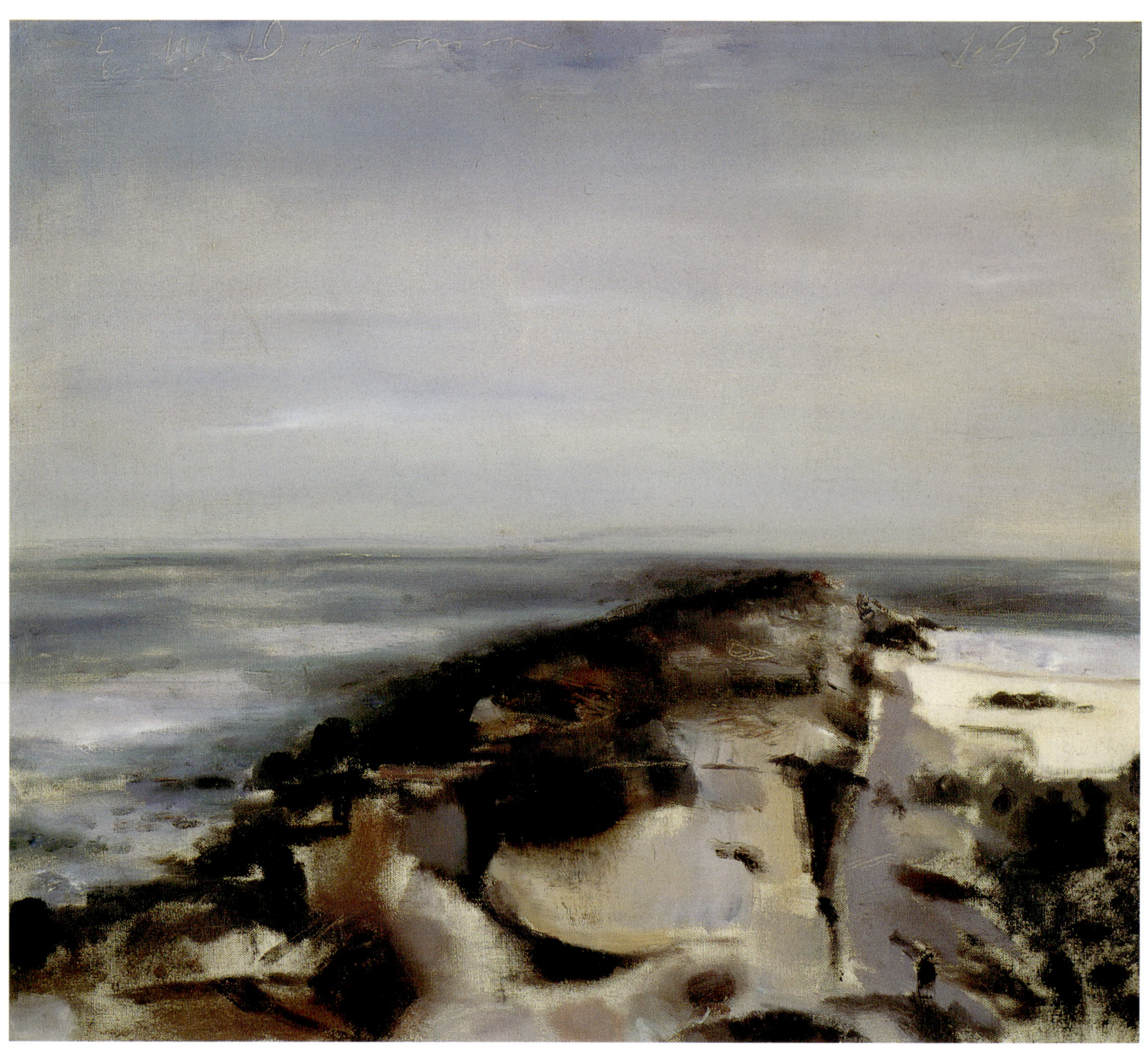

64 *Jetty, Point Lookout,* 1953

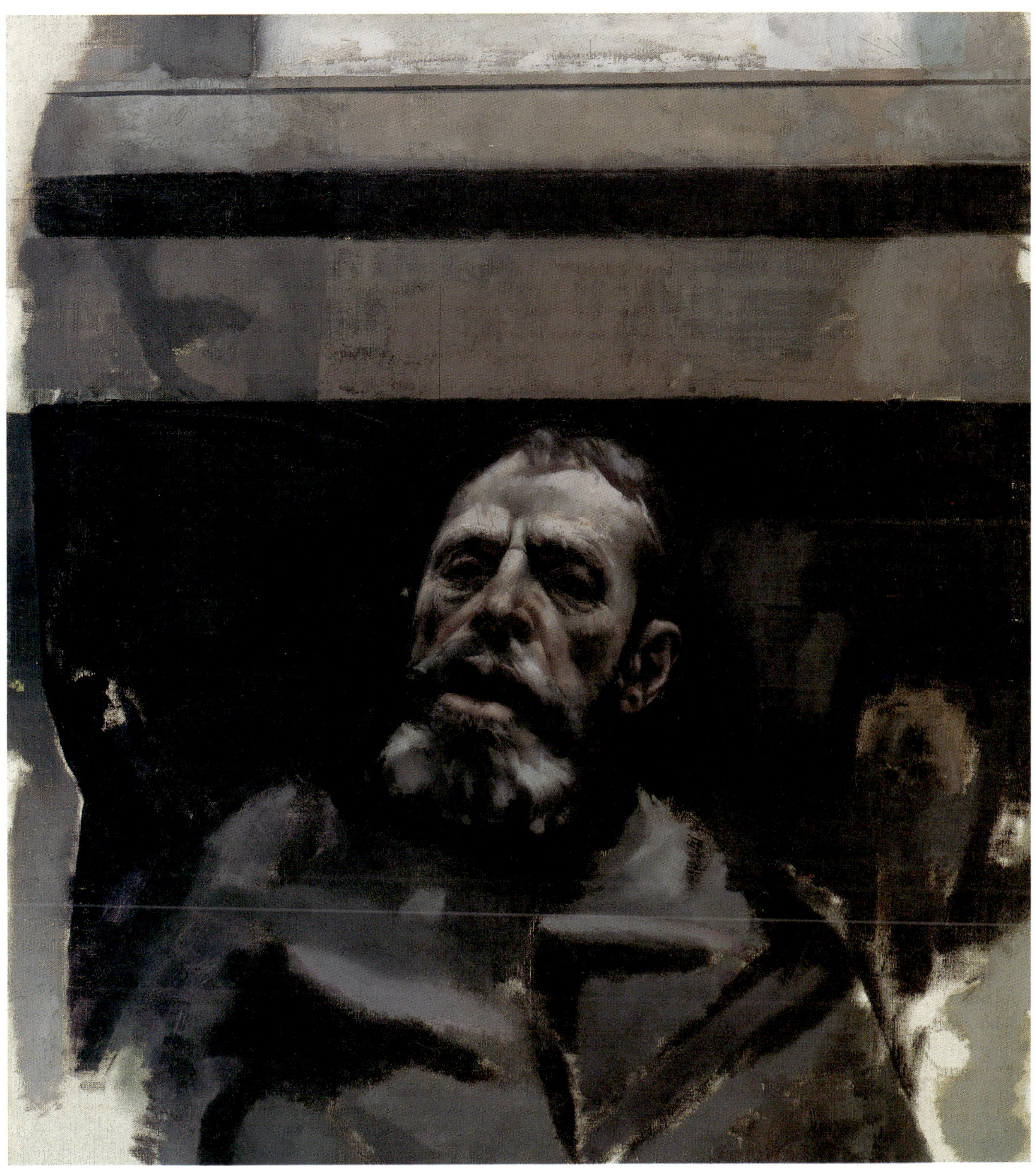

65 *Self-Portrait*, 1954

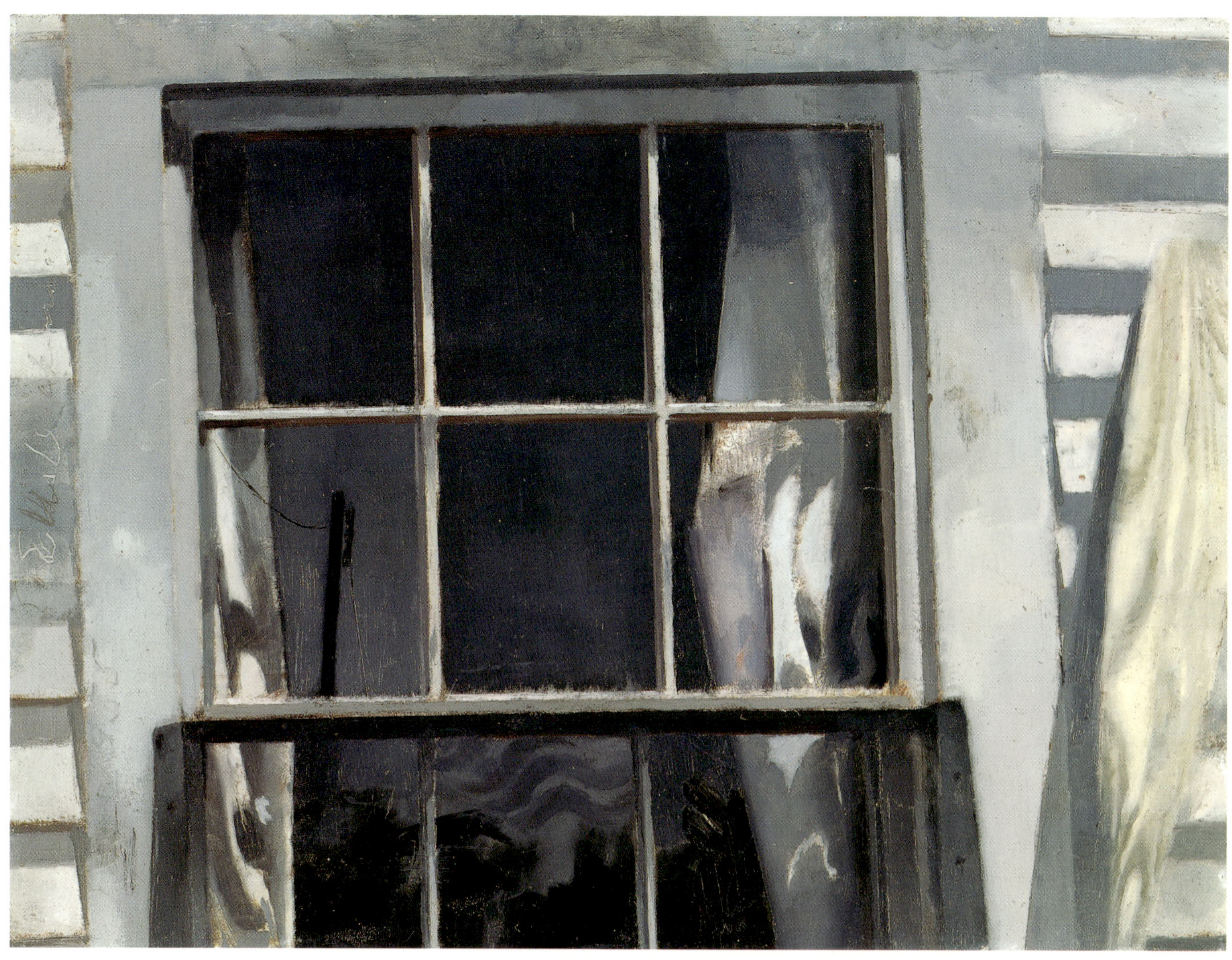

66 *Window and Oar*, 1955

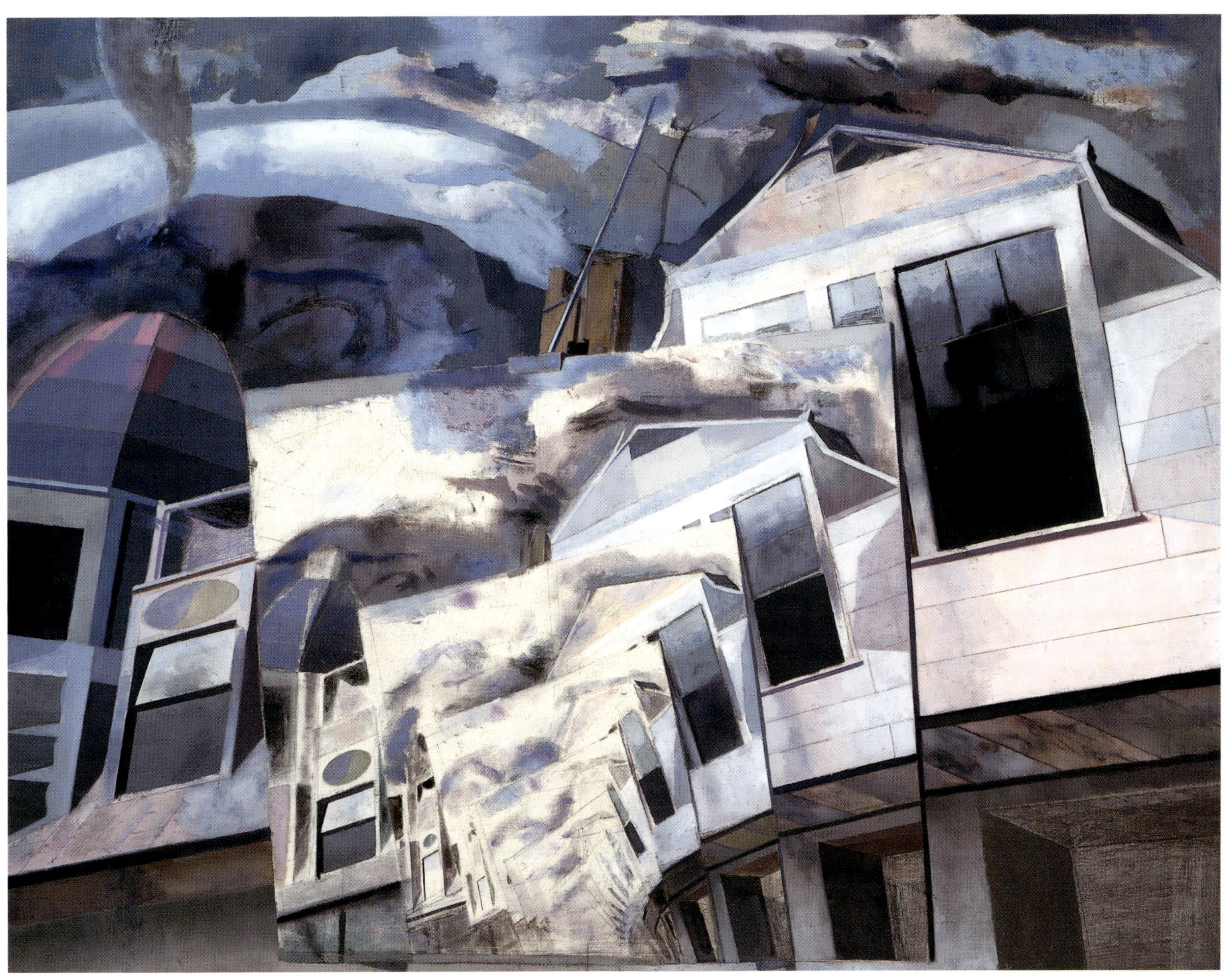

67 *South Wellfleet Inn*, 1955–60

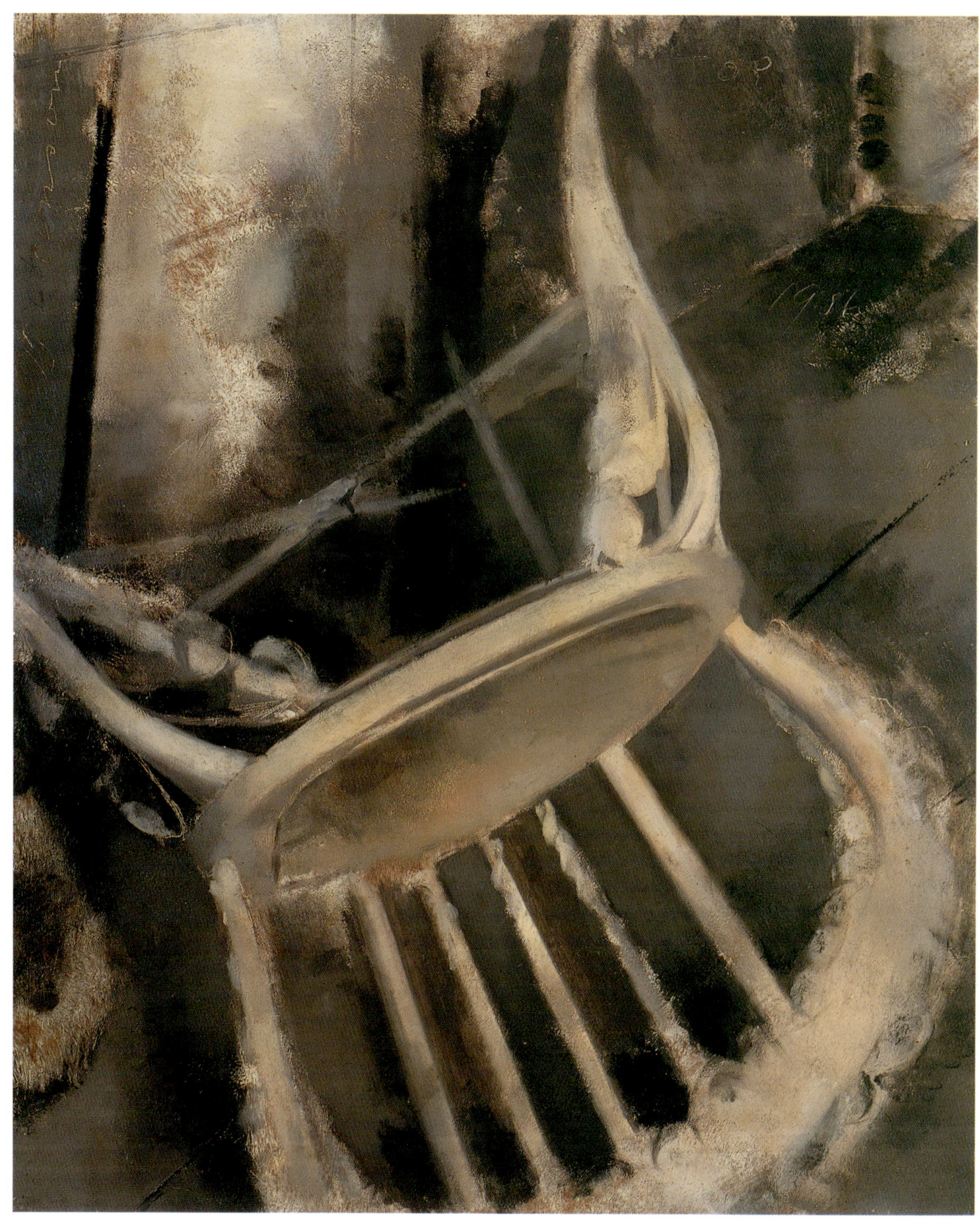

68 *Chair, Skowhegan I*, 1956

Works on Paper

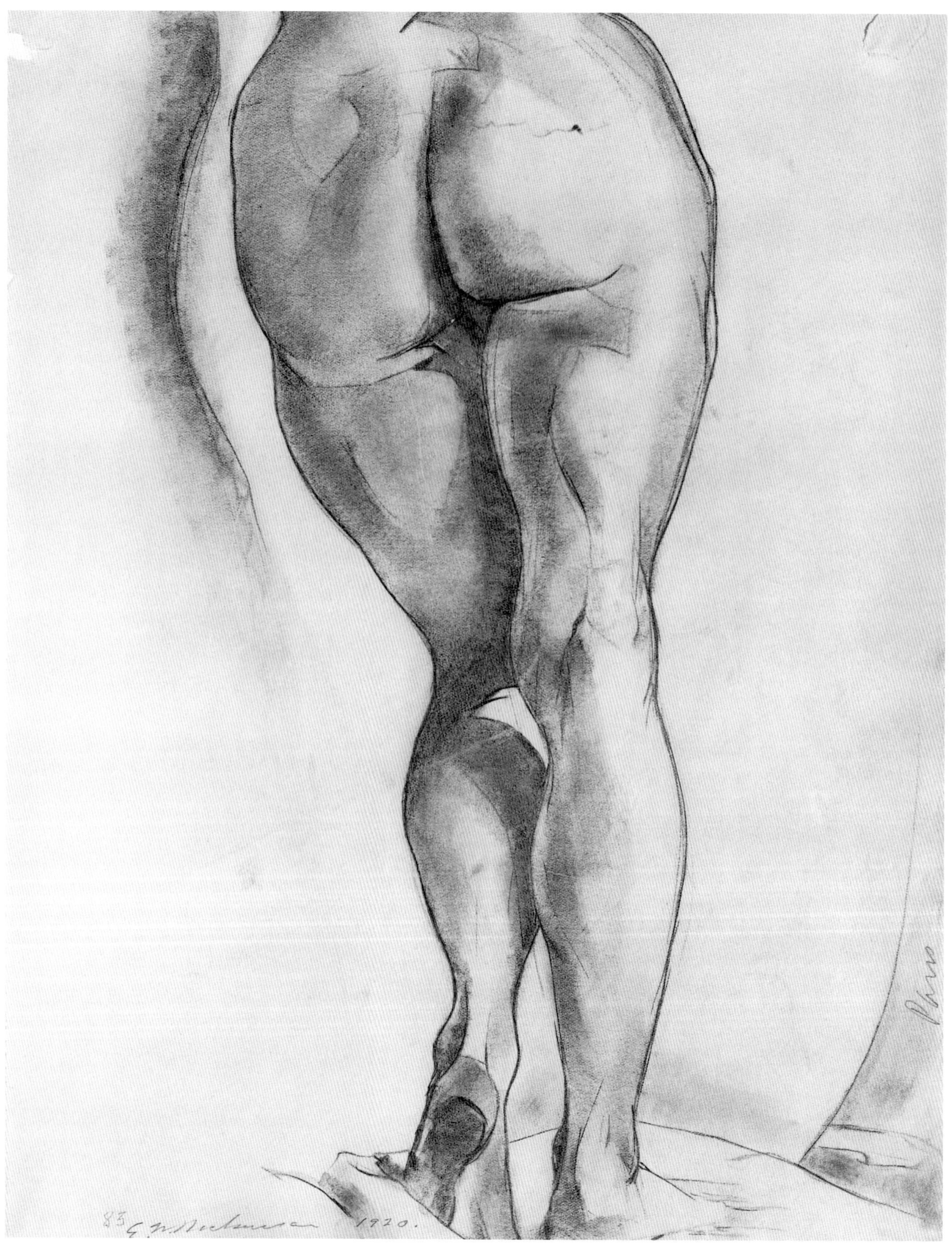

69 *Nude (Standing Nude, Hips and Legs)*, 1920

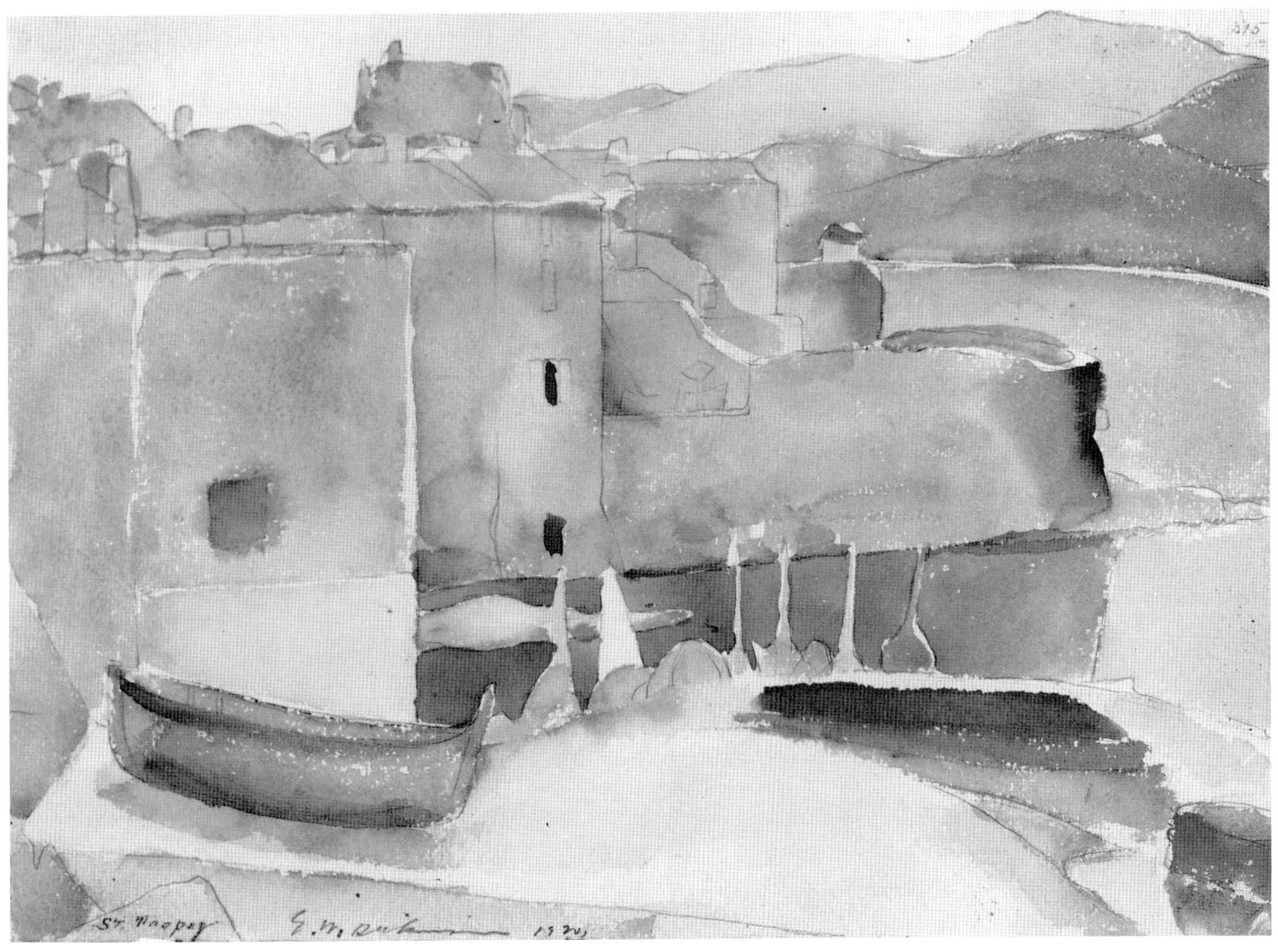

70 *St. Tropez Yacht Basin in Winter*, 1920

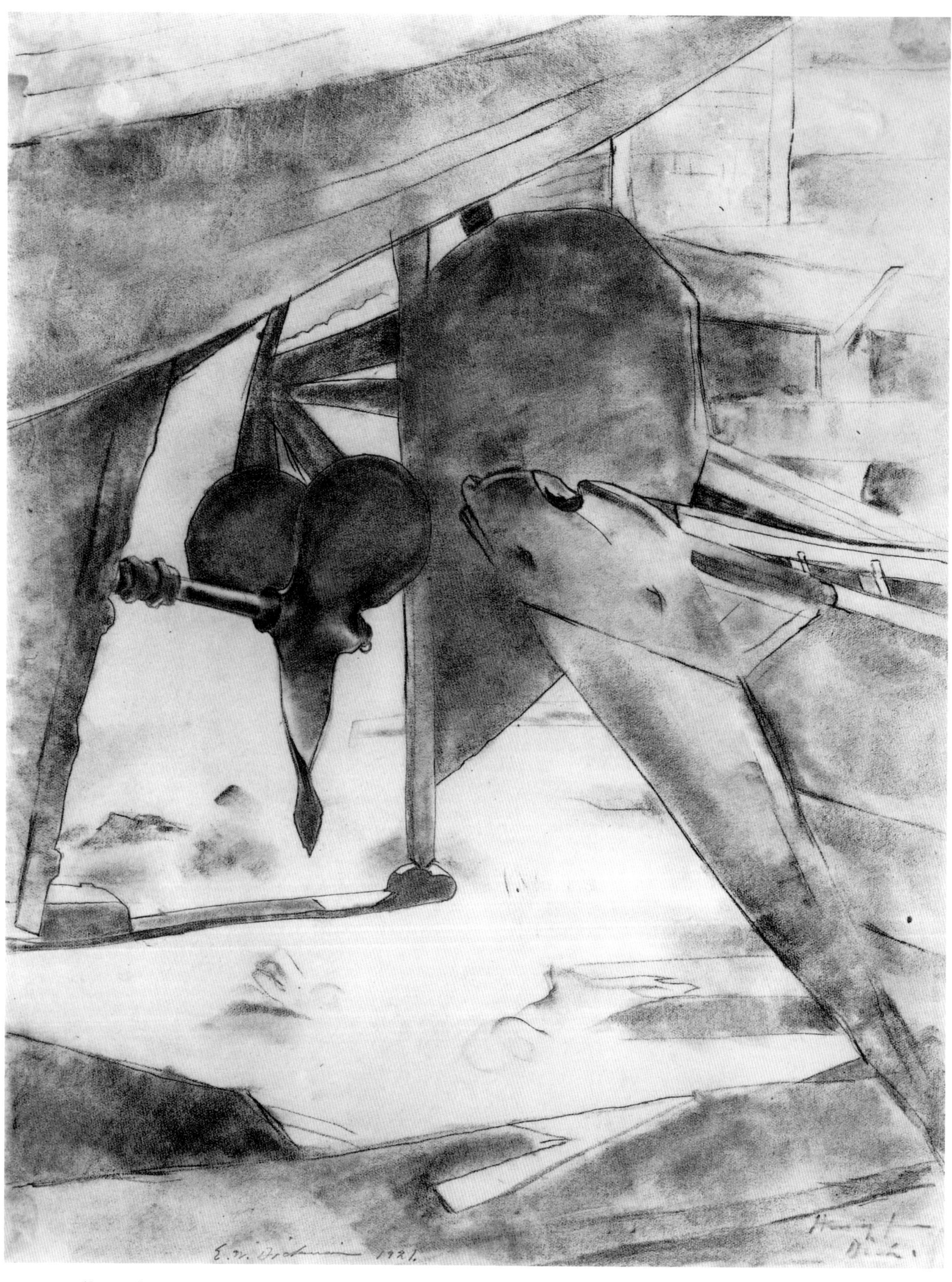

71 *Propeller and Dory*, 1921

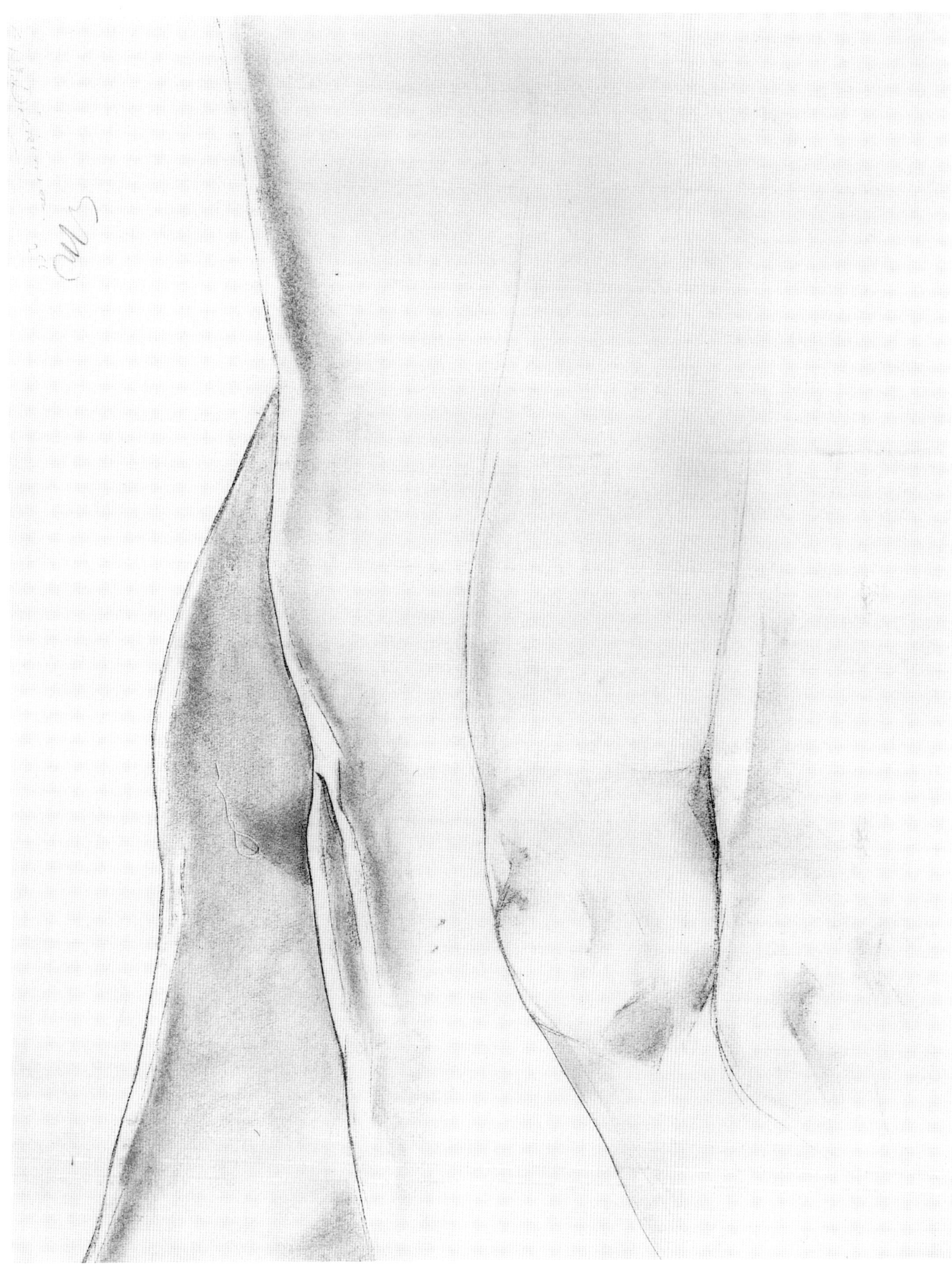

72 *Nude, Helen Souza,* 1925

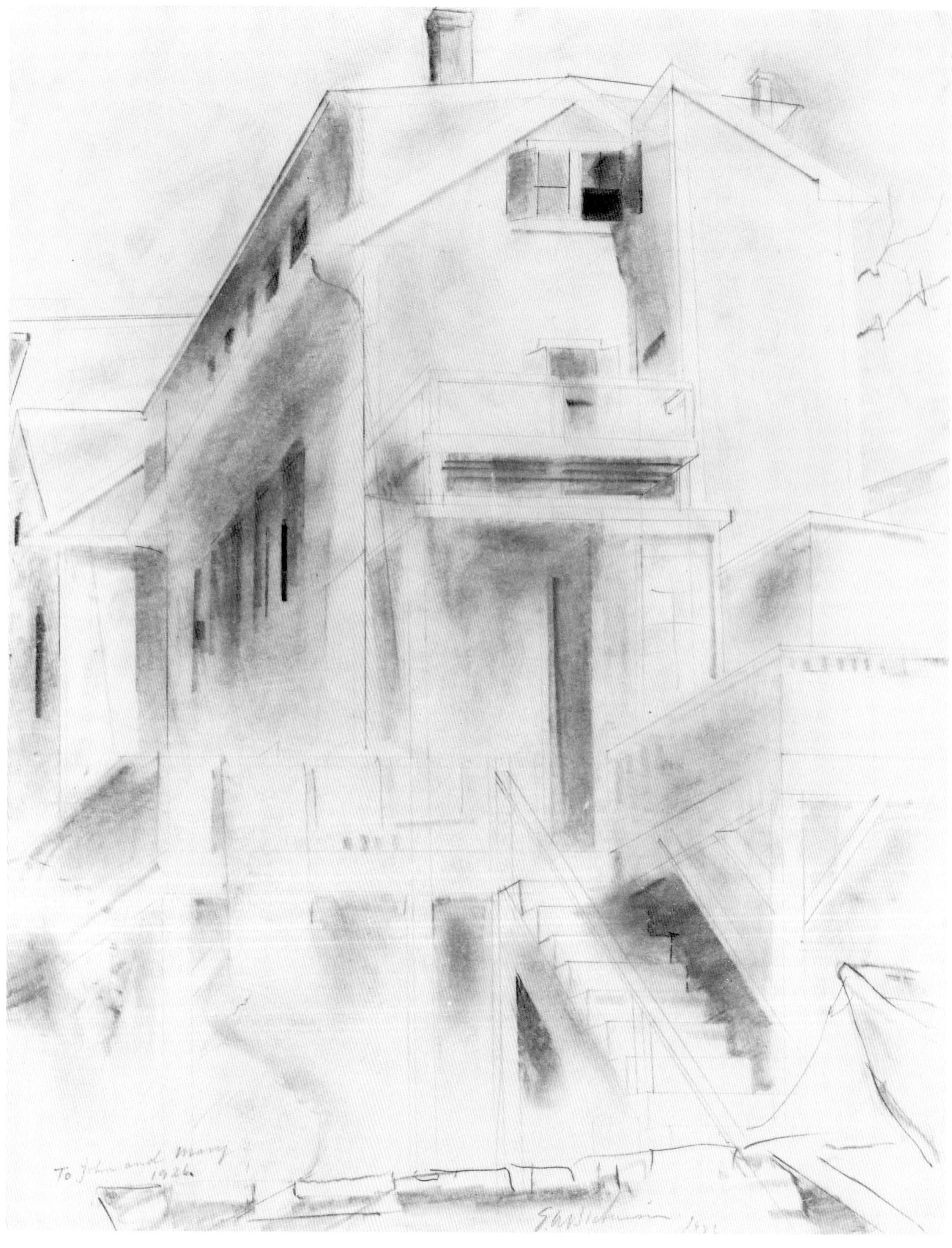

73 *Beach House*, 1926

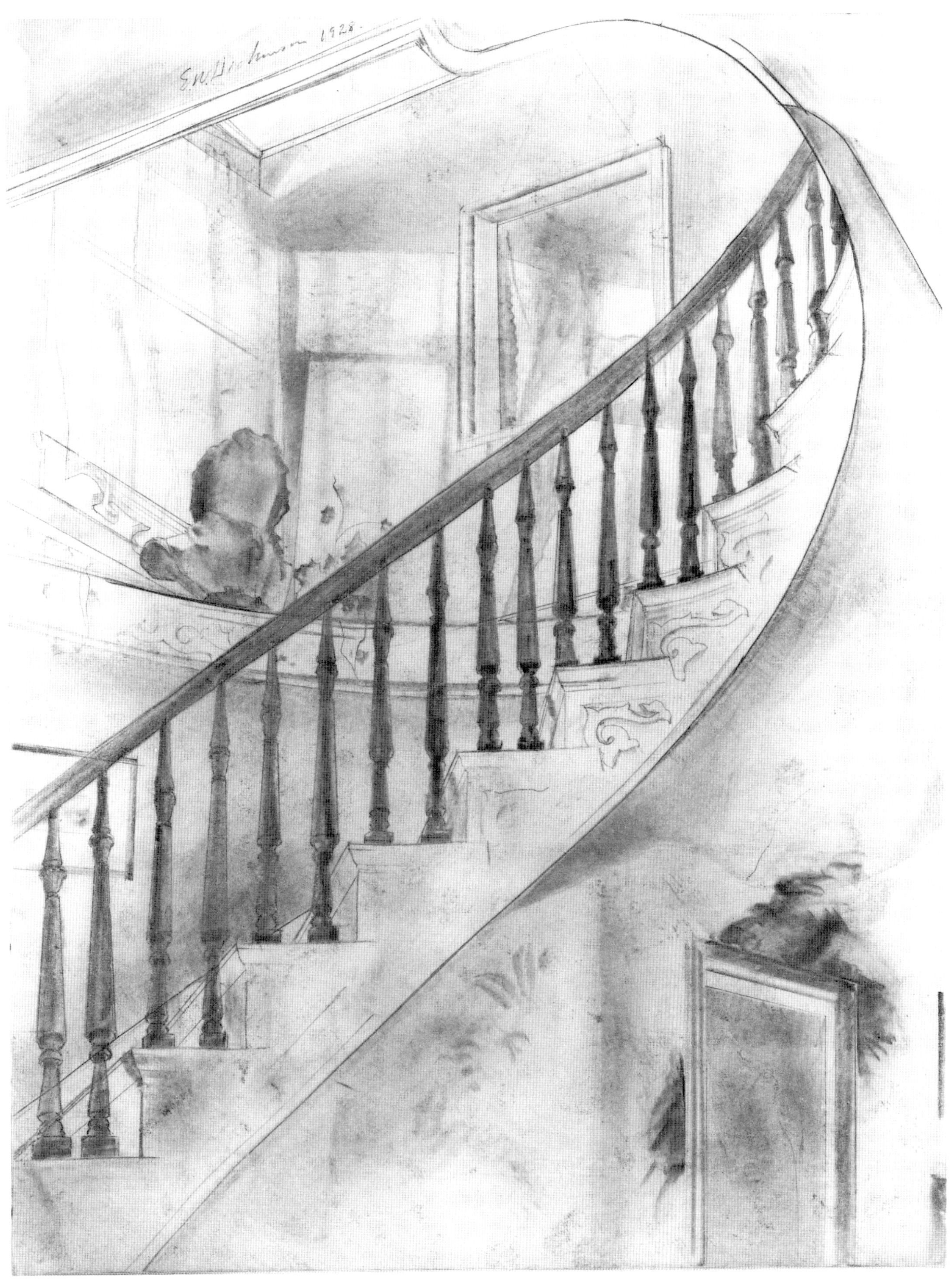

74 *Staircase, The Manse at Ulysses*, 1928

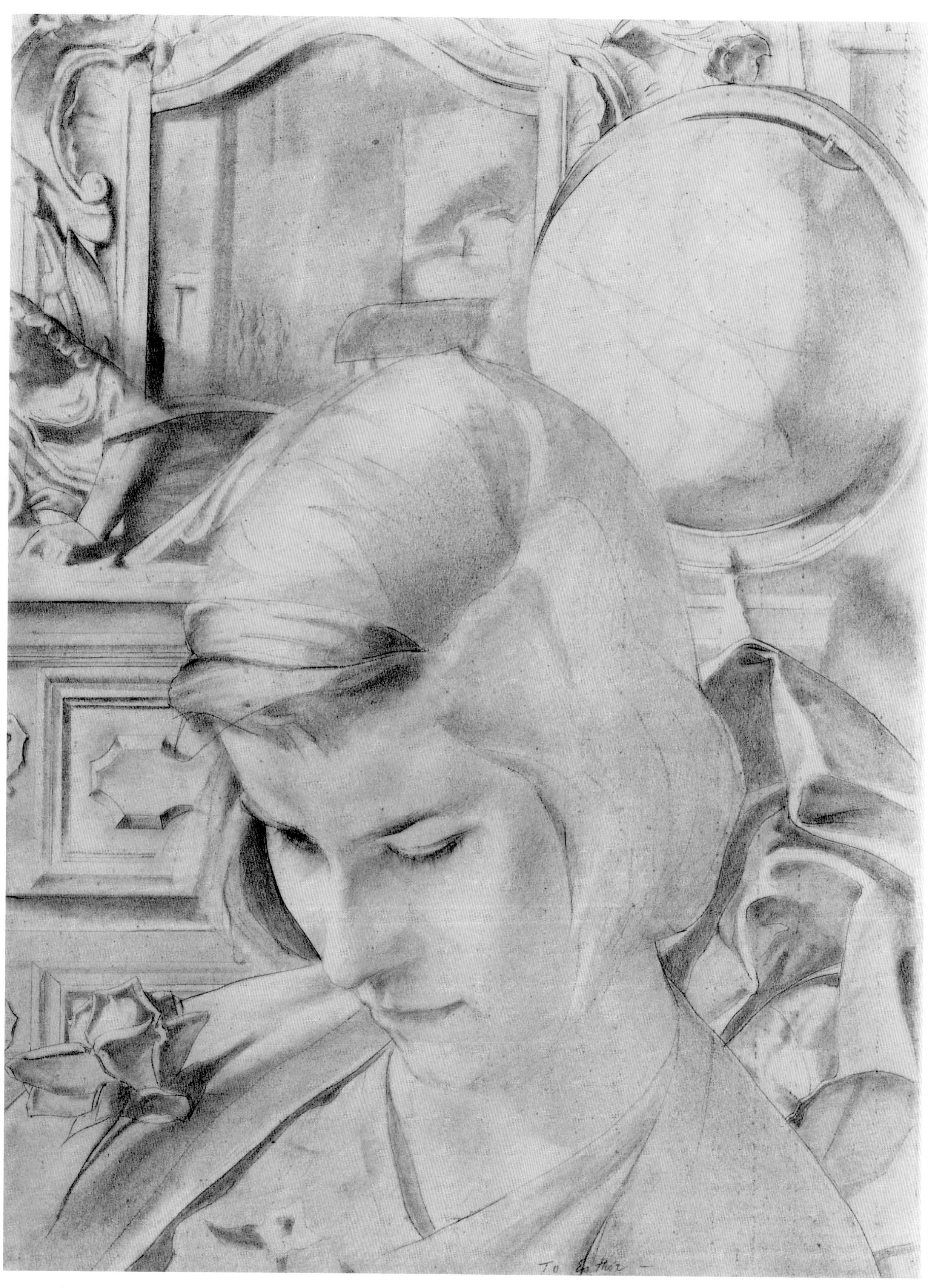

75 *Esther Hill Sawyer*, 1931

76 *Long Point Light, Provincetown*, 1933

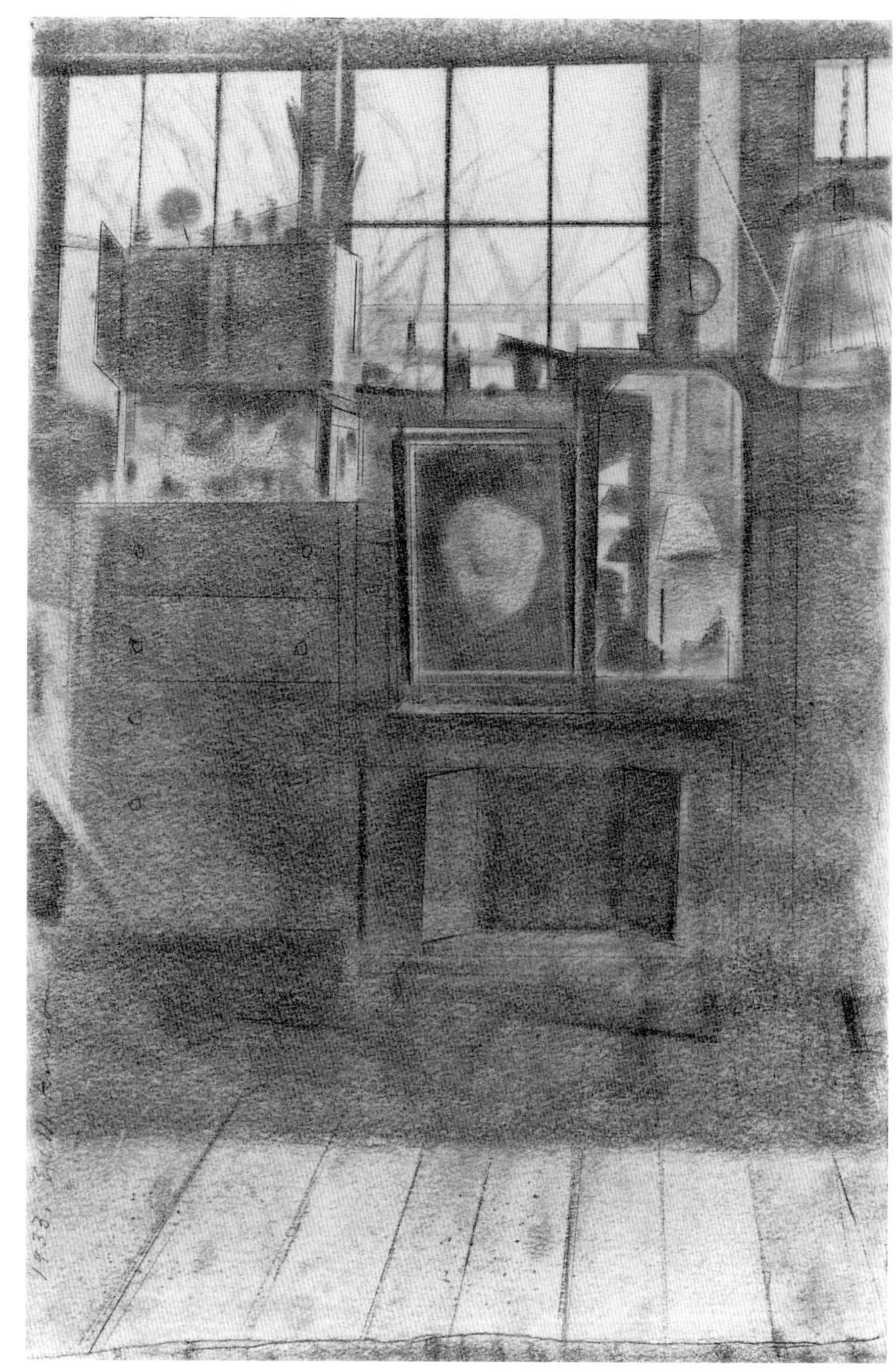

77 *Pat's Studio, Provincetown,* 1933

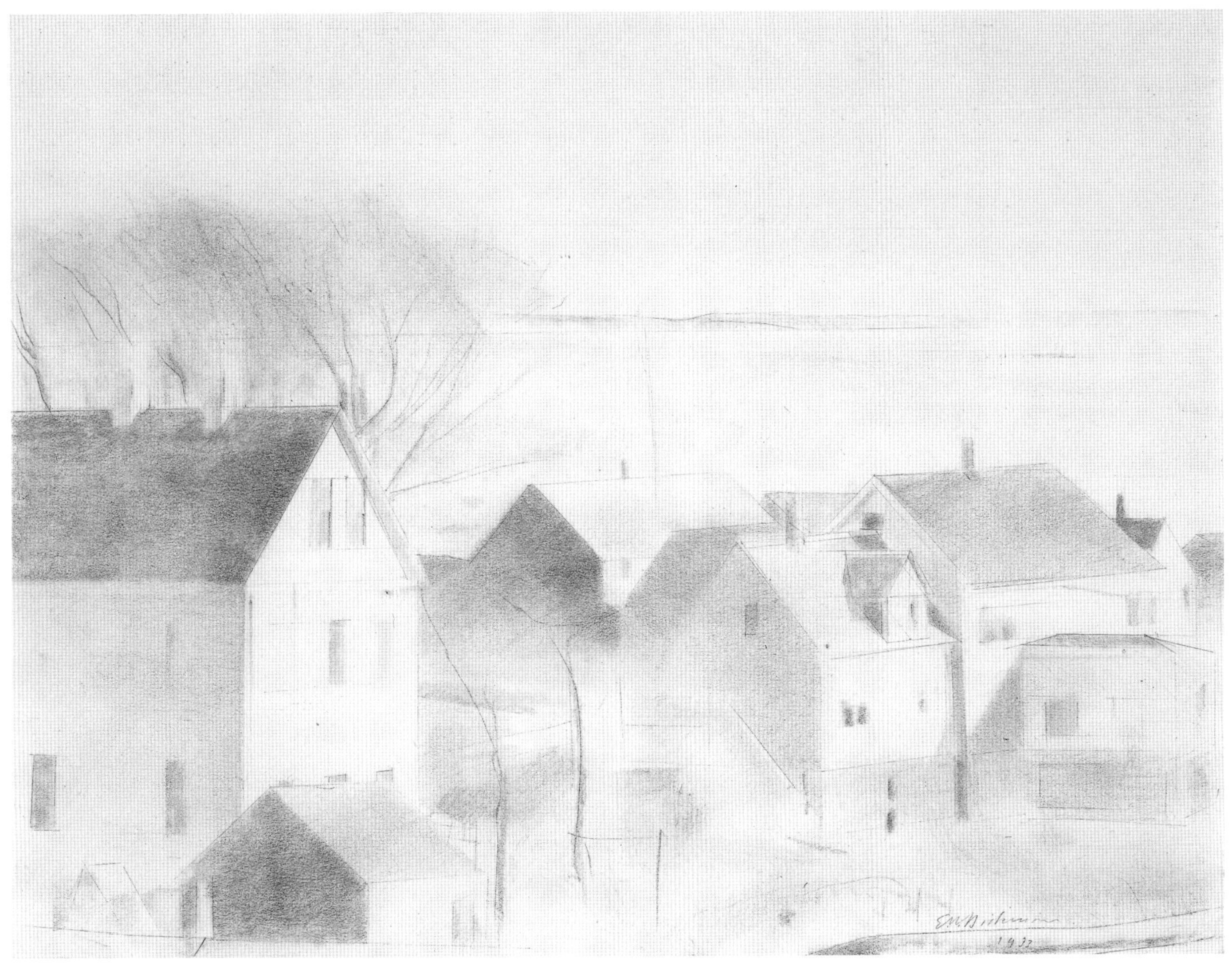

78 *Roofs and Harbor, Provincetown,* 1933

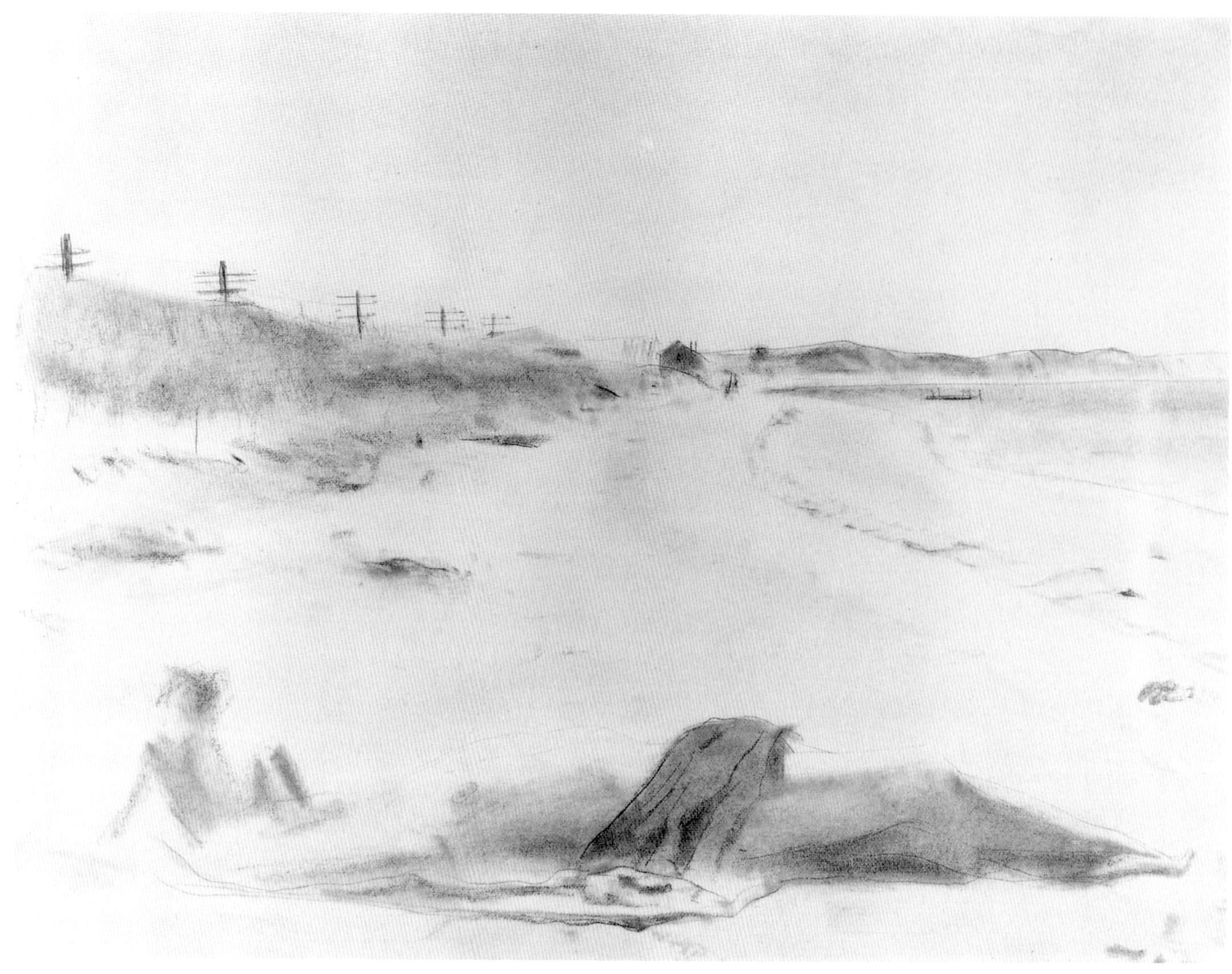

79 *Summer Morning, Beach Point*, 1934

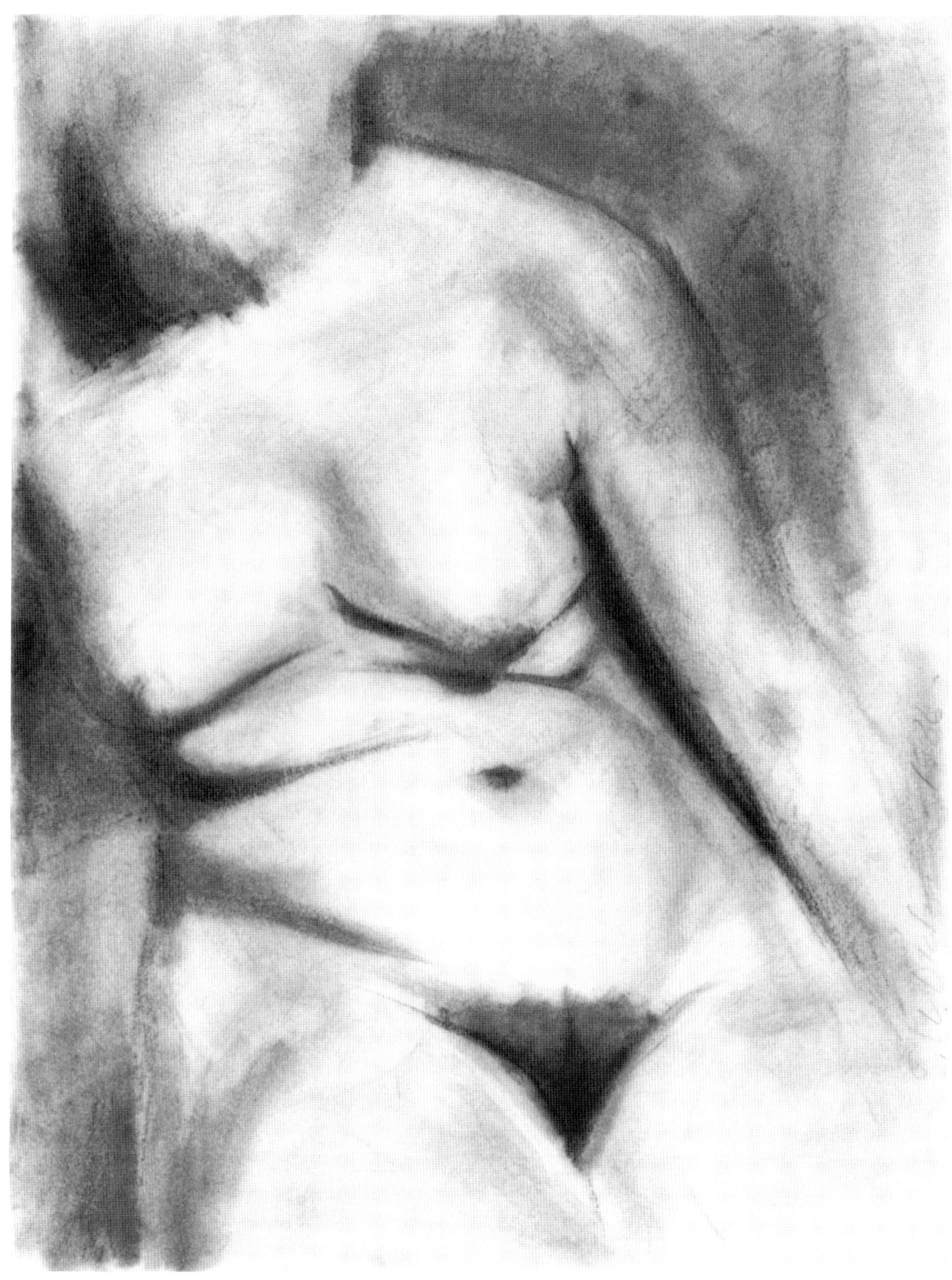

80 *Nude #3*, 1936

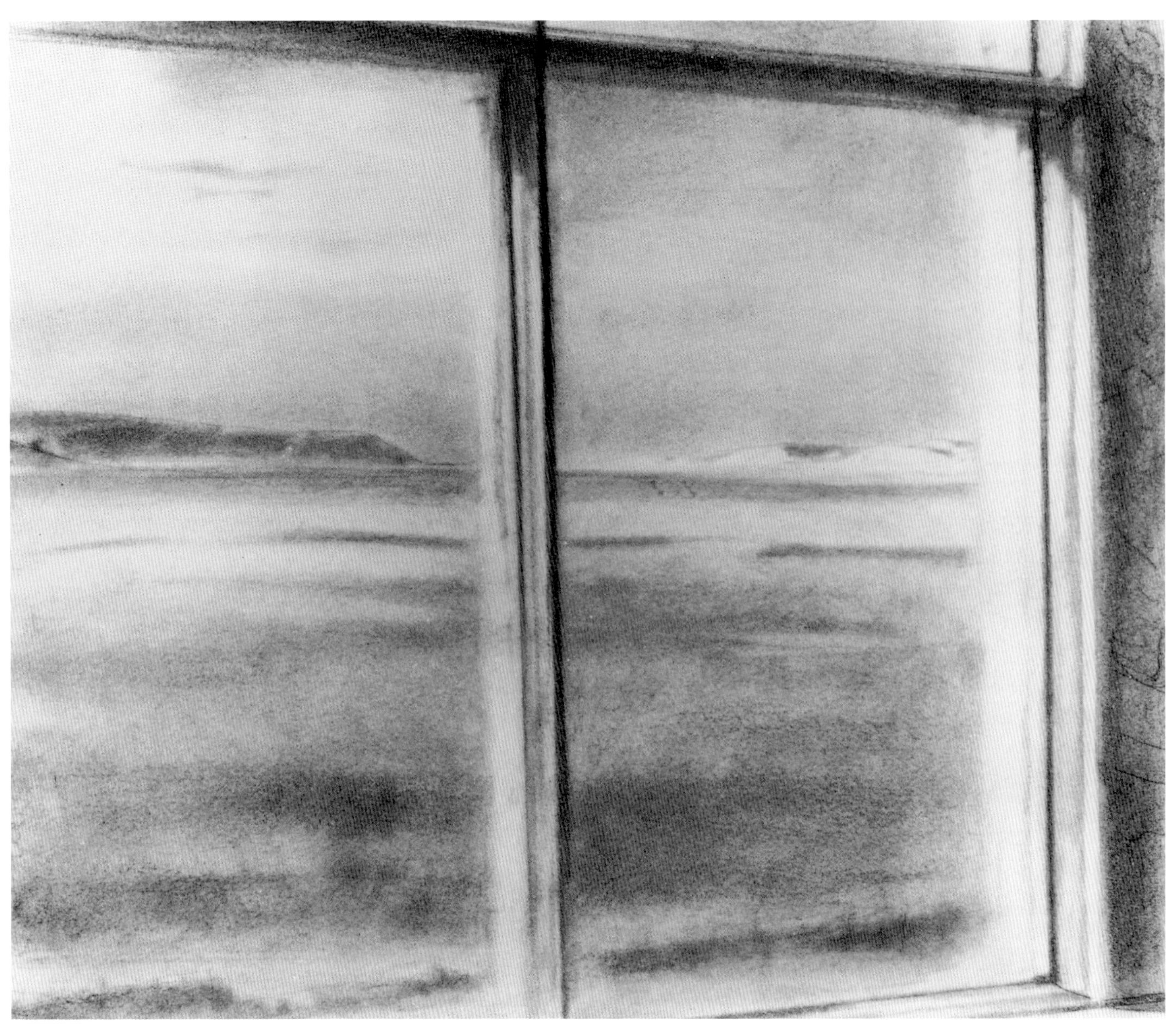

81 *View from a Window at Wellfleet*, 1939

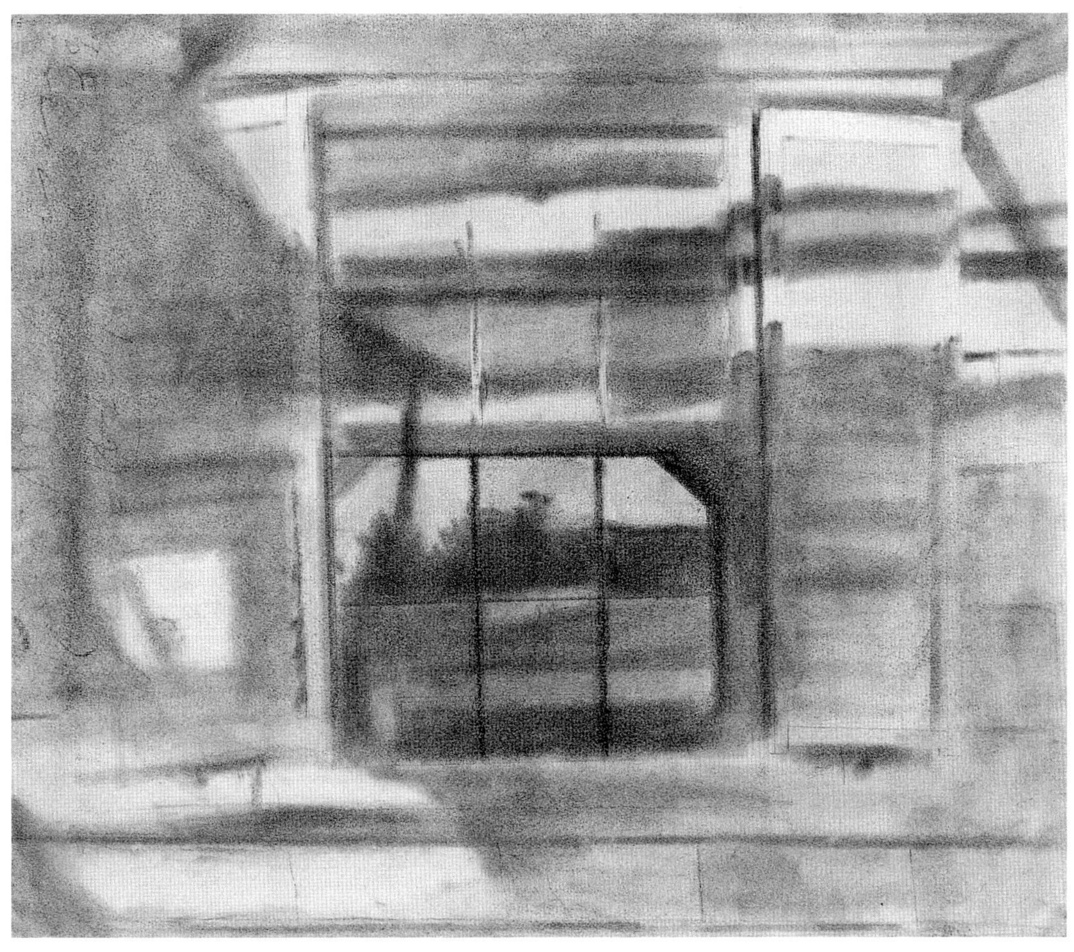

82 *Cottage Window*, 1939

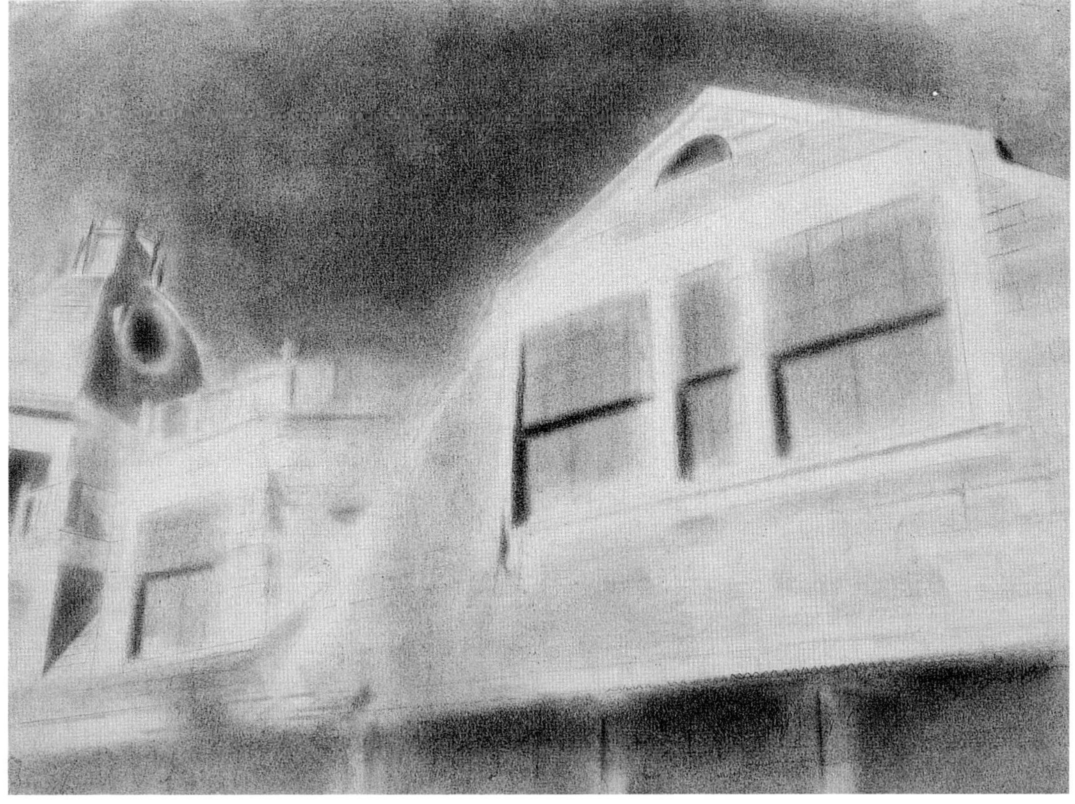

83 *South Wellfleet Inn*, 1939

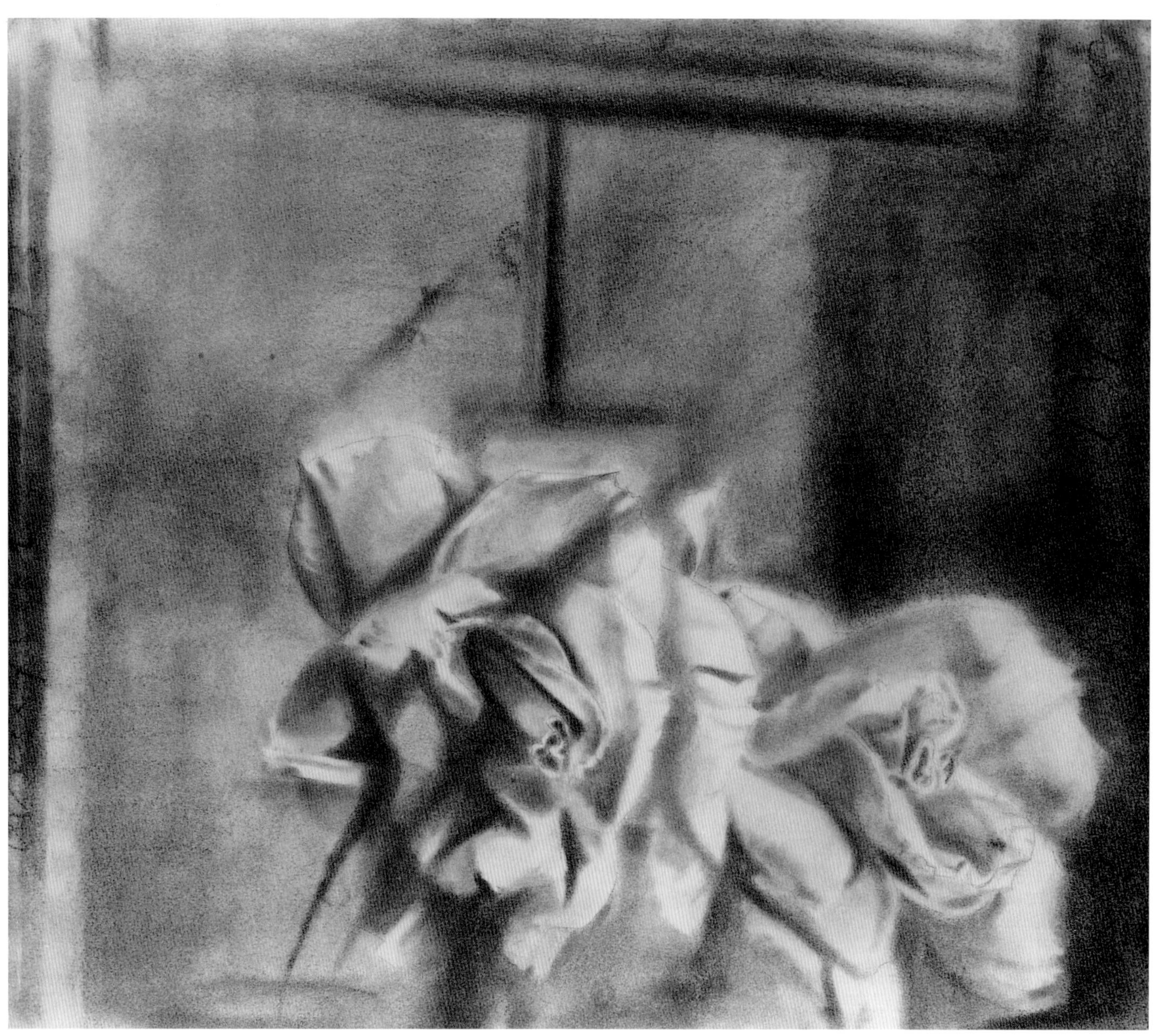

84 *Roses*, 1939

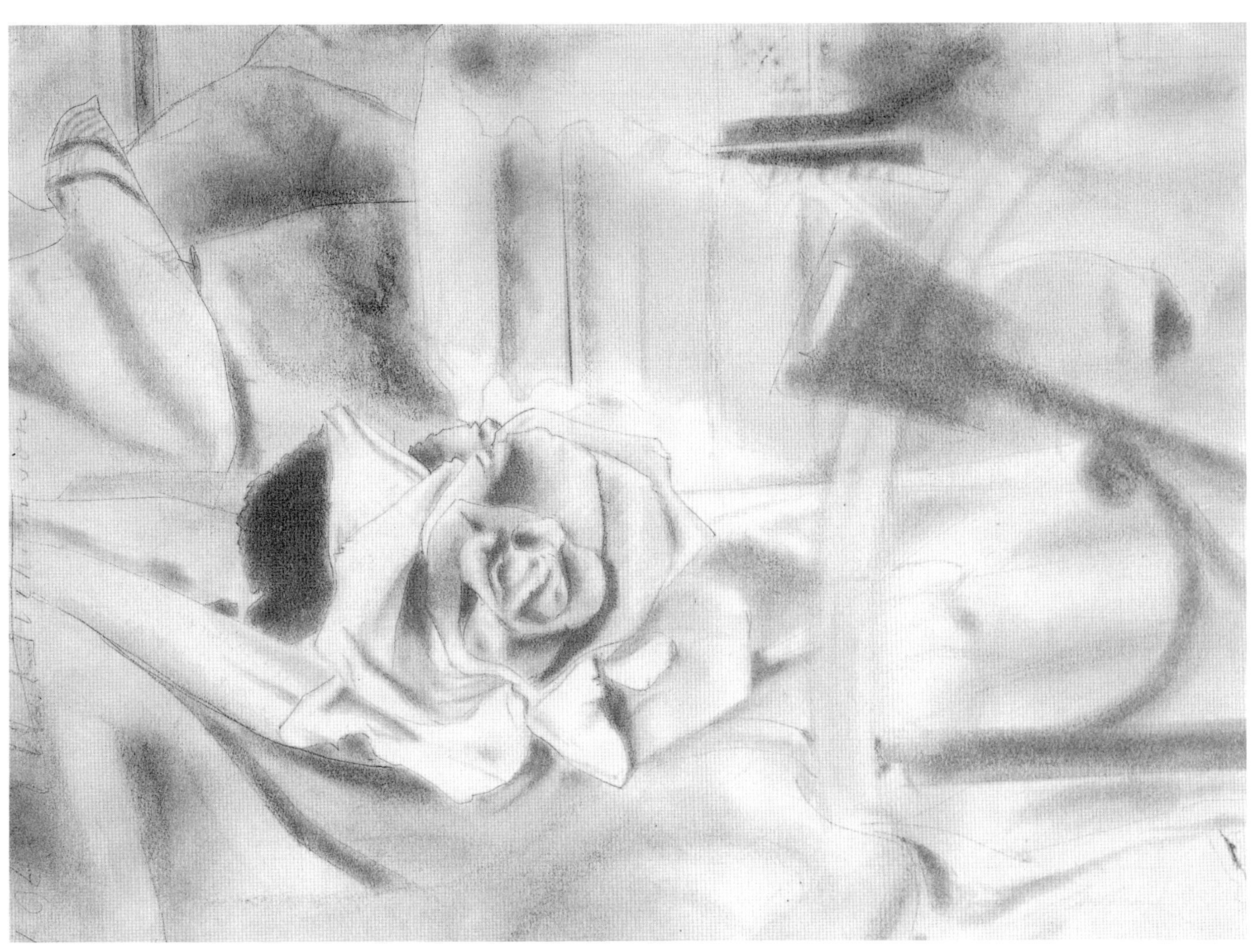

85 *Rose and Sextant*, 1943

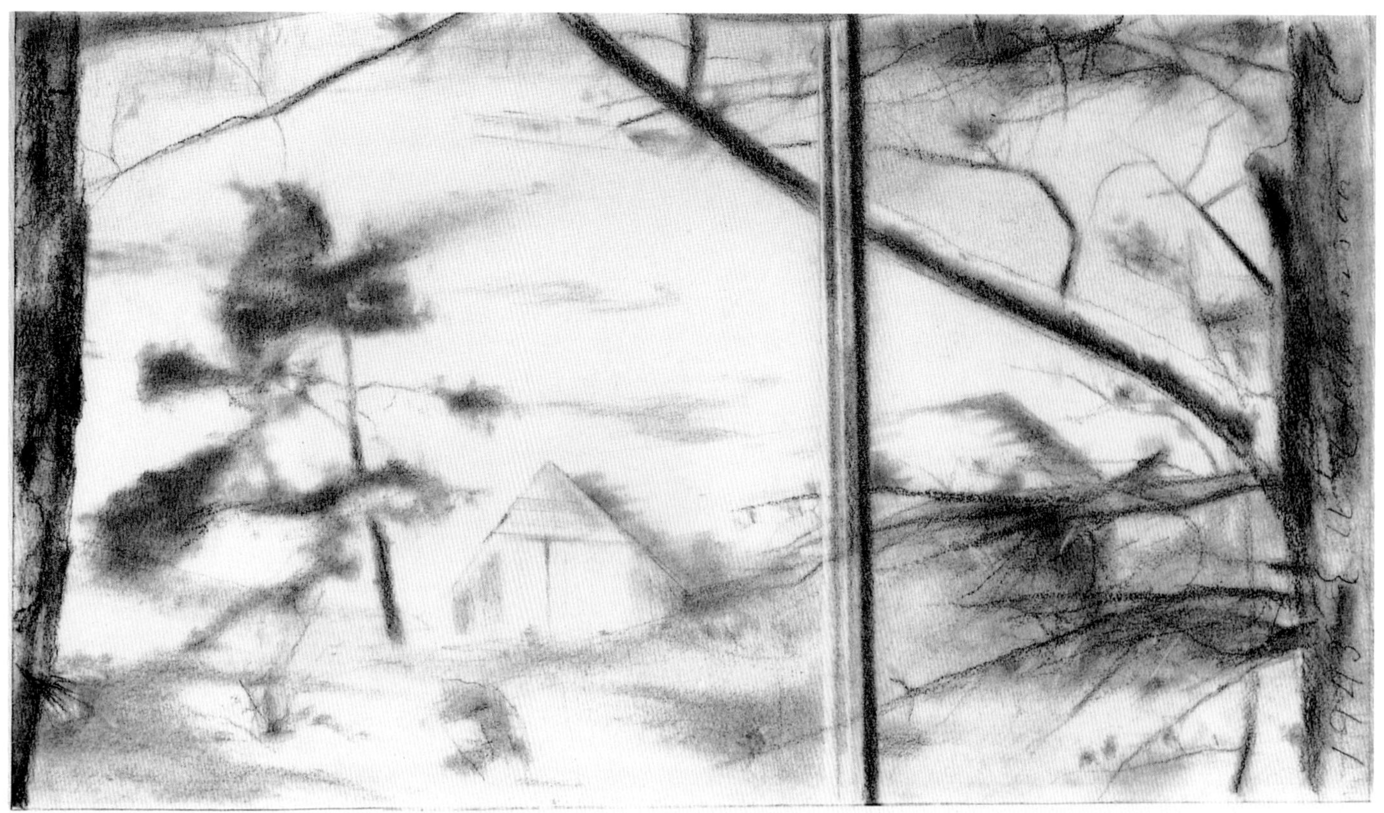

86 *Boathouse, Wellfleet,* 1943

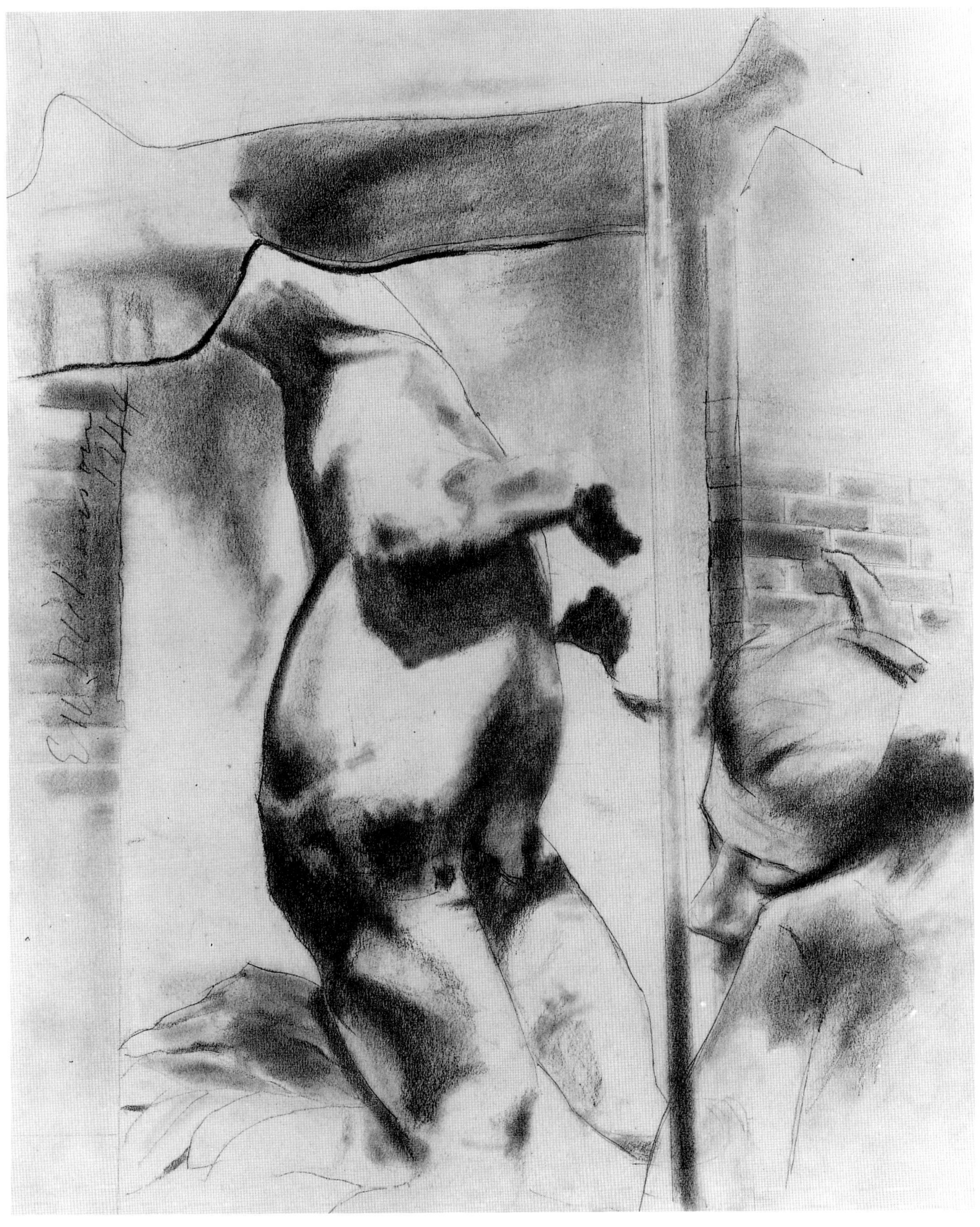

87 *Bear, Sculpture Fragments*, 1944

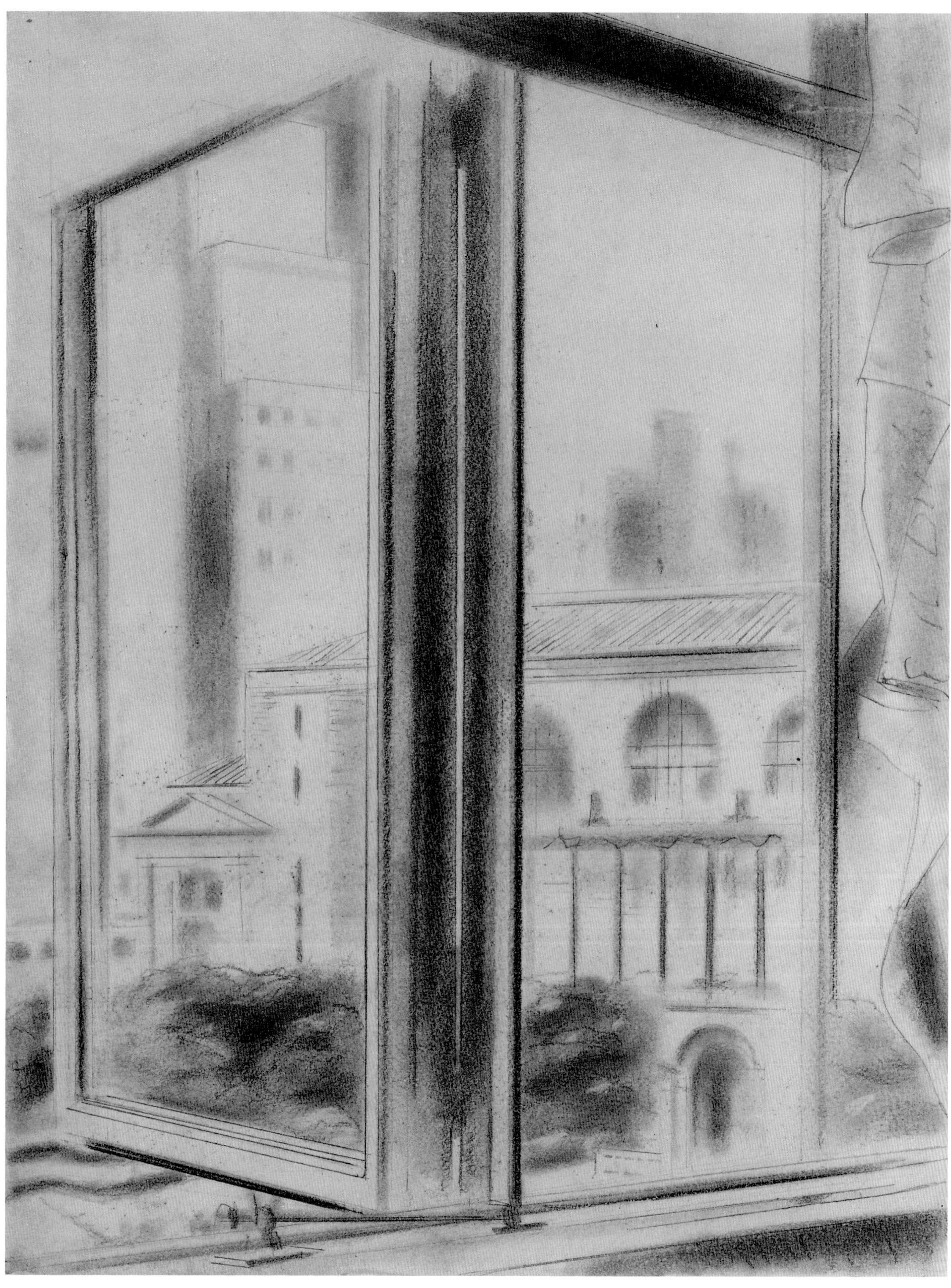

88 *Bryant Park*, 1944

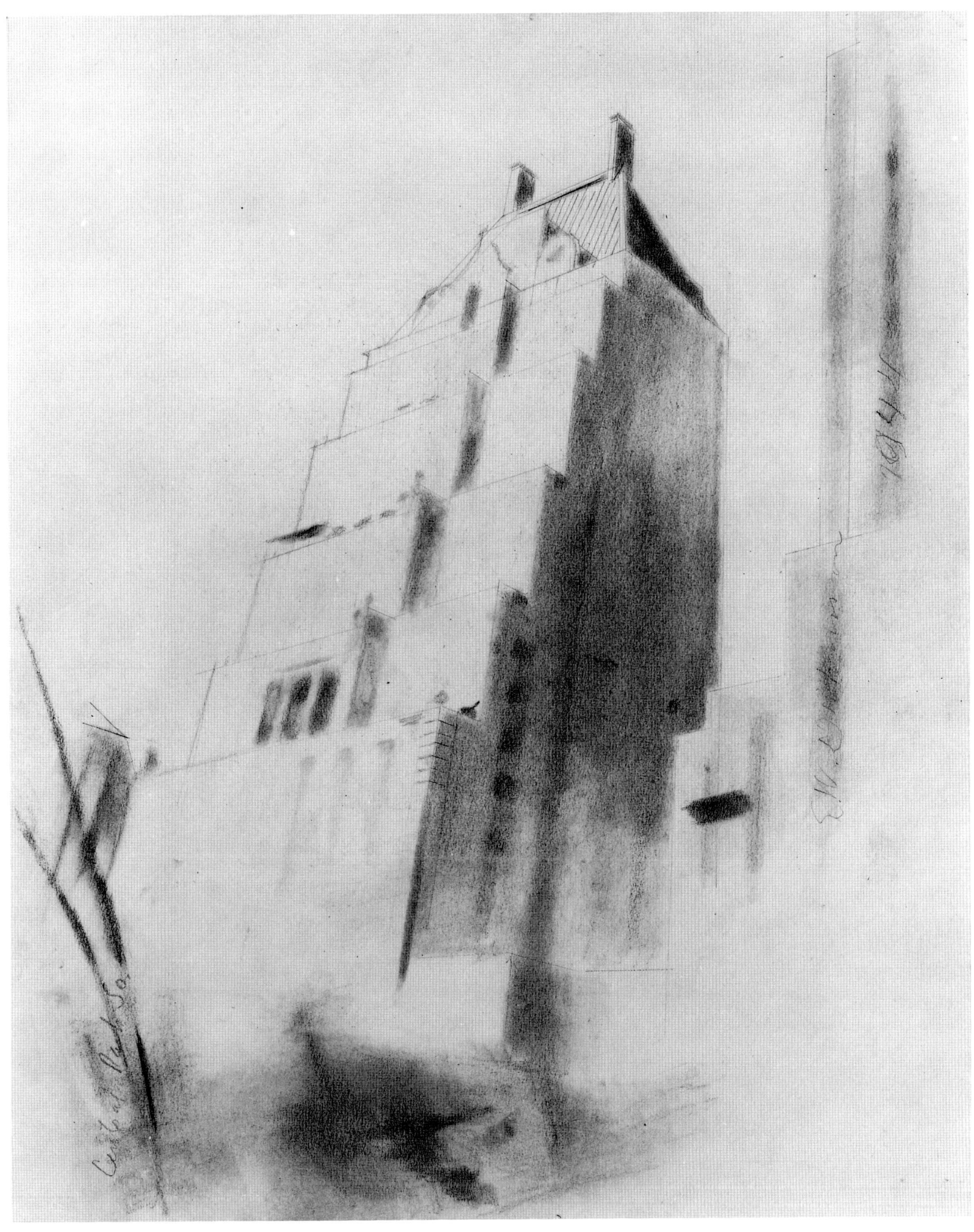

89 *Hampshire House, Central Park South*, 1944

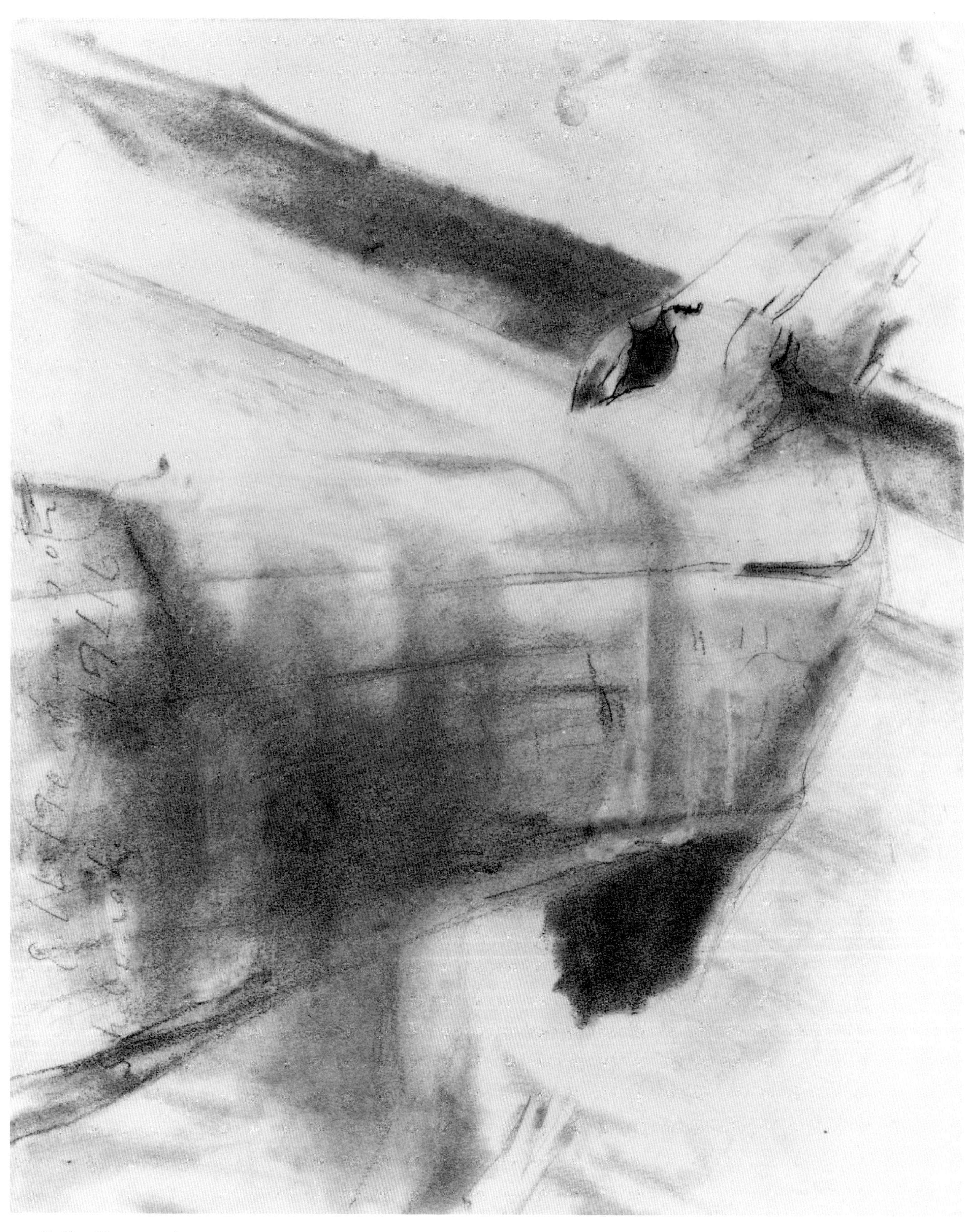

90 *Fallen Tree*, 1946

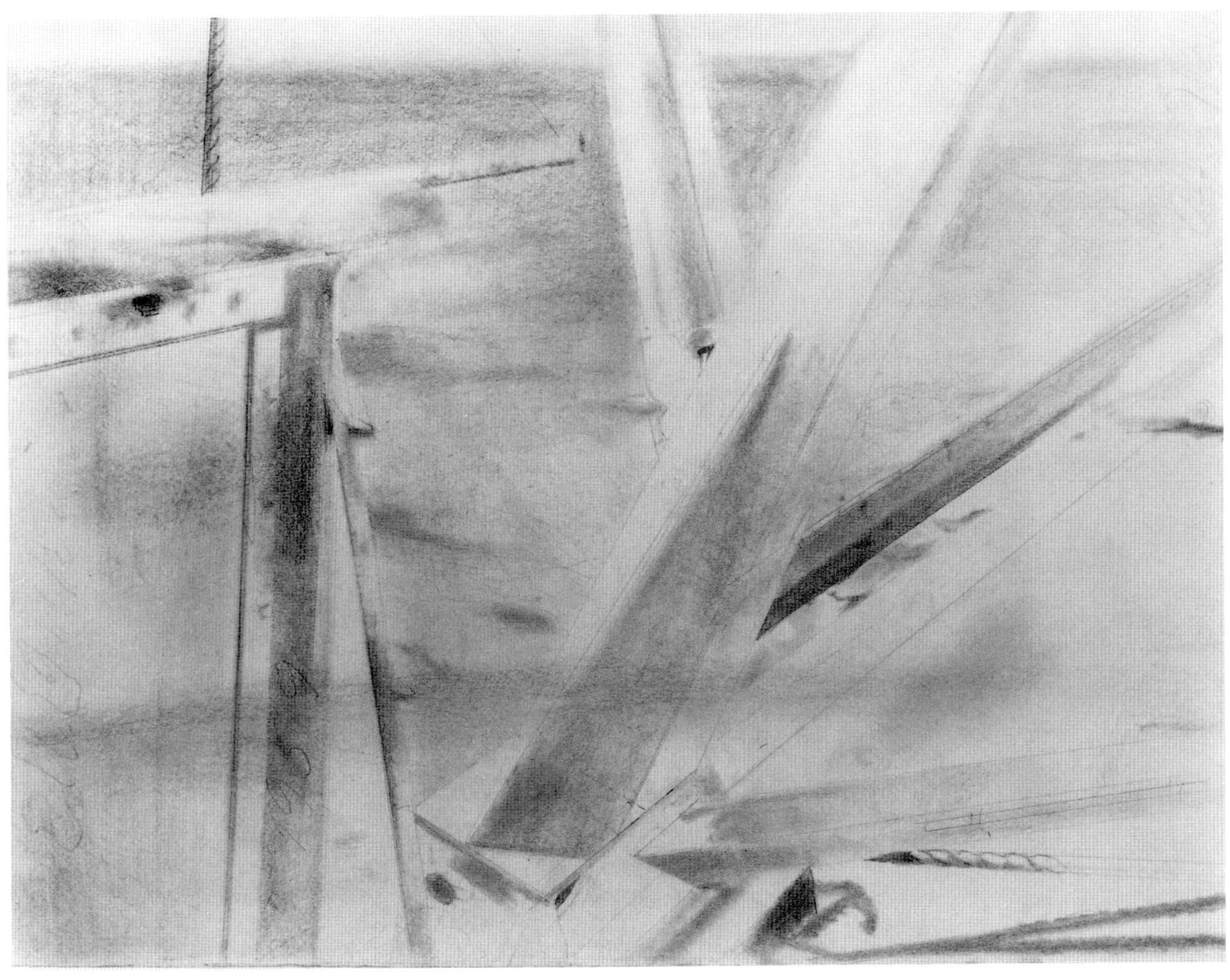

91 *Tekla Torm, Off Algiers,* 1959

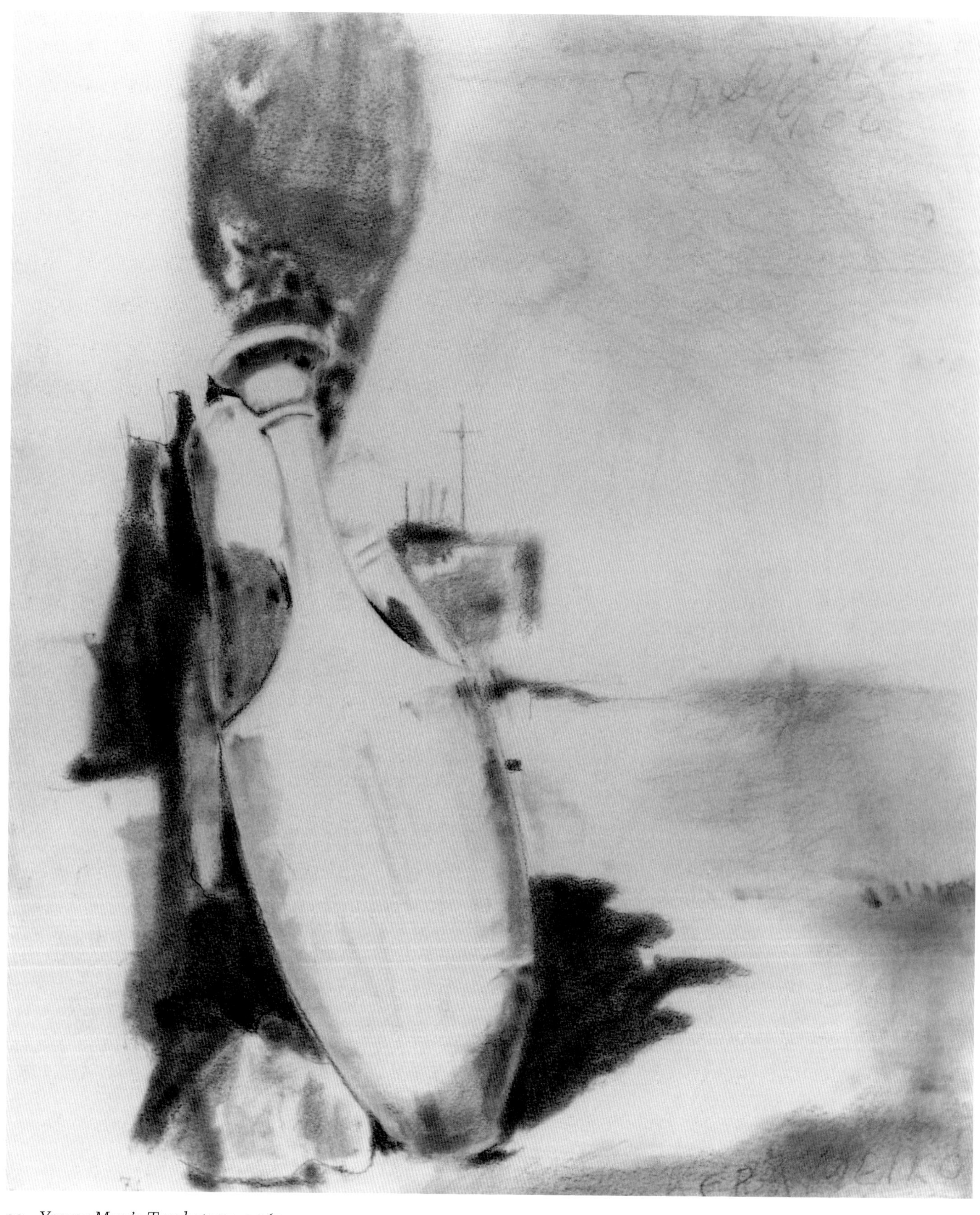

92 *Young Man's Tombstone*, 1962

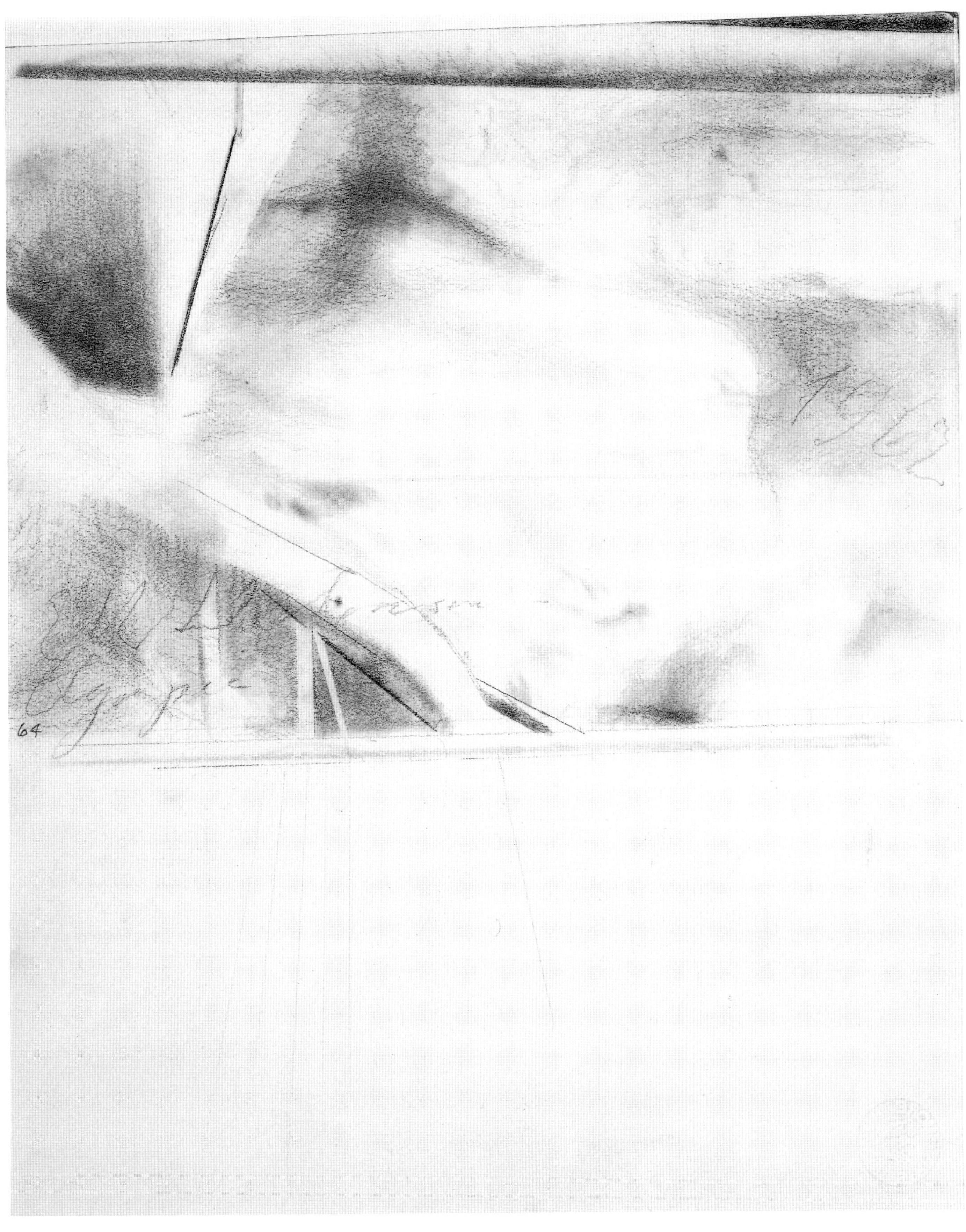

93 *Olympia*, 1962

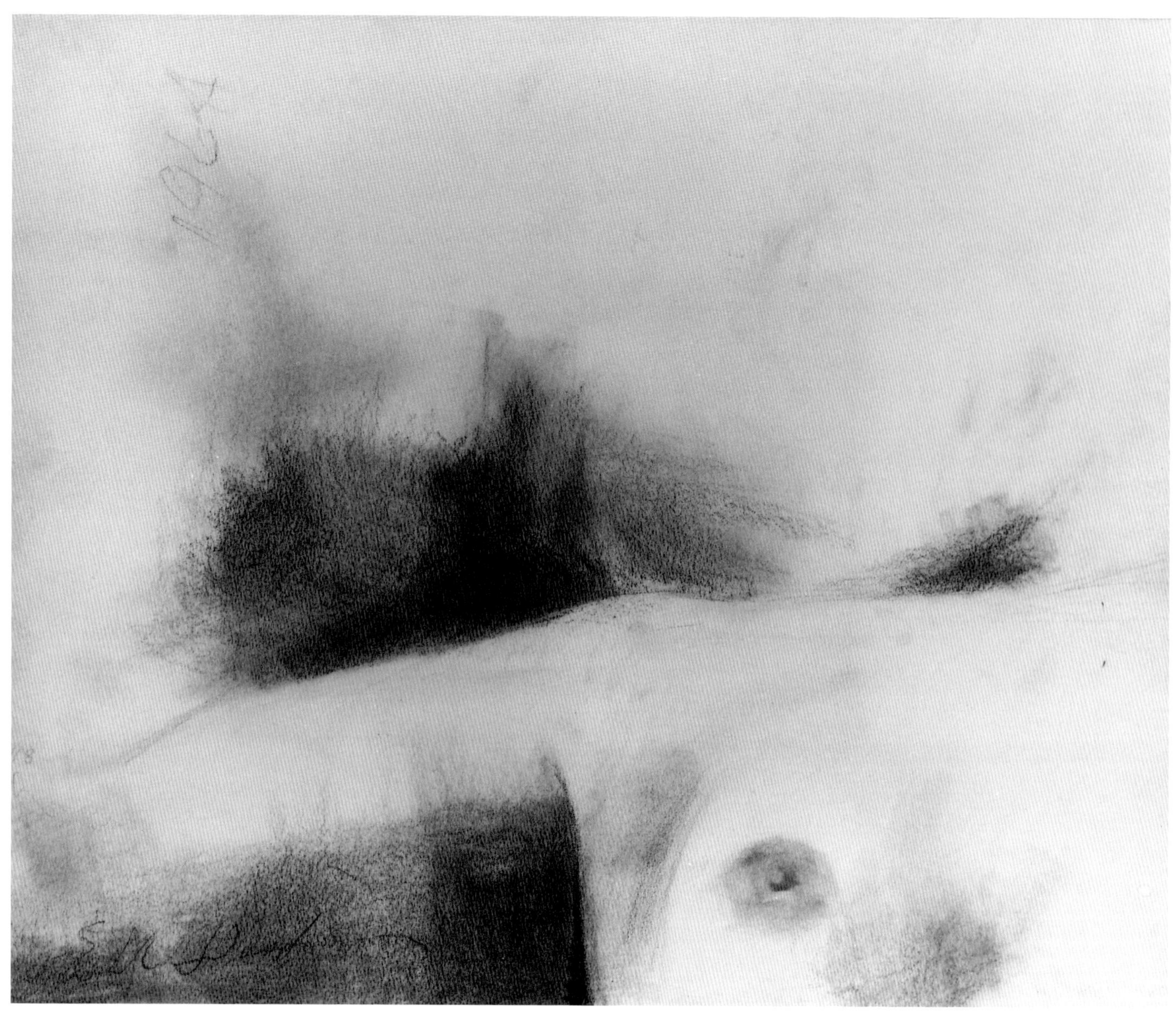

94 *Nude, Breast and Shoulder*, 1964

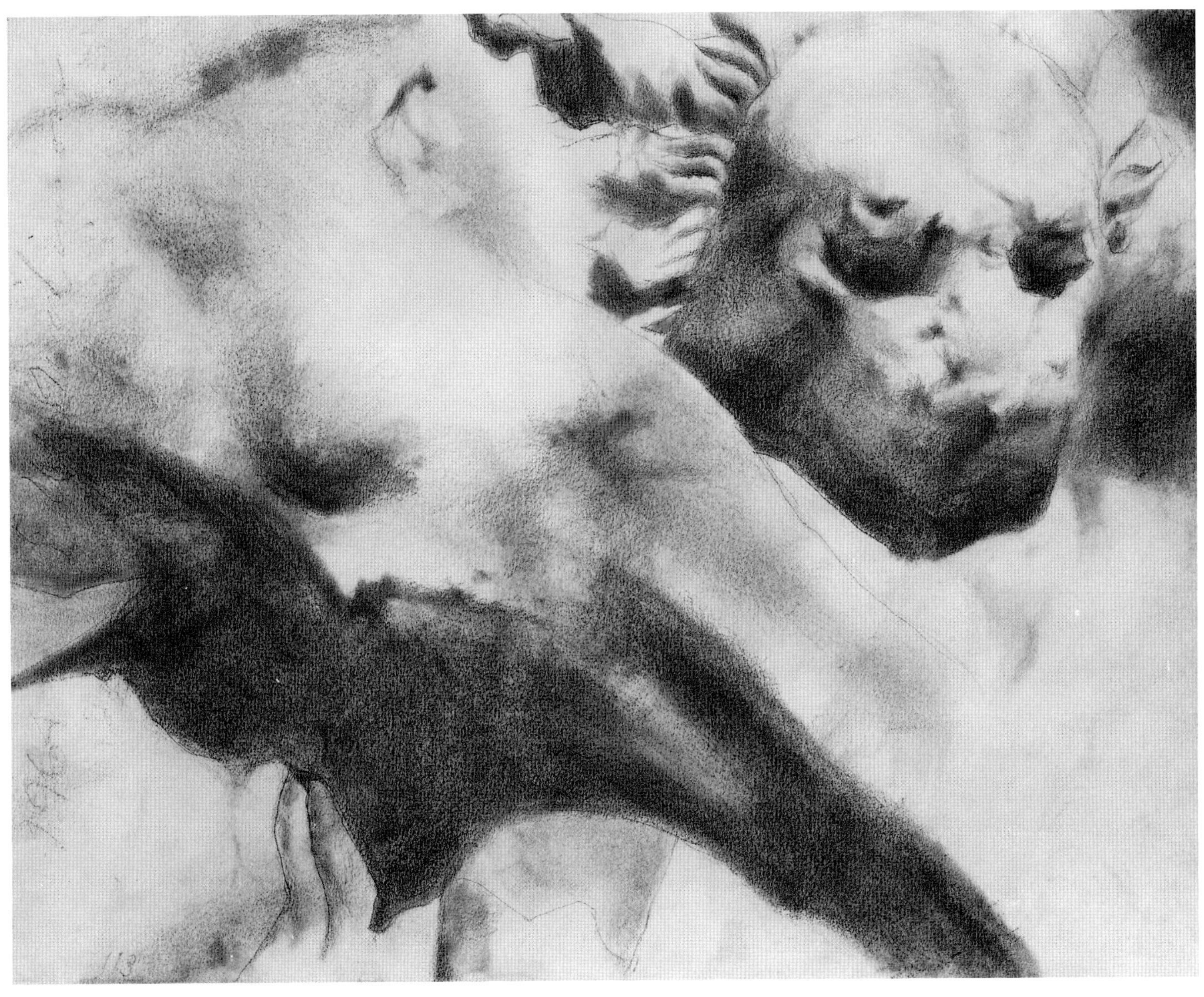

95 *Lion*, 1964

CHRONOLOGY

Helen Dickinson Baldwin

1882 Emma Sophia Carter (1860–1903) marries the Reverend Edwin Henry Dickinson (1855–1951), June 29. Together they have four children: Howard Carter (1883–1935), Burgess (1884–1913), Antoinette ("Tibi") (1889–1968), and Edwin Walter (1891–1978).

1891 Edwin Dickinson born October 11, Seneca Falls, New York. Father, Edwin H., pastor of First Presbyterian Church from January 1, 1889, until moving to Buffalo, Christmas Day, 1897.

1894 Mother Emma ill and often at nearby Clifton Springs Sanatorium; and later at new health resort in Pinehurst, North Carolina, or famed sanatorium at Saranac Lake, New York. Edwin frequently accompanies her, so his schooling is irregular.

1898 Summer at Interlaken, New York, while cottage, "Glen Eyrie," built in nearby Sheldrake.

1899 Celebration of paternal grandparents' golden wedding anniversary, August 14, at new cottage. Entire family present.

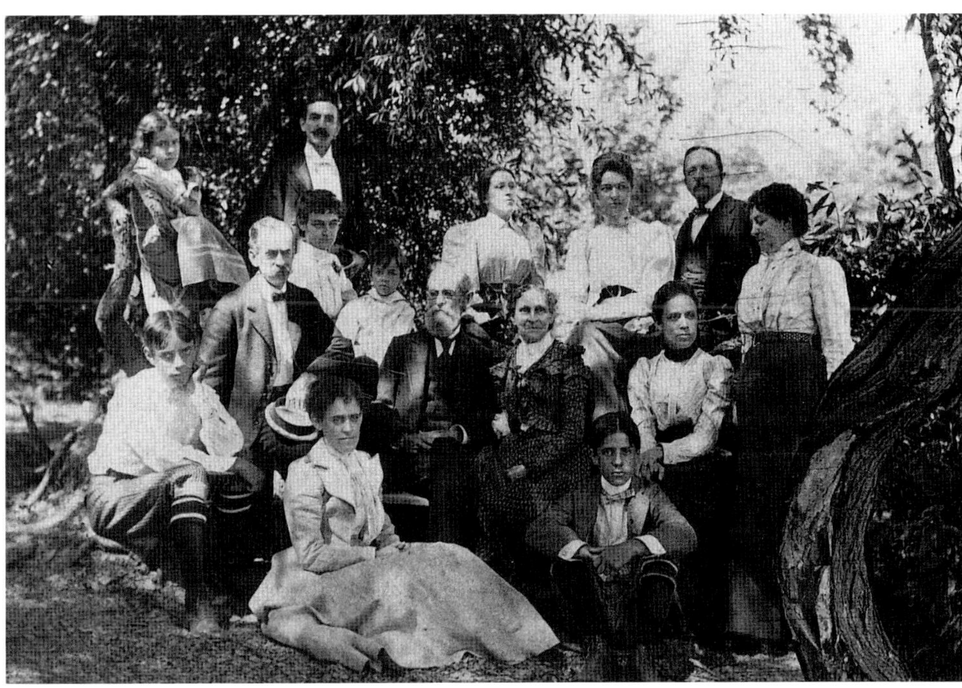

Golden wedding celebration of grandparents Edwin and Paulina Dickinson, August 14, 1899, in Sheldrake, New York. Left to right, bottom row: Howard Dickinson, Marion Dickinson, Burgess Dickinson; second row: The Reverend Edwin H. Dickinson, Edwin Dickinson, Paulina Dickinson, Emma Carter Dickinson, Paulina Dickinson Hand; third row: Antoinette (Tibi) Dickinson, Robert White, Bertha Dickinson White, the artist Edwin W. Dickinson, maid Jane, Elizabeth Hand, Theodore Hand.
Courtesy Dickinson Family Archive

1900 Summers in Sheldrake until 1909.

1902–3 Winter, at Saranac Lake with mother. Attends school there. March 10, with husband and children present, Emma dies of "tuberculosis of the bone." Burial March 13, Pleasant Valley, Connecticut, in Carter family plot established by her father.

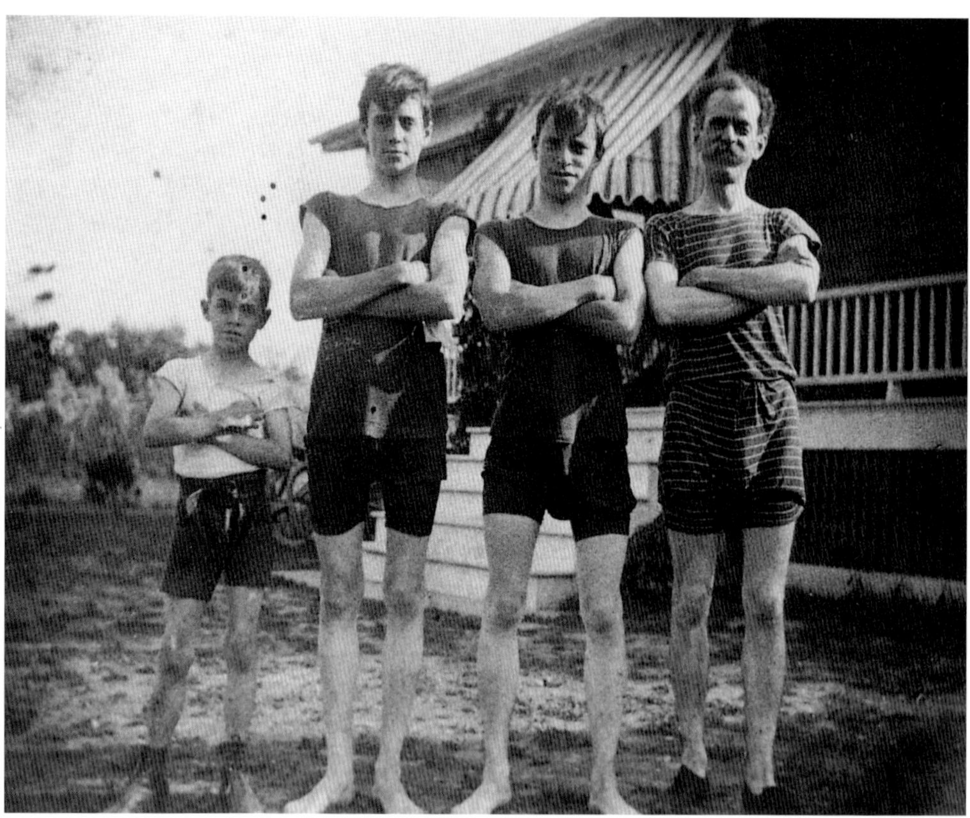

At the cottage in Sheldrake, ca. 1903–4. Left to right: Edwin, Burgess, Howard, the Reverend Edwin H.
Courtesy Dickinson Family Archive

1904 Attends New York State Normal School of Practice of Buffalo.

1909 Appointed to United States Naval Academy. With beginning class, prepares for entrance examinations, but fails mathematics.

1910 Reappointed to Naval Academy and again fails mathematics. Summer in Asheville, North Carolina, with father, who was recuperating there for the season. Studies commercial art and realizes fine art is his calling. October 31, enters Pratt Institute, Brooklyn, living with his brothers in New York.

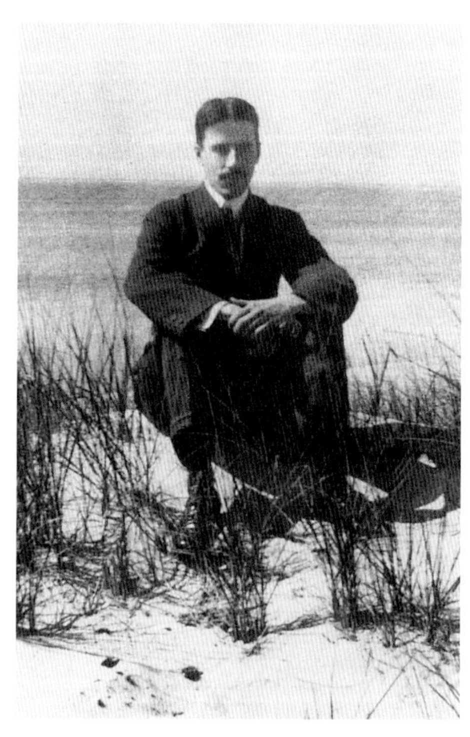

Burgess in Provincetown, summer 1912.
Courtesy Dickinson Family Archive

1911 Fall, enrolls at Art Students League (ASL) in classes of William Merritt Chase and Frank V. DuMond. At ASL, meets Esther Hoyt of Buffalo, who becomes firm friend. Studies briefly at Art School of National Academy of Design.

1912 Receives honors in ASL spring concours of student work. June 6, Howard marries Marjorie Wellstead (1883–1944). Spends summer in Charles W. Hawthorne class at Cape Cod School of Art in Provincetown, Massachusetts. Fall, returns to ASL.

1913 Lives with Burgess on Washington Square in New York. January 28, Burgess jumps from sixth-floor window. Edwin discovers his body in courtyard below. Too devastated to stay in New York, returns home to Buffalo and attends Buffalo Fine Arts Academy. Spends summer again in Provincetown in Hawthorne class. Decides to end formal studies and become an independent artist living in Provincetown year round.

1914 Summer, assistant in Hawthorne class. June 24, father marries Louise [Luty] Walbridge (1876–1949). Nephew Howard Carter Dickinson, Jr., born December 14.

1915 January 27, begins daily journal. Founding member of the Provincetown Art Association. Learns Morse code to support himself as a telegrapher. Esther Hoyt marries Ansley Wilcox Sawyer, who also becomes close friend.

1916 Summer, teaches for a month at Buffalo Fine Arts Academy. *Interior,* 1916, hung in place of honor in the hemicycle at center of ground floor of the Corcoran Gallery of Art, Washington, D.C., for *Sixth Exhibition: Oil Paintings by Contemporary American Artists.* Shown also at the National Academy of Design, New York; the Art Institute of Chicago; and Carnegie International, Pittsburgh.

1917 March 8, moves to New York. Paints and works as telegrapher at Western Union. April, exhibits *Old Ben and Mrs. Marks,* 1916, at *First Annual Exhibition of the Society of Independent Artists.* United States moves closer to involvement in World War I. December 12, enlists in Naval Reserve. Holidays in Sheldrake.

1918 January 9, called up into regular navy. Serves on several ships with longest tours of duty on *Nantucket Light Vessel*, considered to be hard duty. Howard telegraphs of death of close friend Herbert Groesbeck, just ten days before Armistice.

1919 July 19, discharged from navy. Immediately visits Herbert's widow, Amy Groesbeck, and subsequently visits senior Groesbecks periodically for the rest of their lives. To Sheldrake to paint. December 8, sails for France. Arrives Paris, December 19. Sees *Old Ben and Mrs. Marks*, 1916, in exhibition of noted young American artists at the Musée National du Luxembourg. Trip made possible, in large part, by funds given by Amy and the Groesbecks from Herbert's army life insurance.

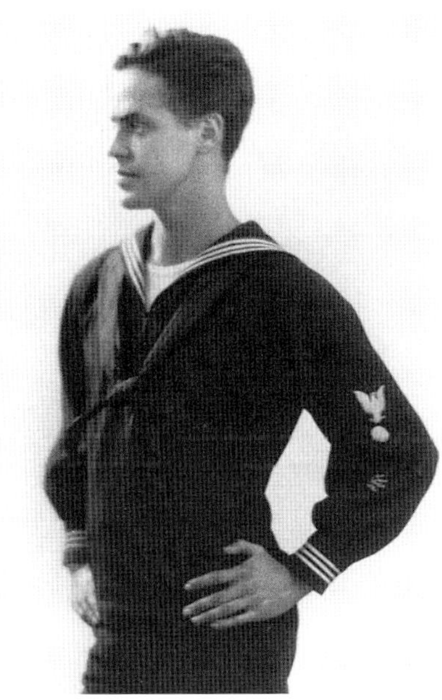

Edwin's navy portrait, 1918–19.
Courtesy Dickinson Family Archive

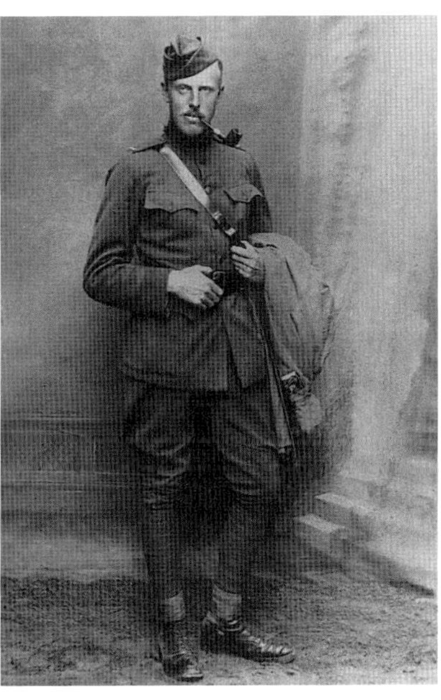

Herbert Groesbeck, Jr. (killed in the Argonne forest, France, November 1, 1918).
Courtesy Dickinson Family Archive

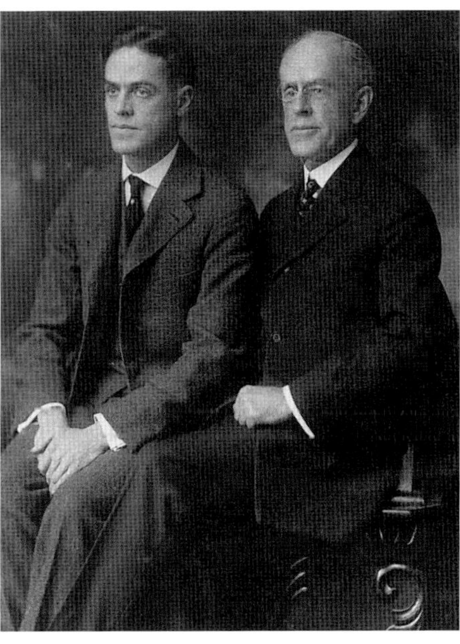

Edwin and his father, the Reverend Edwin H. Dickinson, ca. 1919.
Courtesy Dickinson Family Archive

1920 January 3, at Café Closerie de Lilas, meets Richard Parmenter, who will become lifelong, closest friend. In Paris, paints, makes friends, visits museums and cafés, goes to concerts, plays billiards. March 28 to Verdun, walks twelve kilometers in moonlight to visit Herbert Groesbeck's grave.

After March, draws often at the Académie de la Grande Chaumière. Visits Saint-Tropez, Madrid, Toledo, and London. July, sails for home. To Sheldrake, then Provincetown. Fall, begins *An Anniversary*.

1921 Lives in Provincetown, visits Buffalo and Sheldrake. Christmas in Geneva, New York, with family.

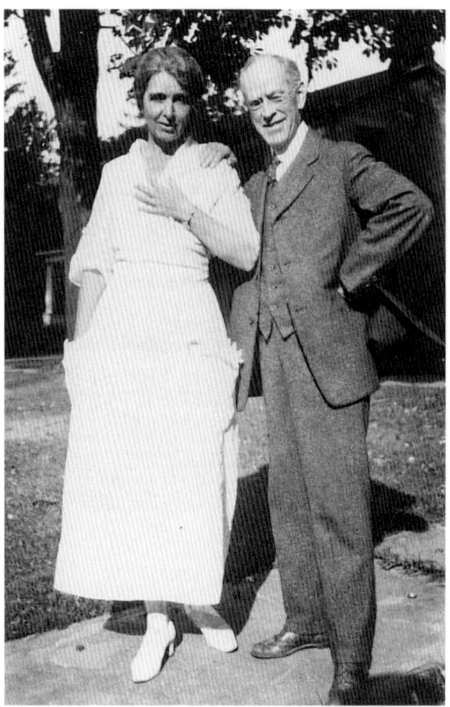

Edwin's stepmother, Louise (Luty) Walbridge Dickinson, and his father the Reverend Edwin H. Dickinson, September 12, 1921.
Courtesy Dickinson Family Archive

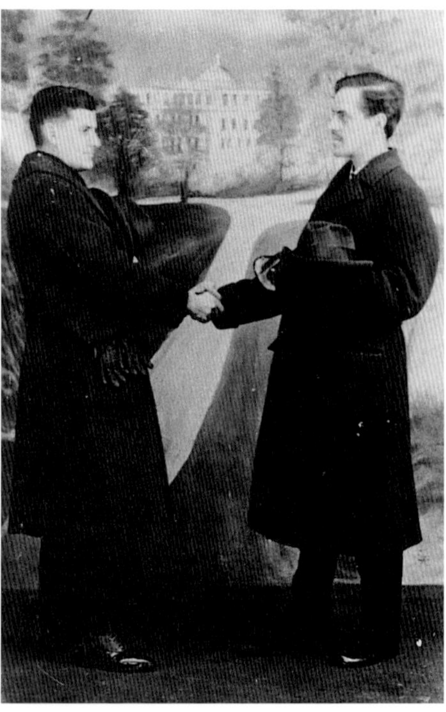

Richard Parmenter (left) and Edwin (right), Bronx Park, January 25, 1923.
Courtesy Dickinson Family Archive

1922 Paints portraits of Hoyt/Sawyer families in Buffalo. Spends summer with family and paints the Sheldrake "X-Cliff" series. October, goes to New York to teach evening life class at ASL until spring.

1923 Summer, in Provincetown teaching sketch class. Sails often with Dick Parmenter. October, to Washington, D.C., to paint portrait of uncle, Charles Evans Hughes, then secretary of state. Christmas at Howard's.

1924 In Provincetown. March 4, begins *The Cello Player*, completing it August 27, 1926, after 290 sittings. Summer, crews on Parmenter's vessel, *Yvonne*, sailing all over Cape Cod Bay collecting marine specimens. Esther and Ansley Sawyer offer a monthly stipend of $50 to alleviate financial worries somewhat, in return for pick of paintings. Takes on Janice Tworkov as a student in Provincetown. Tibi in Provincetown. She visits regularly and often with father and Luty during Provincetown years, a reflection of close family ties. Cards and dancing on New Year's Eve in studio at 46 Pearl Street.

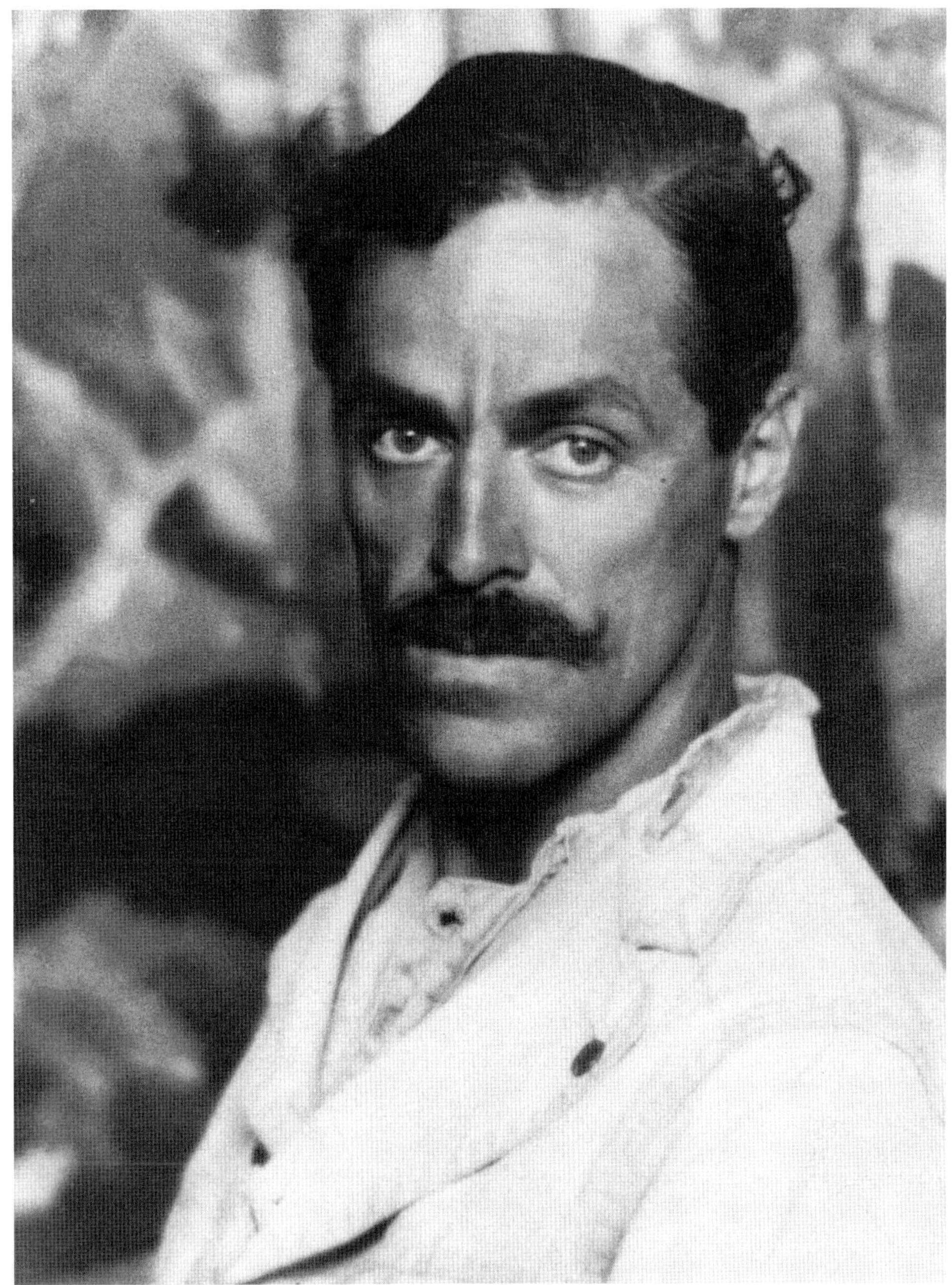

Portrait of Edwin taken in 1924.
Courtesy Dickinson Family Archive

1925 Lives in Provincetown, with visits to Howard and Tibi. Teaches in summer. Small house, to be Tibi's own home, is moved to sit just beside studio.

1926 Winter, in Provincetown with Tibi. Most of summer, paints in Sheldrake. September, in Provincetown, meets Frances ("Pat") Foley. Late September, with Tibi to Trumansburg for father's installation as new pastor of Presbyterian Church of Ulysses.

1927 Sees Pat often in Hawthorne class and around Provincetown. November, hangs exhibition in Springfield, Massachusetts, with help of Pat's brother Sherwood. Returns in time for Mrs. Foley's evening party where he and Pat declare their love. December, Pat travels to Chicago to visit friends.

1928 To Buffalo to try to obtain a portrait commission in Chicago. Succeeds and in Chicago he and Pat become engaged, pending Mrs. Foley's consent. [Pat's father died in 1926.] February, to Provincetown; Pat to Winter Park, Florida. Working hard to finish *The Fossil Hunters*, begun November 16, 1926, and finished September 2, 1928, in 192 sittings; largest painting to date at 96½ by 73¾ inches. August 21, Pat to Provincetown. October 31, wedding in New York, at Hotel Brevoort. After wedding supper, board night train Star; Howard arranges for special stop at Sheldrake. Winter, in Sheldrake cottage, painting, reading aloud, taking long walks on frozen lake, along the lake shore, and up the glen. *The Fossil Hunters* installed on its side at Carnegie International, Pittsburgh, resulting in unwelcome public mockery.

1929 April 29, with Pat to Provincetown. Teaches at Provincetown Art Association. November, *The Fossil Hunters* shown at National Academy of Design, New York, and awarded Second Altman Prize for Landscape. More unwelcome publicity, as work is hung on its side, once again, in spite of *TOP* and *BOTTOM* written in large letters on reverse. Becomes member of Grand Central Art Galleries. To Sheldrake for Christmas.

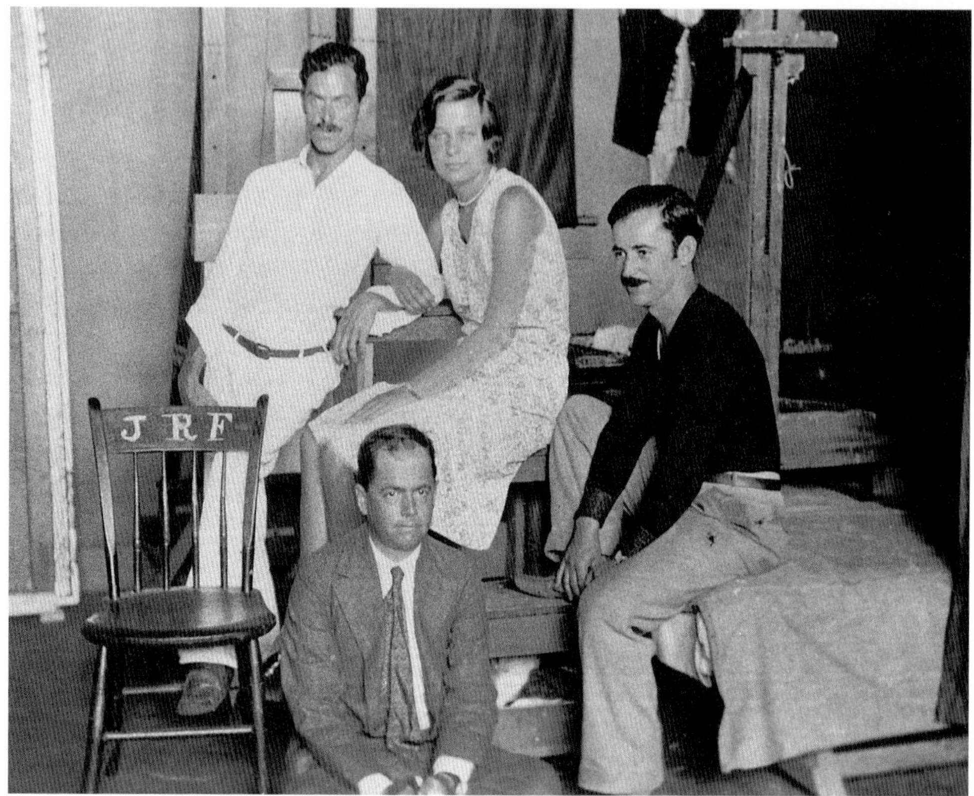

Left to right: Edwin, R. H. Ives Gammell (seated), Pat Dickinson, Raymond J. Eastwood. Portraits of this group, which included John Robinson Frazier, were taken regularly. In this sitting, Frazier was not available, so the artist's daughter believes that Dickinson pulled up a chair and painted the initials *JRF* on it to stand in for their absent friend. Taken in Dickinson's Provincetown studio, 1929. Courtesy Dickinson Family Archive

1930 To Buffalo until February 7 to draw a number of portrait commissions arranged by Esther Sawyer. Summer and winter, in Provincetown.

1931 January, to Fall River, Massachusetts, to visit old friend Florida Duncan a day before her death. Pat pregnant, they decide a girl will be named Florida. February, to Trumansburg and Buffalo for more portrait drawings. Pat to Winter Park, then Brookline, Massachusetts, with her mother and sister, Isabel. Joins her April 16 to await birth of baby. Helen Florida born May 16 in Cambridge, Massachusetts. They return to Provincetown, July 8. Paints steadily on *Woodland Scene*, 1929–35, which proves difficult as its size changes three times. Also paints other compositions. Pat begins histology studies with Dr. Frederick Hammett. November 6, Tibi and Henry Van Sickle married by her father in Pearl Street studio. November 29, Helen Florida baptized by her grandfather Dickinson.

1932 Pat continues histology studies. First visit from Patty Rich, a Boston orphan who lives with them each summer through 1936.

1933 Sign on house offers drawings for fifteen dollars each. August 30, after difficult pregnancy, Pat gives birth to Constant in Provincetown. At ten days old, Constant has sudden, serious eye infection with blindness feared. Dick Parmenter rushes him to Massachusetts Eye and Ear Hospital in Boston. October 16, Constant finally comes home, entirely cured, after long hospital stay. Largest painting ever, 97 by 77¾ inches, stretched November 5 with help of Philip Malicoat, to be *Composition with Still Life*, 1933–37. November 8, Constant baptized by his grandfather Dickinson, making the day a triple event: Constant's baptism, start of large canvas, and anniversary of Pat and Edwin's declaration of love in 1927. December 19, they give a large party.

1934 Paints *Stranded Brig* under WPA. Entire family has chicken pox in winter. Family well enough to spend May in Sheldrake, then return to Provincetown. October, with family moves to Buffalo, living in cottage on Sawyer property and painting in Esther's studio. Teaches art classes through the year.

1935 June 27, family drives to Provincetown, stopping for night at Cazenovia, New York. There state police find them with shocking news of Howard's murder in Detroit earlier that day. He had been killed by a trio who had read about his arrival in Detroit to settle a large estate. June 30, Howard buried next to his mother and brother at Pleasant Valley. Rest of year in Provincetown.

1936 February, with Pat to New York to see Georgette Passedoit Gallery show. April to Andover, Massachusetts; New Haven, Connecticut; and New York to do portrait drawings of the four sons of Anna and John Williamson Bird of Bradford, Pennsylvania. Elected president of Provincetown Art Association.

1937 January, February, and April, meets Esther Hoyt Sawyer in New York as artist-advisor to her Association of Collectors and Artists, a project intended to bring collectors and artists together. May, organizes exhibition in Buffalo, resulting in first sale of a work by Jackson Pollock, *The Cotton Pickers*. To Bradford, Pennsylvania, to do portrait drawings of Anna and John Williamson Bird. His accepted, hers rejected. Much later, sells the latter. Summer in Provincetown. November 20, family sails for Europe on freight ship *Ilsenstein*. First to Paris. In Arles for Christmas, settling December 26 in little port of Sanary-sur-Mer.

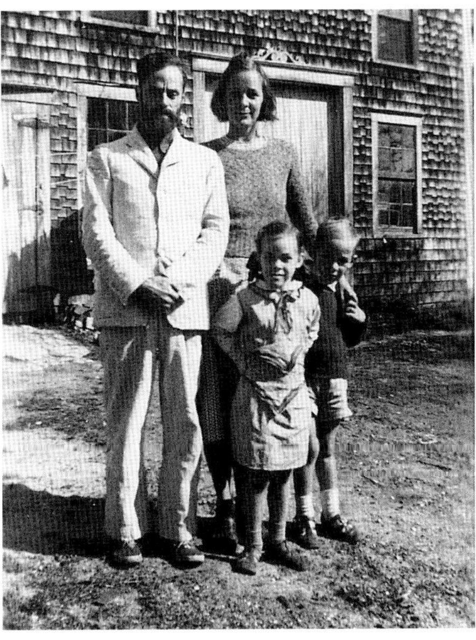

At the barn on Pearl Street in Provincetown with Pat, Helen, and Constant, summer 1937. Courtesy Dickinson Family Archive

1938 January 11, family rents Villa Sinaia. Paints every day in this new landscape. April, new

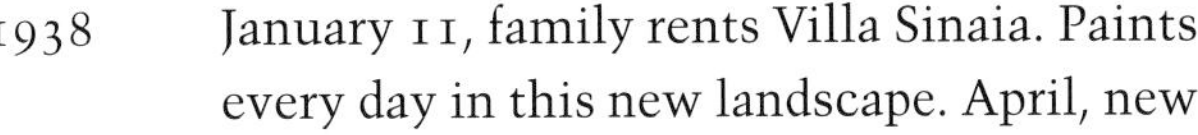

paintings shipped to Georgette Passedoit Gallery for show. Family to Rome for a week; travels alone to Florence and Venice. Metropolitan Museum purchases *Villa la Mouette*. Late May and June, in Paris. July 3, to Brittany, living in stone farmhouse in Lancieux. Paints inland orchards because beaches are so windy. Life characterized by long walks, exploration of local châteaus, beaches, swimming, and reading aloud in evenings. Trips to St. Briac and Mont St. Michel. September 11, packing canvases. September 12, Hitler's designs on Czechoslovakia are clear. September 24, family leaves Lancieux for London. Given exceptional permission to enter Britain without visas. There, he is the last of family to see Frances Wellstead (sister of Marjorie Wellstead Dickinson, Howard's wife), who was never found after the Blitz. Secures passage for family to sail September 29 on the *Transylvania*, Glasgow to Boston. To Provincetown to stay with Pat's mother, and then to Sheldrake. To Buffalo, October 11, to live again in Sawyer cottage and use Esther's studio. November 19, Helen has pneumonia. Start of winter of relentless family sickness, with painting time much curtailed. Pat's bronchitis so severe that doctor requires Helen to recuperate away from home, living with Esther's sister Albertine Glenny.

1939 Teaches at Art Institute of Buffalo. April 5, attends opening of one-artist show in Rochester, New York, and then to New York to hang Georgette Passedoit Gallery exhibition. Summer, family rents old parsonage in Sheldrake, with no utilities, seven dollars per month. No longer content to live in Provincetown; considering Maryland or Connecticut. Finally returns to Cape, purchasing old house on cove off Wellfleet harbor. Declares it perfect, right on the water. October 22, family arrives. House in dreadful condition. Reroof and reshingle house, and make most interior repairs themselves. No utilities and difficult to keep warm. Makes many drawings for Georgette Passedoit Gallery show of drawings in December.

1940 Attempts to make a studio upstairs but light is poor. Works as best he can, producing new pieces for April show at Georgette Passedoit Gallery. Pat's mother offers to pay to install bathroom and running water; work completed that fall. One of the 1939 drawings of South Wellfleet Inn shows turret with large round window. Inn burns that winter but round window survives; arranges for its installation in peak of house. Summer, teaches life class on upper Cape in Centerville. With Pat, paints twice weekly

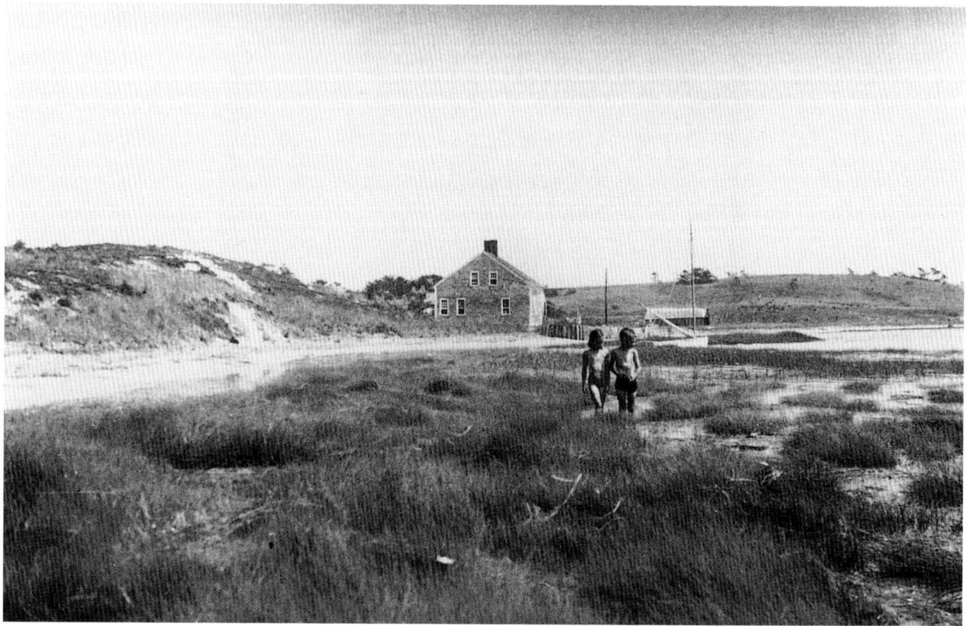

Helen and Constant at Wellfleet, taken by their father, ca. 1940–41.
Courtesy Dickinson Family Archive

in Brewster where Helen has music and dance lessons. Family given a chicken house and thirteen silver-spangled Hamburg chickens; in summer, fresh eggs are a source of revenue. Constant and Helen pick out puppy, their beloved dog "Whistle." Need for studio urgent. November, borrows funds from Dick Parmenter to buy land and build. December 18, studio completed. Years later, Dick forgives debt. Portrait of Constant, 1940–41 and 1944, first work begun in new studio.

1941 Elected to Federation of Modern Painters and Sculptors. Begins teaching at Stuart School of Design, Boston. A largely tranquil year—happy with home and studio—filled with painting, taking long walks, collecting driftwood for fireplace. Teaches telegraphy class at Wellfleet high school. Children have measles. Pat and children join pottery class, digging and cleaning their own clay. Paints portrait of Helen, still lifes, self-portraits, and landscapes.

We also learn that to be different can be dangerous. Wellfleet was a town of about eight hundred fishermen, and our house was isolated from town. My father's beard was then a rarity. Everyone (not unreasonably) feared German U-boats, and the idea grew up that we were German spies. Because my father often drew and painted on beaches, it was thought that he was making maps for the Germans. There was nothing too ridiculous for people to believe, and attitudes toward us became hostile; Constant and I were badly bullied in school. The anti-Dickinson talk became so alarming that Pat's sister, Edith, who lived in town, urged us to take some action to clear ourselves. My father immediately went to a meeting of the American Legion in Provincetown, declared us to be loyal American citizens, said he himself was a veteran of World War I and a member of the American Legion, Paris Post #1. Further, he said it was the clear duty of this American Legion post to state publicly that we were loyal citizens and that all talk against us must stop. A resolution was passed, though by a close vote. It was very sobering and not yet over. Rumors still circulated, and in 1943, American soldiers arrived at our house, threatened to shoot our dog, and said German propaganda had been found nearby. We were astonished, but they had already searched the studio and found two German propaganda magazines of 1936. This was easily explained. Our friend John Dos Passos had seen them in Germany and brought them home to my father because The Cello Player *was mocked and cartooned as an example of "degenerate" art.*

1942 February, family to Boston as a treat. To New York, for Georgette Passedoit Gallery show. Constant, a good rower, learns to sail a homemade craft, with sailing becoming a lifelong interest. Stuart School closes for good, dealing a blow to family. Fall, during a trip to New York, meets Elaine Fried (who will soon marry Willem de Kooning). Visits de Kooning's studio. Food rationing in effect but family extremely self-sufficient: driftwood in front-room fireplace, coal in dining room (and studio), and kerosene upstairs and in the lamps. An old-fashioned kitchen range burns all night cooking very rough oatmeal ordered from Boston. Large shipment of canned goods delivered each fall and stored in round Cape Cod cellar that has no refrigeration.

1943 January 1, begins *Ruin at Daphne*, 1943–53. Title refers to the Syrian "Daphni," not the Greek. Away much of April and May. Makes several trips to New York in search of employment and living accommodations for family. He and Pat asked to lead and advocate Hoover's "Feed the Children Committee" to get food to children of war-torn Europe. Extremely active in this endeavor; much of the Cape joins in and helps. Invited by Dorothy C. Miller to exhibit in *Romantic Painting in America*, exhibition at Museum of Modern Art in New York. Most regular exhibitions closed down because of the war. Constant adds "Edwin" to his name. Family grows fresh food and takes advantage of everything edible in the wild, walks everywhere, often to town to library. Each year, a bicycle is purchased, and in time every family member has one. Pat's was the first. Great enjoyment of cove wildlife, including a great blue heron.

1944 February, to New York with Pat. June 5, death of Marjorie Wellstead Dickinson, who is buried beside Howard in Pleasant Valley. Nephew Carter, Jr., inducted into army. June 29–August 25, in New York doing commissioned drawings and large painting. Finds apartment and family moves there September 4; believes change necessary for work and for children's education. Pat begins work at Hewitt School; Helen and Constant meet Aunt Antoinette and Uncle Charles Evans Hughes and Mr. and Mrs. Groesbeck. Requests that support from Sawyers end.

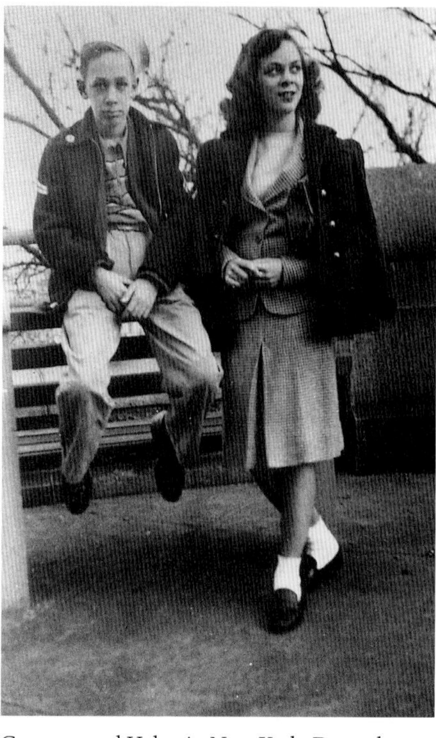
Constant and Helen in New York, December 1945. Courtesy Dickinson Family Archive

1945 May, to Wellfleet to prepare house for rental. New life in New York. Fall, begins teaching at ASL, Cooper Union, and Midtown School of Art. Pat given a better, full-time job at Hewitt School. Every Saturday is "Field Day," cleaning, doing laundry, ironing, marketing. Helen babysits and earns enough money to buy fabric to make her own clothes by hand. December 5, funeral of Aunt Antoinette Hughes.

1946 First public showing of unfinished *Ruin at Daphne* at Provincetown Art Association. September, with Helen to Sheldrake to sort contents of his father's "barn." September 16, barn burns to the ground. Countless early drawings and Chase class still lifes lost, as well as his father's sermons, family memorabilia, and everything Carter, Jr., owned. In New York, amicable parting from Georgette Passedoit after seven one-artist exhibitions. No longer wishes to show there but does not wish to affiliate with a new gallery immediately even though opportunities are many. Pat continues to rise at Hewitt School, becoming expert remedial reading teacher, and later, head of art department.

1947 Summer, Pat teaches remedial reading at Hessian Hills School in Croton, New York. July 24, through carelessness of tenant, Wellfleet house burned. Second floor and roof destroyed. Swift action of Wellfleet Volunteer Firemen saved the rest. Annual search for a new studio resumes each fall as many buildings torn down in postwar building boom. September, entire Lower Cape shocked and sorrowed by sudden death of Katy Dos Passos, who, with her husband, John, was a close family friend. Ends teaching at Midtown School of Art. Appears in many exhibitions, with more paintings sold.

1948 Elected Associate of National Academy of Design. Helen and Constant's high school, Horace-Mann–Lincoln, to close. Helen's class can finish senior year; Constant goes to Friends Seminary. Edwin, an ardent Beethoven admirer like Burgess, who was able to play piano transcription of Beethoven's Ninth Symphony entirely from memory, visits New York Public Library vaults to see Beethoven's piano. Friend Sheldon Dick purchases *Composition with Still Life,* 1933–37, and other canvases. Goddaughter Elizabeth Dick born July 2. Pat's mother, in Provincetown with daughter Isabel, suffers stroke and dies a month later.

1949 Paints *Self-Portrait,* 1949, for National Academy of Design, his "diploma" portrait. Awarded Evelyn Clair Lockman First Prize for Portraiture by National Academy of Design. Begins teaching at Art School of the Brooklyn Museum. Spring, finishes teaching at Cooper Union. Helen graduates from high school, entering Oberlin College in fall. June 30, death of stepmother, Luty Dickinson; service in Shushan, New York, with burial in Buffalo. Father visits Wellfleet in August.

1950 January, begins ambitious composition to include nude self-portrait. Unsatisfied, cuts it up in May, saving head and still-life. February, lectures at American University, Washington, D.C. February 25, in Tokyo, Japan, Carter, Jr., marries Rose Marie Pindat. May 12, sudden death of old friend Sheldon Dick. May 26, cousin Bessie Hand Barr dies Springfield, Massachusetts; her Dickinson paintings lost. To Martha's Vineyard to visit Dick Parmenter. Elected full academician National Academy of Design. Teaches at Pratt Institute, Brooklyn, for one year.

1951 Becomes particularly absorbed in perspective exercises during 1950s, often doing them in evenings. Constant graduates high school, going on to St. Lawrence University. June 10, with Tibi, spends night with their father, who dies quietly in Sheldrake the next day. Funeral Geneva, New York; burial in Buffalo next to Luty. Loss of father, even at age ninety-six, extremely difficult. Pat purchases Dickinson paintings from Sheldon Dick's estate.

1952 Reputation, though strong since 1916, becomes even more widespread. Invited to show work in many exhibitions, serves on numerous juries and committees. Included as one of *15 Americans* in exhibition at Museum of Modern Art. *Carrousel Bridge, Paris,* 1952, purchased by National Academy of Design, Henry Ward Ranger Bequest. Family to Wellfleet for Christmas. Engagement of Helen to Robert (Bob) Ashworth Baldwin. Graduating from Oberlin, Bob begins graduate work at Yale Drama School as scene designer. Summer, spends a month in France with Helen, first in Paris and then in

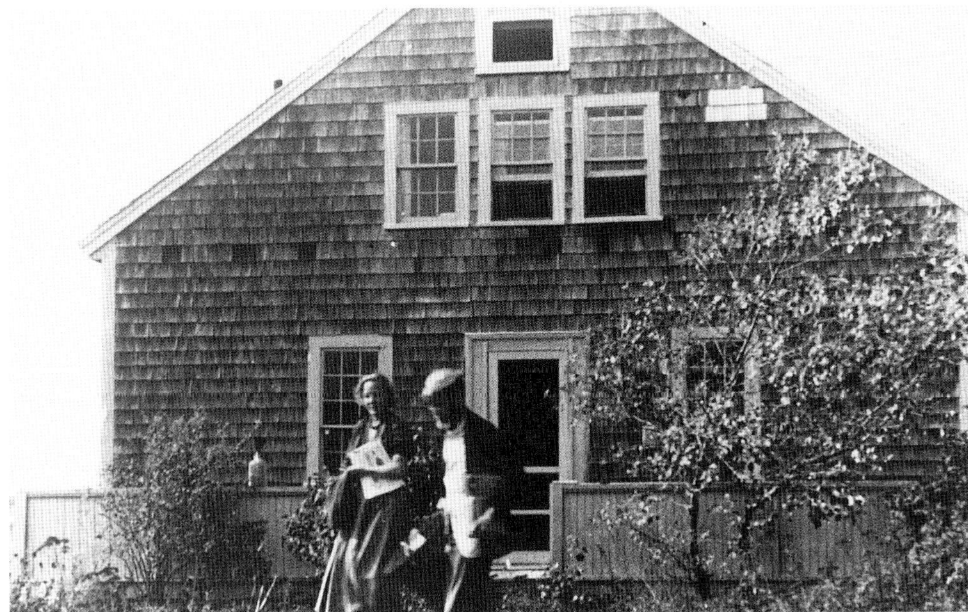

Pat and Edwin at the house at Wellfleet, 1952. Courtesy Dickinson Family Archive

Montignac-sur-Vézère, site of the great prehistoric cave paintings of Lascaux. Visits the cave every day, overwhelmed by the skill and artistry of these artists of fifteen thousand years ago. Pays them homage in 1953, when he paints *Still Life, Lascaux* (cat. no. 61).

1953 Helen graduates from Oberlin and on June 14, married in Wellfleet house to Bob Baldwin by his father, the Reverend A. Graham Baldwin, of Phillips Academy, Andover, Massachusetts. Edwin in exceedingly poor health; in and out of hospital all summer with intractable infections. Helen and Bob live in New Haven, Connecticut. All to Wellfleet for Christmas.

1954 Elected to Century Association. Awarded National Institute of Arts and Letters grant. *Ruin at Daphne* sold to Metropolitan Museum of Art. August, with Pat to Martha's Vineyard.

1955 Constant graduates St. Lawrence University. Bob receives M.F.A. from Yale Drama School. Both drafted, Constant into navy, Bob into army. December 1, Edwin awarded Century Association Medal for Art. Christmas in Wellfleet.

1956 April 19, resigns from Century Association. May 23, inducted into Art Department of National Institute of Arts and Letters. June, Helen goes for year in Germany where Bob is stationed. Edwin to Skowhegan with Pat to teach during August. September 1, returns to Wellfleet. To Sheldrake for Thanksgiving and Florida for Christmas.

1957 January 12, grandson David Graham Baldwin born Stuttgart, Germany. Summer, Constant and Bob discharged. Glen Eyrie sold. Illegal destruction of much of cove. Wellfleet

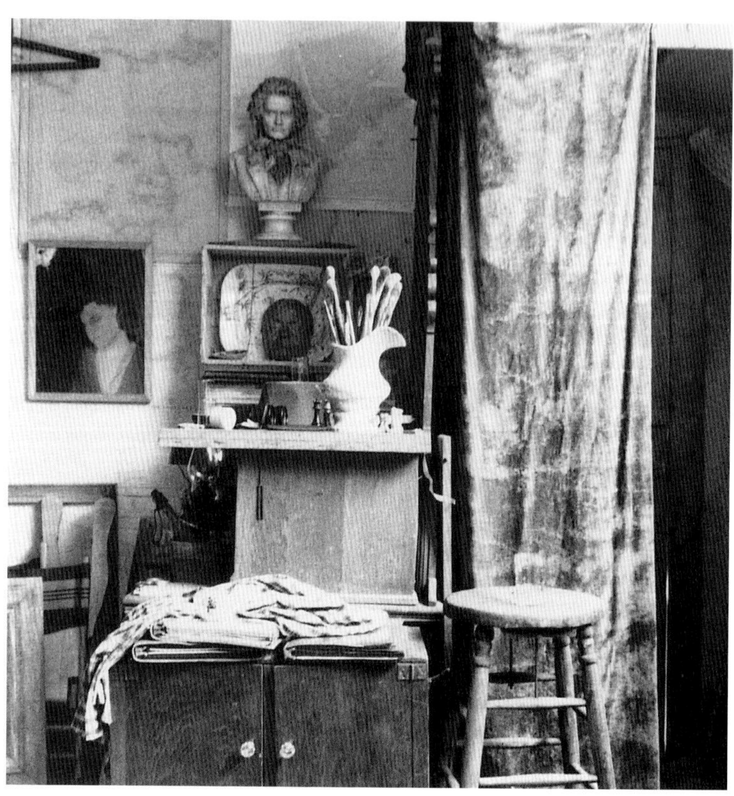

A view of the studio at Wellfleet, August 1957.
Photograph by R. A. Baldwin
Courtesy Dickinson Family Archive

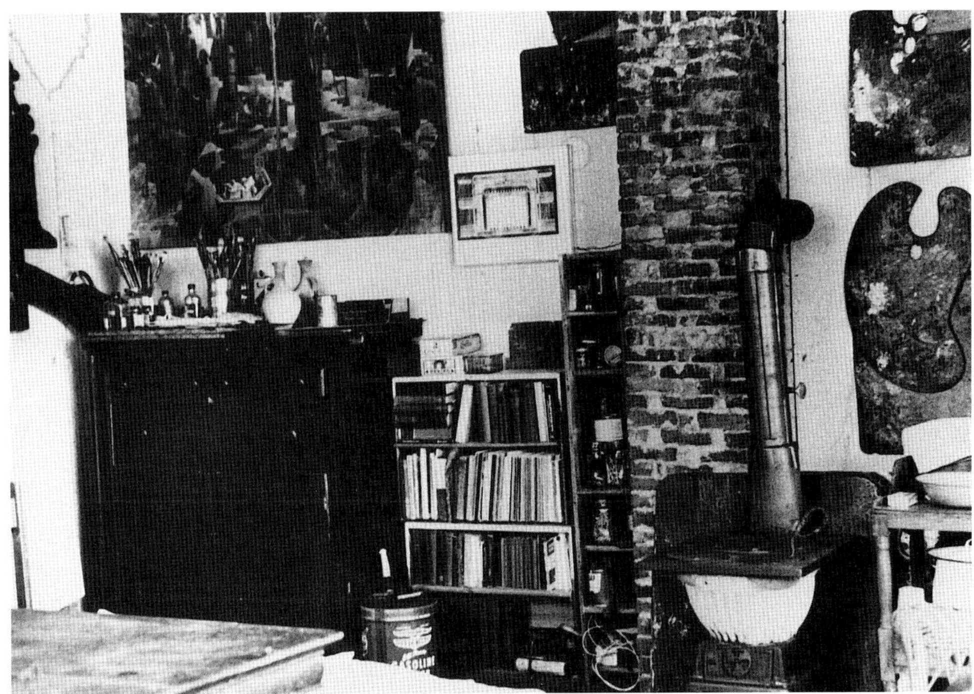

A view of the studio at Wellfleet, August 1957.
Photograph by R. A. Baldwin. Courtesy Dickinson Family Archive

harbor dredged, with dredgings dumped in cove, reducing its size and character dramatically. House no longer by the water. First wish is to sell but no one knows who owns vast new acreage in front of house. Dickinsons gain title to new land from Commonwealth of Massachusetts finally in 1976. Baldwins move to Nashville, Tennessee, where Bob will teach at Vanderbilt University.

1958 Again awarded National Academy of Design's Second Altman Prize for Landscape for *Paris Windows*, 1952. May, elected a vice president of National Institute of Arts and Letters. Large retrospective held at Cushman Gallery in Houston, Texas. July, at Skowhegan with Pat. Late July, diagnosed with tuberculosis. Surgery in Boston in early September for removal of upper part of right lung. Constant visits every day; Pat, who has to continue teaching at Hewitt's, comes every weekend. November 15, grandson Steven Carter Baldwin born in Nashville.

1959 February 10, receives grant of $10,000 from Ford Foundation. Large exhibition held at Boston University. April 7, awarded Brandeis University Creative Arts Award Medal. July 2, with Pat boards freighter *Tekla Torm*; cruising all summer visiting Mediterranean ports. Pat falls in love with Greece. Upon return, they visit Baldwins. To Nashville for Christmas.

1960 Agrees with James Graham & Sons, New York, to a large retrospective of work. Grandson John Frederick Baldwin born in Nashville on his mother Helen's birthday, May 16. Like brothers, christened with salt water from the Wellfleet cove. June 2, Edwin receives honorary D.F.A. from Pratt Institute. Visits Mediterranean with Pat for summer.

1961 All family present for the opening, February 1, of exhibition at James Graham & Sons. July 10, elected Benjamin Franklin Fellow of the Royal Society for the Encouragement of Arts, Manufactures and Commerce, London. With Pat to Nantucket to sail with Chauncey and Catherine Hughes Waddell on their yacht. He and Catherine are close cousins and Waddells have bought his paintings steadily since the 1930s. Sails for

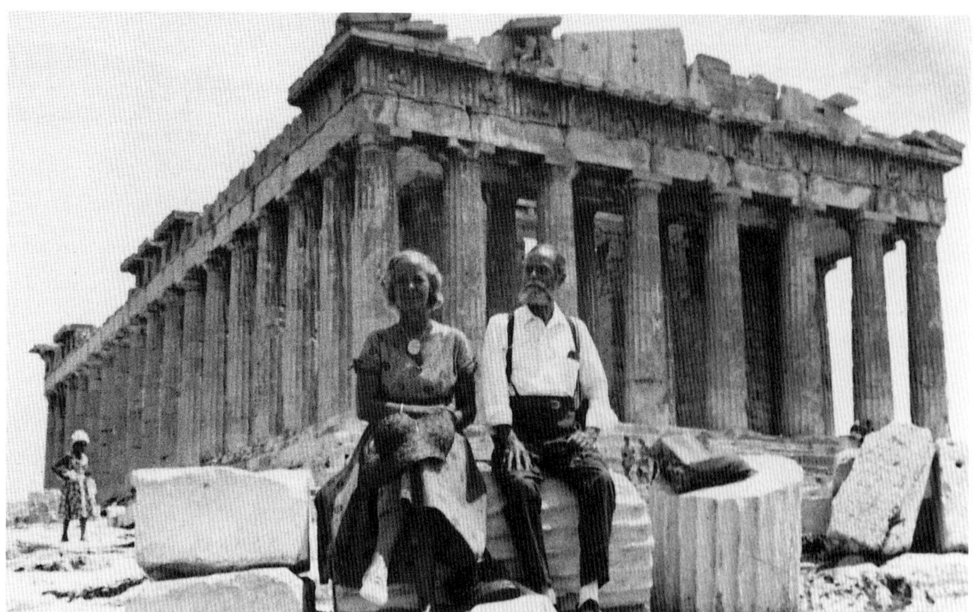

Pat and Edwin at the Parthenon, ca. 1960s.
Courtesy Dickinson Family Archive

Greece with Pat October 16 on *Queen Frederica* for a year's sabbatical. December 12, learns of sudden death of Catherine Hughes Waddell and December 17, of sudden death of Pat's sister, Edith Foley Shay. Both women important in their lives and loss is deeply felt.

1962 Travels in Near East and visits Baalbek with Esther Sawyer. Syrian coup closes borders for three days. Inducted into American Academy of Arts and Letters, one of only fifty

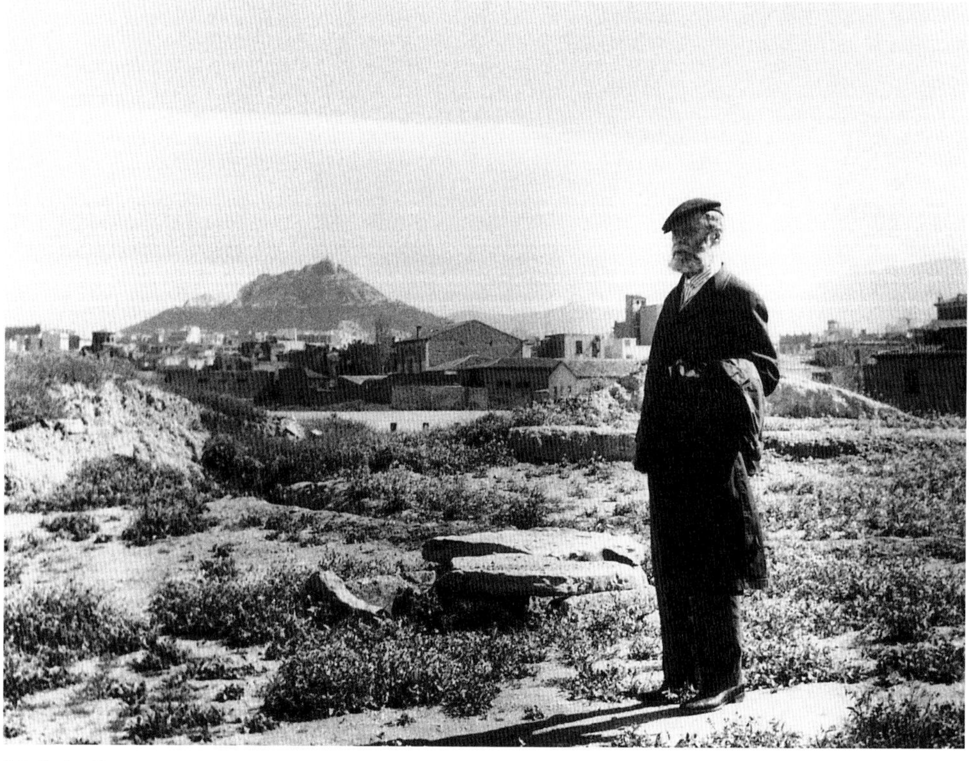

Edwin in Greece, 1962.
Photograph by Michael Tzovaras
Courtesy Dickinson Family Archive

members. Awarded Benjamin West Clinedinst Memorial Medal by Artists Fellowship, Inc.

1963 January, and spring, makes several trips to Sheldrake, visiting Tibi often. June 22, Nancy Constance Snider and Constant are married in New York. Next day, with Pat, flies to Paris to meet Baldwins, who have spent previous year teaching for Vanderbilt in Aix-en-Provence. Travels through Greece and the islands. November 10–15, in New Haven for festivities surrounding the publication by Yale University Press and the Drawing Society of *The Drawings of Edwin Dickinson*, 1963. Lectures as Chubb Fellow of Timothy Dwight College at Yale. Christmas in Nashville.

1964 In New York, then Sheldrake, finally to Washington, D.C. To Nashville with Pat to help with grandsons while Helen recovers from surgery. Sails for Athens June 5, traveling through new areas of Greece. September 10, flies to New York to help settle Tibi and Henry in nursing home. To Nashville for Christmas.

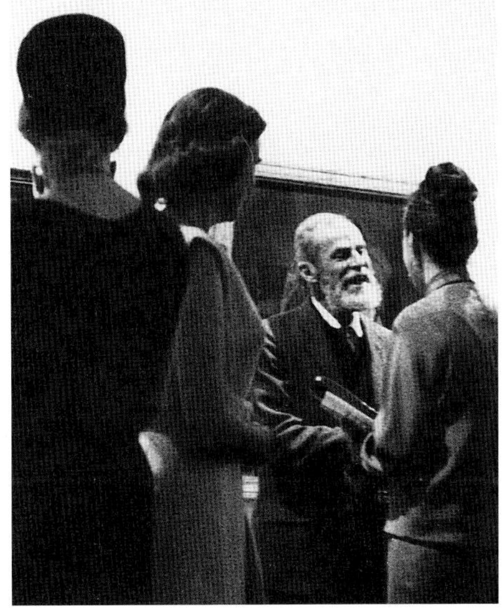

The artist at the opening of his retrospective at the Whitney Museum of American Art, New York, 1965.
Courtesy Dickinson Family Archive

1965 Lectures at Columbia University and University of Hartford. Invited to lecture or teach at many universities but will only consider those near New York. Awarded Brevoort-Eickemeyer Prize, given every five years by Columbia University. Sails June 10 for Piraeus with sojourn in Sicily. September 4, to New York. October 19, all family present for largest show ever, one-artist retrospective at New York's Whitney Museum of American Art.

1966 March, short trip to Greece. Granddaughter Sarah Elizabeth Dickinson born New York, March 26. Prepares for retirement, with last day at ASL May 2. Pat retires June 2. Awarded honorary D.F.A. by Philadelphia College of Art; September 20, sails for Greece with Pat.

1967 Together with Pat, travels in Greece. March 31, flies to London, visiting Stonehenge, Salisbury, and Canterbury. April 29, to Bloomfield Hills, Michigan, for his cousin Elizabeth Hughes Gossett's presentation of Dickinson's 1923 portrait of her father to Oakland University. On to Wellfleet. Baldwins there. August 3, large exhibition of his work opens at Provincetown Art Association and Museum. October, to New York for treatment of glaucoma. December, in Nashville.

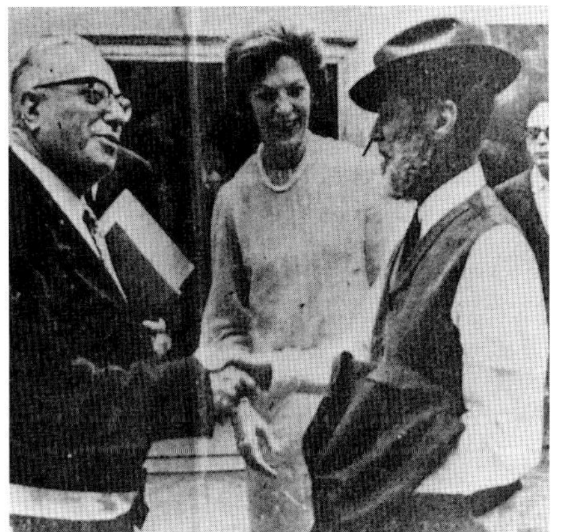

Dickinson (right) greeting the mayor of Venice in June 1968 during the XXXIV Biennale, published in *Stampa Sera* (Venice), June 24–25, 1968. Reprinted in *Triptych* (San Francisco), Sept.–Oct. 1988, p. 15.
Courtesy Dickinson Family Archive

1968 Year in Greece. January 26, death of Henry Van Sickle in Geneva; burial in Interlaken. May 26, Tibi dies in Geneva; burial in Interlaken. Arrives Venice, June 18, as principal painter in American Pavilion of XXXIV

Venice Biennale. Sails for New York, June 24. To Carter, Jr., and Marie's, then to Wellfleet. Baldwins there. Death of Carter, Jr., of cancer, September 7; burial in Alexandria, Virginia. To New York for arrival of Constant, Nancy, and Sarah, who have lived previous two years in Tokyo.

1969 January 25, boards *Cristoforo Columbo* for Greece. March, Pat alone to Macedonia, while Edwin remains in Athens, due to ill health. April 15, returns to New York with Pat; by May 7 in Wellfleet. Birth of grandson Andrew Burgess Dickinson, May 27. To New York to see him, May 31. June 6, to Sheldrake to empty Tibi's house. To Wellfleet, June 10. Helen, sons, and Constant and family visit Wellfleet. Declines a D.F.A from University of Nebraska at Lincoln, saying those already received have not been "used."

1970 January 23, with Pat takes the *Cristoforo Columbo* for Piraeus. Travels more at sea and returns to New York, April 30. Summer, visits with children and grandchildren, returning to Greece in December.

1971 May, returns to New York, then to Riverside, Connecticut, to visit Constant and family, then to Wellfleet. December 11, to Nashville, then to Riverside, flying to Athens, December 24.

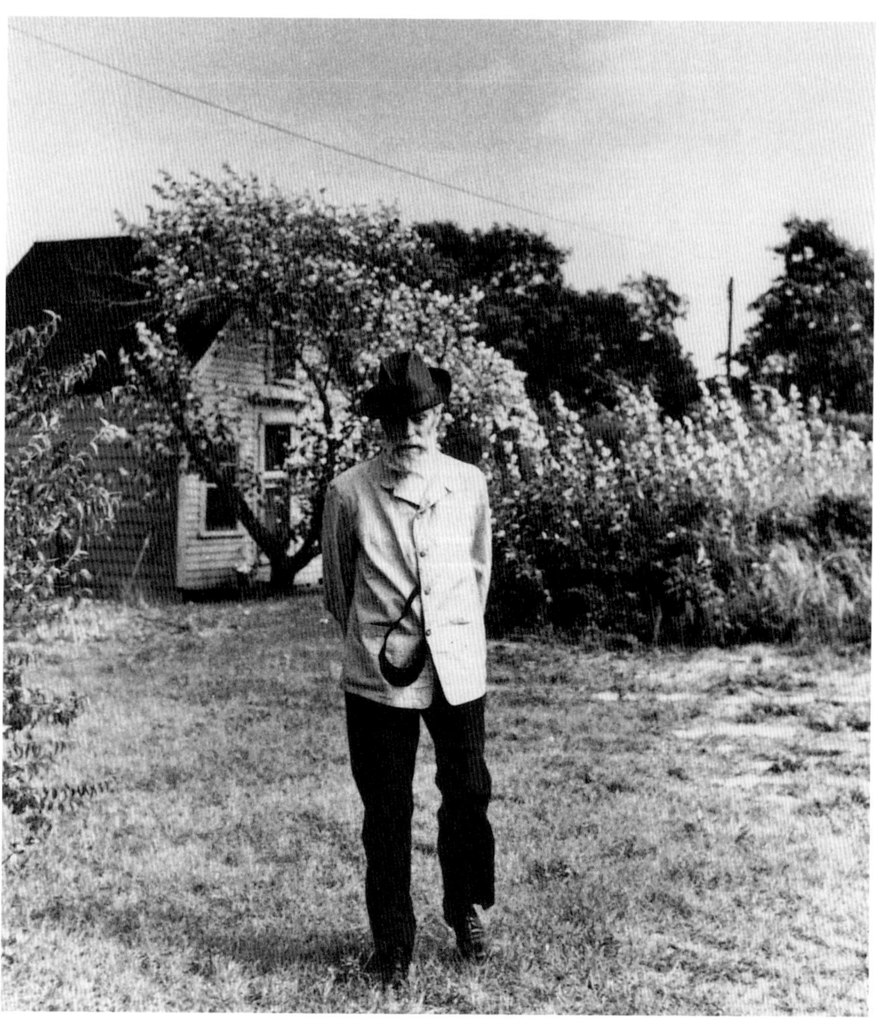

The artist at Wellfleet, September 13, 1972.
Photograph by Tom Breuer
Courtesy Dickinson Family Archive

1972 Spring, Helen and Bob to Athens to travel and experience Greek Orthodox Easter together. April, another cataract operation in Boston, with long recuperation. August, Dick Parmenter visits. October, suffers cerebral hemorrhage.

1973 May 30, awarded honorary D.F.A. from the Maryland Institute, College of Art; received at private home ceremony in Wellfleet. November 17, flies to Greece.

1974 Home from Greece, May 6. Undergoes another cataract operation in New York.

1975 January, to Athens with Pat. Difficulty walking despite much physical therapy. Requires constant care. Only after his death is it realized he had surely had Alzheimer's disease for years. May 27, returns to Wellfleet.

1976 January, to Athens for last time, returning in May. August, the Provincetown Art Association mounts retrospective of his work. Derives enormous pleasure from it. Paintings and drawings are all old friends; asks Pat to take him every day. Each piece recalls something of his fifty years as an artist. Everything about Provincetown brings back a former self.

After 1976 he is no longer able to travel, and he and Pat live quietly in Wellfleet. But as anyone who knows Alzheimer's disease understands, the demands of care overwhelm the caregiver. Pat was herself seventy-three, and it all but broke her heart to take him to a nursing home in April of 1978. She visited him every day and remained able to "reach" him right up until his death.

The night of December 1, he was clearly dying. He and Pat spent the night together, sometimes talking, sometimes reading from his beloved Shakespeare sonnets. And he could recognize them! He died in the early morning of December 2. Constant and I were not able to arrive in time. His closest family took his ashes to a favorite ocean beach and there Constant and I waded into the December water to spread them. In the afternoon, innumerable friends of his eighty-seven years packed the Provincetown Art Association for a short "remembrance."

Pat was born January 2, 1905, and died June 1, 1996. Again, the family gathered, and again, Constant and I spread her ashes in the ocean where our father's had been. We had a remembrance gathering at the Audubon Society in South Wellfleet and then a huge party in the studio. Over one hundred people, from all over New England, came to give love and honor to Pat Dickinson.

2001 June 22, death of Edwin Constant Dickinson.

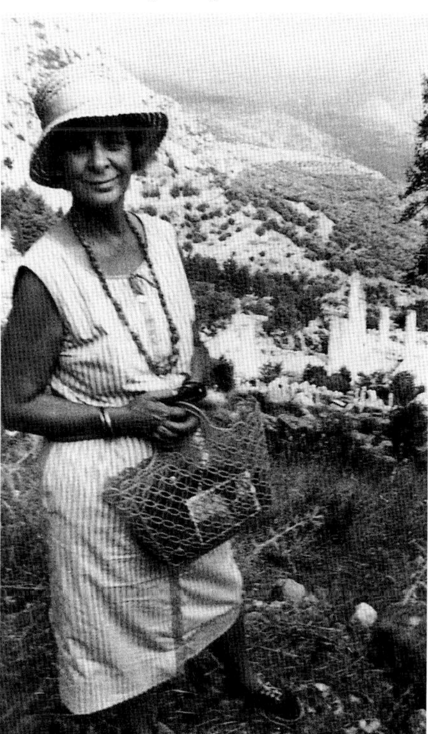

Pat at Delphi, ca. 1960s.
Courtesy Dickinson Family Archive

SELECTED BIBLIOGRAPHY

BY THE ARTIST

1916–71 Journals, Special Collections Library, Syracuse University, New York.

Letters to Ansley W. Sawyer and Esther Hoyt Sawyer. Archives of American Art, Washington, D.C.

1951 "A Painter's Attitude toward Color." *The League* (New York), Spring 1951, p. 14.

1960 Introduction in *Hawthorne on Painting*. Compiled by Mrs. Charles W. Hawthorne. New York and Chicago: Pitman Publishing Corporation, 1938. Reprint, New York: Dover Publications, 1960, p. V.

1963 "On My Way of Painting." In Potter, Eric, ed. *Painters on Painting*. New York: Grosset and Dunlap, 1963, p. 223.

1966 "The Artist on His Work—10: Housekeeping of the Palette." *The Christian Science Monitor* (Boston), Jan. 25, 1966, p. 8.

ON THE ARTIST

Books

1963 Goodrich, Lloyd. *The Drawings of Edwin Dickinson*. New Haven, Conn.: Yale University Press in association with The Drawing Society, 1963.

1985 Driscoll, John Paul. "Edwin Walter Dickinson: An Iconological Interpretation of the Major Symbolical Paintings." Ph.D. dissertation, Pennsylvania State University, 1985. Ann Arbor, Mich.: UMI Research Press, 1985.

1989 Devaney, John. "Full Attention—The Art of Edwin Dickinson." Independent research paper for M.F.A. candidacy, Tufts University/School of the Museum of Fine Arts, Boston, 1989.

1994 Theoret, Michelle S. "The Self-Portraits of Edwin Walter Dickinson." M.A. thesis, Temple University, 1994.

2001 Abell, Mary Ellen. "Edwin Dickinson: His Work, Teaching, and Critical Reception." Ph.D. dissertation, City University of New York, 2001.

Interviews with the Artist

1945 Wolf, Ben. "The Digest Interviews: Edwin Dickinson." *The Art Digest* (New York), Aug. 1, 1945, p. 13.

1957–58 Gruber, Carol S. "The Reminiscences of Edwin Dickinson." Oral History Research Office, Columbia University, New York, 1957–58.

1960 Kuh, Katharine. "Edwin Dickinson." In *The Artist's Voice: Talks with Seventeen Artists*, pp. 69–80. New York: Harper and Row, 1962. Reprint, New York: Da Capo Press, 2000.

1962 Seckler, Dorothy. "Tape-Recorded Interview with Edwin Dickinson. Provincetown, Mass., Aug. 22, 1962." Oral History Collection, Archives of American Art, Washington, D.C.

1963 Louis Finkelstein. "Interview with Edwin Dickinson." New Haven, Conn.: Yale University, Timothy Dwight College, Nov. 13, 1963. Archives of American Art, Washington, D.C.

1966 Wilson, Patricia Boyd. "Angle of Light on Dickinson's Art." *The Christian Science Monitor* (Boston), Jan. 25, 1966, p. 4.

1970 Fortess, Karl. "Karl Fortess Taped Interviews: Edwin Dickinson. Wellfleet, Mass., Aug. 5, 1970." Oral History Collection, Archives of American Art, Washington, D.C.

Articles

1927 H[ekking], W[illiam] M. "Buffalo Given an E. Dickinson." *The Art News* (New York), Oct. 29, 1927, p. 12.

1935 Hekking, Dr. William M. "Dickinson Shows Three Paintings." *The Buffalo Evening News*, Apr. 30, 1935, page unknown.

1938 Burrows, Carlyle. "Four New Canvasses Bought by Museum." *New York Herald Tribune*, July 17, 1938, page unknown.

G., E. "Met Buys Four Paintings by Americans of Today." *New York World Telegram*, July 16, 1938, p. 17.

1939 Rohr, Nora Lee. "Science Museum Adds 4000 B.C. Pottery to Collection Devoted to Primitive Art; Dickinson Awaited." *Buffalo Evening News*, Feb. 25, 1939, page unknown.

1949 Adlow, Dorothy. "'Self Portrait': A Painting by Edwin Dickinson." *The Christian Science Monitor* (Boston), Dec. 19, 1949, p. 8.

de Kooning, Elaine. "Edwin Dickinson Paints a Picture." *Art News* (New York), Sept. 1949, pp. 26–28, 50–51.

McBride, Henry. "The National Academy: The Several Juries of Prize Awards Render Unexpected Justice." *The New York Sun*, Nov. 18, 1949, page unknown.

Rondell, Lester. "Editor's Letters." *Art News* (New York), Nov. 1949, p. 6.

1950 "Edwin Dickinson." *Art Students League News* (New York), Feb. 16, 1950, p. 3.

1951 Adlow, Dorothy. "Windmills on Cape Cod." *The Christian Science Monitor* (Boston), Mar. 26, 1951, p. 8.

1952 de Kooning, Elaine. "The Modern Museum's Fifteen: Dickinson and Kiesler." *Art News* (New York), Apr. 1952, pp. 20–23, 66–67.

1953 Kneeland, Paul F. "Cape Cod Artist Paints Portraits to Please Himself, Not the Subjects." *The Boston Sunday Globe*, Apr. 26, 1953, sec. A, p. 9.

1955 "America, 1953: for the Metropolitan." *Art News* (New York), Mar. 1955, p. 47.

1957 "Three American Artists." *Vogue* (New York), Oct. 15, 1957, pp. 78–79.

"Edwin Dickinson." In Baur, John I. H., ed. *New Art in America: Fifty Painters of the 20th Century*, pp. 216–17. Greenwich, Conn.: New York Graphic Society, 1957.

Smith, Jacob Getlar. "Edwin Dickinson: American Mystic." *American Artist* (New York), Jan. 1957, pp. 54–59, 73–75.

1959 "10 Americans Get Ford Art Grants." *The New York Times*, Feb. 18, 1959, page unknown.

"Edwin Dickinson Wins Ford Foundation Grant of $10,000" and "News from the Institute." *Art Students League News* (New York), mid-Mar. 1959, p. 1.

1960 Schuyler, James. "No. 2: Edwin Dickinson." *Portfolio and Art News Annual* (New York), 1960, pp. 88–103.

1961 "Defying Time and Fashion." *Time* (New York), Feb. 10, 1961, pp. 60–63.

"Philosopher and Painter Honored." *The New York Times*, Dec. 6, 1961, p. 34.

Levin, Meyer, and Levin, Eli. "Today's Painters Lack Fundamentals." *Newark Star Ledger* (N.J.), Mar. 12, 1961, page unknown.

1963 Garabedian, John H. "Drinks with Dickinson: Inscrutable Flames Brighten T[imothy] D[wight] Party." *Yale Daily News* (New Haven, Conn.), Nov. 13, 1963, pp. 1, 8.

Pease, Roland F., Jr. "Dickinson." In Weller, Allen S. *Art USA Now.* Vol. 1. Edited by Lee Nordness, pp. 54–57. New York: Viking Press, 1963.

1964 Driscoll, Edgar J., Jr. "Eyebrows Raise; Only One Artist on Festival Panel." *Boston Globe*, Mar. 28, 1964, page unknown.

1965 "Edwin Dickinson Wins $1,000 Columbia Prize." *The New York Times*, Oct. 20, 1965, p. 38.

Chanin, A. L. "Ruin at Daphne," "The Fossil Hunters," and "Dickinson, Edwin." In *Artguide/New York*, pp. 100, 196, 263. New York: Horizon Press, 1965.

Delavan, Elizabeth. "A Visit with Edwin Dickinson." *The Reveille of Seneca Falls, New York*, Nov. 10, 1965, page unknown.

Geldzahler, Henry. "Figurative Painters of the Forties and Fifties: Edwin Dickinson." In *American Painting in the Twentieth Century.* New York: The Metropolitan Museum of Art, 1965, pp. 169–71.

1966 Pedersen, Axel Sand. "Edwin Dickinson: Part II." *The Prattler* [Pratt Institute] (New York), Nov. 11, 1966, page unknown.

1967 Preston, Stuart. "Edwin Dickinson." *Art and Artists* (London), Apr. 1967, pp. 28–29.

1968 Schneider, Howard. "The Artist Doesn't Compete with Anybody." *Poor Howard's Wednesday Afternoon Post* (Cape Cod, Mass.), Aug. 7, 1968, p. 5.

Winebrenner, D. K. "Dickinson Innovative, Traditionalist." *Buffalo Courier-Express*, Aug. 18, 1968, p. 92.

1969 Bishop, Isabel. "Commemorative Tribute: Edwin Dickinson (1891–1978), *American Institute of Arts and Letters* (New York), no. 30, 1969.

1970 Hoeffel, Paul H. "Edwin Dickinson: '. . . Never in a Superior Light.'" *The Cape Codder* (Orleans, Mass.), June 25, 1970, pp. 11, 14.

1972 Gussow, Alan. "Edwin Dickinson." In *A Sense of Place: The Artist and the American Land,* p. 153. New York: Friends of the Earth, 1972.

1973 Franc, Helen M. "Edwin Dickinson, *Composition with Still Life*, 1933–37." In *An Invitation to See: 125 Paintings from the Museum of Modern Art,* p. 102. New York: The Museum of Modern Art, 1973.

1975 Loercher, Diana. "A Picture with a Secret." *The Christian Science Monitor* (Boston), Aug. 21, 1975, p. 24.

McBride, Henry. "Edwin Dickinson." In *The Flow of Art: Essays and Criticisms of Henry McBride,* pp. 382–84. New York: Atheneum Publishers, 1975.

1976 Cummings, Paul. "Edwin Dickinson." In *American Drawings: The 20th Century,* pp. 82–83. New York: The Viking Press, 1976.

1977 Cummings, Paul. "Edwin Dickinson." In *Dictionary of Contemporary American Artists,* pp. 168–69. New York: St. Martin's Press, 1977.

1978 "Death of Edwin Dickinson, Instructor Emeritus." *Art Students League News* (New York), Dec. 1978, cover, ff.

"Renowned Artist Dies." *Provincetown Advocate* (Mass.), Dec. 7, 1978, page unknown.

Goodman, George, Jr. "Edwin W. Dickinson Dies at 87; Noted Representational Artist." *The New York Times*, Dec. 3, 1978, p. 44.

1979 "Obituaries: Edwin Dickinson." *Art in America* (New York), May–June 1979, p. 224.

N[ash], S[teven]. "Edwin Dickinson, *An Anniversary*, 1921." In Nash, Steven A., with Katy Kline; Charlotta Kotik; and Emese Wood. *Albright-Knox Art Gallery: Paintings and Sculpture from Antiquity to 1942,* pp. 508–9. New York: Rizzoli International Publications, in association with Albright-Knox Art Gallery, 1979.

1981 Mainardi, Patricia. "Edwin Dickinson." *Arts Magazine* (New York), Mar. 1981, p. 17.

1982 Adler, Elliot. "Observations on Edwin Dickinson." Edited, with note by Matthew Baigell. *Arts Magazine* (New York), Apr. 1982, pp. 124–26.

Shannon, Joe. "Wintry Visions." *Art News* (New York), Oct. 1982, pp. 98–100.

1983 J[affe], I[rma] B. "Edwin Dickinson, *Provincetown*, 1922." In Jaffe, Irma B., and Yvonne Korshak. *Selections from the Permanent Collection of the Arkansas Arts Center Foundation*, pp. 102–3. Little Rock: Arkansas Arts Center Foundation, 1983.

Kind, Joshua. "Edwin Dickinson." In Emanuel, Muriel; Sharon Harris; Michael Held; Christopher Lyon; Colin Naylor; Roland Turner; and George Walsh, eds. *Contemporary Artists*, p. 259. New York: St. Martin's Press, 1983.

Kuspit, Donald B. "American Romantic." *Art in America* (New York), Feb. 1983, pp. 108–11.

1986 Lieberman, William S. "Dickinson: Ruin at Daphne." In Lieberman, William S.; Lisa Mintz Messinger; Sabine Rewald; and Lowery S. Sims. *20th Century Art, Painting, 1945–1985: Selections from the Collection of the Metropolitan Museum of Art, New York*, p. 26. New York: The Metropolitan Museum of Art, 1986.

Raynor, Vivien. "Art: Whitney Displays Some New Acquisitions." *The New York Times*, Sept. 26, 1986, page unknown.

1987 Johnson, Robert Flynn. "Forum: Edwin Dickinson's 'Long Point Light.'" *Drawing* (New York), Jan.–Feb. 1987, pp. 107–8. Reprinted in *Triptych* (San Francisco), Feb.–Mar. 1987, pp. 18–19.

"Edwin Dickinson, *Gas Tanks*." In Pisano, Ronald G. *The Art Students League: Selections from the Permanent Collection*, pp. 76–77. Hamilton, N.Y.: Gallery Association of New York State, 1987.

1988 Baldwin, Helen Dickinson. "Edwin Dickinson." *Provincetown Arts* (Mass.), 1988, pp. 64–67, 168–69.

G[eske], N[orman] A. "Edwin Dickinson: *Girl on Tennis Court*, 1926." In *The American Painting Collection of the Sheldon Memorial Art Gallery*, pp. 46–47, 242. Compiled and edited by Norman A. Geske and Karen O. Janovy. Lincoln: University of Nebraska Press, 1988.

Simpson, Marc. "Recent Acquisitions: *The Cello Player*." *Triptych* (San Francisco), Sept.–Oct. 1988, pp. 14–20.

1989 Ashbery, John. "Edwin Dickinson." In *Reported Sightings: Art Chronicles, 1957–1987*. Edited by David Bergman. New York: Alfred A. Knopf, Inc., 1989, pp. 209–11.

Kahan, Mitchell D. "Edwin Dickinson, *Bible Reading aboard the Tegetthoff*." In *Masterworks of American Art from the Munson-Williams-Proctor Institute*, pp. 130–31. Edited by Paul D. Schweizer. New York: Harry N. Abrams, Inc., 1989.

Lublin, Mary. "Edwin Dickinson." In *19th and 20th Century Paintings*, pp. 80–81. New York: The Jordan-Volpe Gallery, 1989.

S[impson], M[arc]. "Edwin Dickinson [The Cello Player]." In Simpson, Marc; Sally Mills; and Jennifer Saville. *The American Canvas: Paintings from the Collection of the Fine Arts Museums of San Francisco*, pp. 222–23, 246. New York: Hudson Hills Press in association with the Fine Arts Museums of San Francisco, 1989.

Tarshis, Jerome. "Suspended in a Dreamlike Space: The Isolation of Painter and Painting." *The Christian Science Monitor* (Boston), Jan. 13, 1989, p. 16.

1991 "Edwin Dickinson (1891–1979 [*sic*]), *Shiloh*, 1940 [*sic*]." In Adams, Henry. *Handbook of American Paintings in the Nelson-Atkins Museum of Art*, pp. 174–75. Kansas City, Mo.: Nelson-Atkins Museum of Art, 1991.

Messinger, Lisa M. "Edwin Dickinson." In Sims, Lowery Stokes, and Lisa M. Messinger. *The Landscape in Twentieth-Century Art: Selections from the Metropolitan Museum of Art*, p. 134. New York: The American Federation of Arts and Rizzoli, 1991.

1993 Macmillan, Kyle. "Oft-Ignored Dickinson: 'Pertinent, Influential.'" *Omaha World-Herald* (Nebr.), Aug. 18, 1993, pp. 41–43.

Morgan, Jeffrey. "Brun-Rouge: An American Enigma." *Modern Painters* (London), Autumn 1993, pp. 64–66.

1996 Baldwin, Helen Dickinson. "Edwin W. Dickinson, *Rock of Port Issol, West Side*, 1938." In Faxon, Susan C.; Avis Berman, and Jock Reynolds. *Addison Gallery of American Art 65 Years, A Selective Catalogue*, pp. 357–58. Andover, Mass.: Addison Gallery of American Art, Phillips Academy, 1996.

Kramer, Hilton. "Return of Dickinson: He's Obscure No More." *The New York Observer*, Nov. 18, 1996, pp. 1, 33.

1999 Abell, Mary E. "Edwin Dickinson: The Site Taken as Seen." *Provincetown Arts* (Mass.), 1999, p. 44.

Baldwin, Helen Dickinson. "A Drawing by Edwin Dickinson: The Studio at 46 Pearl Street." *Provincetown Arts* (Mass.), 1999, pp. 45–46.

THE ARTIST AS STUDENT AND TEACHER

1947 McCausland, Elizabeth. *Charles W. Hawthorne, An American Figure Painter*. New York: privately printed, 1947.

1966 Soyer, Raphael. *Homage to Thomas Eakins, etc.* Edited by Rebecca L. Soyer. New York: Thomas Yoseloff, 1966.

1977 Soyer, Raphael. "Homage to Eakins (III)." In *Diary of an Artist*. Washington, D.C.: New Republic Books, 1977.

1981 Smith, Donald. Interview with Francis Cunningham. Audiocassette, 1981. Oral History Collection, Archives of American Art, Washington, D.C.

1982 Koslow, Susan. "Empirical Realism and Poetic Form in the Paintings of Lennart Anderson." *Arts Magazine* (New York), Dec. 1982, pp. 90–99.

Smith, Donald. Interview with Lennart Anderson. Audiocassette, 1982. Oral History Collection, Archives of American Art, Washington, D.C.

1983 Blake, Wendon. "Self-Portrait in Gray Shirt by Edwin Dickinson." In *Creative Color for the Oil Painter: Paintings from the National Museum of American Art, Smithsonian Institution, Washington, D.C.*, p. 127. New York: Watson-Guptill Publications, 1983.

1984 Orsini, Nicholas. "In Pursuit of Light: The Art of Roger Van Damme." *American Artist* (New York), Nov. 1984, pp. 64–67.

Smith, Donald. Interview with Edward Denyer. Audiocassette, 1984. Oral History Collection, Archives of American Art, Washington, D.C.

Smith, Donald. Interview with Denver Lindley. Audiocassette, 1984. Oral History Collection, Archives of American Art, Washington, D.C.

1985 Peterson, Roger Tory. "The Unseen World of John J. Audubon." *The New York Times Magazine*, Mar. 10, 1985, pp. 48–56.

1988 Mendelowitz, Daniel M., and Duane A. Wakeham. *A Guide to Drawing*, pp. 86, 91, 178–79, 211, 286. New York: Holt, Rinehart and Winston, 1988.

GENERAL

Books

1983 Kahan, Mitchell Douglas. "Subjective Currents in American Painting of the 1930s." Ph.D. dissertation, The City University of New York, 1983. Ann Arbor, Mich.: UMI Research Press, 1983.

1989 Arthur, John. *Spirit of Place: Contemporary Landscape Painting and the American Tradition*, pp. 37–38, 41. Boston: Little, Brown and Company, 1989.

Ward, John L. *American Realist Painting, 1945–1980*, pp. 40, 44. Ann Arbor, Mich.: UMI Research Press, 1989.

Articles

1926 Lockett, Elizabeth. "Provincetown." *The Arts* (New York), July 1962, pp. 49–55.

1938 "Metropolitan Buys Native Canvases." *The New York Times*, July 17, 1938, sec. 9, p. 7.

"Debut This Year, Metropolitan Honors Them." *The Art Digest* (New York), Aug. 1, 1938, p. 7.

1954 "15 Picked for Aid by Arts Institute." *The New York Times*, Apr. 30, 1954, p. 21.

"Arts Groups Plan Joint Ceremonial." *The New York Times*, May 23, 1954, p. 87.

1956 "Two Arts Groups Make 24 Awards." *The New York Times*, May 24, 1956, p. 25.

1957 Hess, Thomas B. "For Spacious Skies, and All That." *Art News* (New York), Nov. 1957, pp. 28–31, 58–60.

1959 "10 Americans Get Ford Art Grants." *The New York Times*, Feb. 18, 1959, p. 30.

"Brandeis Presents Awards in the Arts." *The New York Times*, Apr. 8, 1959, sec. L, p. 19.

Hess, Thomas B. "The Year's Best: 1958." *Art News* (New York), Jan. 1959, pp. 44–45, 60–61.

1961 Baur, John I. H., and Lloyd Goodrich. "Fantasy." In *American Art of Our Century*, pp. 104–5. New York: Frederick A. Praeger, 1961.

Baur, John I. H. "Portfolio of American Drawings." *Art in America* (New York), vol. 49, no. 4, 1961, pp. 64–73.

Hatch, Robert. "At the Tip of Cape Cod." *Horizon* (New York), July 1961, pp. 10–29.

Hawthorne, Roger. "One of America's Oldest Summer Art Groups Is The Provincetown Art Association." *American Artist* (New York), June 1961, pp. 36–41, 82–83.

1962 Frankfurter, Alfred. "The Year's Best: 1961." *Art News* (New York), Jan. 1962, pp. 23, 49.

1969 Jacobs, Jay. "Collector: Joseph H. Hirshhorn." *Art in America* (New York), July–Aug. 1969, pp. 56–71.

1973 Ratcliff, Carter. "New York Letter." *Art International* (Zurich), Jan. 1973, pp. 58–63.

1976 Glueck, Grace. "Art People." *The New York Times*, July 30, 1976, sec. C, p. 16.

1978 Davidson, Abraham A. "Visionaries, 1900–1950." In *The Eccentrics and Other American Visionary Painters*, pp. 183–85. New York: E. P. Dutton, 1978.

1986 Russell, John. "Two Summer Havens on Whose Sands Art Was Writ Large." *The New York Times*, July 13, 1986, p. 29.

1987 Jencks, Charles. "True Classical Sensibility." In *Post-Modernism: The New Classicism in Art and Architecture*. New York: Rizzoli International Publications, 1987, pp. 151–52, 154, 163, 174.

1988 Scott, Nancy. "Museums in the City Shift Focus: Trustees Plan to Buy 20th Century U.S. Art, Move de Young Works." *San Francisco Examiner*, Apr. 24, 1988, page unknown.

1990 Gregor, Katherine. "Harry S. Parker III: Shaking Things Up." *Art News* (New York), Dec. 1990, pp. 97–98.

PUBLIC COLLECTIONS

Achenbach Foundation for Graphic Arts, The California Palace of the Legion of Honor, Fine Arts Museums of San Francisco

Addison Gallery of American Art, Phillips Academy, Andover, Massachusetts

Albright-Knox Art Gallery, Buffalo, New York

The American Academy and Institute of Arts and Letters, New York

The Arkansas Arts Center, Little Rock

The Art Institute of Chicago

The Art Museum, Princeton University, New Jersey

The Art Students League of New York

The Baltimore Museum of Art

Boston University

Brooklyn Museum of Art

Burchfield-Penney Art Center, Buffalo, New York

Cape Museum of Fine Arts, Dennis, Massachusetts

The Chrysler Museum, Norfolk, Virginia

Clark Atlanta University Art Galleries, Georgia

College Art Galleries, Sweet Briar College, Virginia

Corcoran Gallery of Art, Washington, D.C.

The Detroit Institute of Arts, Michigan

El Paso Museum of Art, Texas

Emerson Gallery, Hamilton College, Clinton, New York

William A. Farnsworth Art Museum and Library, Rockland, Maine

The Henry Art Gallery, University of Washington, Seattle

Hirshhorn Museum and Sculpture Garden, Smithsonian Institution, Washington, D.C.

The Hood Museum of Art, Dartmouth College, Hanover, New Hampshire

Hudson Gallery, Flint Institute of the Arts, Michigan

The Israel Museum, Jerusalem

Herbert F. Johnson Museum of Art, Cornell University, Ithaca, New York

Kansas City Art Institute, Missouri

Kresge Art Center Gallery, Michigan State University, East Lansing

The Mead Art Museum, Amherst College, Massachusetts

Meadowbrook Art Gallery, Oakland University, Rochester, Michigan

Memorial Art Gallery of the University of Rochester, New York

The Metropolitan Museum of Art, New York

Middlebury College Museum of Art, Vermont

Minnesota Museum of Art, St. Paul

The Montclair Art Museum, New Jersey

Munson-Williams-Proctor Institute, Museum of Art, Utica, New York

Museum of Art, Rhode Island School of Design, Providence

Museum of Fine Arts, Boston

Museum of Fine Arts, Springfield, Massachusetts

The Museum of Modern Art, New York

National Academy of Design, New York

The Nelson-Atkins Museum of Art, Kansas City, Missouri

The Palmer Museum, Pennsylvania State University, University Park

The Pennsylvania Academy of the Fine Arts, Philadelphia

Philadelphia Museum of Art

Provincetown Art Association & Museum, Massachusetts

Provincetown Heritage Museum, Massachusetts

Sheldon Memorial Art Gallery and Sculpture Garden,
University of Nebraska–Lincoln

The David and Alfred Smart Museum of Art, The University of Chicago

Smithsonian American Art Museum, Washington, D.C.

Tacoma Art Museum, Washington

The University Gallery, University of Massachusetts, Amherst

University Museum, Southern Illinois University at Carbondale

Watson Gallery, Wheaton College, Norton, Massachusetts

T. W. Wood Art Gallery, Vermont College Arts Center, Montpelier

The Weatherspoon Art Gallery, University of North Carolina at Greensboro

Whitney Museum of American Art, New York

M. H. de Young Memorial Museum, Fine Arts Museums of San Francisco

SELECTED ONE-ARTIST EXHIBITIONS AND REVIEWS

Two commercial galleries in New York that figured prominently in Edwin Dickinson's career have been identified by several names through the years. One, founded as James Graham & Sons, has been known periodically as Graham Gallery. The other, Georgette Passedoit's gallery, as confirmed by checklists, brochures, reviews, and ephemera from 1936 to 1942, was referred to interchangeably as Georgette Passedoit, Passedoit Galleries, Passedoit Gallery, Georgette Passedoit Gallery, and Gallery of Georgette Passedoit. After 1942 the name consistently appears as Passedoit Gallery. For the purposes of the documentation in this publication, citations will refer to James Graham & Sons and Georgette Passedoit Gallery.

1926 Provincetown Art Association, Massachusetts. *Edwin Dickinson, A Collection of Small Paintings: Second 1926 Show*, Aug. 22–Sept. 7, 1926.

1927 Albright Art Gallery, Buffalo, New York. *Paintings by Edwin H.* [sic] *Dickinson*, Apr. 17–May 15, 1927. Brochure, foreword by W[illiam] M. H[ekking].

"Buffalo Men Show Own Works." *The Buffalo Sunday Times*, Apr. 24, 1927, p. 60.

1931 Twentieth Century Club, Buffalo, New York. *Edwin Dickinson, Paintings and Drawings*, Feb. 25–Mar. 7, 1931.

"20th Century Club Committee to Give Its Final Program." *Buffalo Evening News*, Feb. 21, 1931, p. 7.

"Twentieth Century Club Art, Music Programs." *Buffalo Courier-Express*, Mar. 1, 1931, sec. 8, p. 9.

Garret Club, Buffalo, New York. *Edwin Dickinson, Painting and Drawings*, Mar. 1931.

1936 Georgette Passedoit Gallery, New York. *Drawings: Edwin W. Dickinson*, Feb. 3–18, 1936.

"Drawings by Dickinson." *The Art Digest* (New York), Feb. 1, 1936, p. 19.

Review of exhibition at Georgette Passedoit Gallery. *New York Sun*, Feb. 9, 1936, page unknown.

Burrows, Carlyle. "Notes and Comment on Events in Art: Landscape Drawings." *New York Herald Tribune*, Feb. 9, 1936, sec. V, p. 10.

Devree, Howard. "A Reviewer's Notebook." *The New York Times*, Feb. 9, 1936, sec. 10, p. 10.

Sayre, Ann Hamilton. "Current Drawings by Four Artists: Iacovleff, Dickinson, Wortman, Kirby." *The Art News* (New York), Feb. 15, 1936, p. 7.

1938 Georgette Passedoit Gallery, New York. *Paintings by Edwin W. Dickinson*, Apr. 11–30, 1938.

"The Visions of Dickinson, 'Lone Spirit.'" *The Art Digest* (New York), Apr. 15, 1938, p. 13.

Review of exhibition at Georgette Passedoit Gallery. *New York Post*, Apr. 16, 1938, page unknown.

Bird, Paul. "The Fortnight in New York." *The Art Digest* (New York), May 1, 1938, pp. 18–19, 31.

Burrows, Carlyle. "Notes and Comment on Events in Art: Edwin Dickinson." *New York Herald Tribune*, Apr. 17, 1938, sec. VI, p. 5.

Devree, Howard. "Four Solos." *Magazine of Art* (Washington, D.C.), May 1938, pp. 308–10.

Jewell, Edward Alden. "Edwin W. Dickinson Exhibits Canvases." *The New York Times*, Apr. 16, 1938, p. 14.

Jewell, Edward Alden. "Edwin W. Dickinson." *The New York Times*, Apr. 17, 1938, sec. X, p. 7.

L., J. "Latest Works by a Capable American Painter, Edwin Dickinson." *The Art News* (New York), Apr. 30, 1938, pp. 11–12.

McB[ride], H[enry]. Review of exhibition at Georgette Passedoit Gallery. *New York Sun*, Apr. 23, 1938, page unknown.

1939 Memorial Art Gallery of the University of Rochester, New York. *Paintings by Edwin Dickinson*, Apr. 6–30, 1939. Checklist.

Georgette Passedoit Gallery, New York. *Recent Paintings and Drawings by Edwin W. Dickinson*, Apr. 10–29, 1939.

Review of exhibition at Georgette Passedoit Gallery. *New York Sun*, Apr. 15, 1939, page unknown.

Bird, Paul. "The Fortnight in New York." *The Art Digest* (New York), Apr. 15, 1939, pp. 18–19, 34.

Burrows, Carlyle. "Notes and Comment on Events in Art: Edwin Dickinson." *New York Herald Tribune*, Apr. 16, 1939, sec. VI, p. 5.

Devree, Howard. "A Reviewer's Notebook." *The New York Times*, Apr. 16, 1939, sec. X, p. 10.

L., J. "Objective Scenes in Oil and Black and White by Edwin Dickinson." *The Art News* (New York), Apr. 15, 1939, p. 14.

Rohr, Nora Lee. "Society of Artists Reviews the Past in Spirited, Well-Balanced Exhibit." *The Buffalo Evening News Magazine*, Apr. 15, 1939, p. 9.

Georgette Passedoit Gallery, New York. *Drawings: Edwin W. Dickinson*, Dec. 11–23, 1939.

"Roundabout the Galleries: Seven New Exhibitions." *The Art News* (New York), Dec. 16, 1939, pp. 15–17.

Review of exhibition at Georgette Passedoit Gallery. *New York Sun*, Dec. 16, 1939, p. 11.

Burrows, Carlyle. "Notes and Comment on Events in Art: Edwin Dickinson." *New York Herald Tribune*, Dec. 17, 1939, sec. VI, p. 8.

Devree, Howard. "A Reviewer's Notebook." *The New York Times*, Dec. 17, 1939, sec. 9, p. 12.

1940 The Art Institute of Buffalo, New York. *Exhibition of Drawings by Edwin W. Dickinson*, Feb. 20–Mar. 2, 1940. Organized by Students' Guild of the Art Institute.

Georgette Passedoit Gallery, New York. *Paintings, Edwin Dickinson*, Apr. 8–27, 1940.

"Dickinson Exhibition." *New York Post*, Apr. 13, 1940, page unknown.

Davis, Stuart. "Other Shows." *The New York Times*, Apr. 14, 1940, sec. 9, p. 9.

Devree, Howard. "Edwin Dickinson; Nordfelt." *Magazine of Art* (Washington, D.C.), May 1940, pp. 299–300.

L., J. "Edwin Dickinson: Dulcet and Romantic." *The Art News* (New York), Apr. 13, 1940, p. 14.

McBride, Henry. Review of exhibition at Georgette Passedoit Gallery. *New York Sun*, Apr. 13, 1940, page unknown.

The Art Museum of Wellesley College, Massachusetts. *Exhibition of Paintings by Edwin W. Dickinson*, Oct. 15–Nov. 5, 1940. Checklist.

1941 Monomoy Theatre, Chatham, Massachusetts. *Work by Edwin Dickinson*, dates unknown, 1941.

Olivet College, Michigan. *Drawings by Edwin W. Dickinson*, Mar., dates unknown, 1941.

Georgette Passedoit Gallery, New York. *Paintings, Edwin Dickinson*, Apr. 1–21, 1941.

"Nostalgic Mysticism of Edwin Dickinson." *The Art Digest* (New York), Apr. 1, 1941, p. 19.

Review of exhibition at Georgette Passedoit Gallery. *The New York Times*, Apr. 6, 1941, page unknown.

Jewell, Edward Alden. "In the Realm of Art: An April Shower of Exhibitions." *The New York Times*, Apr. 6, 1941, sec. 9, p. 9.

L., J. W. "Edwin Dickinson." *Art News* (New York), Apr. 1, 1941, p. 33.

McBride, Henry. "Integrity in Art: with How Much Hokus-Pokus Is an Artist Allowed to Fool the Public?" *New York Sun*, Apr. 5, 1941, page unknown.

1942 Stuart School of Design, Boston. *Paintings and Drawings by Edwin Dickinson*, Feb. 18–27, 1942.

Adlow, Dorothy. "Edwin Dickinson Paintings." *The Christian Science Monitor* (Boston), Feb. 26, 1942, p. 11.

Georgette Passedoit Gallery, New York. *Paintings: Edwin Dickinson*, Mar. 9–28, 1942.

Boswell, Helen. "Fifty-seventh Street in Review." *The Art Digest* (New York), Mar. 15, 1942, p. 23.

Cortissoz, Royal. "Architecture by Stanford White: Three More Shows." *New York Herald Tribune*, Mar. 15, 1942, sec. VI, p. 8.

Jewell, Edward Alden. "In the Realm of Art: Group Annuals and Other Events." *The New York Times*, Mar. 15, 1942, sec. VIII, p. 5.

L., J. W. "Dickinson." *Art News* (New York), Mar. 15, 1942, p. 26.

Monomoy Theatre, Chatham, Massachusetts. *Work by Edwin Dickinson*, Aug. 11–18, 1942.

1944 Washington Art Club, Washington, D.C. *Edwin Dickinson*, Mar. 1944.

1947 Kenneth Taylor Galleries, Nantucket Foundation, Massachusetts. *Edwin Dickinson, Paintings*, July 14–Aug. 1947.

1954 Stable Gallery, New York. *Paintings by Edwin Dickinson*, Oct. 12–Nov. 30, 1954.

Audubon Artists, National Academy of Design, New York. *Paintings by Edwin Dickinson*, Nov. 11–closing date unknown, 1954.

1957–58 Andrew Dickson White Museum of Art, Cornell University, Ithaca, New York. *Edwin Dickinson, Visiting Artist: An Exhibition of Paintings, 1912–1956*, Dec. 10, 1957–Jan. 10, 1958. Brochure.

1958 The Cushman Gallery, Houston, Texas. *Edwin Dickinson: A Retrospective*, Mar. 30–Apr. 25, 1958. Brochure, text by Dorothy C. Miller.

1959 Boston University Art Gallery. *Edwin Dickinson, Retrospective Exhibition*, Mar. 7–Apr. 4, 1959. Brochure.

"Dickinson Retrospective." *Art News* (New York), Apr. 1959, p. 8.

Adlow, Dorothy. "The Untypical Paintings of Dickinson." *The Christian Science Monitor* (Boston), Mar. 14, 1959, p. 8.

Driscoll, Edgar J., Jr. "Not a Fly-by-Night Work in the Whole Lot." *The Boston Sunday Globe*, Mar. 15, 1959, p. 42.

Wien Faculty Center, Brandeis University, Waltham, Massachusetts. *Art on the Campus: Selected Paintings by Edwin Dickinson*, May 21–June 10, 1959.

1960 World House Galleries, New York. *A Selection of Paintings and Drawings Dating from 1920–1959 by Edwin Dickinson*, June 22–July 29, 1960.

1961 James Graham & Sons, New York. *Edwin Dickinson: Retrospective*, Feb. 1–Mar. 11, 1961. Catalogue.

Adlow, Dorothy. Review of exhibition at James Graham & Sons. *The Christian Science Monitor* (Boston), Mar 6, 1961, p. 12.

Ashton, Dore. "Art: Edwin Dickinson." *Arts and Architecture* (Los Angeles), Apr. 4, 1961, pp. 4–5.

Campbell, Lawrence. "Three Painters of Interior Light." *Art News* (New York), Feb. 1961, pp. 47–49, 61–62.

Canaday, John. "An Art Almanac: If the Stars Have Anything to Do with It, 1961 Holds Lessons for 1962." *The New York Times*, Dec. 24, 1961, sec. X, p. 14.

Clark, Eliot. "Edwin Dickinson." *The Studio* (London), Oct. 1961, pp. 138–40, 155.

Coates, Robert M. "The Art Galleries: Backward, O Time." *The New Yorker*, Feb. 18, 1961, pp. 112–17.

Emmons, E. Thayles. "Edwin Dickinson—Geneva Native's Art Exhibited." *The Geneva Times* (Geneva, N.Y.), Feb. 13, 1961, page unknown.

G[enauer], E[mily]. "Long-Overdue Homage Paid to Edwin Dickinson." *New York Herald Tribune*, Feb. 5, 1961, sec. 4, p. 21.

Kuh, Katharine. "Art without Isms." *Saturday Review* (New York), Mar. 4, 1961, pp. 37, 45.

Porter, Fairfield. "Art." *The Nation* (New York), Feb. 18, 1961, pp. 175–76.

Preston, Stuart. "Art: Dickinson's Works Displayed." *The New York Times*, Feb. 4, 1961, p. 16.

Seckler, Dorothy Gees, ed. "1961 Preview." *Art in America* (New York) vol. 48, no. 4, 1960, pp. 84–87, 106, 108, 110.

Tillim, Sidney. "Month in Review." *Arts* (New York), Mar. 1961, pp. 46–49.

Philadelphia Art Alliance. *Edwin Dickinson*, Nov. 29–Dec. 31, 1961.

"Edwin Dickinson Shows Paintings This Month." *Art Alliance Bulletin* (Philadelphia), Dec. 1961, pp. 5, 14.

1961–63 Cheekwood Museum of Art, Nashville, Tennessee. *Edwin Dickinson*, Nov. 15–Dec. 5, 1961. Organized by the Museum of Modern Art, New York. Traveled to Columbia Museum of Art, South Carolina, Jan. 5–26, 1962; Chatham College, Pittsburgh, Pennsylvania, Feb. 5–25, 1962; University of Texas, Austin, May 8–29, 1962; Art Center of La Jolla, California, June 22–July 13, 1962; Hunter Gallery of Art, Chattanooga, Tennessee, Sept. 7–28, 1962; Auburn University, Alabama, Oct. 15–Nov. 5, 1962; Quincy Art Club, Illinois, Nov. 20–Dec. 11, 1962; Telfair Academy of Arts and Science, Savannah, Georgia, Jan. 7–28, 1963; Delaware Art Center, Wilmington, Feb. 15–Mar. 17, 1963; University of Connecticut, Storrs, Apr. 2–23, 1963; Madison Art Association, Wisconsin, May 8–29, 1963.

1962 Vassar Art Gallery, Poughkeepsie, New York. *Paintings by Edwin Dickinson*, Dec. 6, 1962–closing date unknown.

"Amer. Painter Exhibits Work, Gives Lecture." *Vassar Miscellany News* (Poughkeepsie, N.Y.), Dec. 6, 1962, pp. 1, 8.

1963 James Graham & Sons, New York. *Drawings by Edwin Dickinson*, dates unknown, 1963.

Rose Art Museum, Brandeis University, Waltham, Massachusetts. *Paintings by Edwin Dickinson*, dates unknown, 1963.

1964 Charlotte Crosby Kemper Gallery, Kansas City Art Institute, Missouri. *Paintings by Lennart Anderson and Edwin Dickinson*, Apr. 14–May 20, 1964.

HCE Gallery, Provincetown, Massachusetts. *Edwin Dickinson*, Summer 1964.

1965 HCE Gallery, Provincetown, Massachusetts. *Edwin Dickinson*, Summer 1965.

Whitney Museum of American Art, New York. *Edwin Dickinson, Major Retrospective*, Oct. 20–Nov. 28, 1965. Catalogue, text by Lloyd Goodrich.

Canaday, John. "One City and One Painter." *The New York Times*, Oct. 24, 1965, sec. X, p. 33.

Frankenstein, Alfred. "A Rare Breed—A Grand Paradox." *San Francisco Sunday Examiner & Chronicle*, Nov. 21, 1965, This World section, p. 37.

Genauer, Emily. "Dickinson's Retrospective." *New York Herald Tribune*, Oct. 20, 1965, p. 23.

Hoene, Anne. "In the Museums, Recent Exhibitions: Edwin Dickinson." *Arts Magazine* (New York), Dec. 1965, pp. 42–43.

Kay, Jane H. "Dickinson Exhibition: Self-Studies Worked Well." *The Christian Science Monitor* (Boston), Nov. 19, 1965, p. 6.

Pincus-Witten, Robert. "New York: Edwin Dickinson, Whitney Museum." *Artforum* (Los Angeles), Jan. 1966, pp. 54–57.

Smith, Miles A. "Artist Adept at Fooling the Viewer." *Times Enterprise* (Thomasville, Ga.), Nov. 12, 1965, page unknown. Associated Press Wire Story printed as "Dickinson Was Many Painters in One." *Gastonia Gazette* (N.C.), Nov. 14, 1965, page unknown, and "Art Exhibition." *Baltimore Sun* (Md.), Nov. 17, 1965, page unknown.

Waldman, Diane. "Dickinson: Reality and Reflection." *Art News* (New York), Nov. 1965, pp. 28–31, 70–71.

Wilson, Patricia Boyd. Untitled review. *The Christian Science Monitor* (Boston), Nov. 26, 1965, p. 12.

James Graham & Sons, New York. *Paintings by Edwin Dickinson in Retrospective, Selected by Lloyd Goodrich*, Oct. 20–Nov. 28, 1965.

Hoene, Anne. "In the Galleries: Edwin Dickinson." *Arts Magazine* (New York), Dec. 1965, p. 58.

1966 Gilman Galleries, Chicago. *Edwin Dickinson, Paintings*, Jan. 8–closing date unknown, 1966.

The Pennsylvania Academy of the Fine Arts, Philadelphia. *Paintings by Edwin Dickinson*, Apr. 21–May 29, 1966.

The Katonah Gallery, New York. *Edwin Dickinson*, June 12–July 12, 1966.

"Large Reception Greets Dickson [*sic*] in Katonah." *Reporter-Dispatch* (Katonah, N.Y.), June 13, 1966, page unknown.

"At Katonah Gallery: Many Artists Attend Dickinson Reception." *Patent Trader* (Mt. Kisco, N.Y.), June 16, 1966, page unknown.

1967 Hawthorne Memorial Gallery, Provincetown Art Association, Massachusetts. *Selections from the Work of Edwin Dickinson*, Aug. 2–Sept. 4, 1967.

"Display of Dickinson Works Slated at Cape-Tip." *Cape Cod Standard-Times* (Hyannis, Mass.), July 28, 1967.

"Edwin Dickinson Shoe Set in Provincetown." *Sunday Standard-Times* (New Bedford, Mass.), July 30, 1967, page unknown.

"Dickinson Exhibition at Art Association." *Provincetown Advocate* (Mass.), Aug. 3, 1967, p. 1.

Dane, Eva Marie. "Dickinson the Artist Shown in Exhibition; Dickinson the Man Revealed in Interview." *Cape Cod Standard-Times* (Hyannis, Mass.), Aug. 9, 1967.

Driscoll, Edgar J., Jr. "The Art World: Old Pro Dickinson." *Boston Globe*, Aug., 1967, page unknown.

1968 Wellfleet Art Gallery, Palm Beach, Florida. *Edwin Dickinson, Drawings and Oils*, Jan. 6–11, 1968.

James Graham & Sons, New York. *Edwin Dickinson: A Selection of Drawings Including Paintings Not Previously Exhibited*, May 25–June 28, 1968. Brochure.

"Edwin Dickinson at Graham." *Arts Magazine* (New York), June/Summer 1968, p. 20.

Ashbery, John. "Reviews and Previews: Edwin Dickinson." *Art News* (New York), Summer 1968, pp. 14–18, 54.

Canaday, John. "Edwin Dickinson Exhibition at Graham." *The New York Times*, June 1, 1968, p. 23.

1968–69 XXXIV Biennial Exhibition of Art, Venice, Italy. *Venice 34: The Figurative Tradition in Recent American Art*, June 22–Oct. 20, 1968 [Dickinson featured as principal painter]. Catalogue, text by Norman Geske. Traveled to National Collection of Fine Arts, Washington, D.C., Dec. 19, 1968–Feb. 2, 1969; Sheldon Memorial Art Gallery, University of Nebraska, Lincoln, Mar. 17–Apr. 13, 1969.

"Tranquilla apertura a Venezia della contestata Biennale d'arte." *Stampa Sera* (Venice, Italy), June 24–25, 1968, p.3.

Getlein, Frank. "Art: Refreshing Change in America's Stance at Venice." *Washington Star*, Jan. 28, 1968, page unknown.

Harlepp, Marjorie. "The Arts in Venice." *Milan Daily American* (Italy), June 14, 1968, page unknown.

Paris, Jeanne. "Revolt in Venice Sparked by Revival of Recognizable." *Long Beach Press* (Calif.), June 23, 1968, p. 69.

1969 W. T. Bandy Center for Baudelaire Studies, Vanderbilt University, Nashville, Tennessee. *Edwin Dickinson*, July 13–closing date unknown, 1969.

1970 Pratt Manhattan Center, New York. *Paintings and Drawings by Edwin Dickinson*, Mar. 9–26, 1970.

Wellfleet Art Gallery, Massachusetts. *Special Exhibition: Edwin Dickinson Painting—Drawing, 1911–1950*, June 26–July 5, 1970.

"Edwin Dickinson to Exhibit One-Man Show; Was One of First Artists to Settle Here." *Provincetown Advocate* (Mass.), June 25, 1970, page unknown.

"Review of Exhibition/Edwin Dickinson." *The Cape Codder* (Orleans, Mass.), July 2, 1970, p. 12.

Cape Cod Conservatory of Music and Arts, Barnstable, Massachusetts. *Paintings and Drawings by Edwin Dickinson*, July 12–Aug 1, 1970.

Bristol Art Museum, Rhode Island. *An Exhibition of Paintings by Edwin Dickinson*, Aug. 13–24, 1970.

Institute of Contemporary Art and Weeden Gallery, Boston. *"The Dickinson Family Heritage": Paintings and Drawings by Edwin Dickinson*, Oct. 11–Nov. 7, 1970. Catalogue, foreword by Andrew C. Hyde; texts by John Chandler, Ross Moffett, and Dorothea Weeden.

Baker, Kenneth. "A Dickinson Retrospective." *The Christian Science Monitor* (Boston), Nov. 3, 1970, page 5.

Danikan, Caron Le Brun. "Art: A Dickinson Exhibit." *Boston Herald*, Oct. 25, 1970, page unknown.

Grillo, Jean Bergantini. "Art: The Elusive Edwin Dickinson." *The Phoenix* (Boston), Oct. 6, 1970, pp. 22–23.

1972 Wellfleet Art Gallery, Massachusetts. *Paintings and Drawings by Edwin Dickinson*, July 10–17, 1972.

Schwartz, Sanford. "New York Letter." *Art International* (Zurich), Nov. 1972, pp. 43–46.

James Graham & Sons, New York. *Edwin Dickinson: An Exhibition of Paintings and Drawings*, Oct. 24–Nov. 18, 1972. Brochure.

Campbell, Lawrence. "Reviews and Previews: Edwin Dickinson." *Art News* (New York), Nov. 1972, p. 76.

Kramer, Hilton. "Dickinson Motifs Keep Tradition Alive." *The New York Times*, Oct. 28, 1972, p. 23.

Ratcliff, Carter. "New York Letter." *Art International* (Zurich), Jan. 1973, pp. 58–63.

Schwartz, Laura Sue. "Galleries." *Arts Magazine* (New York), Dec. 1972–Jan. 1973, pp. 88–89.

1973 Wellfleet Historical Society, Samuel Rider House, Massachusetts. *Edwin Dickinson: Nine Wellfleet Paintings*, Aug. 16–Sept. 3, 1973.

"Edwin Dickinson Exhibit to Open August 16 in Wellfleet." *Lower Cape Cod Chronicle* (Chatham, Mass.), Aug. 9, 1973.

"Edwin Dickinson Paintings Will Be on Exhibit." *The Cape Codder* (Orleans, Mass.), Aug. 9, 1973, p. 11.

1974 Cape Cod Conservatory of Music and Arts, West Barnstable, Massachusetts. *An Exhibition by Edwin Dickinson*, May 19–closing date unknown, 1974.

Doll & Richards Gallery, Boston. *Six Edwin Dickinsons*, Sept. 1974.

1975 Wellfleet Art Gallery, Massachusetts. *Edwin Dickinson, Drawings and Etchings*, Aug. 1975.

1976 Wellfleet Art Gallery, Massachusetts. *Edwin Dickinson: Select Group of Works*, July 19–31, 1976.

Provincetown Art Association, Massachusetts. *Edwin Dickinson Retrospective*, Aug. 14–Sept. 7, 1976. Catalogue, text by Nathan Halper.

"Dickinson Work to Be Exhibited." *Provincetown Advocate Summer Guide* (Mass.), Aug. 12, 1976, page unknown.

Baldwin, Carol. "Dickinson Retrospective in Provincetown." *Nauset Weekly Calendar* (Cape Cod, Mass.), Aug. 27, 1976, pp. 11–12.

McManus, Otile. "The Depth of Edwin Dickinson." *The Boston Globe*, Aug. 26, 1976, p. 29.

1977–78 Burchfield Center, State University College at Buffalo, New York. *Tribute to Edwin Dickinson: Emphasizing the Buffalo and Sheldrake Years*, Sept. 18–Nov. 6, 1977. Catalogue, texts by Edna M. Lindemann, Thomas W. Leavitt, and Frances Dickinson. Traveled to Herbert F. Johnson Museum, Cornell University, Ithaca, New York, Nov. 16–Dec. 23, 1977; Albany Institute of History & Art, New York, Jan. 14–Feb. 19, 1978.

Crowther, Hal. "A Native Genius." *The Buffalo Evening News*, Sept. 23, 1977, *Gusto* section, p. 21.

Willig, Nancy Tobin. "Dickinson Paintings Sought." *Buffalo Courier-Express*, July 3, 1977, p. 30.

Willig, Nancy Tobin. "On the Art Scene: Dickinson Subject of Show to Open Tonight." *Buffalo Courier-Express*, Sept. 17, 1977, page unknown.

Willig, Nancy Tobin. "Exhibit Emphasizes Dickinson's Buffalo Years." *Buffalo Courier-Express*, Sept. 23, 1977, p. 10.

Willig, Nancy Tobin. "Bordering on the Surreal." *Art News* (New York), Nov. 1977, pp. 195–200.

1980–81 Hirshhorn Museum and Sculpture Garden, Smithsonian Institution, Washington, D.C. *Edwin Dickinson: Selected Landscapes*, Sept. 18–Dec. 14, 1980. Catalogue, text by Joe Shannon. Traveled to J. B. Speed Museum, Louisville, Kentucky, Jan. 19–Mar. 1, 1981.

Ashbery, John. "Coups de Grace." *New York*, Oct. 13, 1980, pp. 59–60.

Dillinger, Jack. "Premier Coups." *Columbia Flyer* (Md.), Oct. 2, 1980, page unknown.

Forgey, Benjamin. "The Steadfast Career of a Somber Romantic." *Washington Star*, Sept. 21, 1980, pp. C7, C10.

Mainardi, Patricia. "Edwin Dickinson." *Arts Magazine* (New York), Mar. 1981, p. 17.

Richard, Paul. "The Swift Strokes of Hurried Summers." *The Washington Post*, Sept. 23, 1980, p. B4.

1982 James Graham & Sons, New York. *Edwin Dickinson: Exhibition of Paintings and Drawings*, Apr. 6–May 15, 1982.

National Academy of Design, New York. *Edwin Dickinson: Draftsman/Painter*, Apr. 7–May 9, 1982. Catalogue, texts by John H. Dobkin, John Ashbery, and Elaine de Kooning. Traveled to Museum of Fine Arts, Springfield, Massachusetts, July 3–Aug. 15; Norton Gallery and School of Art, Inc., West Palm Beach, Florida, Sept. 10–Oct. 17.

Kohen, Helen L. "Museums Open Season with Shows of Great Strength." *Miami Herald*, Sept. 12, 1982, page unknown.

Rose, Barbara. "Talking about . . . Art." *Vogue* (New York), May 1982, p. 120.

Russell, John. "Art: Edwin Dickinson, Enigmatic, Unforgotten." *The New York Times*, Apr. 23, 1982, sec. C, p. 22.

Smith, Don C. "Edwin Dickinson Draftsman Painter." *Art New England* (Newtonville, Mass.), July/August 1982, p. 4.

Taylor, Robert. "Critic's Choice: Edwin Dickinson." *The Boston Globe*, July 2, 1982, p. 27.

Tuby, Heidi S. "Digging Dickinson: Artist's Imagination Was Surpassed Only by His Versatility." *Boca Raton News* (Fla.), Sept. 22, 1982, page 6C.

Tully, Judd. "The Stunning Ferocity of Edwin Dickinson." *Art/World* (New York), Apr. 22–May 20, 1982, pp. 1, 5.

1983 Hirschl & Adler Modern, New York. *Edwin Dickinson, 1891–1978*, Nov. 3–30, 1983. Catalogue.

Glueck, Grace. "Art: Haunting Moods of Edwin Dickinson." *The New York Times*, Nov. 11, 1983, sec. C, p. 26.

1985 Alpha Gallery, Boston. *Edwin Dickinson*, Mar. 9–Apr. 3, 1985.

1986 Hirschl and Adler Modern, New York. *Edwin Dickinson: The Figure*, Sept. 9–Oct. 1, 1986. Catalogue, text by Klaus Kertess.

James Graham & Sons, New York. *Edwin Dickinson: Rare Perspectives*, Oct. 29–Dec. 20, 1986. Catalogue, foreword by Elizabeth Dailey Kvam and Sandra Leff; text by April Kingsley.

1990 Babcock Galleries, New York. *Edwin Dickinson: A Vision of Coast and Sea*, May 19–June 29, 1990. Catalogue, introduction/acknowledgments by John Driscoll and Michael St. Clair; text by Norman Geske.

Geske, Norman. "Dickinson's Inner Sea." *Art/World* (New York), Summer 1990, p. 8.

1991 Babcock Galleries, New York. *Edwin Dickinson 1891–1978: Centennial Exhibition*, Oct. 11–Nov. 22, 1991. Brochure.

1993 Babcock Galleries, New York. *Edwin Dickinson, Drawings*, Mar. 5–27, 1993. Catalogue, text by Paul Cummings.

1996 Babcock Galleries, New York. *Edwin Dickinson: Revelations*, Oct. 15–Nov. 22, 1996. Brochure, text by John Driscoll.

"Edwin Dickinson Revelations on View at Babcock Galleries through Nov. 22." *Antiques and the Arts Weekly* (Newton, Conn.), Oct. 18, 1996, p. 4.

Grimes, Nancy. "Edwin Dickinson at Tibor de Nagy and Babcock." *Art in America* (New York), Mar. 1997, pp. 98–99.

Worth, Alexi. "Edwin Dickinson: Babcock, Tibor de Nagy." *Art News* (New York), Jan. 1997, p. 114.

Tibor de Nagy Gallery, New York. *Edwin Dickinson: Paintings and Drawings*, Oct. 17–Nov. 30, 1996. Catalogue, text by Avis Berman.

"Edwin Dickinson." *The New Yorker*, Nov. 18, 1996, p. 23.

Cotter, Holland. "Art in Review." *The New York Times*, Nov. 8, 1996, sec. C, p. 23.

Grimes, Nancy. "Edwin Dickinson at Tibor de Nagy and Babcock." *Art in America* (New York), Mar. 1997, pp. 98–99.

Stevens, Mark. "Great Outdoors." *New York*, Nov. 11, 1996, pp. 81–82, 99.

Worth, Alexi. "Edwin Dickinson: Babcock, Tibor de Nagy." *Art News* (New York), Jan. 1997, p. 114.

1997 Cape Museum of Fine Arts, Dennis, Massachusetts. *Edwin Dickinson Paintings and Drawings from 1913 to 1961*, Sept. 21–Nov. 16, 1997.

McGuiness, Sheila Sinead. "Cape Museum of Fine Arts/Dennis: Edwin Dickinson." *Art New England* (Brighton, Mass.), Dec. 1997/Jan. 1998, p. 54.

1998 Tibor de Nagy Gallery, New York. *Edwin Dickinson: Selected Paintings*, Jan. 8–Feb. 7, 1998.

Babcock Galleries, New York. *Edwin Dickinson*, Oct. 15–Dec. 15, 1998. Brochure.

SELECTED GROUP EXHIBITIONS

Edwin Dickinson's work was shown in group exhibitions at the Provincetown Art Association, Massachusetts, in the following years: 1915–16; 1918; 1921–22; 1924–40; 1945; 1947–59; 1961–75; 1977–78.

1914 Vinton Studios, Provincetown, Massachusetts. *Group Exhibition*, opening and closing dates unknown, 1914.

1916–17 MacDowell Club, New York. *Contemporary American Oil Paintings and Sculpture*, Oct. 12, 1916–May 22, 1917.

Corcoran Gallery of Art, Washington, D.C. *Sixth Exhibition: Oil Paintings by Contemporary American Artists*, Dec. 17, 1916–Jan. 21, 1917. Catalogue.

1917 The Pennsylvania Academy of the Fine Arts, Philadelphia. *112th Annual Exhibition*, Feb. 4–Mar. 25, 1917.

Grand Central Palace, New York. *First Annual Exhibition of the Society of Independent Artists*, Apr. 10–May 6, 1917. Catalogue.

Albright Art Gallery, Buffalo, New York. *Eleventh Annual Exhibition of Selected Paintings by American Artists*, May 12–Sept. 17, 1917. Catalogue, prefatory by Cornelia Sage.

1918 The Pennsylvania Academy of the Fine Arts, Philadelphia. *113th Annual Exhibition*, Feb. 3–Mar. 24, 1918.

1918–19 National Academy of Design, New York. *Winter Exhibition*, Dec. 11, 1918–Jan. 12, 1919.

1919 Musée National du Luxembourg, Paris. *Exposition d'artistes de l'école américaine*, Oct.–Nov. 1919. Catalogue, introduction by Léonce Bénédite.

1920 The Art Institute of Chicago. *33rd Annual Exhibition of American Oil Paintings and Sculpture*, Nov. 4–Dec. 12, 1920. Catalogue.

1921 Art Gallery of Ontario, Toronto, Canada. *Paintings by Contemporary American Artists*, Jan. 8–Feb. 6, 1921. Catalogue.

Carnegie Institute, Pittsburgh, Pennsylvania. *Twentieth Annual International Exhibition of Paintings*, Apr. 28–June 30, 1921. Catalogue, text by John W. Bealty with Homer Saint-Gaudens.

1922 The Pennsylvania Academy of the Fine Arts, Philadelphia. *117th Annual Exhibition*, Feb. 5–Mar. 26, 1922.

Galerie Intime, New York. *Special Exhibition by a Group of Younger American Painters*, Apr. 11–25, 1922.

Art Association of Newport, Rhode Island. *Eleventh Annual Exhibition of Pictures by American Painters*, July 15–Aug. 12, 1922. Catalogue.

National Academy of Design, New York. *Winter Exhibition*, Nov. 17–Dec. 17, 1922.

1923 Carnegie Institute, Pittsburgh, Pennsylvania. *Twenty-second Annual International Exhibition of Paintings*, Apr. 26–June 17, 1923. Catalogue, text by Homer Saint-Gaudens.

The Art Institute of Chicago. *36th Annual Exhibition of American Paintings and Sculpture*, Nov. 1–Dec. 9, 1923. Catalogue.

1924 Garret Club, Buffalo, New York. *Drawings and Watercolors: Edwin Dickinson and Ross Moffett*, Mar. 3–May 13, 1924.

Albright Art Gallery, Buffalo, New York. *Eighteenth Annual Exhibition of Selected Paintings and Small Bronzes by American Artists*, Apr. 20–June 30, 1924. Catalogue, prefatory by Cornelia B. Sage Quinton.

The Art Institute of Chicago. *37th Annual Exhibition of American Paintings and Sculpture*, Oct. 30–Dec. 14, 1924. Catalogue.

1926 The Art Institute of Chicago. *Selected Group of Paintings from the Twenty-fifth International Exhibition at the Carnegie Institute*, Mar. 15–Apr. 17, 1926.

Carnegie Institute, Pittsburgh, Pennsylvania. *Twenty-fifth Annual International Exhibition of Paintings*, Oct. 4–Dec. 5, 1926. Catalogue, text by Homer Saint-Gaudens.

1927 New Gallery of the Flint and Brickett Company, under the auspices of the Junior League of Springfield, Massachusetts. *An Exhibition of Paintings by American Artists of Provincetown*, Nov. 8–18, 1927. Checklist.

1928 Carnegie Institute, Pittsburgh, Pennsylvania. *Twenty-seventh Annual International Exhibition of Paintings*, Oct. 18–Dec. 9, 1928. Catalogue, text by Homer Saint-Gaudens.

Corcoran Gallery of Art, Washington, D.C. *Eleventh Exhibition of Contemporary American Oil Paintings*, Oct. 28–Dec. 9, 1928. Catalogue.

1929 The Pennsylvania Academy of the Fine Arts, Philadelphia. *124th Annual Exhibition*, Jan. 27–Mar. 17, 1929.

National Academy of Design, New York. *Winter Exhibition*, Nov. 12–Dec. 1, 1929.

1930 Grand Central Art Galleries, New York. *Exhibition of Paintings and Sculpture Contributed by Artist Members*, opening and closing dates unknown, 1930.

The Pennsylvania Academy of the Fine Arts, Philadelphia. *125th Annual Exhibition*, Jan. 26–Mar. 16, 1930.

Toledo Museum of Art, Ohio. *Eighteenth Annual Exhibition of Selected Paintings by Contemporary Artists*, June 1–July 31, 1930. Organized by the American Federation of Arts. Checklist.

The Art Institute of Chicago. *Forty-Third Annual Exhibition of American Paintings and Sculpture*, Oct. 30–Dec. 14, 1930. Catalogue.

1930–31 Corcoran Gallery of Art, Washington, D.C. *Twelfth Exhibition of Contemporary Paintings*, Nov. 30, 1930–Jan. 11, 1931.

1931 The Pennsylvania Academy of the Fine Arts, Philadelphia. *126th Annual Exhibition*, Jan. 25–Mar. 15, 1931.

Albright Art Gallery, Buffalo, New York. *Twenty-fifth Annual Exhibition of Selected Paintings by American Artists*, Apr. 26–June 22, 1931. Catalogue, prefatory by William M. Hekking.

1932 Nebraska Art Association, Morrill Hall, University of Nebraska, Lincoln. *Forty-second Annual Exhibition of Paintings 1932*, Feb. 11–Mar. 13, 1932. Brochure.

1934 Herron Art Gallery, Indianapolis, Indiana. *Contemporary American Artists*, Jan. 1–30, 1934.

1935 Albright Art Gallery, Buffalo, New York. *Second Annual Exhibition: Artists of Buffalo and Western New York*, Mar. 2–31, 1935. Brochure.

Worcester Art Museum, Massachusetts. *Second Biennial Exhibition of American Painting of Today*, Nov. 1–Dec. 15, 1935. Brochure.

1937 Corcoran Gallery of Art, Washington, D.C. *Fifteenth Biennial Exhibition of Contemporary American Oil Paintings*, Mar. 28–May 9, 1937. Catalogue.

1938 Ogunquit Art Center, Maine. *Annual National Exhibition of Paintings*, opening and closing dates unknown, 1938.

Grand Central Art Galleries, New York. *Art without Isms*, opening and closing dates unknown, 1938.

Albright Art Gallery, Buffalo, New York. *Art Collectors and Artists Association*, Apr. 23–29, 1938.

The Art Institute of Chicago. *Forty-ninth Annual Exhibition of American Paintings and Sculpture*, Oct. 20–Dec. 4, 1938. Catalogue.

Riverside Museum, New York. *Buffalo Artists: Members of the Patteran Society*, Nov. 2–Dec. 18, 1938. Catalogue.

Montclair Art Museum, New Jersey. *Twenty-five Years of American Art*, Dec. 1–24, 1938. Brochure.

1939 Albright Art Gallery, Buffalo, New York. *Sixth Annual Exhibition at Buffalo by Artists of Western New York*, Mar. 16–Apr. 17, 1939. Brochure.

Corcoran Gallery of Art, Washington, D.C., *Sixteenth Biennial Exhibition of Contemporary American Oil Paintings*, Mar. 26–May 7, 1939. Catalogue.

Georgette Passedoit Gallery, New York. *Group Show: Paintings*, opening date unknown–Oct. 31, 1939.

Paper Mill Playhouse Gallery, Millburn, New Jersey. Title unknown, Nov. 12–Dec. 26, 1939.

1940 460 Park Avenue Gallery with Georgette Passedoit Gallery, New York. *Americans Then and Now*, Oct. 7–25, 1940.

1941 Georgette Passedoit Gallery, New York. *In Praise of Music*, Jan. 7–31, 1941.

National Academy of Design, New York. *115th Annual Exhibition*, Mar. 11–Apr. 9, 1941.

Willard Straight Hall, Cornell University, Ithaca, New York. *Invitation Show of Oil Paintings by Contemporary Americans*, May 13–30, 1941.

1941–42 The Art Institute of Chicago. *The Fifty-second Annual Exhibition of American Paintings and Sculpture*, Oct. 30, 1941–Jan. 4, 1942. Catalogue.

1942 Virginia Museum of Fine Arts, Richmond. *Third Biennial Exhibition of Contemporary American Painting*, Mar. 4–Apr. 14, 1942. Brochure.

Wildenstein & Co., New York. *Second Annual Federation of Modern Painters and Sculptors*, May 21–June 10, 1942. Brochure.

1943 The Art Students League of New York and The American Fine Arts Society, New York. *50 Years on 57th Street*, Feb. 7–28, 1943. Catalogue, foreword by Stewart Klonis.

National Academy of Design, New York. *117th Annual Exhibition*, Feb. 17–Mar. 9, 1943.

Corcoran Gallery of Art, Washington, D.C. *Eighteenth Biennial Exhibition of Contemporary American Oil Paintings*, Mar. 21–May 2, 1943. Catalogue.

Ogunquit Art Center, Maine. *21st Annual National Exhibition of Paintings*, July 1–Sept. 5, 1943.

Georgette Passedoit Gallery, New York. *Exhibition of Drawings*, Sept. 13–Oct. 10, 1943.

Carnegie Institute, Pittsburgh, Pennsylvania. *Painting in the United States*, Oct. 14–Dec. 12, 1943. Catalogue, text by John O'Conner, Jr.

1943–44 The Museum of Modern Art, New York. *Romantic Painting in America*, Nov. 17, 1943–Feb. 6, 1944. Catalogue, texts by James Thrall Soby and Dorothy C. Miller.

1944 The Pennsylvania Academy of the Fine Arts, Philadelphia. *139th Annual Exhibition*, Jan. 23–Feb. 27, 1944.

Wildenstein & Co., New York. *An Exhibition of Paintings and Sculpture by Members of the Federation of Modern Painters and Sculptors and Guest Artists*, June 8–July 1, 1944. Checklist.

Carnegie Institute, Pittsburgh, Pennsylvania. *Painting in the United States*, Oct. 12–Dec. 19, 1944. Catalogue, text by John O'Conner, Jr.

1945 Georgette Passedoit Gallery, New York. *A Green Exhibition*, opening date unknown–January 31, 1945. Brochure.

Bertha Schaefer Gallery, New York. *Landscapes and Seascapes in Modern Painting*, Feb. 10–closing date unknown, 1945.

Corcoran Gallery of Art, Washington, D.C. *Nineteenth Biennial Exhibition of Contemporary American Oil Paintings*, Mar. 18–Apr. 29, 1945. Catalogue.

Carnegie Institute, Pittsburgh, Pennsylvania. *Painting in the United States, 1945*, Oct. 11–Dec. 9, 1945. Catalogue, text by John O'Conner, Jr.

1945–46 Denton, Cottier and Daniels, Buffalo, New York. *The Patteran Society*, Nov. 15, 1945–Jan. 1, 1946.

Whitney Museum of American Art, New York. *Annual Exhibition of Contemporary American Painting*, Nov. 27, 1945–Jan. 10, 1946. Catalogue.

1946 Wellfleet Town Hall, Massachusetts. *Wellfleet Artists*, opening and closing dates unknown, 1946.

The Pennsylvania Academy of the Fine Arts, Philadelphia. *141st Annual Exhibition*, Jan. 23–Mar. 3, 1946.

1947 Institute of Modern Art, Boston. *Thirty Massachusetts Painters in 1947*, Nov. 7–Dec. 21, 1947. Brochure, introduction by Bartlett H. Hayes, Jr.

1948 Hawthorne Memorial Art Gallery, Provincetown, Massachusetts. *Special Group Exhibition*, Aug. 1–Sept. 6, 1948.

Albright Art Gallery, Buffalo, New York. *La Tausca Art*, Sept. 28–Oct. 24, 1948. Brochure, foreword by Peyton Boswell, Jr.

1949 The Pennsylvania Academy of the Fine Arts, Philadelphia. *144th Annual Exhibition*, Jan. 23–Feb. 27, 1949.

National Academy of Design, New York. *124th Annual Exhibition*, Mar. 10–23, 1949.

The Buffalo Seminary, New York. *Exhibition of Portraits of and by Seminarians Past and Present*, Apr. 7–11, 1949.

Art Association of Newport, Rhode Island. *Thirty-eighth Annual Exhibition of Pictures by American Painters*, July 1949. Catalogue.

The Brooklyn Museum, New York. *38 Artists Who Teach*, Sept. 14–Oct. 9, 1949. Catalogue.

National Arts Club, New York. *The Federation of Modern Painters and of Sculptors 9th Annual Exhibition*, Oct. 12–29, 1949. Checklist.

Carnegie Institute, Pittsburgh, Pennsylvania. *Painting in the United States, 1949*, Oct. 13–Dec. 11, 1949. Catalogue, text by Homer Saint-Gaudens.

National Academy of Design, New York. *124th Annual Exhibition II*, Nov. 11–Dec. 11, 1949.

1950 Salmagundi Club, New York. *Annual Oil Exhibition*, Mar. 18–Apr. 7, 1950.

The Metropolitan Museum of Art, New York. *100 American Painters of the 20th Century*, June 16–Oct. 29, 1950. Catalogue.

The Brooklyn Museum, New York. *Artists Who Teach*, Sept. 16–Oct. 15, 1950.

National Academy of Design, New York. *1875–1950: The Art Students League Diamond Jubilee*, Oct. 8–29, 1950. Catalogue, foreword by E. Leslie Waid.

1951 National Academy of Design, New York. *Audubon Artists*, Jan. 18–Feb. 4, 1951.

National Academy of Design, New York. *126th Annual Exhibition*, Mar. 23–Apr. 8, 1951. Catalogue.

Corcoran Gallery of Art, Washington, D.C. *Twenty-second Biennial Exhibition of Contemporary American Oil Painting*, Apr. 1–May 13, 1951. Catalogue.

The Brooklyn Museum, New York. *32 Artists Who Teach*, Oct. 5–Nov. 11, 1951.

1952 National Academy of Design, New York. *127th Annual Exhibition*, Mar. 21–Apr. 13, 1952. Catalogue.

The Museum of Modern Art, New York. *15 Americans*, Apr. 8–June 22, 1952. Catalogue, text by Dorothy C. Miller et al.

National Academy of Design, New York. *A Memorial Exhibition of Paintings by Frank Vincent DuMond, N. A. with Some Distinguished Former Students*, May 25–June 22, 1952. Catalogue.

1953 The Art Students League of New York. *Artists' Faces*, opening and closing dates unknown, 1953.

Riverside Museum, New York. *Federation of Modern Painters and Sculptors*, opening and closing dates unknown, 1953.

National Academy of Design, New York. *Audubon Artists*, Jan. 12–Feb. 8, 1953.

The Museum of Modern Art, New York. *New Acquisitions*, Feb. 11–Mar. 15, 1953.

National Institute of Arts and Letters, New York. *Exhibition of Works by Candidates for Grants in Art for the Year 1953*, Feb. 18–Mar. 4, 1953.

National Academy of Design, New York. *128th Annual Exhibition*, Apr. 2–26, 1953.

Nita Cole Gallery, Orleans, Massachusetts. Exhibition title unknown, Aug. 19–Sept. 22, 1953.

Whitney Museum of American Art, New York. *1953 Annual Exhibition of Contemporary American Painting*, Oct. 15–Dec. 6, 1953. Catalogue.

Stable Gallery, New York. Exhibition title unknown, Nov. 13, 1953–closing date unknown.

American Academy of Arts and Letters, New York. *Exhibition of American Drawings*, Dec. 4–23, 1953.

1954 Riverside Museum, New York. *Federation of Modern Painters and Sculptors*, Jan. 10–31, 1954.

Stable Gallery, New York. *Third Annual Exhibition of Painting and Sculpture*, Jan. 27–Feb. 10, 1954.

National Academy of Design, New York. *129th Annual Exhibition*, Apr. 1–25, 1954. Catalogue.

Walker Art Center, Minneapolis, Minnesota. *Reality and Fantasy 1900–1954*, May 23–July 2, 1954. Catalogue, text by H. H. Arnason.

American Academy of Arts and Letters and the National Institute of Arts and Letters, New York. *Exhibition of Work of Newly Elected Members, Recipients of Honors, and Childe Hassam Fund Purchases*, May 27–June 27, 1954. Brochure.

The Art Institute of Chicago. *61st American Exhibition*, Oct. 21–Dec. 5, 1954.

1955 Whitney Museum of American Art, New York. *Annual Exhibition of Contemporary American Sculpture, Watercolors, and Drawings*, Jan. 12–Feb. 20, 1955. Catalogue.

University of Illinois, Champaign-Urbana. *Contemporary American Painting and Sculpture*, Feb. 27–Apr. 3, 1955. Catalogue.

Korman Gallery, New York. *Selected Drawings*, June 7–July 1, 1955.

The Museum of Modern Art, New York. *Selections from the Art Lending Service*, Oct. 6–24, 1955.

National Academy of Design, New York. *Five Arts*, Dec. 1–18, 1955. Catalogue.

1956 National Academy of Design, New York. *Audubon Artists*, opening and closing dates unknown, 1956.

The Brooklyn Museum, New York. *Brooklyn Artists Biennial Exhibition*, Jan. 18–Feb. 1956. Brochure.

Thomas Welton Stanford Art Gallery, Stanford University, California. *Contemporary American Painters, 1950–55*, Apr. 15–May 20, 1956.

American Academy of Arts and Letters and the National Institute of Arts and Letters, New York. *Exhibition of Work by Newly Elected Members, Recipients of Honors, and Childe Hassam Fund Purchases*, May 23–June 24, 1956. Brochure.

Cabinet des Estampes, Château des Rohan, Strasbourg, France. *Dessins américains contemporains*, Sept. 29–Oct. 28, 1956. Catalogue, text by Arthur W. Heintzlman.

National Academy Galleries, New York. *Allied Artists America, 43rd Annual Exhibition*, Oct. 1–28, 1956.

1957 Corcoran Gallery of Art, Washington, D.C. *Twenty-fifth Biennial Exhibition of Contemporary American Oil Painting*, Jan. 13–Mar. 10, 1957. Catalogue, introduction by Hermann Williams, Jr. Traveled to Toledo Museum of Art, Ohio. Apr. 1–30, 1957.

The Art Institute of Chicago. *Society for Contemporary Art: 17th Annual Exhibition*, May 8–June 9, 1957.

Greenwich Gallery, New York. *Painting and Sculpture*, Oct. 17–Nov. 16, 1957.

1957–58 The Brooklyn Museum, New York. *Face of America: The History of Portraiture in the United States*, Nov. 13, 1957–Jan. 26, 1958. Catalogue, foreword by Edgar C. Schenck.

1958 Chrysler Art Museum, Norfolk, Virginia. *Provincetown Past and Present*, opening and closing dates unknown, 1958.

National Academy of Design, New York. *133rd Annual Exhibition*, Feb. 20–Mar. 16, 1958. Catalogue.

Albright Art Gallery, Buffalo, New York. *Privately Owned*, May 23–June 30, 1958. Catalogue, foreword by Gordon M. Smith.

1959 HCE Gallery, Provincetown, Massachusetts. *Paintings and Drawings by Three Artists: Janice Biala, Edwin Dickinson, Jack Tworkov*, opening and closing dates unknown, 1959.

Whitney Museum of American Art, New York. *The Collection of the Sara Roby Foundation*, Apr. 29–June 14, 1959. Catalogue, foreword by Sara Mary Roby; introduction by Lloyd Goodrich.

American National Exhibition, Moscow, USSR. *American Painting and Sculpture*, July 25–Sept. 5, 1959. Catalogue, text by Lloyd Goodrich. Traveled to Whitney Museum of American Art, New York, as *Painting and Sculpture from the American National Exhibition in Moscow*, Oct. 28–Nov. 15, 1959.

Stable Gallery, New York. Exhibition title unknown, Sept. 28–closing date unknown, 1959.

The Pennsylvania Academy of the Fine Arts, Philadelphia. *Paintings, Drawings, and Prints Collected and Owned by Fourteen Philadelphia Artists*, Nov. 7–Dec. 6, 1959. Checklist.

1960 Albright Art Gallery, Buffalo, New York. *The T. Edward Hanley Collection*, Jan. 6–Feb. 14, 1960. Brochure.

The Pennsylvania Academy of the Fine Arts, Philadelphia. *155th Annual Exhibition*, Jan. 24–Feb. 28, 1960.

World House Galleries, New York. *Summer International 4*, June 22–July 29, 1960. Catalogue. Traveled to Tennessee Fine Arts Center, Nashville, Aug. 14–Oct. 2, 1960.

Albright Art Gallery, Buffalo, New York. *The Patteran Artists Exhibition*, Nov. 1–30, 1960. Brochure, foreword by Mary Elizabeth Letchworth.

1961 Colby College Art Museum, Waterville, Maine. *Exhibition of Art by the Faculty and Visiting Artists of the Skowhegan School of Painting and Sculpture*, opening and closing dates unknown, 1961. Catalogue.

Goddard-Riverside Community Center, New York. *Annual Fine Arts Exhibition*, opening and closing dates unknown, 1961.

University of Nebraska Art Galleries, Lincoln. *A Selection of Works from the Art Collections*, opening and closing dates unknown, 1961.

Whitney Museum of American Art, New York. *The Theatre Collects American Art: Fourth Loan Exhibition by the Whitney Museum of American Art*, Apr. 10–May 16, 1961. Catalogue, foreword by Eloise Spaeth.

The Art Institute of Chicago. *Society for Contemporary Art*, May 17–June 4, 1961.

The Finch College Museum of Art, New York. *American Drawings (Benjamin West to the Present) from the Paul Magriel Collection*, June 9–Aug. 31, 1961. Checklist.

Cape Cod Conservatory of Music and Arts, Hyannis, Massachusetts. *2nd Annual Cape Cod Festival of the Arts*, July 18–23, 1961.

Joslyn Art Museum, Omaha, Nebraska. *100 Works from the Collections at the University of Nebraska*, Oct. 1–29, 1961. Brochure.

James Graham & Sons, New York. *Two Hundred Years of American Painting*, Nov. 1–Dec. 2, 1961.

The Isaac Delgado Museum of Art, New Orleans, Louisiana. *The Magriel Collection of American Drawings*, Nov. 1–Dec. 31, 1961. Brochure.

Wildenstein & Co., New York. *Loan Exhibition of Paintings and Drawings from the Hanley Collection*, Nov. 22–Dec. 30, 1961. Brochure.

Decorative Arts Gallery, New York. *The Contemporary Collector's Home*, Dec. 7–22, 1961.

1961–62 Krannert Art Museum, University of Illinois, Champaign-Urbana. *A Selection from the Josephine and Phillip A. Bruno Collection*, Nov. 11–Dec. 3, 1961. Checklist. Traveled to Tennessee Fine Arts Center at Cheekwood, Nashville, Jan. 20–Feb. 20, 1962.

Yale University Art Gallery, New Haven, Connecticut. *Contemporary Paintings Selected from 1960–1961 New York Gallery Exhibitions*, Dec. 7, 1961–Feb. 4, 1962.

1962 James Graham & Sons, New York. *Benefit Exhibition: CORE*. Organized by the American Federation of Arts. Opening and closing dates unknown, 1962.

Norfolk Museum of Arts and Sciences, Virginia. *American Drawing Annual XIX*, Jan. 12–Feb. 1, 1962. Brochure.

Montclair Art Museum, New Jersey. *American Drawings: A Selection from the Paul Magriel Collection*, Mar. 11–25, 1962. Brochure.

American Academy of Arts and Letters and the National Institute of Art and Letters, New York. *Exhibition of Work of Newly Elected Members and Recipients of Honors and Awards,* May 24–June 17, 1962. Brochure.

Silvermine Guild of Arists, New Canaan, Connecticut. *Ford Foundation Winners' Exhibition*, Oct. 6–25, 1962.

1962–63 Whitney Museum of American Art, New York. *Annual Exhibition: Contemporary Sculpture and Drawings*, Dec. 12, 1962–Feb. 3, 1963. Catalogue.

1962–64 Milwaukee Art Museum, Wisconsin. *Art:USA:Now*, Sept. 20–Oct. 21, 1962. Catalogue, text by Allen S. Weller. Traveled to Royal Academy of Arts, London, Feb. 15–Mar. 17, 1963; Zappeion, Athens, Greece, Apr. 2–15, 1963; Palazzo Venezia, Rome, May 7–24, 1963; Haus der Kunst, Munich, Germany, June 13–July 14, 1963; Salons Privée, Monaco, Aug. 8–31, 1963; Congress Hall, Berlin, East Germany, Sept. 22–Oct. 6, 1963; Charlottenborg, Copenhagen, Denmark, Oct. 20–Nov. 10, 1963; Liljevalchs Konsthall, Stockholm, Sweden, Nov. 23–Dec. 18, 1963; Sala delle Cariatidi Palazzo Reale, Milan, Italy, opening and closing dates unknown, 1964; Palais des Beaux Arts, Brussels, Belgium, Feb. 15–Mar. 15, 1964; Municipal Museum, Dublin, Ireland, Apr. 17–May 10, 1964; Cason del Buen Retiro, Madrid, Spain, June 6–28, 1964; Kunstmuseum Luzern, Switzerland, Aug. 1–31, 1964; Musée d'Art Moderne de la Ville de Paris, Sept. 8–27, 1964; Akademie Bildende Kunste, Vienna, Austria, opening and closing dates unknown.

1963 Wilmington Society of the Fine Arts, Delaware. *Provincetown: A Painter's Place*, Jan. 11–Feb. 1, 1963. Organized by the American Federation of Arts, New York. Catalogue. Traveled to University of Missouri, Columbia, Feb. 15–Mar. 8, 1963; Quincy Art Center, Illinois, Mar. 22–Apr. 12, 1963; Fort Wayne Art Museum, Indiana, Apr. 30–May 29, 1963; Brooks Memorial Art Center, Memphis, Tennessee, July 5–Aug. 5, 1963; Utah Museum of Fine Arts, Salt Lake City, Aug. 19–Sept. 9, 1963; Tyler School of Fine Arts, Temple University, Philadelphia, Sept. 23–Oct. 14, 1963.

Bradley Museum, Columbus Museum of Arts and Crafts, Georgia. *American Traditionalists of the 20th Century*, Feb. 15–Mar. 17, 1963.

Cleveland Museum of Art, Ohio. *Shadowed Images*, Feb. 19–Mar. 31, 1963. Brochure.

National Academy of Design, New York. *138th Annual Exhibition*, Feb. 21–Mar. 17, 1963.

Sheldon Memorial Art Gallery, University of Nebraska, Lincoln. *A Selection of Works from the Art Collections at the University of Nebraska*, May 1963. Catalogue.

Whitney Museum of American Art, New York. *26 American Artists from Museums and Friends Collections*, July 16–Sept. 1, 1963.

The Katonah Gallery, New York. *Sea and Shore. Exhibition of 20th Century Paintings and Sculpture*, July 21–Sept. 3, 1963.

Beaverbrook Art Gallery, Fredericton, New Brunswick, Canada. *The Dunn International: An Exhibition of Contemporary Painting*, Sept. 7–Oct. 6, 1963. Catalogue. Traveled to Tate Gallery, London, Nov. 14–Dec. 14, 1963.

Whitney Museum of American Art, New York. *60 Years of American Art*, Sept. 17–Oct. 20, 1963.

Philadelphia Museum of Art. *Philadelphia Collects 20th Century*, Oct. 3–Nov. 17, 1963. Catalogue, text by Henry Gardiner.

The American Federation of Arts Gallery, New York. *Painters and Sculptors, Winners of the Brandeis University Creative Arts Awards*, Oct. 21–Nov. 5, 1963.

1963–64 Allen Memorial Art Museum, Oberlin College, Ohio. *U.S. Government Art Projects: Some Distinguished Alumni*, Feb. 11–Mar. 4, 1963. Circulated by the Museum of Modern Art, New York. Traveled to Mercer University, Macon, Georgia, Mar. 19–Apr. 9, 1963; University of Nevada, Reno, Apr. 24–May 19, 1963; Tacoma Art League, Washington, May 30–June 20, 1963; Washington Gallery of Modern Art, Washington, D.C., July 8–Sept. 1, 1963; State University of New York, Oswego, Sept. 18–Oct. 9, 1963; Cranbrook Academy of Art, Bloomfield Hills, Michigan, Oct. 21–Nov. 11, 1963; Carleton College, Northfield, Minnesota, Nov. 22–Dec. 13, 1963; Coe College, Cedar Rapids, Iowa, Jan. 2–23, 1964; Pomona College, Claremont, California, Feb. 7–29, 1964.

Colby College Art Museum, Waterville, Maine. *Maine and Its Artists: 1710–1963*, May 4–Aug. 31, 1963. Catalogue, text by William B. Miller. Traveled to Museum of Fine Arts, Boston, Dec. 12, 1963–Jan. 26, 1964; Whitney Museum of American Art, New York, Feb. 10–Mar. 22, 1964.

National Gallery of Art, Washington, D.C. *Paintings from the Museum of Modern Art*, Dec. 17, 1963–Mar. 22, 1964. Catalogue, text by Alfred H. Barr, Jr.

1964 The Pennsylvania Academy of the Fine Arts, Philadelphia. *159th Annual Exhibition*, Jan. 25–Mar. 1, 1964.

Marquette University Committee on the Fine Arts, Milwaukee, Wisconsin. *Great Art from Private Colleges and Universities*, Feb. 20–27, 1964. Brochure, text by John Pick.

Bayonne Jewish Community Center, New Jersey. *Trends in American Painting—1964, 11th Annual Exhibition of Contemporary American Painting*, Feb. 24–Mar. 6, 1964.

The Brooklyn Museum, New York. *10th Annual Brooklyn Heights Art Show*, Apr. 17–26, 1964.

Whitney Museum of American Art, New York. *The Friends Collect: Recent Acquisitions by Members of Friends of the Whitney Museum of American Art, 7th Friends Loan Exhibition*, May 8–June 16, 1964. Catalogue.

Art Gallery, Better Living Center, Hall of Education, New York World's Fair, New York. *Four Centuries of American Masterpieces*, May 22–Oct. 18, 1964. Organized by the Skowhegan School of Painting and Sculpture, Maine.

Colorado Springs Fine Arts Center, Colorado. *New Acquisitions USA*, June 15–Sept. 14, 1964. Catalogue, introduction by Fred S. Bartlett.

Whitney Museum of American Art, New York. *Between the Fairs: 25 Years of American Art, 1939–1964*, June 24–Sept. 23, 1964. Catalogue, foreword by Lloyd Goodrich; text by John I. H. Baur.

Provincetown Art Association, Massachusetts. *Second 1964 Show*, Aug., opening date unknown–Sept., closing date unknown, 1964.

The Baltimore Museum of Art. *"1914,"* Oct. 6–Nov. 15, 1964. Catalogue, *1914: An Exhibition of Paintings, Drawings and Sculpture in Celebration of the 50th Anniversary of The Baltimore Museum of Art.*

The Armory, Englewood, New Jersey. *Englewood Armory Art Show*, Oct. 18–21, 1964.

1964–66 Everson Museum of Art, Syracuse, New York. *One Hundred Years of American Realism. Watercolors and Pastels from the Paul Magriel Collection*, Jan. 4–25, 1964. Circulated by the American Federation of Arts. Traveled to Public Library, Winston-Salem, North Carolina, Feb. 8–29, 1964; St. Lawrence University, Canton, New York, Mar. 14–Apr. 4, 1964; Frye Art Museum, Skagit Valley College, Seattle, Washington, Apr. 18–May 9, 1964; Brooks Memorial Art Gallery, Memphis, Tennessee, June 27–July 25, 1964; Ohio State University, Columbus, Aug. 8–29, 1964; Art Associates of Lake Charles, Louisiana, Sept. 12–Oct. 3, 1964; Fort Lauderdale Museum of Art, Florida, Oct. 17–Dec. 12, 1964; New Britain Museum of American Art, Connecticut, Jan. 3–24, 1965; Currier Gallery of Art, Manchester, New Hampshire, Feb. 2–18, 1965; University of Wyoming, Laramie, Apr. 18–May 6, 1965; American Federation of Arts Gallery, New York, May 20–June 12, 1965; Howard University, Washington, D.C., Sept. 14–Oct. 5, 1965; Huntington Galleries, West Virginia, Oct. 19–Nov. 9, 1965; Canton Art Institute, Ohio, Nov. 23–Dec. 14, 1965; Andrew Dickson White Museum of Art, Cornell University, Ithaca, New York, Dec. 28, 1965–Jan. 18, 1966; J. B. Speed Art Museum, Louisville, Kentucky, Feb. 1–22, 1966; Decatur Art Center, Illinois, Mar. 6–27, 1966; Hackley Art Gallery,

Muskegon, Michigan, Apr. 12–May 3, 1966; Charleston Civic Center, West Virginia, May 17–June 7, 1966.

The American Federation of Arts Gallery, New York. *Fifty Years of American Art from the Provincetown Golden Anniversary*, Oct. 13–30, 1964. Circulated by the American Federation of Arts. Traveled to Bacardi Imports, Miami, Florida, Nov. 27–Dec. 18, 1964; Watkins Institute, Nashville, Tennessee, Jan. 1–22, 1965; Schenectady Museum Association, New York, Feb. 5–26, 1965; University of North Carolina, Greensboro, Mar. 12–Apr. 2, 1965; Charleston Civic Center, West Virginia, May 20–23, 1965; Canton Art Institute, Ohio, June 6–July 5, 1965; Eastern Illinois University, Charleston, Sept. 3–24, 1965; Fort Lauderdale Museum of the Arts, Florida, Oct. 8–29, 1965; Christopher Newport College, Huntington, Pennsylvania, Jan. 7–28, 1966; Austin College, Sherman, Texas, Feb. 11–Mar. 4, 1966; Southern Illinois University, Alton, Apr. 22–May 13, 1966; Hofstra University, Hempstead, New York, opening and closing dates unknown.

1965 Forum Gallery, New York. *Artists by Artists: An Exhibition of Portraits of Artists by Their Contemporaries: Paintings, Sculpture and Drawings*, Jan. 9–30, 1965.

Gallery of Modern Art, New York. *The Drawing Society*, Jan. 26–Mar. 14, 1965.

The Brooklyn Museum, New York. *11th Annual Brooklyn Heights Art Show*, Apr. 23–May 2, 1965.

James Graham & Sons, New York. *Artists for CORE: Exhibition and Sale*, Apr. 28–May 8, 1965.

Whitney Museum of American Art, New York. *A Decade of American Drawings: 1955–1965*, Apr. 28–June 6, 1965. Catalogue, foreword by Donald M. Blinken.

The White House, Washington, D.C. *The White House Festival of the Arts*, June 14, 1965.

The Brooklyn Museum, New York. *Herbert A. Goldstone Collection of American Art*, June 15–Sept. 12, 1965. Catalogue, preface by Axel von Saldern.

The Brooklyn Museum, New York. *12 Years of Collecting Drawings & Prints 1953–1965*, June 21–Dec. 26, 1965. Brochure, text by Una E. Johnson.

Wellfleet Art Gallery, Massachusetts. *Group Exhibition*, Summer 1965.

Bowdoin College Museum of Art, Brunswick, Maine. *Collecting Privately*, July 1–Sept. 5, 1965. Catalogue, foreword by Marvin S. Sadik.

Art and Home Center, Exhibition Grounds, Syracuse, New York. *Five Distinguished American Artists: Dickinson, Hofmann, Hopper, Shahn, Soyer*, Aug. 31–Sept. 6, 1965.

James Graham & Sons, New York. *In Honor of the International Council of Museums: A Special Exhibition*, Sept. 20–Oct. 2, 1965.

ACA Gallery, New York. *The Artist Sees Himself*, Oct. 11–30, 1965.

Wilmington Society of the Fine Arts, Delaware. *Trends in Contemporary American Painting*, Oct. 13–Nov. 7, 1965. Brochure, text by Rowland Elzea.

The Armory, Englewood, New Jersey. *Englewood Armory Art Show*, Oct. 23–closing date unknown, 1965.

Lenox Hill Hospital and Skowhegan School of Painting and Sculpture, Lenox Hill Hospital, New York. *Annual Art Exhibition and Sale*, Nov. 10–23, 1965.

1965–66 DeWaters Art Center, Flint Institute of Arts, Michigan. *The Drawing Society National Exhibition: 1965*, Oct. 1–22, 1965. Organized by the American Federation of Arts. Traveled to University of Massachusetts, Amherst, Nov. 5–26, 1965; Oklahoma Art Center, Oklahoma City, Dec. 10–31, 1965; Atlanta Art Association, Georgia, Jan. 24–Feb. 4, 1966; University of Kansas Museum of Art, Lawrence, Feb. 18–Mar. 11, 1966; Colorado Springs Fine Arts Center, Colorado, Mar. 25–Apr. 14, 1966; Frederick & Nelson, Seattle, Washington, Apr. 22–May 2, 1966; Long Beach Museum of Art, California, June 5–26, 1966.

Finch College Museum of Art, New York. *The Josephine and Phillip A. Bruno Collection*, Nov. 23, 1965–Jan. 9, 1966. Traveled to Saint Paul Art Center, Minnesota, Mar. 3–May 15, 1966.

Wadsworth Atheneum, Hartford, Connecticut. *56th Connecticut Academy of Fine Arts Exhibition*, Dec. 11, 1965–Jan. 2, 1966.

1966 National Academy of Design, New York. *141st Annual Exhibition*, Feb. 24–Mar. 20, 1966.

Stephen Mazoh Gallery, Baltimore. *20th Century American Landscapes*, Mar. 1–Apr. 15, 1966.

The Larry Aldrich Museum, Ridgefield, Connecticut. *Brandeis University, Creative Arts Awards 1957–1967*, Apr. 17–June 26, 1966. Brochure.

Goddard-Riverside Community Center, New York. *West Side Artists*, Apr. 19–May 8, 1966.

San Francisco Museum of Art. *Art for the Collector (Accessions Committee Exhibition) 20th Century American Master Drawings*, Apr. 20–May 29, 1966.

Virginia Museum of Fine Arts, Richmond. *American Paintings 1966*, May 16–June 12, 1966. Catalogue, text by Cecil Vincent Donovan.

Storm King Art Center, Mountainville, New York. *79 Original Drawings by 20th Century Masters*, June 28–Aug. 28, 1966. Brochure.

Whitney Museum of American Art, New York. *Art of the United States: 1670–1966*, Sept. 28–Nov. 27, 1966. Catalogue, text by Lloyd Goodrich.

1967 Gallery of Modern Art, New York. *Selections from the Collection of Dr. and Mrs. T. Edward Hanley*, Jan. 3–Mar. 4, 1967. Catalogue, text by Margaret Potter and Evan H. Turner. Traveled to Philadelphia Museum of Art, Apr. 6–May 28, 1967.

Henry Art Gallery, University of Washington, Seattle. *Drawings by Americans: Recent Work by Thirteen Contemporary Artists*, Feb. 12–Mar. 19, 1967. Catalogue.

Storm King Art Center, Mountainville, New York. *Original Works of Art in a Variety of Mediums Selected from the Permanent Collection of the Art Students League of New York*, July 1–Aug. 30, 1967. Brochure.

James Graham & Sons, New York. *The 110th Anniversary Graham Gallery, 1857–1967*, Sept. 20–Oct. 18, 1967.

Visual Arts Gallery, New York. *Perspective: An Exhibition of Early and Current Work*, Nov. 28–Dec. 22, 1967.

1967–68 Georgia Museum of Art, University of Georgia, Athens. *American Painting: The 1940s*, Apr. 19–May 10, 1967. Organized by the American Federation of Arts. Catalogue, texts by Lamar Dodd and William D. Paul, Jr. Traveled to Art Club of Erie, Pennsylvania, Aug. 6–27, 1967; Roberson Center for the Arts & Sciences, Binghamton, New York, Sept. 10–Oct. 1, 1967; Everson Museum, Syracuse, New York, Oct. 15–Nov. 15, 1967; Kent Boys' School, Connecticut, Nov. 19–Dec. 10, 1967; Museum of Fine Arts, St. Petersburg, Florida, Jan. 28–Feb. 18, 1968; Bacardi Imports, Miami, Florida, Mar. 3–24, 1968; Greenville County Museum of Art, South Carolina, Apr. 7–28, 1968; Nassau Community College, Garden City, New York, May 12–June 2, 1968.

Quincy Art Club, Illinois. *American Masters: Art Students League.* Organized by the American Federation of Arts to celebrate the start of the tenth decade of the Art Students League of New York, Oct. 8–29, 1967. Traveled to Art Students League, New York, Nov. 12–Dec. 3, 1967; School of Fine Arts, Arkansas State College, Jan. 21–Feb. 12, 1968; Norton Gallery and School of Art, West Palm Beach, Florida, Feb. 26–Mar. 17, 1968; Abilene Fine Arts Museum, Texas, Mar. 31–Apr. 21, 1968; Montgomery Museum of Fine Arts, Alabama, May 5–26 1968; Laguna Gloria Art Museum, Austin, Texas, June 9–30, 1968; Cummer Gallery of Art, Jacksonville, Florida, Aug. 18–Sept. 18, 1968.

American Academy of Arts and Letters and the National Institute of Arts and Letters, New York. *Drawings by Members*, Nov. 17, 1967–Feb. 4, 1968. Brochure.

1968 Peridot Gallery, New York. *The American Landscape: A Living Tradition*, Jan. 30–Feb. 24, 1968.

The Slater Memorial Museum, Norwich, Connecticut. *A Survey of American Art*, Feb. 4–25, 1968. Catalogue, text by Janet Shafner.

Fine Arts Gallery, Vanderbilt University, Nashville, Tennessee. *The Faculty Collects*, Feb. 4–27, 1968.

Minneapolis Institute of Arts, Minnesota. *A Selection of Drawings from the David Daniels Collection*, Feb. 22–April 21, 1968. Catalogue, introduction by Agnes Mongan. Traveled to The Art Institute of Chicago, May 3–June 23; Nelson-Atkins Museum of Art, Kansas City, Missouri, July 11–Sept. 29; Fogg Art Museum, Harvard University, Cambridge, Massachusetts, Oct. 16–Nov. 25.

The Century Association, New York. *Centurions Associated with the Art Students League. Part Two: The Present*, Mar. 6–30, 1968.

Museum of Art, Rhode Island School of Design and Annmary Brown Memorial, Brown University, Providence. *The Neuberger Collection: An American Collection of Paintings, Drawings, and Sculpture*, May 8–June 30, 1968. Catalogue, foreword and introduction by Daniel Robbins. Traveled to National Collection of Fine Arts, Smithsonian Institution, Washington, D.C., Aug. 15–Sept. 25, 1968.

James Graham & Sons, New York. *Dickinson, Gallo and Glarner*, Summer 1968.

Art Association of Newport, Rhode Island. *Third Harrison S. Morris Memorial Exhibit: Landscapes by 20th Century American Artists*, Aug. 3–Sept. 2, 1968.

Sheldon Memorial Art Gallery, University of Nebraska, Lincoln. *Painting and Sculpture from the Collection of Mr. and Mrs. Louis Sosland*, Sept. 17–Oct. 13, 1968. Brochure. Traveled to Mulvane Art Center, Washburn University, Topeka, Kansas, Nov. 3–Dec. 1, 1968.

Whitney Museum of American Art, New York. *The 1930s: Paintings and Sculpture in America*, Oct. 15–Dec. 1968. Catalogue, text by William C. Agee.

American Academy of Arts and Letters and the National Institute of Arts and Letters, New York. *Paintings by Members*, Oct. 25–Dec. 22, 1968. Brochure.

Art Department Galleries, University of Northern Iowa, Cedar Falls. *Unidrawings '68 Invitational*, Nov. 4–22, 1968.

Columbus Gallery of Fine Arts, Ohio. *Works from the Hanley Collection*, Nov. 7–Dec. 15, 1968. Catalogue, text by Mahonri Sharp Young.

San Francisco Museum of Art. *Untitled '68*, Nov. 9–Dec. 29, 1968. Catalogue, foreword by Gerald Nordland.

1969 The Brooklyn Museum, New York. *Thirty Years of Collecting by Una E. Johnson*, Feb. 25–Apr. 27, 1969. Catalogue.

Wilmington Society of the Fine Arts, Delaware. *Contemporary American Painting and Sculpture from New York Galleries*, Mar. 28–Apr. 27, 1969. Brochure.

High Museum of Art, Atlanta, Georgia. *The Collection of Peggy and David Steine*, May 18–June 15, 1969. Catalogue, introduction by David Steine.

Southern Vermont Art Center, Manchester. *Contemporary Masters*, July 12–27, 1969.

Cape Cod Art Association, Hyannis, Massachusetts. *An Exhibition of the Work of 40 Distinguished Guest Artists from Cape Cod and the Islands*, July 27–Aug. 8, 1969.

Montclair Art Museum, New Jersey. *100 Paintings from the 20th Century*, Sept. 7–28, 1969.

Institute of Contemporary Art, Boston. *A Memorial Exhibition: Selections from the Nathaniel Saltonstall Collection*, Nov. 11–Dec. 14, 1969. Catalogue, introduction by Andrew Hyde; text by Michael Phillips.

Canisius College, Buffalo, New York. *Works from the T. Edward Hanley Collection*, Nov. 23–Dec. 23, 1969.

James Graham & Sons, New York. *Contemporary American Drawings and Watercolors*, Dec. 2–24, 1969.

1969–70 Museum of Art, University of Connecticut, Storrs. *Contemporary Portraits*, Feb. 2–23, 1969. Organized by the Museum of Modern Art, New York. Brochure, text by Alicia Legg. Traveled to Flint Institute of Art, Michigan, Mar. 21–Apr. 13, 1969; J. B. Speed Art Museum, Louisville, Kentucky, Apr. 28–May 26, 1969; Abilene Fine Art Museum, Texas, June 9–30, 1969; University of North Carolina, Greensboro, Oct. 3–24, 1969; Cummer Gallery of Art, Jacksonville, Florida, Dec. 8, 1969–Jan. 5, 1970; Middlebury College, Vermont, Feb. 1–22, 1970.

1970 Sheldon Memorial Art Gallery, University of Nebraska, Lincoln. *Selected Works from the Collection of Mrs. A. B. Sheldon*, Jan. 20–Feb. 15, 1970. Catalogue.

Charles Burchfield Center, State University College at Buffalo, New York. *Art in the Buffalo Area: 1920–1930*, Apr. 19–Sept. 27, 1970. Brochure.

The Art Institute of Chicago. *A Quarter Century of Collecting: Drawings Given to The Art Institute of Chicago 1944–1970, by Margaret Day Blake*, Apr. 28–June 7, 1970.

Montclair Art Museum, New Jersey. *Blanche P. Pleasants Fund Purchases*, Sept. 16–Oct. 13, 1970. Brochure.

1971 Birmingham Museum of Art, Alabama. *Contemporary Selections 1971*, Jan. 24–Feb. 20, 1971. Catalogue, text by Edward F. Weeks.

M. Knoedler and Company, New York. *What Is American in American Art. An Exhibition in Memory of Joseph B. Martinson for the Benefit of the Museum of American Folk Art*, Feb. 9–Mar. 6, 1971. Catalogue, text by Mary Black.

Delaware Art Museum, Wilmington. *American Painting since World War II*, June 8–July 11, 1971. Catalogue, text by Rowland Elzea.

Charles Burchfield Center, State University College at Buffalo, New York. *Our Legacy of Art in Western New York*, Sept. 14–Oct. 24, 1971. Catalogue, preface by Edna M. Lindemann.

The Baltimore Museum of Art. *Maryland Collectors*, Oct. 5–Dec. 5, 1971.

Weatherspoon Art Gallery, The University of North Carolina, Greensboro. *Art on Paper Invitational*, Nov. 14–Dec. 17, 1971. Catalogue, text by James Tucker.

1971–72 A. M. Sachs Gallery, New York. *The Artist and the American Landscape: 1908–1971*, Nov. 30, 1971–Jan. 5, 1972.

1972 Bacon Farm Barn Gallery, Barnstable Village, Massachusetts. *Mid-Summer Invitational Exhibition*, Aug. 5–24, 1972. Organized by Cape Cod Art Association.

Washburn Gallery, New York. *Mind over Matter: Painters of the Immanent Things*, Sept. 20–Oct. 21, 1972. Brochure.

Portland Museum of Art, Maine. *Spaces and Places*, Sept. 22–Nov. 12, 1972.

Cleveland Institute of Art, Ohio. *32 Realists*, Oct. 8–Nov. 10, 1972. Brochure.

American Academy of Arts and Letters and the National Institute of Arts and Letters, New York. *Paintings by Members*, Nov. 10–Dec. 17, 1972. Brochure.

Allen Priebe Gallery, University of Wisconisin, Oshkosh. *American Representational Painting*, Nov. 27–Dec. 14, 1972. Catalogue, brochure by Ron Weaver and Sam Yates.

1973 Heckscher Museum, Huntington, New York, and The Parrish Art Museum, Southampton, New York. Heckscher: *The Students of William Merritt Chase: Shinnecock Group*, Sept. 28–Nov. 11, 1973, and *The Students of William Merritt Chase: Major Artists*, Nov. 18–Dec. 30, 1973. Parrish: *The Students of William Merritt Chase: Major Artists*, Sept. 28–Nov. 11, 1973, and *The Students of William Merritt Chase: Shinnecock Group*, Nov. 18–Dec. 30, 1973. Catalogue, foreword by Eva Ingersoll Gatling and Jean M. Weber; text by Ronald G. Pisano.

American Academy of Arts and Letters and the National Institute of Arts and Letters, New York. *Exhibition of Graphics and Sculpture by Members*, Nov. 9–Dec. 16, 1973. Brochure.

1974 National Portrait Gallery, Smithsonian Institution, Washington, D.C. *American Self-Portraits: 1670–1973*, Feb. 1–Mar. 15, 1974. Organized and circulated by the International Exhibitions Foundation. Catalogue, texts by Ann C. VanDevanter and Alfred V. Frankenstein with Shirley S. Simpson. Traveled to Indianapolis Museum of Art, Indiana, Apr. 1–May 15, 1974.

Charles Burchfield Center, State University College at Buffalo, New York. *Works by Living American Artists*, Mar. 16–Apr. 21, 1974. Brochure, text by Edna Lindemann.

Lowe Art Museum, University of Miami, Coral Gables, Florida. *Contemporary Portraits by American Painters*, Oct. 3–Nov. 10, 1974. Catalogue, preface by John J. Baratte; introduction by John Gruen.

Museum of Art, The Pennsylvania State University, University Park. *Living American Artists and the Figure*, Nov. 2–Dec. 22, 1974. Catalogue.

1974–75 The Hirshhorn Museum and Sculpture Garden, Smithsonian Institution, Washington, D.C. *Inaugural Exhibition*, Oct. 4, 1974–Sept. 15, 1975. Catalogue, text by Abram Lerner.

Charles Burchfield Center, State University College at Buffalo, New York. *Young Collectors. An Exhibition of Their Favorite Selections*, Dec. 8, 1974–Jan. 12, 1975. Catalogue, text by Edna M. Lindemann.

1975 Kennedy Galleries, New York. *The Kennedy Galleries Are Host to the Hundredth Anniversary Exhibition of Paintings and Sculptures by 100 Artists Associated with the Art Students League of New York*, Mar. 6–29, 1975. Catalogue, introduction by Lawrence A. Fleischman.

Montgomery Museum of Fine Arts, Alabama. *Selected Works from the Dillard Collection*, Apr. 15–May 18, 1975. Catalogue, introduction by James E. Tucker.

Whitney Museum of American Art, New York. *The Whitney Studio Club and American Art 1900–1932*, May 23–Sept. 3, 1975.

Charles Burchfield Center, State University College at Buffalo, New York. *Western New Yorkers Collection*, May 25–June 3, 1975. Checklist.

Henry Art Gallery, University of Washington, Seattle. *Selections from the Collections*, Sept. 10–Oct. 12, 1975.

1976 The Katonah Gallery, New York. *American Painting 1900–1976: The American Scene and New Forms of Modernism 1935–1954*, Jan. 17–Mar. 14, 1976. Catalogue, text by John I. H. Baur.

Chrysler Museum, Norfolk, Virginia. *Three Hundred Years of American Art in the Chrysler Museum*, Mar. 1–July 4, 1976. Catalogue, text by Dennis R. Anderson.

New Jersey State Museum, Trenton. *This Land Is Your Land*, Apr. 17–Sept. 6, 1976.

Museum of Art, The Pennsylvania State University, University Park. *Portraits USA 1776–1976*, Apr. 18–June 6, 1976. Catalogue, text by Harold Dickson.

The Pennsylvania Academy of the Fine Arts, Philadelphia. *In This Academy: The Pennsylvania Academy of the Fine Arts, 1805–1976*, Apr. 22–Dec. 31, 1976. Catalogue, texts by Frank H. Goodyear, Jr., Doreen Bolger, Louise Lippincott, Mark Thistlethwaite, Richard J. Boyle, Carolyn Diskant, and Joan M. Marter.

Institute of Contemporary Art, Boston. *A Selection of American Art: The Skowhegan School, 1946–1976*, June 16–Sept. 5, 1976. Catalogue, text by Gabriella Jeppson, Lloyd Goodrich, Bernarda B. Shahn, and Allen Ellenzweig. Traveled to Colby Museum of Art, Waterville, Maine, Oct. 1–30, 1976.

The Museum of Modern Art, New York. *The Natural Paradise: Painting in America 1800–1950*, Oct. 1–Nov. 30, 1976. Catalogue, texts by Barbara Novak, Robert Rosenblum, and John Wilmerding.

1976–77 Burchfield Center, State University College at Buffalo, New York. *First Decade*, Nov. 14, 1976–Jan. 23, 1977.

Whitney Museum of American Art, New York. *American Master Drawings and Watercolors: A History of Works on Paper from Colonial Times to the Present*, Nov. 23, 1976–Jan. 23, 1977. Catalogue, texts by Theodore E. Stebbins, Jr., et al.

1976–78 Corcoran Gallery of Art, Washington, D.C. *America 1976: A Bicentennial Exhibition Sponsored by the United States Department of the Interior*, Apr. 27–June 6,

1976. Catalogue, texts by Robert Rosenblum and Neil Welliver. Traveled to Wadsworth Atheneum, Hartford, Connecticut, July 4–Sept. 12, 1976; Fogg Art Museum, Cambridge, Massachusetts, and Institute of Contemporary Art, Boston, Oct. 19–Dec. 7, 1976; Minneapolis Institute of Arts, Minnesota, Jan. 16–Feb. 27, 1977; Milwaukee Art Center, Wisconsin, Mar. 19–May 15, 1977; Fort Worth Art Museum, Texas, June 18–Aug. 14, 1977; San Francisco Museum of Modern Art, Sept. 10–Nov. 13, 1977; High Museum of Art, Atlanta, Georgia, Dec. 10, 1977–Feb. 5, 1978; Brooklyn Museum, New York, Mar. 11–May 21, 1978.

1977 Henry Art Gallery, University of Washington, Seattle. *Henry Gallery/Five Decades*, Feb. 10–Mar. 13, 1977. Catalogue.

Everson Museum of Art, Syracuse, New York. *Provincetown Painters: 1890's to 1970's*, Apr. 1–June 26, 1977. Catalogue, text by Dorothy Gees Seckler. Traveled to Provincetown Art Association, Massachusetts, Aug. 15-Sept. 5, 1977.

The Brooklyn Museum, New York. *Artists' Lives in American Prints and Drawings*, Apr. 9–May 22, 1977. Brochure.

Heritage Plantation of Sandwich, Massachusetts. *Cape Cod as an Art Colony*, Apr. 30–Oct. 16, 1977. Catalogue, texts by H. R. Bradley Smith, April Kingsley, and Fritz Bultman.

National Academy of Design, New York. *Invited Paintings Eligible for Purchase for the Henry Ward Ranger Fund*, Sept. 21–Oct. 8, 1977.

Harbor Gallery, Cold Spring Harbor, New York. *Hawthorne and His Circle*, Nov. 11–Dec. 10, 1977. Catalogue.

1977–78 Whitney Museum of American Art, New York. *American Art 1920–1945*, Oct. 29, 1977–Feb. 12, 1978.

1978 Whitney Museum of American Art, New York. *American Art 1950 to the Present*, May 3–Sept. 10, 1978.

Provincetown Art Association and Museum, Massachusetts. *Works on Paper, Members' Exhibition*, July 31–Aug. 18, 1978.

Corcoran Gallery of Art, Washington, D.C. *Artists and Their Circles*, Aug. 1–Oct. 1, 1978. Brochure, text by Linda C. Simmons.

Provincetown Art Association and Museum, Massachusetts. *Days Lumberyard Studios: Provincetown 1914–1971*, Aug. 18–Oct. 1, 1978.

Henry Art Gallery, University of Washington, Seattle. *Works from the Henry Gallery Collection*, Aug. 24–Sept. 24, 1978.

Mint Museum of Art, Charlotte, North Carolina. *American Painting and Sculpture: 1900–1945*, Nov. 12–Dec. 23, 1978. Brochure, texts by Jerald Melbery and Virginia F. Conder.

1978–79 The Metropolitan Museum of Art, New York. *Tribute to a Curator: Robert Beverly Hale*, Nov. 17, 1978–Mar. 18, 1979.

1979 Hirshhorn Museum and Sculpture Garden, Smithsonian Institution, Washington, D.C. *Artists and Others: Some Portraits from the Collection*, Jan. 11–Apr. 29, 1979.

Montgomery Museum of Fine Arts, Alabama. *Art Inc.: American Paintings from Corporate Collections*, Mar. 7–May 6, 1979. Catalogue, introduction by Mitchell Douglas Kahan. Traveled to Corcoran Gallery of Art, Washington, D.C., June 12–July 14, 1979; Indianapolis Museum of Art, Indiana, Aug. 8–Sept. 23, 1979; San Diego Museum of Art, California, Nov. 17–Dec. 30, 1979.

Heckscher Museum, Huntington, New York. *As We See Ourselves: Artists' Self-Portraits*, June 22–Aug. 5, 1979. Catalogue, text by Katherine Lochridge with contributions by Janet Culbertson and Mary Vaughan.

Kornblee Gallery, New York. *Artists Choose: Figurative/Realist Art. A Benefit Exhibit for the Artists' Choice Museum*, Sept. 8–22, 1979. Catalogue, texts by Robert Godfrey and Howard Kalish.

Whitney Museum of American Art, New York. *Tradition and Modernism in American Art, 1900–1930*, Sept. 11–Nov. 11, 1979.

American Academy and Institute of Arts and Letters, New York. *Memorial Exhibition: Edwin Dickinson, Charles Eames, Eugene Francis Savage, Edward Durell Stone, Stow Wengenroth*, Nov. 19–Dec. 30, 1979. Catalogue.

1979–80 The Solomon R. Guggenheim Museum, New York. *Master Drawings and Watercolors of the Nineteenth and Twentieth Centuries: The Baltimore Museum of Art*, Aug. 24-Oct. 7, 1979. Organized by Baltimore Museum of Art and American Federation of Arts. Catalogue, introduction by Victor Carlson; catalogue entries by Carol Hynning Smith. Traveled to Des Moines Art Center, Iowa, Nov. 19, 1979–Jan. 6, 1980; Art Museum of South Texas, Corpus Christi, Texas, Feb. 8–Mar. 16, 1980; Museum of Fine Arts, Houston, Texas, May 1–June 22, 1980; Denver Art Museum, Colorado, July 12–Aug. 24, 1980.

1980 Whitney Museum of American Art, New York. *The Figurative Tradition and the Whitney Museum of American Art*, June 25–Sept. 28, 1980. Catalogue, texts by Patricia Hills and Roberta K. Tarbell.

1981 Buscaglia-Castellani Art Gallery of Niagara University, Lewiston, New York. *A Legacy of Friendship: Esther Hoyt Sawyer, Edwin W. Dickinson, Nicholas Vasilieff*, May 22–June 21, 1981. Catalogue, text by Sandra H. Olsen.

Cherrystone Gallery, Wellfleet, Massachusetts. *Wellfleet Artists Invitational*, July 18–24, 1981.

Whitney Museum of American Art, New York. *Drawing Acquisitions: 1978–1981*, Sept. 17–Nov. 15, 1981. Catalogue, text by Paul Cummings.

Museum of Art, Rhode Island School of Design, Providence. *Rhode Island Collects Paintings*, Oct. 2–Nov. 15, 1981.

1981–82 Philbrook Art Center, Tulsa, Oklahoma. *Painters of the Humble Truth: Masterpieces of American Still Life, 1801–1939*, Sept. 27–Nov. 8, 1981. Catalogue, text by William H. Gerdts. Traveled to Oakland Museum, California, Dec. 8, 1981–Jan. 24, 1982; Baltimore Museum of Art, Mar. 2–Apr. 25, 1982; National Academy of Design, New York, May 18–July 4, 1982.

Burchfield Center, State University College at Buffalo, New York. *One Hundred and Fifty Years of Portraiture in Western New York*, Dec.9, 1981–Jan. 31, 1982. Catalogue, foreword by Edna M. Lindemann.

1982 Miami University Museum of Art, Oxford, Ohio. *Twentieth Century American Masters: 1911–1957*, Jan. 16–Feb. 28, 1982. Organized by Cedar Rapids Museum of Art, Iowa. Catalogue, text by John S. Czestochowski. Traveled to Tennessee Botanical Gardens and Fine Arts Center, Nashville, Mar. 20–May 2, 1982; Cedar Rapids Museum of Art, Iowa, June 25–Sept. 19, 1982; Springfield Art Museum, Missouri, Oct. 3–Nov. 14, 1982.

Rutgers University Art Gallery, The State University of New Jersey, New Brunswick. *Realism and Realities: The Other Side of American Painting, 1940–1960*, Jan. 17–Mar. 26, 1982. Catalogue, texts by Greta Berman and Jeffrey Wechsler. Traveled to Montgomery Museum of Fine Arts, Alabama, Apr. 15–June 13, 1982; The Art Gallery, University of Maryland, College Park, Sept. 7–Oct. 18, 1982.

Rosa Esman Gallery, New York. *A Curator's Choice 1942–1963: A Tribute to Dorothy Miller*, Feb. 6–Mar. 6, 1982.

Rodman Hall Arts Centre, St. Catharines, Ontario, Canada. *20th Century Drawings from the Collections of Mr. and Mrs. Harvey Breverman*, Sept. 4–26, 1982.

1983 Parrish Art Museum, Southhampton, New York. *The Painterly Figure*, July 24–Sept. 4, 1983. Catalogue, text by Klaus Kertess.

James Graham & Sons, New York. *American Modernism*, Sept. 16–Oct. 20, 1983.

1983–85 National Academy of Design, New York. *Artists by Themselves: Artists' Portraits from the National Academy of Design*, Nov. 3, 1983–Jan. 1, 1984. Catalogue. Traveled to National Portrait Gallery, Washington, D.C., Feb. 10–Mar. 25, 1984; Everson Museum of Art, Syracuse, New York, May 4–June 17, 1984; Joslyn Art Museum, Omaha, Nebraska, July 7–Aug. 19, 1984; Ackland Art Museum, University of North Carolina, Chapel Hill, Sept. 1–Oct. 25, 1984; Norton Gallery and School of Art, West Palm Beach, Florida, Nov. 1, 1984–Jan. 6, 1985; Los Angeles County Museum of Art, Feb. 7–Mar. 15, 1985.

1984 James Graham & Sons, New York. *American Modernism*, Sept. 18–Oct. 20, 1984.

Matthews Hamilton Gallery, Philadelphia. *Landscape Exhibition*, Oct. 20–Nov. 9, 1984.

Artists' Choice Museum, New York. *Artists' Choice Museum: The First Eight Years*, Nov. 17–Dec. 30, 1984.

1984–85 James Graham & Sons, New York. *Small Works, Fine Works: 19th and 20th Century American Painters*, Dec. 13, 1984–Jan. 19, 1985.

1984–86 Munson-Williams-Proctor Institute, Utica, New York. *Order and Enigma: American Art between the Two Wars*, Oct. 13–Dec. 2, 1984. Catalogue, foreword by Paul D. Schweizer; text by Sarah Clark-Langager. Traveled to Herbert F. Johnson Museum of Art, Cornell University, Ithaca, New York, Feb. 16–Apr. 7, 1985; Everson Museum of Art, Syracuse, New York, Apr. 27–June 16, 1985; Albany Institute of History & Art, New York, July 12–Sept. 2, 1985; Memorial Art Gallery of the University of Rochester, New York, Sept. 14–Nov. 3, 1985; Albright-Knox Art Gallery, Buffalo, New York, Jan. 17–Mar. 2, 1986.

1984–87 Robert Hull Fleming Museum, University of Vermont, Burlington. *Artists and Models*, Jan. 5–Feb. 10, 1984. Organized by Smithsonian Institution Traveling Exhibition Service, Washington, D.C. Brochure, text by Frank Gettings. Traveled to Gardiner Art Gallery, Stillwater, Oklahoma, Mar. 2–Apr. 7, 1984; Grinnell College, Grinnell, Iowa, Apr. 27–June 2, 1984; Albrecht Art Museum, St. Joseph, Missouri, June 22–July 28, 1984; Bladen Memorial Art Museum, Fort Dodge, Iowa, Aug. 17–Sept. 22, 1984; Arkansas Arts Center, Little Rock, Oct. 12–Nov. 17, 1984; Anchorage Historical and Fine Arts Museum, Alaska, Dec. 7, 1984–Jan. 12, 1986; Snite Museum of Art, Notre Dame University, Indiana, Feb. 1–Mar. 9, 1986; Alexandria Museum, Louisiana, Mar. 29–May 4, 1986; Pennsylvania State University Museum of Art, University Park, May 24–Aug. 24, 1986; Charles H. MacNider Museum, Mason City, Iowa, Sept. 13–Oct. 19, 1986; University of Southern Mississippi, Hattiesburg, Nov. 8–Dec. 14, 1986; Parkersburg Art Center, West Virginia, Jan. 3–Feb. 8, 1987; Colorado Gallery of the Arts, Littleton, Feb. 28–Apr. 5, 1987.

The Eastern Shore Art Association, Fairhope, Alabama. *Twentieth-Century American Drawings from the Arkansas Arts Center Foundation Collection*, Jan. 15–Feb. 29, 1984. Catalogue, preface by John C. Glover; introduction by Townsend Wolfe. Traveled to Arkansas Art Center, Little Rock, Apr. 27–Sept. 30, 1984; Louisiana Arts & Sciences Center, Baton Rouge, May 7–June 30, 1985; Art Institute for the Permian Basin, Odessa, Texas, Sept. 8–Oct. 21, 1985; Jacksonville Art Museum, Florida, Nov. 14, 1985–Jan. 5, 1986; Cornell Fine Arts Center, Rollins College, Winter Park, Florida, Mar. 14–Apr. 27, 1986; Meadows Museum and Sculpture Court, Southern Methodist University, Dallas, Texas, June 8–Aug. 3, 1986; Sangre de Cristo Arts & Conference Center, Pueblo, Colorado, Sept. 12–Oct. 24, 1986; Alexandria Museum of Art, Louisiana, Nov. 3, 1986–Jan. 3, 1987; Alaska State Museum, Juneau, Mar. 19–Apr. 26, 1987; University of Alaska Museum, Fairbanks, May 8–June 21, 1987.

1985 Smith College Museum of Art, Northampton, Massachusetts. *Dorothy C. Miller: With an Eye to American Art*, Apr. 19–June 16, 1985. Brochure, texts by Betsy B. Jones and Robert Rosenblum.

1985–87 San Francisco Museum of Modern Art. *American Realism: Twentieth Century Drawings and Watercolors from the Glenn C. Janss Collection*, Nov. 7, 1985–Jan. 12, 1986. Catalogue, text by Alvin Martin. Traveled to De Cordova and Dana Museum and Park, Lincoln, Massachusetts, Feb. 13–Apr. 6, 1986; Archer M. Huntington Art Gallery, University of Texas, Austin, July 31–Sept. 21, 1986; Mary and Leigh Block Gallery, Northwestern University, Evanston, Illinois, Oct. 23–Dec. 14, 1986; Williams College Museum of Art, Williamstown, Massachusetts,

Jan. 15–Mar. 8, 1987; Akron Art Museum, Ohio, Apr. 9–May 31, 1987; Madison Art Center, Wisconsin, July 26–Sept. 20, 1987.

1986 Hudson River Museum, Yonkers, New York. *Form and Formula: Drawing and Drawings*, Jan. 22–May 4, 1986. Catalogue, text by Richard Carlson.

Hirschl & Adler Galleries, New York. *Master Drawings from the Drawing Society's Membership*, Feb. 12–Mar. 8, 1986.

CDS Gallery, New York. *Artists Choose Artists IV*, Apr. 3–May 3, 1986. Catalogue, introduction by Max Kozloff.

Guild Hall Museum, East Hampton, New York. *Cross Currents: An Exchange between Guild Hall Museum and the Provincetown Art Association and Museum*, June 22–July 27, 1986. Catalogue, text by B. H. Friedman.

Davenport West Estate, Cape Museum of Fine Arts, South Harwich, Massachusetts. *Art in the Garden*, July 11–Aug. 20, 1986.

New York Studio School of Drawing, Painting and Sculpture, New York. *Founding Faculty of the New York Studio School*, Sept. 12–Oct. 10, 1986.

Washburn Gallery, New York. *15th Anniversary*, Oct. 1–Nov. 1, 1986. Brochure.

1986–88 Montgomery Museum of Art, Alabama. *Two Hundred Years of American Art: The Munson-Williams-Proctor Institute*. Nov. 15, 1986–Jan. 10, 1987. Catalogue, texts by Wayne Craven and Richard Martin. Traveled to the R. W. Norton Gallery, Shreveport, Louisiana, Jan. 21–Mar. 18, 1987; Tucson Museum of Art, Arizona, Mar. 28–June 7, 1987; Sunrise Museums, Charleston, West Virginia, June 19–Aug. 7, 1987; Bass Museum of Art, Miami Beach, Florida, Sept. 19–Nov. 14, 1987; San Antonio Museum of Art, Texas, Dec. 19, 1987–Feb. 13, 1988; Oklahoma Museum of Art, Oklahoma City, Mar. 12–May 7, 1988.

1987 California Palace of the Legion of Honor, San Francisco. *Achenbach Foundation for Graphic Arts, Recent Acquisitions: Part I, 1400–1950*, Mar. 7–May 24, 1987.

Albright-Knox Art Gallery, Buffalo, New York. *The Wayward Muse: A Historical Survey of Painting in Buffalo*, Mar. 28–May 24, 1987. Catalogue, text by Susan Krane with contributions by William H. Gerdts and Helen Raye.

James Graham & Sons, New York. *Modernism*, Apr. 29–June 12, 1987. Brochure.

Tibor de Nagy Gallery, New York. *Still Life*, May 27–June 27, 1987.

Provincetown Art Association, Massachusetts. *Cross Currents*, June 26–July 23, 1987.

The Baltimore Museum of Art. *Figure Drawings from the Thomas E. Benesch Memorial Collection*, July 21–Sept. 27, 1987.

Jordan-Volpe Gallery, New York. *Works from the Gallery's Collection*, Summer 1987.

Metro Nashville Arts Commission Gallery, Tennessee. *The Best of Nashville Arts*, Oct. 18–Nov. 15, 1987.

Middendorf Gallery, Washington, D.C. *En Grisaille: American Painting in Gray*, Nov. 7–Dec. 9, 1987.

1987–88 Hirshhorn Museum and Sculpture Garden, Smithsonian Institution, Washington, D.C. *Sea and Shore: Selections from the Museum Collection*, Oct. 1, 1987–Nov. 7, 1988.

Pinacoteca Ambrosiana, Milan, Italy. *Da pittore a pittore*, Oct. 16–Dec. 18, 1987. Organized by National Academy of Design, based on the exhibition, *Artists by Themselves*. Catalogue, introduction by John H. Dobkin; texts by Russell Lynes and Michael Quick. Traveled to Galleria degli Uffizi, Florence, Italy, Apr. 15–June 15, 1988.

1987–89 National Gallery of Art, Washington, D.C. *American Drawings and Watercolors of the Twentieth Century: Selections from the Whitney Museum of American Art*, May 24–Sept. 7, 1987. Catalogue, *20th Century Drawings from the Whitney Museum of American Art*, by Paul Cummings. Traveled to Cleveland Museum of Art, Ohio, Sept. 30–Nov. 8, 1987; Achenbach Foundation for Graphic Art, California Palace of the Legion of Honor, San Francisco, Mar. 5–June 5, 1988; Arkansas Arts Center, Little Rock, June 30–Aug. 28, 1988; Whitney Museum of American Art at Champion, Stamford, Connecticut, Nov. 17, 1988–Jan. 25, 1989.

1987–90 Heckscher Museum, Huntington, New York. *The Art Students League: Selections from the Permanent Collection*, Sept. 12–Nov. 1, 1987. Circulated by Gallery Association of New York State. Catalogue, text by Ronald G. Pisano; biographical essays by Beverly Road. Traveled to University Art Gallery, State University of New York, Albany, Jan. 20–Feb. 21, 1988; Brush Art Gallery, St. Lawrence University, Canton, New York, Apr. 15–May 30, 1988; Schweinfurth Memorial Art Center, Auburn, New York, July 16–Aug. 30, 1988; Danforth Museum of Art, Framingham, Massachusetts, Sept. 18–Nov. 6, 1988; Everhart Museum of Art, Scranton, Pennsylvania, Nov. 20–Dec. 31, 1988; Tyler Art Gallery, State University of New York, Oswego, Jan. 29–Mar. 25, 1989; Ruth E. Dowd Art Gallery, State University of New York, Cortland, Apr. 7–28, 1989; Hudson River Museum, Yonkers, New York, June 24–Aug. 20, 1989; Metropolitan Life Insurance Gallery, New York, Jan. 9–Mar. 3, 1990; Davenport Museum of Art, Iowa, Mar. 25–May 2, 1990.

1988 Museum of Art, Rhode Island School of Design, Providence. *1900 to Now: Modern Art from Rhode Island Collections*, Jan. 22–May 1, 1988. Catalogue, introduction by Daniel Rosenfeld.

M. H. de Young Memorial Museum, Fine Arts Museums of San Francisco. *American Paintings: Recent Acquisitions*, Apr. 27–Oct. 9, 1988.

Montclair Art Museum, New Jersey. *A Love Affair: 50 Years of Collecting American Art*, Sept. 18–Oct. 30, 1988. Brochure, foreword by Robert J. Koenig; text by Marilyn Kushner.

Washburn Gallery, New York. *Prints and Drawings*, Nov. 29–Dec. 23, 1988.

1989 M. H. de Young Memorial Museum, Fine Arts Museums of San Francisco. *Viewpoints VII: Twentieth-Century American Landscape Drawings from the Achenbach Foundation for Graphic Arts*, Jan. 18–Apr. 9, 1989. Checklist.

Edward Thorp Gallery, New York. *Epiphanies*, Jan. 28–Feb. 25, 1989.

Babcock Galleries, Seventh Regiment Armory, New York. *The Art Show*, Feb. 15–19, 1989. Organized by Art Dealers Association of America.

Provincetown Art Association and Museum, Massachusetts. *The Beginnings of the Provincetown Art Association and Museum, I. Founders of an Art Colony, 1914–1924*, July 14–Oct. 29, 1989. Catalogue, text by Tony Vevers.

Metro Nashville Arts Commission Gallery, Tennessee. *The Best of Nashville: Small Sculpture and Works on Paper from Nashville Collections*, Oct. 11–Nov. 22, 1989.

Museum of Art, Rhode Island School of Design, Providence. *Art for Your Collection XXVI*, Dec. 1–10, 1989.

1989–92 Cheekwood Fine Arts Center, Nashville, Tennessee. *An American Collection: Paintings and Sculpture from the National Academy of Design*, Oct. 7, 1989–Jan. 7, 1990. Catalogue, texts by Abigail Booth Gerdts et al. Organized by National Academy of Design, New York. Traveled to North Carolina Museum of Art, Raleigh, Mar. 4–Apr. 24, 1990; Emory University Museum, Atlanta, Georgia, May 30–July 15, 1990; Triton Museum of Art, Santa Clara, California, Aug. 15–Oct. 31, 1990; Terra Museum of American Art, Chicago, May 18–July 14, 1991; Washington University Gallery of Art, St. Louis, Missouri, Sept. 6–Nov. 3, 1991; Denver Art Museum, Colorado, Nov. 1991–Jan. 1992.

1990 Babcock Galleries, Seventh Regiment Armory, New York. *The Art Show*, Feb. 22–26, 1990. Organized by Art Dealers Association of America.

The Cooley Gallery, Old Lyme, Connecticut. *Influence and Inspiration: The Students of Frank Vincent DuMond*, June 1–July 7, 1990. Brochure.

Provincetown Art Association and Museum, Massachusetts. *The Beginnings of the Provincetown Art Association and Museum: II. A House Divided, 1925–1937*, Aug. 3–Oct. 29, 1990. Catalogue, text by Tony Vevers.

Metro Arts Downtown Gallery, Nashville, Tennessee. *Sitting Pretty: The Art of the Chair*, Sept. 15–Nov. 11, 1990.

1990–91 Louis Stern Galleries, Beverly Hills, California. *Stamens and Pistils: Interpreting the Flower 1790–1990*, Nov. 20, 1990–Jan. 15, 1991.

1990–92 Sheldon Memorial Art Gallery and Sculpture Garden, University of Nebraska, Lincoln. *Of Time and the City: American Modernism from the Sheldon Memorial Art Gallery*, Jan. 9–Mar. 11, 1990. Catalogue. Traveled to J. B. Speed Art Museum, Louisville, Kentucky, Apr. 1–May 27, 1990; Paine Art Center and Arboretum, Oshkosh, Wisconsin, June 24–Aug. 19, 1990; The Art Museum, Florida International University, Miami, Sept. 16–Nov. 11, 1990; Crocker Art Museum, Sacramento, California, Dec. 9, 1990–Feb. 3, 1991; Society of the Four Arts, Palm Beach, Florida,

Mar. 3–Apr. 28, 1991; Louisiana Arts and Science Center, Baton Rouge, May 26–July 21, 1991; Tacoma Art Museum, Washington, Aug. 18–Oct. 18, 1991; Cummer Gallery of Art, Jacksonville, Florida, Nov. 10, 1991–Jan. 5, 1992; Terra Museum of American Art, Chicago, Jan. 25–Mar. 22, 1992.

1991 Thomas Colville, Seventh Regiment Armory, New York. *Eastside House Settlement Winter Antiques Show*, Jan. 26–Feb. 3, 1991.

Babcock Galleries, Seventh Regiment Armory, New York. *The Art Show*, Feb. 15–19, 1991. Organized by Art Dealers Association of America.

The Baltimore Museum of Art. *As Artists See Us: Drawings from the Museum Collection*, May 14–Aug. 11, 1991.

Provincetown Art Association and Museum, Massachusetts. *The Artist's Eye: I*, May 24–June 30, 1991. Brochure.

Provincetown Art Association and Museum, Massachusetts. *The Artist's Eye: II*, July 26–Aug. 20, 1991. Brochure.

Provincetown Art Association and Museum, Massachusetts. *The Last Hundred Years: Selections from the Collection*, Nov. 1–26, 1991. Brochure.

Watson Gallery, Wheaton College, Norton, Massachusetts. *Curator's Choice: Paintings and Drawings from the Wheaton College Collection*, Nov. 25–Dec. 15, 1991.

Forum Gallery, New York. *Drawings*, Dec. 1991.

1991–92 Philbrook Museum of Art, Tulsa, Oklahoma. *The Landscape in Twentieth-Century American Art: Selections from the Metropolitan Museum of Art*, Apr. 14–June 9, 1991. Catalogue, introduction by Robert Rosenblum; texts by Lowery Stokes Sims and Lisa M. Messinger. Traveled to Center for the Fine Arts, Miami, Florida, June 29–Aug. 24, 1991; Joslyn Art Museum, Omaha, Nebraska, Sept. 14–Nov. 10, 1991; Tampa Museum of Art, Florida, Dec. 14, 1991–Feb. 8, 1992; Greenville County Museum of Art, South Carolina, Mar. 17–May 10, 1992; Madison Art Center, Wisconsin, June 6–Aug. 2, 1992; Grand Rapids Art Museum, Michigan, Sept. 11–Nov. 8, 1992.

The Miyagi Museum of Art, Sendai, Japan. *American Realism and Figurative Art, 1952–1990*, Nov. 1–Dec. 23, 1991. Catalogue, texts by Kuwabara Sumio, John Arthur, and Nitta Hideki. Traveled in Japan to Sogo Museum of Art, Tokohama, Jan. 29–Feb. 16, 1992; Tokushima Modern Art Museum, Feb. 22–Mar. 29, 1992; Museum of Modern Art, Shiga, Apr. 4–May 17, 1992; Kochi Prefectural Museum of Folk Art, May 23–June 17, 1992.

1992 Provincetown Art Association, Massachusetts. *Work of Hawthorne Students*, opening and closing dates unknown, 1992.

Museum of Art, Rhode Island School of Design, Providence. *American Prints and Drawings from a Private Collection*, Jan. 17–Mar. 29, 1992. Checklist.

Duke University Museum of Art, Durham, North Carolina. *Twentieth-Century Drawings from the Weatherspoon Art Gallery,* Jan. 31–Mar. 29, 1992.

Provincetown Art Association and Museum, Massachusetts. *The Artist's Eye: Winter*, Feb. 1–Mar. 1, 1992. Brochure.

Babcock Galleries, Seventh Regiment Armory, New York. *The Art Show: 4th Annual Exhibition*, Feb. 27–Mar. 2, 1992. Organized by Art Dealers Association of America.

Forum Gallery, New York. *Figurative Paintings and Drawings*, May 1992.

First Street Gallery, New York. *Through a Glass Darkly*, June 2–20, 1992.

Emerson Gallery, Hamilton College, Clinton, New York. *Highlights of the Hamilton College Collection*, June 5–Sept. 6, 1992. Checklist.

Greenville County Museum of Art, South Carolina. *Edwin Dickinson, Wallace Putnam and Richard Maury*, June 16–July 26, 1992.

Provincetown Art Association, Massachusetts. *Artists and Their Art: The Yater Years*, Aug. 14–Sept. 22, 1992. Catalogue, text by Tony Vevers and Joyce Johnson.

Addison Gallery of American Art, Phillips Academy, Andover, Massachusetts. *Point of View: Landscapes from the Addison Collection*, Oct. 16–Dec. 20, 1992. Catalogue.

The International Fine Print Dealers Association, Seventh Regiment Armory, New York. *The Print Fair*, Nov. 6–8, 1992.

1993 Babcock Galleries, Seventh Regiment Armory, New York. *The Art Show*, Feb. 25–Mar. 1, 1993. Organized by Art Dealers Association of America.

Minneapolis Institute of Arts, Minnesota. *American Masters: Selections from the Richard Lewis Hillston Collection*, Apr. 23–July 3, 1993. Catalogue, text by Dennis Jon.

Provincetown Art Association and Museum, Massachusetts. *The League at the Cape*, Aug. 14–Sept. 20, 1993. Catalogue, texts by Ronald Pisano and Tony Vevers.

1994 Babcock Galleries, Seventh Regiment Armory, New York. *The Art Show*, Feb. 24–28, 1994. Organized by Art Dealers Association of America.

Babcock Galleries, New York. *Current Selections*, Spring 1994. Brochure.

National Academy of Design, New York. *The Artist's Eye: Wayne Thiebaud Selects Paintings from the Permanent Collection*, Apr. 8–Sept. 4, 1994.

Babcock Galleries, New York. *Flowers!!!*, Apr. 28–June 3, 1994.

Cline Fine Art, Sante Fe, New Mexico. *American Realism + Figurative Painting*, May 27–Aug. 18, 1994. Catalogue, text by John Arthur.

Hammer Galleries, New York. *19th and 20th Century American Paintings*, Sept. 26–Oct. 29, 1994.

James Graham & Sons, New York. *American Modernism, 1920s and 1940s*, Nov. 5–Dec. 23, 1994.

1997 Babcock Galleries, New York. *Beyond Modernism: Three Individuals in the Age of 'Isms: E. Ambrose Webster, Charles W. Hawthorne, and Edwin Dickinson*, Oct. 27–Dec. 9, 1997.

1998 Anderson Gallery, Buffalo, New York, *From behind Closed Doors: Twentieth-Century Figuration from the Albright-Knox Art Gallery*, Sept. 12–Nov. 1, 1998. Organized by the Albright-Knox Art Gallery.

2000 James Graham & Sons, New York. *Crossroads: On the Cusp of Modernism in America*, May 23–June 23, 2000. Catalogue, text by Priscilla Vail Caldwell.

Forum Gallery, New York. *Drawings by 20th Century and Contemporary Masters*, Summer 2000. Catalogue.

INDEX

Page numbers in *italics* refer to illustrations.

PHOTOGRAPH CREDITS

© Addison Gallery of American Art, Andover, Massachusetts: Cat. no. 27
Courtesy The Arkansas Arts Center, Little Rock: Cat. no. 79
Courtesy The Art Students League, New York: Cat. no. 23
Courtesy AXA Financial, Inc.: Cat. nos. 22, 29, 46
Courtesy Babcock Galleries, New York: Cat. nos. 14, 25, 39, 51
Courtesy Helen Dickinson Baldwin: Cat. nos. 17, 64, 80
Stephen J. Barao, Seekonk, Minnesota: Cat. no. 73
George Bouret, Hebron, New York: Cat. no. 75
Scott Bowron Photography: Cat. no. 9
Courtesy Dr. & Mrs. Philip L. Brewer: Cat. no. 92
© 2001 Brooklyn Museum of Art: Cat. no. 38
Geoffrey Clements: Figure 16, page 40; Cat. nos. 72, 84
Courtesy College Art Galleries, Sweet Briar College, Virginia: Cat. no. 86
Sheldan C. Collins, New Jersey: Cat. nos. 12, 66
Courtesy Curtis Galleries, Minneapolis, Minnesota: Cat. nos. 2, 5
© 2001 D. James Dee: Cat. nos. 10, 28, 30
Courtesy Dickinson Family Archive: Cat. nos. 4, 34, 35, 42, 43, 45, 48, 53, 55, 56, 62
Courtesy Emerson Gallery, Hamilton College, Clinton, New York: Cat. no. 94
Courtesy Fine Arts Museums of San Francisco: Cat. nos. 8, 76
Courtesy James Graham & Sons, New York: Cat. no. 33
Courtesy Robert C. Graham, Jr.: Cat. nos. 71, 74
Courtesy Julie Heller Gallery, Provincetown, Massachusetts: Cat. no. 78
Biff Henrich, Keystone Productions, Buffalo, New York: Cat. nos. 6, 7, 82, 83, 93
Biff Henrich, Keystone Productions, Buffalo, New York, Courtesy Dickinson Family Archive: Cat. no. 24
Courtesy Hirshhorn Museum & Sculpture Garden, Smithsonian Institution: Cat. nos. 63, 77
Courtesy Herbert F. Johnson Museum of Art, Cornell University, Ithaca, New York: Cat. nos. 16, 70
Courtesy Maurice & Margery Katz: Cat. no. 13
Balthazar Korab, Courtesy Helen Dickinson Baldwin: Cat. nos. 90, 91
Courtesy The Metropolitan Museum of Art, New York: Cat. nos. 50, 87–89, 95
Courtesy Middlebury College Museum of Art, Vermont: Cat. no. 3
Courtesy Mitchell-Innes & Nash, New York: Cat. no. 44
Courtesy Museum of Fine Arts, Springfield, Massachusetts: Cat. no. 21
Courtesy The Museum of Modern Art, New York: Cat. nos. 18, 20
Courtesy National Academy of Design, New York: Cat. no. 54
O. E. Nelson, New York: Figure 6, page 26
Robert Newcombe: Cat. no. 19
Courtesy The Pennsylvania Academy of the Fine Arts, Philadelphia: Cat. no. 15
Courtesy Philadelphia Museum of Art: Frontispiece; Cat. nos. 36, 58, 61
Courtesy Rose Art Museum, Brandeis University, Waltham, Massachusetts: Cat. nos. 59, 85
Courtesy Michael Rosenfeld Gallery, New York: Cat. no. 37
Courtesy Shein Collection: Cat. no. 67
Courtesy Sheldon Memorial Art Gallery & Sculpture Garden, University of Nebraska–Lincoln: Cat. nos. 11, 69
Courtesy The David & Alfred Smart Museum of Art, The University of Chicago: Cat. no. 40
Courtesy Smithsonian American Art Museum, Washington, D.C.: Cat. nos. 49, 60
Gregory Staley, Silver Springs, Maryland: Cat. nos. 1, 47, 52, 68
Lee Stalsworth: Cat. nos. 31, 65
Courtesy Merrill Wagner & Robert Ryman: Cat. no. 81
Paul Waldman, New York: Cat. nos. 26, 32, 41, 57